Coventry

at Highfield Road 1899-2005

GHOSTS OF A VANISHED STADIUM

Series Editor: Clive Leatherdale

Jim Brown

DESERT ISLAND BOOKS

First hardback edition published in 2006
First paperback edition published in 2008
by
DESERT ISLAND BOOKS LIMITED
7 Clarence Road, Southend-on-Sea, Essex SS1 1AN
United Kingdom
www.desertislandbooks.com

© 2006, 2008 Jim Brown

The right of Jim Brown to be identified as author of this work has been
asserted under The Copyright Designs and Patents Act 1988

British Library Cataloguing-in-Publication Data
A catalogue record for this book is available from the British Library

ISBN 978-905328-53-6

Printed in Great Britain
by
4edge Ltd, Hockley. www.4edge.co.uk

Coventry City at Highfield Road
GHOSTS OF A VANISHED STADIUM

Contents

Author's Note

After almost 40 years collecting statistics and researching the history of Coventry City FC, I could not see my football home demolished without recording its past. What, two years ago, set out to be a chronicle of Highfield Road, evolved into the story of the club itself, incorporating many first and second-hand memories of the stadium and a few important happenings away from there.

My first game at the stadium was on 30 April 1962, a Monday evening, when my dad took me to see my home-town team Lockheed Leamington beat Rugby Town 5-1 in the Birmingham Senior Cup final. I was only nine at the time, and it probably meant a late night for me. We sat in the old Atkinson's Stand and I can remember thinking that this was a real football ground rather than the tiny but welcoming Windmill Ground at Leamington.

Ten days later we were back for my first Coventry City game, a friendly against Burnley to commemorate the opening of the city's newly rebuilt cathedral. Burnley were a top First Division club and had lost in the FA Cup final to Spurs just days earlier. Burnley's Ray Pointer, a centre-forward with a mop of blond hair, was one of my earliest football heroes and he scored an amazing goal that night in Burnley's 4-2 victory.

Strangely, it was because of City's left-winger that night that I became a City fan. Stewart Imlach had grown up in the same street as my mother in Lossiemouth, and he had been my idol since I was first introduced to the game.

Imlach soon moved on and City never again wore the all-white strip they had worn that night, but I was hooked. Jimmy Hill introduced the Sky Blue kit and the rest, as they say, is history. My trips to Highfield Road were sporadic until 1964, although my dad did manage to get tickets for that historic Manchester United Cup game. It was a golden period and I can hardly remember seeing the team lose before they reached the First Division.

My most memorable game, of all time probably, was against Wolves in 1967, when I think I was one of the last people into the ground at around 2.30pm and spent the whole match on the running track – apart from the forays onto the pitch when City scored their first two goals. I only missed one home game that season and that was the sole defeat to Crystal Palace.

A major source in writing this book has been the *Coventry Evening Telegraph* (and its predecessor the *Midland Daily Telegraph*), whose archives have filled in the gaps left by my fellow Coventry City authors who, it has to be said, had already left few stones unturned. My gratitude goes to all of the uncredited football writers of these newspapers, the majority of whom wrote under the *nom de plume* of 'Nemo', the Latin for 'no one'. In the 1960s, the last 'Nemo', and in my opinion the finest of them all, Derek Henderson, dropped the pen name and let himself become known. It was Derek who inspired me as a teenager to study the club's history and his match reports from the 1960s are a constant source of pleasure.

Dozens of other people kindly helped on this long project but I am especially indebted to my long-time friend Lionel Bird who gave me loads of assistance with much of the research into the ground's developments over the years.

Thanks, too, to others who gave me assistance, including, in no specific order: Rod Dean, Paul O'Connor, Jonathan Strange, Tom Dentith, Charlie Timmins, Peter & Barbara Hill, Lol Harvey, the late Bert Woodfield and family, Jim Hamill, Mick Kearns, Graham Hover, Joan Barratt, Kevin Monks, David Brassington, Don Chalk, Alan Tyrell, Bob Weeks, George Ling, Geoff Moore, Graeme Baldwin, Barry Ireland, Jack Evans, Neville Hadsley, Eric Howell, Harry Green, Frank Wood, Peter Lea, Jon 'Reg' Rishworth, Dave Long, Paul Howard, Bryan Richardson, the late Sydney Ward, Les Raven, Dennis Coleman, Trevor Lloyd, Phil Snelman, Jed Smith (Twickenham), Andy Turner and Rob Madill (Coventry Evening Telegraph), David Antill, Pam Hindson, the late David Jones, Jenny Poole, Joe Elliott, Paul Fletcher and Ken Sharp (Coventry City), Martin Roberts and Huw Jones (Coventry Museum) and the staff at the British Newspaper Library, Colindale. I am sure there were others and if I have not mentioned you I apologise.

Thanks to Brian Tabner for permission to use his definitive attendance statistics and pointing out that there were only 51,452 people at the Wolves game in 1967!

For permission to reproduce published and unpublished photographs and material in this book I would like to thank Coventry City FC, the *Coventry Evening Telegraph*, Mike Moody and the late Harry Jervis (for the wonderful motorcycle football photos), Action Images, Joan Barratt, John Hyde, Edna Davis, and Martin Winch (BBC Coventry & Warwickshire). I have tried to trace all copyright holders, and the publishers will be pleased to correct any omissions brought to their notice in any future edition.

Last but not least, thanks to my wonderful family, my long-suffering wife Doreen and children Lisa and Alastair for all their invaluable support. Finally, my dad Ernie, who first took me to Highfield Road in 1962. Sadly he did not live to see this book finished.

JIM BROWN
October 2006

CHAPTER ONE

The Dawn of a New Era

The city of Coventry in the last decade of the 19th Century was expanding dramatically. The population rose from around 65,000 in 1891 to close to 88,000 in 1899. The bicycle industry in itself was responsible for a steady influx from the countryside to the city, and the Singers cycle works, in Canterbury Street, Hillfields – one of an estimated 248 such works in the city – was one of the largest in the Midlands. Since its inception in 1883, the Singers works' football team had evolved by 1894 into the top professional team in the city. It played in the Birmingham & District League against the reserve teams of the big Midland clubs such as Aston Villa and West Bromwich Albion.

The original Singers pitch had been at Dowells Field in Binley Road or, if a more definite land or water mark was needed, the stranger was directed 'near the horse-pond'. The club moved in 1887 to a site between Paynes Lane and Swan Lane. It was called the Stoke Road Ground, on space now occupied by Britannia Street and Wren Street, just south of the eventual Highfield Road enclosure. In those days this was virtually the edge of town, with only a few cottages in Paynes Lane and farms to the east and north. The new site enabled the club to start charging its growing band of supporters 2d (two pence) admission. Over the next decade, however, the city's population growth resulted in substantial house building projects in the Hillfields area, as a result of which the ground had to undergo adjustments to cater for new houses and roads. As the turn of the century approached, pressure grew on the football club to move yet again, because of plans to extend King Richard Street.

Although the team's accomplishments in the Birmingham League were unimpressive – they failed to finish higher than 13th out of sixteen in the first three seasons – its status was rising and there were calls from the committee running the club to rename it Coventry City. Resistance came from the Singers directors, and owner George Singer made veiled threats to sack any workers playing for a renamed club.

In the summer of 1898, following the club's best season yet – they finished 7th and gates had crept up to 1,000 – there was a change of heart. An application was proposed to change the name. A last-minute objection from Coventry Rugby Club, on the grounds of possible confusion between the two clubs, was overruled and on 11 August 1898 FA Chairman Frederick Wall wrote to the club permitting the use of the new name. Simultaneously the club switched their colours from the black and red stripes of Singers to blue and white stripes.

Coventry City's first season, 1898-99, was a success on the field and 7th place was again achieved in an expanded eighteen-club league. Off the field, it had been apparent for some time that another move was likely as the Corporation sought more building land for housing development. Tom Cashmore, the secretary, who in those days ran the club, and the committee lost no time in seeking 'fresh woods and pastures new'.

On 31 January 1899 'Centre-Forward' writing in the *Coventry Mercury* spoke of the club's ambitions: 'If not actually known by outsiders, it has been pretty freely conjectured that at the end of the present season the City club would, through the exigencies of building operations, lose their present playing piece ... They [the committee] have secured on lease for a number of years, the two fields adjoining the present ground. As negotiations have only recently been concluded, I am not prepared to go into details this week; but this may be said, that if the expectations of the committee are only realised there is every reason to hope that the club next season will be in possession of an inclosure [sic] which should be an improvement upon the one they now occupy.'

Three weeks later Ian McGhie, football correspondent for the *Midland Daily Telegraph* (and the first to assume the pseudonym 'Nemo'), reported: 'The requisite capital to ensure proceeding with the undertaking was promised in a very short space of time at a committee meeting last week. The ground will afford accommodation for football, cricket and lawn tennis, in addition to other games too numerous to mention, and a golf course being amongst the possibilities. In short, matters are to be made to hum in the Swan Lane vicinity in the near future.'

With a new ground on the horizon, the inspired players remained unbeaten for eleven games from mid-January until early April, lifting them up to 7th. In fact, financial issues caused friction in the dressing room. The new ground had to be funded to the tune of several hundred pounds and there was outstanding rent to pay on the Stoke Road ground. In an effort to meet their liabilities, the club arranged friendlies with 'First League' opponents and almost 3,000 watched Newcastle, the first top-flight club to play in the city, beat Coventry 2-0 at Christmas. Subsequent friendlies against First Division Nottingham Forest and Second Division Barnsley were less well attended. With £100 already outlaid on the site, the committee – as a last resort – asked players to sacrifice wages for the last few weeks of the season. The committee offered to 'defray' all other expenses and provide 'a substantial meal'. The players refused and went on strike: only three of the first team took part in the final league game at Hereford Thistle. Several striking players – including goalkeeper Nat Robinson and long-serving defenders Harry Whitehouse, 'General' Roberts and Charlie Lomas, turned up at Stoke Road instead to watch a minor cup final and 'endeavoured to ventilate their grievance before the spectators'.

By mid-March 1899 the *Mercury* was reporting 'good progress' on the new ground, which would be a 'distinct credit to Association Football in the city'. The paper also pointed out that public support would need 'to be generous' if the club's ambitions were to be met – a clarion call for more money!

City's last game at Stoke Road was the friendly against Second Division Barnsley on 29 April. City lost 1-2 but reports state that 'the gap between Division Two [of the Football League] and the Birmingham League is not a great one'.

The committee had again appealed for a good crowd to enable them to complete the new ground, but receipts were low.

In the meantime, the club had taken over the new six-and-a-half-acre site from the Craven Cricket Club, and 'preparations began for the laying out of a proper ground'.

A row of elm trees was removed (which ran more or less along the modern-day halfway line) and the pitch levelled and re-turfed 'so that when it is properly set a very fine playing piece will be the result. A grass track, four laps to a mile is also being prepared.'

Work then commenced on a twelve-row 'elevation' stand, planned to hold 2,000 spectators, to be built on the south side of the 'enclosure', in other words the King Richard Street side, where the Main Stand was eventually situated. This 'commodious' stand was later referred to as the John Bull Stand, in view of the advertising for the popular magazine carried on the fore-edge of its roof. The magazine's motto: 'If it is in John Bull, it is so,' was painted along the stand facia.

The remaining three sides were boarded around the perimeter with low grassy banks. 'Centre-Forward' wrote in the *Mercury*: 'Part of the ground has been let for cricketing purposes, but considering that the turf must necessarily at present, and for some time to come, be in a loose condition, it cannot be expected to prove a joy to those using it for this season at least.'

The first Annual Meeting of Coventry City FC was held at the Sydenham Palace on 21 June 1899. Secretary Tom Cashmore, a driving force behind the club's development, believed that 'in acquiring the new ground the club had laid the foundation-stone whereon their future would be built'. Acknowledgment was given to the landlords, the Mercers

Company, for their generous terms for the lease and subsequent purchase of the ground. Director Thomas Owen 'considered the new ground to be the best in the Midlands'. His view was supported by fellow director William Penn. Cashmore wrote thanking the Mercers Company 'for the manner in which they had met the club's representatives'.

Early match reports in the *Midland Daily Telegraph* spoke of 'Coventry City Stadium' or the 'Swan Lane Ground', but soon came to refer to it as Highfield Road. In 1899 that was the only route to the ground from the city centre and took its name from Highfield Farm, which once graced the area. The houses in Highfield Road almost adjoined the entrance to that side of the ground, while what is now Thackhall Street petered out into a lane as far as Swan Lane. Two houses in Highfield Road (Nos 2 and 4) were demolished in the 1920s when Thackhall Street was extended to join up with Swan Lane.

On Saturday, 19 August 1899 a practice 'trial' match took place at what was referred to as 'Swan Lane enclosure'. It went ahead in the evening, following the conclusion of the cricket match between Craven and St Michael's. It is unlikely the new stand would have been in use, and from previous comments regarding the pitch it is hard to imagine a decent cricket wicket being ready. In the soccer game one team wore blue and black, whilst the other wore 'chocolate' colours. Interest was 'considerable' and the final score was a 3-0 victory to the blue and blacks. The goals were scored by Crofts (2) and Rideout.

Several of the triallists 'acquitted' themselves well, and the consensus from the committee was that a good squad had been assembled for the coming season. Technically, this was the first match ever played on the new site, although history records the first competitive game as the first league fixture against Shrewsbury three weeks later.

On Saturday, 9 September City's new ground was officially opened for a Birmingham & District League game against Shrewsbury Town. The task of kicking off was given to Mr Walter Hewitt, a manager at the Singers works and described as club president by some reports: 'He set the ball rolling amid the plaudits of the crowd' using a 'brand new ball', kicking towards the 'town-end goal'.

The Chief Constable of Coventry, Charles Charlsley, was present, as was one of the club's founders, a Mr Biggs, who despite 'severe illness' was wheeled out to view the opening fixture. The Shropshire club were defeated 0-1 through a fifth-minute goal from centre-forward Rideout. It was however a mediocre game and it was 'somewhat of a relief when the whistle blew at the end'. The crowd of 3,000 was more than double the previous season's average.

The correspondent of the *Coventry Reporter* described the scene: 'As one enters the ground from Highfield Road, the eye encounters the grand new stand on the opposite side of the enclosure. It is a gigantic wooden structure, roofed with corrugated iron, and is coloured chocolate and light blue. Indeed it presents a fine picture and is an ornament of which the committee might well be proud. The turf looked decidedly fresh and is remarkably level, while the enclosure is banked up well the whole way round, so that each spectator is enabled to have an uninterrupted view.' The weather was perfect and whilst the sun shone 'brilliantly at times', there was a 'refreshing breeze which made matters comfortable for both players and spectators'.

The *Coventry Mercury* said 'there can be little question that the City club now possess one of the very finest junior football arenas in the district'. The new stand, 'a most capacious one,' however, was not completely finished; the committee were keen to have two dressing rooms and a bathroom installed – presumably the players were still getting changed in the Binley Oak, a hundred yards from the pitch.

As there were no press facilities, the *Mercury* correspondent gave this advice to the committee: 'as this highly-necessary adjunct is sure to come, I would suggest ... that they should make the entrance from the back of the stand, and thus put an end to the necessity, which existed last year, of the reporters having to crush their way through a crowd of people to get to the quarters allotted to them.'

The *Midland Daily Telegraph* reported: 'all who visited the new enclosure expressed unbounded satisfaction at its appearance and capabilities. The field of play was well wire-roped in, and the turf looked in splendid trim. The stand is a most capacious one with a variety of accommodation at the rear for the storage of appendages of the game and for dressing purposes. Without doubt it looked what it was declared by visitors to be, one of the finest grounds in the Midlands, surpassing those of several league teams.'

New football grounds were all the craze in 1899, with several clubs opening new stadia. In August, Kilmarnock opened Rugby Park, whilst on the opening day of the League season, 2 September, Sheffield Wednesday's Hillsborough, Grimsby Town's Blundell Park, and Aberdeen's Pittodrie were opened. They were followed by Blackpool's Bloomfield Road and Rangers' Ibrox Park a few days later.

At the AGM the following August, Cashmore gave these figures:

Draining, levelling & relaying new pitch	£179 5s 5d
Fencing	£170 10s 11½d

Ground implements	£4 18s 8d
Total	£354 15s 0½d

The pitch was also sub-let to junior side Clifton Victoria to save costs.

CHAPTER TWO

1899-1919

The first season at Highfield Road, **1899-1900**, was a disaster. The optimism from the last season at Stoke Road vanished. City won only six games, all at their new ground, lost all fifteen away and finished bottom of the Birmingham League. Some of the away losses were embarrassing – 1-9 at Aston Villa's reserves, 0-8 at Halesowen, 0-7 at Dudley. No doubt the team's form contributed to secretary Tom Cashmore leaving in 1900 and moving with his family to the thriving railway town of Wolverton.

In the second home game, almost a month after the first (there were no early midweek games in those days), Dudley won 5-2 in front of 1,200 spectators. One of the six victories was a first ever over Aston Villa, albeit their reserves, who then played in the Birmingham League. A Walker hat-trick – the first by a City player on the new ground – sank Villa on the Saturday before Christmas. A month later came Villa's 9-1 revenge.

By the end of the season attendances were down to a few hundred, and for the Bristol Rovers defeat in April the crowd was estimated at only 200. The financial situation was precarious and rumours abounded that the club may have to fold.

Matters did not improve much the following, **1900-01**, season, Mr Newhall's first season as secretary-manager. At home City managed nine wins, but they failed again to win on their travels, and shocking defeats at Small Heath (0-10) and Villa's reserves (1-14) left City 14th out of eighteen. Another player dispute surfaced early on. The FA found City guilty of not 'fulfilling the contracts' of two players and fined the club £4.

During the 1901 close season efforts were made to address the financial plight. The feasibility of the club becoming a limited liability company was discussed, raising capital by selling shares. Close accounting showed the club was too much in debt to attempt this route – its net liabilities exceeded £300, although some unusual assets came to light. The stand had a dressing room and the pitch a mower and roller, so that total assets amounted to £600. A share flotation of £800-900 would be needed to put the club on a sound footing, but such an appeal 'would meet with poor response'.

The losing ways continued in **1901-02** with 16th place and another re-election, but in **1902-03** things looked up. The side finished 7th, winning ten home games, among them a 9-0 thumping of Ironbridge just before Christmas to avenge a 0-10 loss a year earlier. The *Midland Express* of 11

April 1903 reported that 'recently the fortunes of Coventry City took a change for the better ... they have built up a sound eleven, and have wiped off all their debts and have a balance in hand. And all this has been done in the course of a few months'. New secretary-manager M O'Shea was credited with orchestrating the turnaround, and the article mentions 'a record gate of over £90 for one of their Birmingham league games'. That level of receipts indicates a crowd of 3/4,000.

Generally, however, the club staggered from one crisis to another. An 11th place finish in **1903-04** was followed by another application for re-election in **1904-05**, when the side slumped to 17th. Thirty-five players were used and the inexperienced side at the end contained none who had been on the books a year earlier.

By now, the ground was surrounded on three sides by houses. In addition to Highfield Road, Nicholls Street and Catherine Street had been developed behind the west town end, while Mowbray, Britannia, King Richard and Wren Streets were also established – according to city maps of 1906. Beyond Swan Lane and to the north-east, however, there were open fields with a footpath still leading from the junction of Highfield Road and Thackhall Street to Swan Lane. From the same maps it appears that the ground had three entrances: one at the top of King Richard Street, a second off the aforementioned footpath close to Highfield Road, and a third in the south-east corner from Swan Lane.

In 1905 it was decided to abandon the 'board of directors' style of management and adopt a 'club syndicate' under the direction of Fred Lee (later Mayor of Coventry) as financial secretary. Former player Joe Beaman took over as match secretary-trainer. The syndicate acquired the lease of Highfield Road and authorised ground improvements. A small refreshment bar was constructed, the area in front of the grandstand was terraced with concrete, and a clock placed on the front of the grandstand.

Beaman certainly made a difference in **1905-06**. With a settled line-up which included Harry Whitehouse, a good goalkeeper in the tradition of Nat Robinson, and Jimmy McIntyre, who netted nineteen goals and would later become team manager, a creditable 11th place was achieved. McIntyre only stayed one season, but Beaman replaced him by signing one of the club's legendary goalscorers, Albert Lewis. As a result, City enjoyed their best season in **1906-07**, finishing 7th, and crowds averaged 2,700. Lewis, who stayed two years before joining Herbert Chapman's Northampton, scored 50 goals in that time and helped transform City from Birmingham League strugglers to Southern League aspirants.

A year later a report of the pre-season practice between the blues and the stripes described that summer's ground improvements: 'The enclosure presented a very smart appearance with the improvements that had been effected. The ground was newly mown, and the goal posts and railings were newly painted. Structural improvements had been carried out to the large grandstand, and this was painted in the light and dark blue colours of the City, as was also the commodious new refreshment pavilion which had been erected on the banking at the Wren Street corner of the enclosure. An improvement effected in connection with this department is that the spectators can now imbibe their refreshments in full sight of the game, whereas formerly they had no view of the playing field from the bar. The counter is 44 feet long, with side extensions of eight feet each. In addition to this erection two other refreshment bars are to be erected, one at the Swan Lane end of the ground and one immediately opposite the large grandstand. The banking will be further extended so as to surround three sides of the arena, the fourth being already occupied by the grandstand. A tall flagstaff has been set up, and a large sign under the grandstand clock "Coventry City F.C. Athletic Ground". Altogether the enclosure has a very bright and cheerful appearance, and affords accommodation superior to that of the non-reserve clubs' grounds in the Birmingham League, with the exception, perhaps of Wrexham.'

The 'Wren Street corner' was at the south-west of the ground. It is believed that the catering contract was awarded to John Tipping, landlord of the Vauxhall Tavern in Hillfields, along with a Mr Warden of the Hertford Arms, Gosford Green. Tipping, a 'stout' figure would soon become a director of the club.

In the summer of 1907, following another FA investigation, the syndicate was disbanded and the club registered as a limited liability company. It provided a board of directors and £2,000 in capital. This consisted of 8,000 5 shilling shares, although the first general meeting in December 1907 reported that only 1,317 shares had been allotted. The first chairman was Thomas Owen, and Messrs Tipping, Sage, Clarke, Rollason and Stone were the other directors. Fred Lee was secretary (but was succeeded by Walter Harris during the coming season), with goalkeeper Harry Whitehouse assistant secretary. The first board meetings took place in a shed on the Swan Lane bank, but they soon decamped to the offices of solicitors Maddocks, Ogden & Co, supervised by the club's legal advisor, William Maddocks.

Prior to 1907, Coventry City's FA Cup record was poor. It was three years after the new ground opened before it hosted a Cup-tie. In 1899 City lost at the preliminary round at Stourbridge, the following year they scratched to fulfil a league game the same day, and in 1901 played a league game and Cup-tie on the same day, after the League refused to allow a postponement. Whilst the first team were drawing 0-0 at home with Ironbridge, a team of reserves and local league players crashed 2-11 at Worcester-based Berwick Rangers, still City's heaviest ever Cup defeat. The *Coventry Times* carried a two-column report on the Ironbridge game but the Cup debacle went unreported.

The first Cup-tie at the new stadium was a 3-1 first qualifying round win over Welsh side Aberaman on 1 November 1902, with Taplin scoring twice and Fern once. There followed a 5-2 home win over Stafford Rangers in round two before bowing out in a replay at Kidderminster, following a 2-2 draw at Coventry.

In 1903 fellow Birmingham League side Walsall won 4-2 at Highfield Road in the first qualifying round in front of a ground record 5,000 – the size of the crowd demonstrated the importance and attraction of the Cup. In 1904 the team reached the third qualifying round by defeating Halesowen and Walsall before losing at Stafford Rangers. Defeat at the first hurdle to Worcester City (the former Berwick Rangers) in 1905 was followed by a non-appearance the following year when someone at the club forgot to get the entry forms in on time.

Non-league clubs like City had to survive various qualifying rounds before the Football League Clubs entered in early January, which is little different to today. Prior to 1925, however, today's third round was called the first round, and today's quarter-finals the fourth round.

The **1907-08** Cup campaign began in September with a 6-2 win at Brierley Hill Alliance and progressed through five qualifying rounds (Darlaston, Bilston, Worcester, Oswestry) before the sixth qualifier paired them with Bishop Auckland from the North East. With Cup ties and replays taking priority, City had only played seven league games when the Bishops arrived on 7 December for a game to decide who would progress into the first round proper.

The North East amateurs might have twice won the FA Amateur Cup, but they were no match for Joe Beaman's side. It ended 7-1 in front of a record crowd of 7,820. The first round draw gave City another home tie, with Crystal Palace of the Southern League, then considered on a par with the Football League Division Two. Palace had been Cup giantkillers the previous year, knocking out League champions Newcastle on their way to the quarter-finals.

For City to go so far should not be underestimated. It was almost unheard of for a club of their status to reach the last 64, and the forthcoming tie generated much excitement. Commercialism was rife, then as now, and pressure was put on City to switch the tie to London in order to 'maximise' the gate. These days the FA are a lot less amenable to clubs switching ties, but then it was common for the bigger club to 'compensate' a smaller one for sacrificing home advantage. For example, that season mighty Aston Villa had paid struggling Stockport County to switch grounds – £450 down, half of anything over £900, and all expenses met. In the event, the Villa gate was only enough to pay County's £450, plus expenses. Some said Villa had bought the tie and the Football Association squirmed uncomfortably.

Rumours abounded in Coventry that City were considering a lucrative switch, especially as Palace played at Crystal Palace, the traditional venue for the Cup final, where they had attracted 30,000 crowds for their Cup-ties the previous season. By all accounts Palace did try, but their offer was not enough to persuade City's directors to switch. Director Fred Lee was quoted in the local press as saying they had decided not to switch, but that the club would probably lose £500 by not doing so. He encouraged fans to buy shares in the club and turn up to the forthcoming Christmas games to recoup some of the loss. Some 5,500 paid to see the next home game, against Birmingham Reserves on the Saturday before Christmas, and 4,000 for the Christmas Day game against Kidderminster.

The Crystal Palace game was not all-ticket – few matches were at Highfield Road before the 1960s – and admission prices reflected a pragmatic attitude. Coventry's normal admission was 4d (2p). In those days many clubs might have doubled prices for big Cup-ties, sometimes more, to capitalise on the big crowd. This usually alienated fans and resulted in a less than capacity crowd. City put tickets on sale at 6d, but only up to three days before the game, after which they rose to 1 shilling (5p), thus pacifying the loyal fans while penalising the spur-of-the moment types. Stand tickets were priced similarly at 1s for the wing stand and 3s for the central stand.

Three weeks before the tie, work commenced on constructing more entrances, and banking to improve elevation and increase capacity. The players spent several days at Droitwich Spa, which would become a ritual before Cup-ties over the next 40 years. A regime of brine baths and relaxing country walks prepared them for the biggest game in the club's short history. Player Harry Jones reminisced in 1967: 'We went away for a week's special training, and I can tell you we felt like kings.'

The *Midland Daily Telegraph* issued what might have been the first Coventry City match programme, four pages, printed by Iliffe & Sons of London and Coventry, on a high-quality paper. Headed 'The Midland Daily Telegraph' Official Team-Sheet, it was given away free, if the word 'gratis' on the front top right-hand corner is accurate. The front page shows the teams lined up in a 2-3-5 formation, and in common with other club programmes of the time, confusingly show the players numbered – Palace 1 to 11, and City 12 to 22. These numbers did not appear on players' shirts – shirt numbering would not be introduced for another 30 years. Palace wore 'cardinal and blue jerseys with white knickers' whilst City wore light and dark blue jerseys and white 'knickers'. The rest of the front page was taken up with the History of Crystal Palace. Page 2 had a 'Who's Who' of both teams, which included potted pen pictures. Only two players were over 5ft 9ins tall. Pages three and four reproduced an article by Ian McGhie ('Nemo') previously published in the newspaper regarding City's future direction. He argued, prophetically, that for the club to achieve Football League status it should first consider the Southern League. The programme was advert-free apart from a one-line exhortation to buy the newspaper and read the match report by 'Nemo' and special comments by Mr Charles Charlsley (ex International Goalkeeper). Charlsley (ex-Birmingham) was a club director and Chief Constable of Coventry at the time!

City lost 2-4, but the club's advance planning and hospitality to their London visitors created a sufficiently strong impression for Palace, a few months later, to help vote City into the Southern League. The attendance of 9,884 was disappointing considering the directors had expected 12,000 but nevertheless was a new ground record.

The long Cup run left City with a league backlog, which meant five games in six days in April. Form suffered slightly but it was still City's finest season, finishing fourth and scoring 97 goals, more than any other team. City equalled their record victory at Highfield Road by crushing Stourbridge 9-0 and in their final game topped that with an 11-2 win over West Brom reserves. Billy Smith netted five to take his season's total to 38. It was City's twelfth successive home win and 'Nemo' was ecstatic in the *Midland Daily Telegraph*: 'The distinguishing badge of Coventry City is an elephant. Cartoonists represent him as a playful animal with a bow of blue and white ribbon in his tail. But at Highfield Road what a change is seen. He becomes a tusked and ferocious beast trampling all down before him.'

At season's end the club heeded 'Nemo's' January advice and applied to join the Southern League. Despite the club's raised profile, managing director Fred Lee was not optimistic. Just before the voting, Spurs, QPR and Bradford Park Avenue all resigned to join Division Two of the Football League. With the Southern League expanded by two clubs to twenty, five places were now up for grabs.

Charles Charlsley was the club's representative at the Southern League's AGM on 27 May 1908. City polled 25 votes, which resulted in them being the fifth club elected. The other four were Exeter, Leyton, New Brompton (who later became Gillingham) and Southend.

The club's elevation to the Southern League for **1908-09** generated much activity around Highfield Road, including new dressing rooms, the printing of a regular match programme, and the erection of a wooden half-time scoreboard at the Town end. In that hectic summer a water supply was plumbed in to provide washing facilities. Money was tight, however, and at the AGM in July Fred Lee appealed to local tradesmen to offer their services free of charge.

The first programme explained the scoreboard: 'Arrangements have been made with the Express News Agency, of London and Sheffield, to erect a large Scoring Board on our ground, and to supply us with the half-times and finals of all Southern League matches and several English League games played during the season. The code to this board is in this official programme, and it is hoped that the spectators will show their appreciation of the enterprise of the management by always purchasing a programme, the sale of every one of which means a small addition to the Club funds.' The same programme warned supporters against 'Bogus' programmes being offered for sale outside 'principal grounds'. These, it went on to say 'do not contain any code to the scoring board or official information'. Pirate programme sellers were rife in the inter-war period but must also have been active as early as 1908. The scoreboard displayed letters from A to P and wooden numbers were hung on hooks to display the scores.

Ground admission prices rose from 4d to 6d, with a season ticket costing 7s 6d (38p). The programme, published by Allen Greaves of Sheffield and London, cost 1d. It largely comprised adverts and syndicated articles but did include specific Coventry information, such as a player picture, and fixtures and results for the first team and reserve team. One advert for the first game was for the Sydenham Palace public house in Lower Ford Street, conveniently run by club chairman Thomas Owen.

According to the programme, teams colours for the new league were light and dark blue quarters with white knickers. The first game was at home to Crystal Palace on the late afternoon of Tuesday, 1 September 1908. Before the First World War the football season was barred from starting in August on account of pressure from the cricket world and others who wished football to remain a winter game. The fixture kicked off at 5pm, but heavy rain for most of the day kept the crowd down to 5,000 and receipts to £116. The game ended 1-1, with centre-half William Marvin – one of several close-season signings – scoring City's first goal in the Southern League.

City struggled in their first season in the Southern League. Too many players were not good enough, while an administrative error meant Billy Smith had not been re-signed and had joined Birmingham. The two best newcomers were wingers with nursery rhyme names – Harry Buckle and Charlie Tickle. They would play crucial roles in the club's Cup success over the coming three seasons. Buckle, an Irish international, came from Bristol Rovers with considerable experience of Southern and Football League football, whilst Tickle represented the Football League whilst with Birmingham the previous season.

City started poorly – they lost five out of their first six and never escaped from the bottom two – and finished 20th of 21 clubs with only Brentford below them. Relegation was avoided only because the league was extended to 22 clubs and no teams were demoted. Several gates were above 7,000 and averaged 5,740.

In November 1908 the nickname of 'the Bantams' was adopted after 'Nemo' pointed out in the *Midland Daily Telegraph* that City were one of the few clubs lacking one. He called on supporters for ideas and, being the 'lightweights' in the league, the small domestic fowl seemed appropriate. City were depicted as the Bantams in a newspaper cartoon soon afterwards. The name endured to the 1960s, when another 'Nemo', Derek Henderson, re-christened the team the Sky Blues.

Fundraising to compete in the Southern League was uppermost in the minds of directors in the summer of 1909. David Cooke, a local tobacco magnate, joined the board and immediately invested for new player-manager Harry Buckle to strengthen the side. The directors proposed to raise £1,000 through a share issue and use the proceeds to build a new grandstand. More modifications were made to the existing stand, including new reserved seats for visiting directors and improvements to the dressing rooms.

Buckle's transfer dealings proved shrewd. Welsh international goal-keeper Bob Evans signed from Croydon Common, and half-back Eli Bradley from West Brom. Both would be key players and prove popular with the fans over the next four seasons. Billy Smith returned from Birmingham but failed to rediscover his previous scoring prowess.

1909-10 pre-season warm-ups between the first team and the reserves attracted over 4,000 at the final practice, played at 5.30pm on the Saturday before the start of the season, presumably to avoid upsetting the cricketing fraternity. 'Nemo' remarked on the increasing number of ladies attending Highfield Road – 'many on their own' – and rejoiced in the fact that local professionals, lawyers, doctors and the like were to be seen regularly in the stand at Highfield Road.

The season again began poorly, but in October 1909 – following the signing of Patsy Hendren, the Middlesex and England cricketer – things started to take off. By the New Year, after eight wins out of nine, the club were in the top six pushing upwards. On 28 December around 12,000, a new ground record, saw fellow challengers QPR defeated 4-0, and four days later a similar crowd saw the game with Swindon.

Another FA Cup run saw comfortable wins over Wrexham and Kettering. In the first round proper City were drawn at Preston. Few gave City much hope in the club's first ever game against First Division opponents, with bookies offering 20-1 against a City win. Whilst Preston were not in the same class as the 1889 'Invincibles' who had been the first winners of the League and FA Cup double, they were still felt to be far too good for City. On a mudheap of a pitch City trailed for most of the game but won with goals from Buckle and Hendren. Five hundred City fans were reported to have travelled north, one with a blue and white striped umbrella with a brass figure of a Bantam perched on it. A second round 1-0 win at Portsmouth (City's gate share was £200) set up a third round home tie with another top division side, Nottingham Forest.

Special arrangements were made at Highfield Road to accommodate a large crowd including 'erection of crush barriers on the banks' to 'check swaying movements', the installation of four extra rows of temporary seats in front of the grandstand, and detailed plans to avoid crowding at the entrances. Ground capacity was reportedly increased by 2,000 to an estimated 20,000. City's directors took the rash decision to 'make the price of admission 1s instead of 6d'. The hike caused 'some irritation among a section of the club's supporters' but others argued that the club needed the money. During the build up the *Midland Daily Telegraph* reported that the grandstand had often been overcrowded and talked of a new stand. If not, then a 'covered side' to protect supporters from 'rain and snow' which could in time become a grandstand. 'Nemo' wrote: 'The football enclosure of the not too distant future, I believe, will not have a single seat or standing space where a spectator is liable to a soaking.'

City's players escaped the Cup fever and ticket-price row by returning to the Richmond House, Droitwich Spa. After lunch on the Tuesday they were reported to have had a country walk followed by natural brine baths – said to have miraculous therapeutic powers – and in the evening went to the theatre in Worcester to see 'A White Man'.

As match-day approached it was feared that the raised capacity would not be 'overtaxed', as many floating supporters would be deterred by the high cost. A 'strong' police force of 30 were present for the the 3.30pm kick-off. The official crowd was 12,500 with receipts of £666 5s, a new ground record, but it was reported that there was 'a good deal of stand-ing room on the banks'. Around 2,000 Forest 'excursionists' made the 50-mile journey and 'made things lively in the centre of the city by cheering and the ringing of hand-bells'. 'Vendors of team photographs and club favours did a thriving business in the streets.' The ground opened early at 1pm and slowly filled. The crowd was entertained by 'lively music' from the Coventry Military Band.

After only five minutes City were ahead against 'red-shirted' Forest. 'A rush of the inside forwards carried the ball down' to the Swan Lane End and Billy Smith with a 'lightning shot along the ground' scored. City con-tinued to press, and from a free-kick 'a fierce scrimmage resulted and Chaplin dashing up vollied [sic] the ball into the side net'. After twenty minutes Forest equalised through Welsh international Grenville Morris. George 'Tubby' Warren restored City's lead before the break after a col-lision between two defenders left him with a tap-in. Smith scored again to make it 3-1 in the second half and Forest missed a penalty late on.

The quarter-final draw paired City with Everton, easily the hardest opponents to date: 'the most important and attractive football match yet played in Coventry.' The people of Coventry could speak of little else in the two weeks leading up to the game. There was predictable talk of switching the tie, and it seems the financially adept David Cooke – who was playing an increasingly central role in the club's affairs – was tempt-ed, if not with a switch to Goodison Park, then to nearby Villa Park, where a possible 40,000 crowd could be comfortably handled. In the end, the club resisted the lure of a massive pay-day to stay at home, maximise the potential of Highfield Road, but to make it a shilling gate. If the game was played today it would have surely been made all-ticket, but back then it was hoped to accommodate everyone who turned up, despite the counter-risk of a poor turnout if the weather turned bad.

The *Midland Daily Telegraph* assessed the price increase: 'The decision to again make it a shilling gate', double the normal price, 'with prices ranging up to 4/-, created no irritation among the local public on this occasion, the general feeling being that as the home club showed a sportsmanlike spirit in sticking to their ground, despite the temptations of filthy lucre, a shilling was not an out-of-the-way figure for such a first-class attraction.'

Once again City prepared at Droitwich Spa, although Everton 'whose directors are absolutely averse to the week's "special training" policy' trained quietly at home. On Thursday evening they travelled down from Merseyside and stayed at the Abbey Hotel, Kenilworth, arriving in Coventry on the day of the game by the 2pm train.

The gates opened two hours before the 3.30 kick-off and railway companies made arrangements to cope with an influx of 10,000 visitors to the city, including 2,000 from Merseyside. This was fewer than expected as the cheaper half-day excursion rates would get them to the ground too late. Some Everton fans were observed to be wearing Coventry City 'death-cards' in their hats, foretelling City's demise at the hands of their favourites.

A 34-strong police force apprehended a number of pick-pockets, along with pirate programme sellers, whose 'amateur contents' did not fool many. Some of these 'rogues' even shouted 'important team changes in both teams', which needless to say was 'invention', as both sides lined up as originally selected. Club favours and photographs sold readily in the streets, and 'on every side was apparent the evidence of the absorbing interest that was felt in the match'.

The banks filled up early, and long before the kick-off there appeared 'every prospect of the accommodation of the ground being taxed to the full'. The club had commandeered benches and chairs from local schools and placed them inside the enclosure, close to the touchlines to maximise the capacity, and this temporary seating was 'early taken up'. Large numbers evaded the barriers at the Highfield Road entrance corner and threatened 'the playing pitch from being encroached upon'. Eventually they were cleared away, 'leaving the touch lines quite clear.' 'The time of waiting was passed away by lively music played by the Coventry Military Band.' In the packed stand 'a piece of silverware occupied a prominent position on a pedestal'. This was a silver inkstand in the form of a bantam, which had been presented to the club by David Cooke. Decorated with 'light and dark ribbons it attracted much attention'.

With both teams normally wearing blue, City switched to a brand new kit of white shirts with collar and cuffs 'of the two blues'. Messrs Dowdeswell & Greenway, gentlemen's outfitters of 12 Smithford Street, generously donated them and displayed them in their window. When the teams emerged with City in 'new jerseys' the ground was 'packed'.

Everton boasted seven internationals, one amateur international, and one Scottish League representative. 'Nemo' noticed 'the Northerners were certainly the heavier lot of men'. City captain Charlie Tickle won the toss and chose to attack the Swan Lane End in the first half – a tradition largely observed to the modern day.

Two goals from England centre-forward Bertie Freeman, the first after only four minutes, settled the game in Everton's favour and ended City's glorious Cup run. In the semi-final Everton lost to Barnsley. The attendance of 18,995 produced record receipts of £1,052 and with the proceeds of the Cup run the club budgeted a new barrel-roofed grand-stand on the Highfield Road side at a cost of £1,200.

City's team in that memorable Cup was still talked about by older fans 50 years later. It was full of players who became club legends. In goal was Welshman Bob Evans, the only international in the ranks, 'a daring custodian.' At centre-half was former West Brom pivot Eli Bradley. The captain, Charlie Tickle, was a 'speedy and artistic right-winger' who represented the Football League against the Scottish League two years previously. Billy Smith at centre-forward was 'popular with his comrades' and in his second spell at the club. At inside-left was Patsy Hendren, not only an outstanding footballer but a brilliant 'dashing' batsman for Middlesex and England. He would become one of the century's greatest ever cricketers and his arrival the previous October had sparked City's rich vein of form.

Once again the Cup run meant a backlog of league matches. City had to play fifteen games in seven weeks to finish 8th. The club, however, now boasted a bigger profile than ever before, and home gates were now averaging 6,300.

The directors spent the proceeds of the Cup bonanza on a new 'grandstand' opposite the John Bull Stand on the north side of the enclosure. It would be erected on what had previously been a low bank. On 6 July 1910 the *Midland Daily Telegraph* reported: 'good progress being made in the erection of new grandstand.' On 20 August, during the first public trial, the new stand although 'virtually completed' was not used. The *MDT* reported that afterwards many spectators stayed to 'look over' it, 'which was much commended as a well-designed and substantially built erection, commanding an excellent view of the playing enclosure from all the ranks of its steeply raked tiers of seats.'

The new structure, costing £1,200 and built by Humphreys Ltd, who were well known for their work at football grounds, was some 80 yards long – the pitch was between 100-110 yards – and had a barrel-type roof. Entry was via the front, up wooden steps. Along the facia was painted 'Atkinsons Fine Ales', presumably for a small fee. The dressing rooms were underneath and the players emerged onto the pitch midway between the halfway line and the Swan Lane corner flag. There was seating for around 2,000, with the centre of the stand housing 498 'most comfortable' tip-up seats 'similar to those used in theatres'. The *MDT* asserted that 'there was better accommodation than any other Southern League ground'.

There was, however, grumbling about the prices charged in the new stand – 1s 3d for the wings and 1s 6d for the tip-up seats in the centre.

This compared with 9d and 1s for the old stand. For some weeks empty seats confirmed that spectators were balking at the higher prices.

The official opening was on 3 September 1910 for the reserve team's South East Counties League game against Tunbridge Wells. Councillor Vernon Pugh, vice-president of the club carried out the formalities and Charles Crump represented the Football Association. In his opening speech Pugh attacked the club's critics: 'Since the club got into the Southern League ... have to remember that Association Football appeals to all classes nowadays ... well to do clientele can well afford to pay for superior accommodation.' His words confirmed that City were charging what they thought the market could bear and were targeting a higher class of football fan. One wonders if that 'clientele' would turn up for the cold afternoons in the middle of winter.

The Mayor, Alderman Fred Lee, made an enthusiastic speech: 'looking at the old stand I wonder how we endured it for so many years. It was anything but comfortable but this [one] was beautiful.' The reserves won 5-0 to round off a memorable day and the stand remained for 54 years before being demolished to make way for the Sky Blue Stand.

The club handbook, published to coincide with the new season, was upbeat: 'It is in no boastful or over-reaching spirit that Coventry City may boldly claim to stand higher than ever before in its history, and with every prospect of a steadily successful future.' In October a report in the *MDT* said: 'the new grandstand is indifferently patronised "but old cheers factory is full up".' This suggests that the old stand was still full but the dearer new stand was proving less popular with supporters.

The **1910-11** season was less successful in league terms. City finished 11th in the Southern League, but once again pulled off a Cup giantkilling. Their success the previous year guaranteed an automatic first round place and City were drawn at Sheffield Wednesday, destined to finish 6th in Division One. Two thousand City fans made the trip to Hillsborough, 'outshouted' the home crowd, and were rewarded with a victory – Billy Smith scoring a late goal.

Defending Southern League champions Brighton were next up. After a 0-0 draw on the south coast the clubs met in a Thursday afternoon replay at Highfield Road. It was the first big game since the opening of the new stand. The club charged 6d (2.5p) for the Highfield Road end but 1 shilling (5p) for the Swan Lane bank. The stands were dearer, with seats in the old stand costing 1s 6d (7.5p) or 2s (10p), and in the new stand 2s and 2s 6d (12.5p) for those in the centre, which were reserved and available only from David Cooke's tobacconists in High Street. Boys could get in for 3d, but only at the Highfield Road end.

The club's directors urged local employees to allow workers to work from breakfast until 2pm to allow them to attend. They felt the Cup performances had promoted the city and hoped companies would reciprocate. Three of the biggest – Daimler, Humber, and Deasy – announced a 1pm closing to allow workers to get to the game. What seems on the face of it a magnanimous gesture was not welcomed by all. On the letters page in the *Midland Daily Telegraph* JEH complained: 'What about the scores of workmen who did not wish to attend the match, but who were compelled to lose half a days work [and presumably pay] in consequence of this half holiday.'

The team left for Droitwich on the Monday morning for 'pampering', rest, brine baths, and an 'exciting' whist drive on Wednesday night. They returned to 'lunch at the Queens Hotel and took a brake [a sturdy horse-drawn wagon] to the ground' before beating Brighton 2-0 in front of 15,711 (the second largest crowd at the ground to that date) and receipts of £611 10s 6d. After the game the players had 'tea' at the Kings Head. The following day Coventry Police Court dealt with one of the first incidents of football hooliganism when Thomas Throne, a 42-year-old tool fitter of Thomas Street, was charged with being drunk and disorderly in Spon Street. He said he had been to the match and got a little excited.

The Cup run ended in a third round defeat at Burnley, where City's travelling army of 600 got soaked in 'miserably wet weather' and the team, without the injured Bob Evans, slumped to a 0-5 defeat on 'the worst pitch City have ever played on'. City's share of the £600 gate was a welcome addition to the coffers already boosted by the proceeds from the previous three ties.

Small compensation came when City lifted the Birmingham Senior Cup for the first time by beating Stourbridge at home 2-1 in the final.

One of the ground's zanier moments occurred in January 1911 when on a damp Thursday afternoon a City XI comprising mainly reserves met Fred Karno's XI in a charity game in aid of the Bolton Colliery Disaster Relief Fund. Karno was a Music Hall impresario who employed a travelling band of comedians known as Fred Karno's Fun Factory. That week they were playing the Coventry Hippodrome in Hales Street and possibly included two bright young comics, Charlie Chaplin and Stan Laurel, who were known to be part of Karno's group until at least 1912. It is not known how much the game raised, but £145,000 was collected nationwide to assist families of the 344 men and boys killed in a fire at Pretoria Pit near Bolton just before Christmas.

The *Midland Daily Telegraph* reported on City's 3-2 win: 'A celebrated company of comedians includes some well known professional footballers, also the popular vaudeville artistes, Will Poluski Junior and the Three Prestons.' These acts were household names at the time.

A week later 'Nemo' reporting on a reserve game, was forced to criticise the Highfield Road pitch: 'The ground was in a condition known as "rotten", half frozen and half thawed, flaky and greasy on the surface. There was hardly enough wind to stir the flags.'

At the board meeting of June 1911 it was confirmed that home crowds averaged 5,900 with total gate money received £4,869. The fixed assets of the club were reported to be £1,242 and included the two stands and fencing.

That summer further ground improvements took place. The embankments at the west town end were extended, the original John Bull grandstand was made thoroughly weather-proof and 'comfortable', and a 'well fitted room' for the referee was added to the new stand. On the playing side, several Cup 'heroes' departed, including Hendren, Buckle, Tickle and Percy Saul. New manager Bob Wallace made some useful signings, among them defender Billy Yates from Portsmouth and forwards Ivor Brown from Tottenham and Albert Holmes from Mansfield.

1911-12 was another good season with a 6th-place finish and crowds up to 6,100. In October the club played foreign opposition for the first time when the Canadian champions Hillhurst Amateur Association of Calgary (known as Calgary Hillhursts) visited. The Thursday afternoon attendance is not recorded but was unlikely to be much over 1,000. Full-strength City won 4-3.

On 2 September 1911 the club announced the formation of a 'Supporters Committee', a forerunner of the Supporters Club. It comprised twelve 'gentlemen' supporters who would assist the directors in the running of the football club. It was the first clear evidence of 'ordinary' supporters becoming involved in this way. The committee would 'have the welfare of the club at heart, might be able to promote it, and act as a kind of connecting link between the Board and the general body of City followers'. The identities of those twelve 'gentlemen' is a mystery but they met regularly and in December introduced a £5 gate prize at a reserve game, which was later discovered to be illegal and was a flop anyway.

At Christmas 1911 City played three games on consecutive days. Over 10,000 were inside the ground on Christmas Day to watch City lose to lowly Bristol Rovers. On Boxing Day Rovers completed the double at Eastville, and a tired and sorry-looking City returned to face Brentford the following day. A crowd of 7,000 witnessed a reversal of fortunes, with the Londoners on the end of a nine-goal barrage, and Billy Smith netting five.

Two weeks later in the Cup, City pulled off a minor shock by winning 2-0 at fellow Southern Leaguers Southampton. The match report reveals a wonderful story about City's travelling support. Two hundred City followers gave a 'perfect imitation' of the Chorus of Demons from Berlioz's *Faust*. 'Their shrieks and howls, wild laughter and mocking choruses were a veritable reproduction of the pandemonium let loose which occurs in that terrific opera.'

The draw for the second round paired City with mighty Manchester United, arguably the top team of the age. Under the management of Ernest Magnall, the Reds had won the League championship in 1908 and 1911 and the FA Cup in 1910. They boasted several internationals including legendary Welshman Billy Meredith.

Should Coventry switch to United's new Old Trafford stadium? The ground, opened a year previously, could hold 80,000 on gigantic concrete terracing which covered three of its sides. The board waited on a 'substantial' offer from United which apparently never materialised, because City soon published their ticket prices.

The directors announced another '1 shilling gate', doubling the normal terrace prices, but tickets purchased more than seven days in advance cost just 6d – a praiseworthy gesture to 'poor' supporters. In view of their slice of the gate money, it transpired that Manchester's permission was necessary, and there was much hoo-ing and haa-ing about forged tickets. If tickets went on sale more than two days before the game it would almost certainly provoke a flood of counterfeits by 'certain Birmingham Swindlers who are always on the look-out for such opportunities' and 'whose practices the club have had previous experience'. This presumably referred to the big Cup games in 1910. The outcome is unknown, but there were certainly plenty of cheaper ground tickets purchased before the big day.

Droitwich Spa was again City's venue for preparations, with days 'quietly spent in readiness for the great tussle'. A midweek return to Coventry preceded evening excursions to the Hippodrome Theatre and the Opera House, the latter to view the hit play 'The Whip', about the kidnap of a racehorse on the train to Newmarket where he is a dead cert for the Two Thousand Guineas. The tense tunnel scene as the roaring train came closer and closer provoked the audience to shout out in their attempt to free the horse from the crash.

Light snowfalls preceded the game and the pitch was treacherous, although the lines had been cleared. The club had erected extra crush barriers on the banks, deeper than the Everton game two years earlier, which encouraged directors to anticipate a record 20,000-plus gate.

'Nemo' reported from amongst the mass of standing spectators: 'Standing amongst a knot of enthusiasts from Bedworth it was at all times necessary to take what precautions one might against the shoe-toes of one's neighbours, for the way these miners kick when they are excited is wonderful.'

He described what could be bought inside the ground: 'The cup-tie spectator has plenty of opportunities of parting with his pence. He may purchase from the numerous vendors who squeeze their way through the crowd, pictures of both teams, favours of all styles, chocolates and oranges. That there would be custom for these items can be understood, but what the football crowd wanted were the booklets which were being offered for sale entitled "The Hangman's Record: Executions of the last 400 years", goodness only knows'.

By 2.30 the Old stand was almost full and both banks behind the goals were packed. There were, however, gaps in the centre stands where the prices were 'steep' at 4s 6d for the New, and 3s 6d for the Old. Four hundred makeshift chairs in front of the Old stand (1s 6d) were snapped up. The crowd was entertained by the Broad Street Wesleyan Band's 'popular airs'. A detachment of 30 policemen helped stewards keep the crowd in order, although 'on the whole they didn't require much looking after'.

The Bantams ran out at 2.50 to 'hearty applause' before lining up for their team photo. United kicked off kicking towards the Swan Lane end and proceeded to rip City apart, winning 5-1. Afterwards it was suggested City had the wrong footwear for the icy pitch, but they were probably simply outclassed by a tip-top side for whom Meredith sparkled. The 35-year-old winger didn't score but made endless chances for others. He had been suspended for eighteen months earlier in his career for accepting illegal payments, but would go on to play top-class football until he was 50 years old.

According to one match report: 'considering the condition of the turf, distinctly the finest display of high class football that has been yet given on the Highfield Road enclosure since it was opened.' The attendance, a disappointing 17,251, produced receipts of £908, but the obvious spare room on the banks convinced the club that the ground capacity now exceeded 20,000.

The heavy defeat did not affect City's league form and they ended the season strongly. However, on a Thursday afternoon in March possibly the smallest crowd ever to watch the first team at Highfield Road saw a 2-0 win over Leyton. As the game kicked off with rain 'pelting down mercilessly' it was estimated that there were around 500 people in the ground. As the rain eased slightly that number increased to around 1,000.

On 23 March 1912 Highfield Road registered another first when chosen to host a representative game for the first time – the annual fixture between Birmingham Juniors, the cream of young Midlands talent, and Scotland, similarly the best young players from north of the border. 1,500 spectators watched a 2-2 draw between what was a forerunner of Under-23 internationals.

Three weeks later the *Titanic* sank in the North Atlantic with the loss of 1,500 lives. Collections for survivors were made all over the world, and at City's final home game against West Ham £16 4s 5¾d was raised in a half-time blanket collection. That same week David Cooke stepped up as chairman in place of Councillor Lee, with other directors JF Eales and WH Hattrell retiring. Messrs WM Turrell and A Collingbourne accepted invitations to join the board.

With reduced income from Cup-ties, reduced finances meant that at a shareholders meeting in June 1912 plans to build terraces at the ground were put on hold. Average gates of 6,100 would need to rise to 10,000 for the club to break even.

The team started **1912-13** brightly, but it wouldn't last. Popular player Eli Bradley was sold for a record £500 to Hearts to prop up the finances, and a post-Christmas slump saw the club finish 13th. Attendances were never going to reach 10,000 and bobbed along at 6/7,000 before sinking to 3/4,000 by the season's end.

Once again the Cup came to the rescue. City again landed Manchester United, this time at Old Trafford. In bitterly cold weather, only 11,502 spectators rattled around the 80,000-capacity concrete bowl – justifying City's decision the previous season not to switch the tie. A few hundred supporters battled through snowstorms to follow the club north, one of whom presented a live bantam mascot to the team – cementing the impact of the nickname. Scores were relayed every fifteen minutes back to Highfield Road, where the reserves were playing Darlaston in the Birmingham League. Young Coventry player J Mitchell put the Bantams ahead before England international George Wall equalised, forcing a creditable replay. City's Harry Welch was crocked from several strong challenges from United's Enoch 'Knocker' West. He collapsed in the dressing room, spent the journey home prone on his back, and had his injury diagnosed as a strain of the heart muscle. West was one of the hardest men in a hard game and was later was banned *sine die* for fixing a United game in 1915.

On the Monday before the replay the club followed routine by heading for Droitwich, brine baths and massages. That night they trooped to Birmingham for pantomime. Tuesday was light training at Highfield Road with a whist drive in the evening. Wednesday evening was spent at the Hippodrome where old friend Fred Karno was in town.

On match-day, Thursday, the weather turned warmer and the snow was cleared to avoid a 'slushy' pitch. Supporters were warned to have the right money as no change would be given at the turnstiles. Prices were again 6d at the Highfield Road end and 1 shilling at the Swan Lane end. Chairman David Cooke wrote to local firms asking them to cooperate by closing early, and the scenes outside the ground at lunchtime suggested they had acceded to his request. Thousands were desperate to gain admission. Some climbed trees in Swan Lane to view the game whilst others perched on advertising hoardings.

The lucky bantam mascot was given pride of place on a perch in the centre of the old stand, while Jack Cribdon, a well-known local boxer and City supporter, paraded around the pitch on a donkey waving a blue and white striped umbrella.

United had a big travelling support even in those days, and probably several hundred made the trip to Coventry, up for the Cup, 'carrying their bells and rattles and red and white sunshades.'

On a heavy pitch, City went close on several occasions before Charlie Roberts headed the Reds into the lead before half-time. City continued to press and with six minutes left Harry Parkes headed home Holmes' cross. The roar was such that some said later that it was heard three miles away, but three minutes later the normally reliable keeper Bob Evans slipped and allowed a tame shot to dribble past him. It was the end of City's fourth consecutive exciting Cup campaign, which had become an accepted thing in the city. Little did the fans realise that it would be another seventeen years before Cup fever would return.

The official attendance, 20,042, was a new record, but the receipts of £859 were less than the record set against Everton in 1910.

The summer of 1913 was marked by increasing militancy from the suffragette movement, with arson attacks mounted on churches, country houses and sporting facilities, culminating in Emily Davison being killed by the King's horse on Derby Day. At Highfield Road in July a concert was given on the pitch. A stage was erected facing the new stand, while artistes included the Coventry Musical Club Male Voice Choir and the Chapman and Pool Prize Quartet Parties.

That summer the club's offices moved from Bayley Lane to Highfield Road, situated behind the Atkinson's stand, and improvements were carried out to the pitch's drainage. But money was tight. The club issued a statement: 'Unless we can be assured of better gates, the club cannot go on in its present sphere.' Some good players left, including Bob Evans, defender John Thomson, and Ivor Brown as the club slashed the playing staff from 24 to eighteen. During the **1913-14** season the team failed to win between November and April and were relegated after propping up the league. Attendances, which averaged 6,100, held up surprisingly well, but gates at many clubs were booming, with Chelsea averaging over 37,000. Income from reserve games had slumped, with attendances at some measured in the hundreds.

In the Cup the club were handicapped for not progressing beyond the first round the previous season and forced to take their chances in the fourth qualifying round (the equivalent of today's first round) at the end of November. The disappointment probably went some way to explaining a shock defeat by Port Vale.

The summer of 1914 saw a mass exodus of players, so that virtually the whole team had to be rebuilt by new manager Frank Scott-Walford. Division Two of the Southern League comprised fifteen clubs, the great majority of them from south Wales. Of these, Abertillery and Mardy did not last the season and City's huge wins, 8-0 and 6-0 respectively, were expunged from the records. City racked up ten against Newport County and six against Ebbw Vale, but the goal feasts didn't attract the fans to Highfield Road and attendances slumped.

As the **1914-15** season unfurled, City were forced to rely on grants from the Southern League and even cash from Scott-Walford's own pocket. Players accepted pay-cuts with stoicism, but in March 1915 the final indignity came when the club was summoned for non-payment of rates. The season ended in mid-April with a 5-2 win over Pontypridd, watched by around 1,000 spectators. The result left City 5th, but on the brink of going out of business.

Whilst City were going through the motions in this Mickey Mouse competition, British servicemen were falling in droves on the battlefields of France and Belgium. The Great War had started in August 1914, but the football authorities chose to persevere with a full league programme, which many found distasteful. In Coventry there was criticism of the football club in the *Coventry Herald*: 'It is to be regretted that professional football was not abandoned at the beginning of the war like rugby whose spirited and patriotic policy received general acclamation. The professional footballer is no longer a public idol. When the war is over and football resumes, one certainly expects to see Coventry Rugby Club once again the most popular club as in the older days and Coventry a distinctly rugby town.'

Coventry weren't the only club to suffer a drop in gates. Across the Football League revenues were slashed by more than half. Several clubs were on the verge of collapse and in April 1915, as British and Common-wealth troops prepared for their fateful landings at Gallipoli, the Football and Southern Leagues made plans to reduce the players' maximum wage and to allow clubs to terminate players' contracts at 28 days notice.

In a gamble to improve its sagging fortunes, Coventry City applied for membership of the Central League – the reserve league of the northern Football League clubs – but neither this nor a subsequent application to the Second Division of the Football League were successful. The club had lost £1,500 in the previous season and owed nearly £1,000 to David Cooke and £100 to Scott-Walford, who had left to take up a Government appointment. City now had no officials, no money, very few players and no league to play in.

In July 1915 the football authorities bowed to mounting public pres-sure and suspended competitive football for the duration of the war. The Football League continued to run regional competitions but players were not paid, other than expenses, there were no midweek games, and there would be no cups, medals or other trinkets. Games were reduced to 80 minutes and the referee could dispense with the ten-minute interval. After compulsory military service was introduced in 1916, police kept close watch at matches, trying to catch shirkers, and many players ended up in the armed forces. Clubs found it hard to muster a team – in 1916-17 Blackburn Rovers used 95 different players to fulfil a 36-match pro-gramme – and guest players were used by all teams.

Over the next three years there was little or no football at Highfield Road. Although the ground was effectively mothballed and all the players released, there was still rent and rates to pay, plus interest on loans. Losses of £500 in 1916 and £564 in 1917 were reported before David Cooke came to the club's rescue. Cooke, by now a prominent local businessman, paid off three and a half years' rent owing on Highfield Road and became sole tenant of the ground.

The ground hosted a number of sporting events over this period, including two celebrity charity football games. The first, on 5 February 1916, was between teams representing the Midlands and the Rest of England. Three former Bantams turned out: Harry Parkes (now of West Brom), for the Midlands, and Fred Jones (Manchester City) and Albert Feebury (Crystal Palace) for the Rest of England. It was a star-studded game and gave City's long-suffering fans the opportunity to see top-class international players including Harry Hampton (Aston Villa), Jesse Pennington (West Brom), the Reverend Kenneth Hunt (Wolves) and Jimmy Windridge (Birmingham). The match report described a 'large crowd' but gives no figures and the Midlands team lost 2-4. The proceeds went to the British Red Cross Society and reports describe wounded soldiers being driven to the match in motor cars lent by the Coventry and Warwickshire Motor Club.

A year later on 20 January 1917 a similar game was contested between Coventry City and a Midlands XI. City put out a team comprising pre-war players and a few guests, including Tottenham's Middlemiss, but lost 3-6 to a strong select XI which included internationals Andy Ducat (Aston Villa) and Bertie Freeman, the former Everton forward who had ended City's Cup dreams in 1910, who now played for Burnley.

Boxing was staged at Highfield Road on 5 May 1917. A ring was erected in front of the Atkinson's Stand and 'a goodly number' watched an attractive bill made up of mainly Midland boxers. Top billing was a heavyweight bout between Tango Debney and Jean Barr. Debney hailed from West Bromwich whilst Barr was a Belgian residing in Coventry. In a fifteen-round contest Debney was declared the winner on points.

That summer the club opened its grounds for two sports days. First, the Coventry Advisory Committee for Womens War Employment organised a benefit for the city's female munitions workers. Among the events was an egg and spoon race, a skipping race, a tug of war, and something called cutting-the-ham. Then on 30 June around 5,000 spectators attended the Coventry Ordnance Works Sports Carnival. The men's events included 100 yards sprint, high jump, a 50 yards wheelbarrow race, a tug of war, relay races and a novelty cycle race. Events for the ladies included an egg and spoon race, a tug of war and a 70 yards skipping race. The proceeds were shared between the Coventry and Warwickshire Hospital and the Hillcrest Military Hospital.

Coventry Godiva Harriers also used the Highfield Road facilities for their training headquarters. At weekly sessions the runners would set off on a course from the ground, up Binley Road, across fields to the Craven Arms pub, along the Sowe Road, across Wyken Church fields, up to Stoke Heath Common and back to the ground for a lap around the pitch.

Later in 1917 the city's female munitions workers held their football tournament at Highfield Road. On 19 October 1917 the *Coventry Graphic* reported that the Coventry Ordnance Main Shop team had reached the semi-final of the competition. Three months later there were reports of a Rudge-Whitworth ladies team playing a Coventry Army Service Forces team at Highfield Road.

In early 1918, with the club's debts cleared and the war on the Western Front apparently turning in the Allies' direction, the board looked ahead to peacetime football, with their key objective being entry to the Football League. A manager, William Clayton, had been appointed in 1917, and although he was only employed on a part-time basis, it marked the start of the club's rejuvenation.

In January 1918 City played their first home game for almost three years, drawing 1-1 with an Aston Villa XI. The players were virtual unknowns, and details of the game sketchy, but that friendly match was soon followed by others with Birmingham Works Association, Leicester Fosse, and Birmingham FC. By May 1918, when Leicester returned to Highfield Road for a National War Fund game, Clayton had developed a useful team which thumped the visitors 5-0.

A new sport appeared at Highfield Road in July 1918 when US servicemen stationed in Britain played the first baseball match at the ground. Teams representing Waddington and South Canton played out a nine-innings game to raise funds for the Coventry Prisoner of War Fund. A crowd estimated at 4,000 raised several hundred pounds and saw South Canton triumph 3-1.

City's **1918-19** season was destined to be the last on a regional basis, as the club applied to be co-opted to the Midland Section of the Football League. After much lobbying by Clayton, director Alf Collingbourne and secretary Harry Harbourne, City were duly elected and drooled at a fixture list that included five First Division sides and the likes of Sheffield United and Wednesday, Huddersfield, Birmingham and Leicester Fosse. City were one of only two non-league clubs in the league and knew that a strong showing in this temporary competition would help secure a League place when post-war football started.

The opening game against Grimsby Town was watched by 10,000 and resulted in a 7-4 victory, with Bantams centre-forward Chris Sambrooke scoring a hat-trick. Home performances were good, and the side defeated Huddersfield 7-1, with another Sambrooke hat-trick, and Notts County 5-1 on the Saturday before the Armistice was signed on 11 November.

It is estimated that over one million British soldiers died in the Great War. Every football club in the country lost players in action. According to the 1919-20 Club Handbook, the following City players died in action: George Warren, Steven Jackson, Tom Morris, Jack Harkins and Walter Kimberley. Several others were wounded in service.

Crowds at Highfield Road were remarkable, with 10,000 the norm and the highest being 12,000 to see Sheffield United and Leicester Fosse. Attending matches was a popular pastime for returning soldiers, as well as the general public starved of entertainment during the war.

The Coventry team had a pretty settled look, with six or seven players virtually ever-present, but still had to rely on guests, and in total used 47 different players in 36 games. The guests included West Brom's English international full-back Jesse Pennington and Scottish international George Chaplin, both of whom were employed in the city's munitions factories. Chaplin would stay with the club after the war and become captain. Many of the guests, however, were one-game wonders, thrown into the fray when the club couldn't put a full side out. Among them was the team's trainer, Fulljames, who had to don the shirt against Sheffield Wednesday. The team finished 9th but by January 1919 the directors felt sufficiently confident to resign from the Southern League and start their campaign to join the Football League.

Coventry's outlook was nothing less than professional and their case was persuasive: City had a 'fine, well-equipped' ground holding 24,000 spectators; attendances were good; the team was a 'big-draw' at away grounds; the financial position of the club was sound; the city had good railway facilities and the population had more than doubled in the last twenty years to close to 200,000.

Collingbourne, Cooke, Clayton and Harbourne lobbied hard and the club's fate was determined at the Football League's Special General Meeting in Manchester on 10 March 1919. The meeting was dominated by the vote to fill two extra places in the First Division, a ballot which controversially saw Second Division Arsenal receive more votes than Tottenham, despite their North London rivals having been relegated from the top division in 1914-15. Seven clubs faced City in the fight for four places in Division Two, and City topped the poll with 35 votes. West Ham (32), South Shields (28), Rotherham (28) were also elected, but Port Vale (27), Southport (7) and Rochdale (7) were unsuccessful.

Coventry looked forward to their first season in the Football League.

CHAPTER THREE

The 1920s

Coventry City's preparation for life in the Football League started as soon as their election had been confirmed. In the *Midland Daily Telegraph* on 15 March 1919, 'Nemo' interviewed director Mr W Carpenter, who said: 'The matter of first importance will be the Club's ability to get together a team sufficiently strong to uphold the reputation of the City in the Second Division.' He added that it was impossible to say what the composition of the team would be, but hoped that there would be a number of local players in it.

Many believed entry to the League would herald a golden age in the club's history: in fact it would be the start of a period later described as the 'Stormy Period', which lasted twelve years until the arrival of Harry Storer as manager in 1931.

Elsewhere in 1919 it was clear the transition from war to peace would not be easy for many clubs. Some still awaited the demobbing of players from the armed services, others were given dispensation to pay players extra travelling expenses because of housing shortages.

A potentially serious problem for City arose when the Southern League barred their players from registering with the Football League. This was in retaliation for perceived League heavy-handedness towards the Southern League. The club were 'advised' to ignore the ban, but the frosty relationship between the leagues continued. City were, in effect, struck off from the Southern League, a situation which could have had catastrophic implications nine months later.

Off the field, much work was carried out on the ground in anticipation of larger crowds. On 15 August 1919 the *Coventry Herald* reported:

'Those who attend the Highfield Road ground on Saturday will find plenty to claim their attention. During the close season the enclosure has been greatly improved and the structural work will be finished this week. The extensive terracing in front of the new (1910) stand will provide capital accommodation, the banking on the Nicholls Street side (West end) of the ground has been extended, and the Swan Lane end improved. Extra standing room has also been provided in front of the old stand. All these improvements have meant taking of a small portion of the playing field, but this has been accomplished without detriment or cramping. The playing pitch has been marked out a couple of yards nearer the old stand and a fair distance nearer Swan Lane. Additional entrances and turnstiles have been provided, and it should be a great deal easier this season to gain admission. The chief improvement in this direction is a new entrance with several turnstiles at the top of King Richard Street, their being sufficient room at this spot for spectators to queue up on the club's own ground. The players will find much more comfortable quarters on the ground. A fine new Recreation room is now approaching completion, where they will be able to enjoy billiards and other games. The Dressing rooms have been much improved, particularly bathing facilities, and a new arrangement will give both teams protracted entrance to the field of play.'

The pitch movement described as 'a couple of yards' was actually four or five yards, and allowed not only a larger bank at the west end, but also the terraced enclosure in front of the newer stand. An early programme that season showed a 'sketch plan' showing the stands, entrances and transfers. In total there were seventeen external turnstiles, two designated as 'boys only', plus a further seven internal 'stiles' allowing transfer from the ground into the stands or the enclosures in front of the stands. Increased prices now showed ground entrance 1 shilling (5p) and entrance to the stands from 1s 6d (7.5p) to 3 shillings (15p).

Jim Hamill, president of the supporters club (a turnstile operator during the Second World War), remembers those turnstiles well: 'Those old stiles were so thin that you had to go through them sideways. A lot of the modern day fans wouldn't have been able to get through them as they are too large. Boys could be lifted over the stiles if their dad knew the turnstile operator.'

The **1919-20** season kicked off on 30 August with an attractive home game against Tottenham, relegated from Division One in 1915 and, in many people's eyes, cheated of a place in the enlarged post-war top division by Arsenal. City fielded many of the better players from the previous season but included four new signings, all with top-flight experience. The game kicked off at 3.30 and the Coventry Silver Band entertained the crowd beforehand.

City were outclassed by the Londoners and crashed 0-5 in front of a 16,500 crowd. To rub salt in the wounds, Spurs' goalkeeper was former City custodian Bill Jacques. It was the start of a miserable run of nine successive defeats, and City's first win did not arrive until Christmas Day, after nineteen winless games. By then, the entire team had been scrapped, except for two players, and manager Clayton had quit seven games into the season. Harry Pollitt took over in mid-November and was given several thousand pounds to strengthen the woeful team. By the season's end the club had used a record 43 different players. Despite the team being several points adrift at Christmas, Pollitt turned things around. With two games remaining City were next to bottom, a point behind Lincoln but with a game in hand. With the bottom two facing re-election, it was widely feared that City would be voted out. With the Football League and the Southern League still at loggerheads, City might even find themselves with nowhere to go.

The final games were home and away to fifth-placed Bury. City drew 2-2 at Gigg Lane and needed to win the final game to avoid re-election. In front of a record crowd of 23,506 a nervous City trailed 0-1 at half-time. Two second-half goals from Alec Mercer saved their bacon. Dark rumours persisted about the result, and three years later in 1923 the FA conducted an inquiry, the conclusion of which was that the two clubs had colluded to allow City to win. All told, six players and five directors and officials were suspended for life. Directors David Cooke and Jack Marshall, manager Harry Pollitt and captain George Chaplin were City's culprits. Both clubs were fined £100. Ironically, City would have been safe even in defeat, as Lincoln lost at Huddersfield, making the score from Highfield Road immaterial.

Some twenty years later details of the scandal emerged in a newspaper interview with Chaplin. He had taken £200 to Bury before the first game, feeling confident the incentive would ensure City at least three points from the two matches. At half-time at Highfield Road a Bury players entered the home dressing room and told him City were so poor that Bury could not lose. Later that night Chaplin handed over the final instalment of the bribe in the cloakroom of the Kings Head.

Despite poor home performances and the plight of the team, attendances were a record high and averaged 16,899, the fourth highest in the division, with several exceeding 20,000. Contemporary match photographs generally show a healthy, full crowd. After the austere war years, crowds were flocking to watch football across the country, with Chelsea topping the averages with over 42,000 – a new League record. Prior to 1925 City's attendances were estimates only, apart from Cup games which – with proceeds split three ways with the opposition and the FA – had to be exact. In the Cup, City drew 1-1 at Southern League Luton and in the Thursday afternoon replay Highfield Road's highest recorded crowd of 21,893 saw the Hatters snatch a 1-0 win. Despite healthy gates, the club reported a loss of £7,000, mainly down to transfer fees, and these were only possible thanks to David Cooke's deep pockets.

The **1920-21** season saw no improvement on the pitch. Despite keeping the team up, Pollitt had been sacked and replaced by Albert Evans, a member of Aston Villa's double-winning team of 1897. The side were bottom for most of the season and finished 21st out of 22, avoiding relegation to the new Third Division because only one team went down. Average crowds were up to 16,992 with the highest – 22,800 – recorded for the December local derby with Birmingham.

Long-time supporter Sydney Ward remembers his first City game that season: 'I was about thirteen years old and my father took me to the home game with Cardiff City on Boxing Day. Boys got in for sixpence in those days and a programme was one penny. City's goalkeeper was Jerry Best and he was carried off injured that day and we lost 4-2. We stood on the Swan Lane end, which later was built up with soil and other materials. A lot of the gardens of houses around the ground were full of bicycles. People would charge 2d to leave your bike in their garden.'

1920 saw the formation of the Coventry City supporters club. Within six months the 1,000 early members were enjoying social events and trips to away games. In early 1921 the supporters club and the football club formed a joint council to work in unison for the betterment of the club. At a meeting in March 1921 it was proposed to raise finance for a cover over the 'popular side' (the west end).

In February 1921 ladies football arrived at Highfield Road. A girls team from Dick, Kerr – a firm of tram makers from Preston – made headlines after the First World War with their exciting brand of football. The undefeated ladies champions of England hired League grounds and staged matches for charitable causes. England's biggest ever crowd for a women's game in England took place at Goodison Park on Boxing Day 1920 when 53,000 people watched Dick, Kerr's Ladies beat their closest rivals, St Helens Ladies, 4-0.

On 26 February the same teams played at Highfield Road in aid of the Mayor's Fund for the Relief of Distress, a local charity for the benefit of poor families. Advance publicity stirred the interest, and a crowd nearing 25,000 was reported in attendance. If that figure is accurate it would have constituted a new ground record, but in 1929 when discussing record crowds that gate was confirmed as 22,920, 600 short of the record. The team from Preston were again too strong and ran out 8-1 winners. Lily Parr netted a hat-trick.

In October 1921 the Football Association banned women from playing on Football League grounds. The reason given was that: 'Complaints have been made as to football being played by women, the council feel impelled to express their strong opinion that the game of football is quite unsuitable for females and ought not to be encouraged.' Though ladies football continued to take place, there was a considerable decrease in interest. The FA ban lasted until 1971.

In **1921-22**, for the third season running, City struggled in Division Two and in early 1922 there was more talk of financial difficulties. The supporters club tried to discover the true situation via the Joint Council and the club's shareholders called an Extraordinary General Meeting. The move prompted David Cooke to write off £13,835 owed to him and persuade other directors to cancel loans due to them. Up to this time he had been the sole guarantor of the club's debt. At the same time the entire board of directors resigned. Cooke's initiative undoubtedly saved the club from disaster. He was appointed President, with Walter Harris – chairman of the supporters club – forming a new board. Harris said: 'What money I possess I have made in Coventry, and if I can do anything to further the interests of Coventry City I feel I should do it.'

On the field, relegation was averted with a 4-2 home win over Notts County in front of a new record crowd of 25,000. In the Cup, City's prewar cup-fighting tradition was a distant memory – once again they failed to reach the competition proper, losing to Third Division Southport Central.

The new board favoured a new club image. Out went the old blue and white, and in came red and green, 'in harmony' with the civic colours. Red and green halves was introduced for **1922-23**, and the club's offices and stands were repainted in the new colours.

Walter Harris encouraged the supporters club in ground development and set up an Appeal Fund. In the summer of 1922 they helped out with a number of tasks, including the repainting. Herbert Kendall, secretary of the supporters club, handed out brushes and paint kettles each evening during the summer and volunteers painted away until dusk. A 100-yard cinder sprint track was laid alongside the touchline in front of the new stand, as a welcome addition to the 'training appointments' of the stadium. The stands underwent renovation with the roofs tarred, better-quality seats provided for visiting directors, and additional crush barriers erected at the Swan Lane end. The *Midland Daily Telegraph* complimented the work: 'The workmanship is excellent and the effect will certainly be bright and pleasing. The upper portions of the insides of the two stands are being painted white. The ironwork and uprights are red, and the woodwork is to be green. The boarded fence which skirts the playing pitch is to be painted white, the barriers have been creosoted, and all the turnstiles will be painted. The whole scheme is admirable.' It was a fine testament to the volunteers, whether they be amateur painters or professional glaziers, plumbers or carpenters.

Another major project in the summer of 1922 was the extension of the Swan Lane end into what became as the 'Spion Kop' or the 'Kop' for short. The name originates from a mountain in the Natal province of South Africa where a battle took place in 1900 during the Boer War. The words are Dutch, meaning 'Look-out hill', and it was famously used at Liverpool's Anfield to describe the massive terracing which could accommodate 20/25,000 spectators. Other clubs aped the expression, including Sheffield Wednesday, Leeds United and Birmingham City. Coventry's Kop was smaller than all of these, but in 1922 was a substantial improvement on the small banks that preceded it. Waste material – mainly shale and waste concrete from excavations around the city, including that for relaying the city's tramway system – was conveyed to Highfield Road and used to form a large bank later described as 'a steep, scarred and totally shapeless mess'. It increased the capacity by a few thousand and formed an integral part of the ground for many years.

Reminiscing in 2002, Sydney Ward recalled: 'In the early 1920s I witnessed several attempts to build up the Kop. Tons of soil were ferried by horse and cart to Swan Lane. The soil came from footings being dug in Gosford Street for the new Hotchkiss Car Engine Works.'

1922-23 was another struggle but 18th was the club's best finish in four seasons of League football, although they were still just two points above the drop zone. Opponents included Manchester United, West Ham (who would appear in the first Wembley Cup final that season) and local derbies against Leicester City, Wolves and Derby. It was against Wolves on Christmas Day that City recorded their best result since joining the League, 7-1, with Bill Toms scoring three. The stars of the side were goalkeeper Jerry Best, forward Frank 'Cute' Herbert and right-winger Jimmy Dougall. Best, who although only 5ft 6ins tall and carrying a war injury which restricted movement in one arm, performed heroics in City's goal for five and a half years. Herbert was a local lad supposedly signed at the colliery pithead by Albert Evans. Dougall was a winger with a deadly cross who graced City's team for almost seven years.

Attendances fell that season with an average of 13,500. Times were hard, unemployment was rising, and fewer could afford to go to 'the match'. For the Monday afternoon visit of Fulham in December, with most supporters at work, only 4,000 turned up. In the Cup, City again slumped to a lower-status team, losing 0-3 at Lancashire Combination side New Brighton. Rumours later circulated that City's players threatened strike action in protest at a lack of a win bonus for the game against inferior opponents.

The **1923-24** season followed a similar pattern. Plenty of optimism at the start, a big opening home game crowd watching a defeat, then inconsistency and disgrace in the Cup against a lower league team, this time

Tranmere Rovers from the Third Division (North). City signed veteran former England international Danny Shea, and he showed glimpses of good form but stayed only eighteen months.

A new match programme attracted praise from the *Coventry Standard*: 'The City Football Club is to be complimented on its official weekly organ. A new cover has been designed; its principal feature is a depiction of the three tall spires, drawn with a great deal more accuracy than is often the case, for the flying buttresses of the Cathedral steeple and the octagonal shape of the Christ Church tower are shown. Above are the City Arms, and the whole is printed in the City colours – red and green. The contents are well suited to the purpose of the publication; all the writers put football on a high plane, some excellent advice to spectators and players is tendered, and most of the paragraphs are written in a style which is both pointed and breezy. People who do not care for football one bit may read the official organ and be interested in it.'

A different sport arrived at Highfield Road in April 1924 when prior to a reserve game against Folkestone there was an exhibition of lacrosse. A Midlands 12 played a Yorkshire 12, and the City programme advised of a 'Face' not a 'Kick-off' at 2pm. The score is unknown.

In the summer of 1924 the 'special' relationship between the football club and the supporters club came under strain, with directors accusing the supporters club of interference. Following an enquiry by senior members of each organisation, a bombshell was dropped. The details of the sensitive report were only made public to shareholders, but the entire board was forced to resign as a result. In the midst of this catastrophe David Cooke, probably frustrated by the internal wrangling, announced the withdrawal of his personal guarantee on the club's £2,500 overdraft. A reconstituted new board comprised just three members of the previous one.

Relegation, which had loomed over the club for six years, finally descended in **1924-25**. A twelve-game winless autumn run left City anchored at the bottom. The annual scramble for safety seemed to have paid off in March, when a five-game unbeaten run lifted them out of the bottom two. But City were finally relegated with 31 points, four short of safety, along with Crystal Palace. Evans had been dismissed in November 1924 and secretary Harbourne took over on a caretaker basis. For the first time in five years City reached the first round of the Cup and hosted First Division Notts County. Over 21,000 saw County win 2-0.

In December 1924 the club hosted top-class rugby union for the first time when the touring New Zealand All Blacks were entertained by a Warwickshire team. At Highfield Road the tourists performed the Haka, their famous war dance, before winning 20-0 with winger Jack Steel scoring three tries. That tour saw the All Blacks remain unbeaten after 30 matches in Britain and France. They were dubbed The Invincibles, and George Nepia, a nineteen-year-old Maori, became a star. He was ever present, but two years later was barred from playing in South Africa because of the colour of his skin.

The three years following City's relegation in 1925 were as dark as they have ever known. **1925-26** was spent in Division Three (North) due to a geographical quirk. Coventry – who had reverted to blue and white after three seasons in green and red – were the most southerly side in the northern section. Their only 'local' derby was Walsall, and the next nearest opponents, Crewe, were 75 miles away. With many long trips to places like Ashington, Durham City and Hartlepools in the North East, and Barrow, Nelson and Wigan Borough in the North West, it was financially ruinous. New manager, Scotsman James Kerr, took charge to find players disgruntled by the sacking of Evans. Many of those he inherited were jettisoned and replaced by none-too-impressive Scots. Hopes of a quick return to Division Two were shattered after losing 1-5 at Wigan in the first away game. Eighteen of 21 away games were lost, the biggest defeat being 1-8 at Doncaster. The season's nadir, however, came in the Cup when Midland Leaguers Worksop Town inflicted a 1-0 defeat. The score was bad enough, but it was made worse when it came to light that most of the Worksop team had spent the morning of the game working down the mine. By the season's end the average attendance of 8,461 was 3,000 down on the previous season and marked the club's lowest since the entry into the League. Sixteen players were released and Kerr headed to Scotland in search of replacements.

One of those freed was goalkeeper Jerry Best, who held the club's appearance record with 236 games. Not for the first or last time, the disposal of a popular, long-serving player angered supporters. Best at least had the honour of being the first City player to be granted a benefit. In those days players' long service was rewarded with benefits. After five years with the same club the player was normally awarded a sum in recognition of his loyalty. The player could choose a particular League game as his benefit, and would receive an agreed sum from the gate receipts. Should those receipts be too small, the club would normally make up the difference. In addition, the player could have a collection at their designated match, when the fans could show their appreciation by making a donation. Best had chosen the local derby with Walsall, and at half-time four members of the supporters club carried an open blanket slowly around the pitch, with the crowd lobbing coins into the blanket.

Needless to say, lobbing coins from a great height ran the risk of missing the blanket, striking those manning it, or worse, striking the heads of children, who often took up position at the foot of the banking so that they would not have to peer over the heads of adults. It remains an oddity that coin throwing was tolerated for so long when the risk of serious injury was so high. Those readers old enough to remember pre-decimal currency will not need reminding of the size and weight of pennies, half-crowns and florins, and threepenny bits were like miniature slabs of lead. Those coins missing the blanket, and mercifully any human target, would be snatched up from the running track by a further attendant.

The money collected was generally more than a few weeks' wages. Best's decision to choose the Walsall game was wise: around 14,500, the second biggest gate of the season, were present and when the proceeds of a benefit concert at the Sydenham Palace pub were added to the fund he received a 'substantial quantity of Treasury Notes'.

In the summer of 1926, with Stoke and Stockport relegated from Division Two, a reshuffle was necessary to accommodate the two 'northern' clubs. Coventry were switched to the southern section to join the likes of Northampton, Watford, Luton and five London clubs, including QPR, Charlton and Millwall. The longest journey was now the 200-mile trip to Plymouth. The supporters club again assisted the club, donating a new set of goalposts featuring oval crossbars, an innovation replacing the old-fashioned square-faced type.

Kerr's new team – with a club record ten debutants on **1926-27**'s opening-day 0-3 home defeat by Northampton (in which only full-back Charlie Houldey survived the purge) – took time to gel. Embarrassing defeats at Brentford (3-7) and Exeter (1-8) were countered by big victories over Bournemouth (6-2), Merthyr Tydfil (5-1) and Aberdare Athletic (7-0). The supporters preferred the southern section to the northern and average gates were surprisingly good, considering the economic hardships attending the General Strike. In fact, 17,000 saw the Christmas game with Swindon. Yet the team finished 15th and there was another early Cup exit at Lincoln. 'Cute' Herbert, one survivor of Kerr's clearout, ended up top scorer with 26 goals.

The summer of 1927 saw Highfield Road host motorcycle football matches – played by six-man teams riding 350cc bikes and trying to get a large ball into goals stationed at either end. Little is known about the rules but curious photographs came to light in 2004. On researching the subject it was discovered that Coventry Motor Cycle Club (CMCC), formed in 1924, were the undefeated champions of England in 1926 and won the National Cup in 1927 defeating a team from Douglas, Isle of Man 12-1 in the final. On 6 August 1927 around 1,500 spectators watched CMCC play ACO MCFC in the semi-final of the Auto Cycle Union Cup. Heavy rain during the game forced the referee to withdraw the teams but they returned 'soon after in fine weather'. One wonders what the groundsman felt about these large bikes roaring around his pristine turf three weeks before the new season. Photographs exist of a motorcycle football game at Highfield Road against Wolverhampton in May 1929. A crowd of possibly 5,000 was present, but it is likely that CMCC had their headquarters elsewhere in the city and hired Highfield Road for big games during the close season. It is known that the Coventry team won the Motor Cycle Football Cup final for the third successive year in 1929, having beaten Wolverhampton 2-1 in the final at Kings Heath.

Back to conventional football. In April 1927 City played at Luton, where officials of City and the supporters club were taken aback by the 'canopy extension' to the Kenilworth Road grandstand which protected spectators from the elements. The supporters club raised funds to pay for more covering at Highfield Road. The roof of a stand at Twickenham rugby ground was identified as being ideal to cover the 'popular side', namely the Nicholls Street or west end.

The Rugby Union were in the process of adding a new tier to the East Stand at Twickenham and the old roof was surplus to requirements. It was dismantled and sold to Coventry City. The supporters club agreed to fund it, but hadn't the money, so the club lent the supporters club £1,700 to be repaid in annual instalments. The surveyor then discovered a seven-foot north-to-south slope across the 278 feet to be covered by the new structure. Work, carried out by Messrs W Humphreys, was delayed whilst new stanchions were manufactured to compensate for the slope.

On 13 August 1927 the *Midland Daily Telegraph* reported that the scoreboard had been partially removed for re-location to the Kop, excavation was underway for support for the new cover, and the cover was sure to be ready for 3 September, the date of the first home League game. On 20 August, the day of the final public trial, the *Telegraph* reported on progress: 'The Cover is coming on well – lots of big hefty men have been digging tremendous holes all over the place and within a day or two the main iron supports will be duly installed in beds of concrete. Quite a lot of iron girder work has arrived safely and soundly and some massive stuff it is. The main site girders are 46 feet long and weigh over one ton each. This cover isn't going to be nearly the half-hearted affair which the price might suggest, and it is estimated that a new one of the same size and type would cost over £7,000. Residents of Nicholls Street made an official objection to the new structure but their appeal was dismissed.

The 'new' roof would provide cover for 11,000 spectators as well as necessitate that the scoreboard be shifted to the opposite end of the ground. The club recognised the need for concrete terracing under the new roof, and although it was too expensive to completely terrace the bank, a start was made by carving seven steps at the rear of the bank. Eventually the whole bank would be equipped with 13½ins by 4ins steps. The substantial roof added to the advertising potential, and at some stage the Rex cinema was emblazoned in large white letters. In the post-war period Sam Robbins motor car dealership was advertised in a similar way.

Within months of the new cover being erected the supporters club raised £500 towards its £1,700 cost but by the end of 1928 faced difficulties in making a repayment. 'Nemo' in the *MDT* appealed for City fans to step in and make a donation: 'The Supporters Club want that cover to be paid for by a voluntary effort. So come along and let's have it paid for.' Other appeals by the supporters club were necessary before the debt was finally cleared in March 1933. Press photographs of matches in the 1930s show crowds packed under the cover on wet days with the surrounding open banks empty, apart from a few hardy souls.

On the pitch, **1927-28** went from bad to worse. Heavy defeats were suffered at Millwall (1-9), Swindon (0-6) and Walsall (0-7) before Kerr was relieved of his duties in February 1928. He was on the receiving end of blistering attacks from the *MDT* which on one occasion explained the slump in attendances: 'City fans have little desire to watch Coventry Celtic' – an indictment of the influx of Scots players.

Director Albert Saunders took temporary charge, and re-election remained a threat on the final day when City travelled to Northampton. Several thousand City supporters made the trip but a controversial goal for the Cobblers provoked a riot amongst City fans and the referee was knocked unconscious by a stone. It was all unnecessary, as Merthyr had lost and City's League status was assured.

More financial support from David Cooke was required towards the end of the season when a cheque for £500 paid to Notts County for two players bounced. The bank refused the club further credit and President Cooke came to the rescue once again, paying Notts County and making further guarantees of debts.

That year, on the advice of former director Fred Lee, a committee of enquiry was set up and in May 1928 reported to a special meeting of shareholders at Union Street Assembly Rooms. The enquiry's recommendation for the chairman and vice-chairman to resign was accepted, only for the entire board to resign in protest. It was a classic example of shareholders' (and the supporters club) power. The two groups had worked together to dethrone an inefficient board who had bankrolled James Kerr's investments in inferior players. The supporters club again facilitated the raising of money by selling new shares in the football club. Within days Walter Brandish become chairman in place of W Carpenter and other new board members included FW Kimberley, Fred Stringer and Bill Slade.

Ex-player James McIntyre was appointed new manager soon afterwards, and once again it was all change as the new man brought in his own players. There were seven debutants for the opening League game with Norwich, which attracted 18,000, the biggest home crowd for four years. Following years of criticism over players' fitness and discipline, the new manager introduced 'McIntyre's ticket', a set of rules for the players which forbade, among other things 'attendance at whist drives' and 'driving automobiles'.

1928-29 saw a good run before Christmas, but home and away defeats to leaders Charlton over the holiday were a big blow and the side slipped to finish 11th. The average attendance of 15,610 was the highest for six years. The biggest crowd was for the Cup-tie against Fulham. A record 26,000 passed through the turnstiles to see City humbled. It was one of 'Cute' Herbert's final games for the club and his goal tally of 82 from 187 League games was a club record that would stand until Clarrie Bourton broke it. Herbert's replacement, Billy Lake, would also become a Coventry legend.

The supporters club's role in City's affairs was increasing and in 1929 membership exceeded 400. The *MDT* reported on their AGM: 'the sum of £980 had been raised in aid of the City's finances in the course of the past twelve months. No more fuss was made about it and not a word was said about the work involved in selling nearly 86,000 penny-on-the-ball tickets.' The supporters club were funding the terrace cover, all the team's footballs, and helping supporters to buy season tickets on hire purchase, not to mention providing volunteers to do odd jobs and painting around the stadium.

With a settled side, McIntyre's men started **1929-30** by remaining unbeaten for seven games, the best start ever. Goals were flowing in from Lake and Jimmy Loughlin. After almost twenty years without any real Cup success, the Bantams reached the third round, which since 1925 had been when Division One and Two clubs entered. Victories over Norwich (after a replay) and non-league Bath set up a plum tie with Sunderland on 11 January 1930. The ground record would certainly be smashed for arguably the most attractive game at the ground since the end of the Great War.

Beforehand, City had a Christmas double-header against runaway leaders Plymouth Argyle. On Christmas morning, in front of another record crowd of 26,400, City inflicted the Devon side's first defeat, 1-0, with Loughlin grabbing the vital goal.

The 11am kick-off caused havoc at Highfield Road, described by the *MDT*: 'Long after the kick-off people were clamouring at the turnstiles. Even with a tremendous crowd one could perceive gaps in various parts of the ground and it should be possible to accommodate 30,000 spectators on January 11. Given a favourable day, that figure should be reached, for the City's match with Sunderland should prove more attractive to outside fans than the games in the neighbouring city (Birmingham). I understand that many outside Coventry have made up their minds to visit Highfield Road that day.'

Following the Argyle match, players and officials enjoyed Christmas dinner at the Craven Arms Hotel. Turkey and trimmings were on the menu but trainer Kimpton was reported to have banned Christmas pudding. At 3.15pm the team left by train for Plymouth, along with their opponents, for the return game at Home Park the following afternoon.

As the club prepared for the Sunderland Cup-tie there appeared to be light at the end of a long dark tunnel. The club's finances were still a source of concern, with debts of around £10,000, but performances on the pitch were heartening, and healthy attendances proved that Coventry was a football city. As the decade ended, 'Nemo' in the *MDT* wrote: 'I anticipate that the season 1929-30 will live to be regarded as the period during which Coventry City got back on its feet again, and as the weeks advance the conviction grows stronger.'

CHAPTER FOUR

The 1930s

Ever since the FA Cup draw in mid-December 1929, interest in the Sunderland game had been immense. The club's board quickly agreed neither to make the game all-ticket nor raise the general admission prices, keeping the terrace price at one shilling (5p), but they did increase the price of 'grandstand' seats.

The *MDT* reported chairman Brandish as saying: 'If one must be perfectly candid supporters have been paying their shillings regularly for years for football which at times has not been worth it, and if we can't give them a little treat on this occasion without muleting them for more of their pocket money, we don't deserve to have support at all … Here is an opportunity of showing that we appreciate their support, and we are taking advantage of it.'

Manager McIntyre was confident of a big crowd: 'I have not the slightest doubt that there will be a record gate, and given good weather, I anticipate there will be over 30,000 to see the match. I am already having applications for tickets from the most unexpected quarters and Sunderland have demanded their full quota (25 per cent) of all the reserved accommodation, i.e. the big stand. They are bringing down two excursion loads of supporters.'

McIntyre also anticipated that the club would engage the services of one or two megaphone men, who would stand on the running track and help pack the crowds evenly on the terraces to make room for the greatest possible number. They would be advised 'where space was abundant' and instruct the supporters to stand closer to their neighbour or take a step aside to let more in. This would be a first for Coventry, but would ensure a massive crowd.

On Saturday, 4 January 1930, after the *Midland Daily Telegraph* reported stand seats still available, the club were inundated by requests. It transpired that only 40 tickets were left unsold. Sunderland meanwhile had taken up their full allocation of around 600 stand tickets.

On the Monday before the game the City team visited their old haunt at Droitwich to test the 'toning properties' of the Worcestershire spa town. On Tuesday they trained at Highfield Road, but no 'high-velocity' training. Wednesday consisted of a 'short char-a-banc' tour around the countryside during the morning; lunch at Brandon, and a walk in the afternoon. Thursday was light training at the ground with light road work on Friday and a visit to the theatre. On match day an early lunch was planned at the Craven Arms.

During the build up, the *Midland Daily Telegraph* described the tie as the Match of the Midlands, and the Coventry and North Warwickshire Football League cancelled all fixtures to allow players to attend. 'Nemo' in the *MDT* felt that if City, who he believed had their 'best fighting' side since the Great War, could reproduce their Christmas Day form then Sunderland would go home a 'disappointed' team.

Sunderland might have been bottom of Division One, but they had a superb pedigree, having won five League titles around the turn of the century. Although they had not won a major trophy since before the Great War, they had finished in the top four five times and had 38 unbroken years of top-flight service. Their team included four Scottish internationals, plus emerging stars Bobby Gurney and Patsy Gallacher, whose grandson Kevin would play for Coventry 60 years later.

Much work had been done to the Swan Lane 'bank' during the week, including 'crush' barriers and 'sway' barriers to prevent excessive movements of the crowd. The gates were opened at noon (for a 2.30 kick-off) and 'all wounded soldiers in bath chairs had to be at the King Richard Street entrance before 12 noon – otherwise they may be impeded in the rush.' Thirty police officers were on duty at the ground.

Long before the gates were opened long queues extended down King Richard Street and hundreds of schoolboys already 'cheering lustily' had gathered at the entrances. Street musicians 'whiled' away the time. By 1.15, an hour and a quarter before the kick-off, the ground looked 'comfortably full'. At 1.30 the banks and terraces were full and 'every road' within a mile of Highfield Road was bringing 'streams of spectators'. They were pouring in at every gate, filling up 'almost indiscernable' gaps round the enclosure.

The *MDT* painted the scene: 'Occasionally the din became deafening. Someone would start a rattle, and it would be responded to by a hundred bells carried by ultra enthusiasts. Paper streamers began to make their appearance in such quantities that very soon the main stand was festooned from end to end. Snow began to fall and the end of the big stand resembled a Christmassy appearance. The Coventry Silver Band was finding it just a little too hard to make much impression upon the continued din and the cheering, bell-ringing, chattering and excited crowd, which was still being rapidly augmented. The explosion of fireworks at the thickest part of the throng was adding to the din and the gaiety.'

The pitch, after a night of heavy rain, was a swamp and threatened to cut up badly. With both sides usually wearing striped shirts, Sunderland were asked to wear an alternative and chose white with black shorts. City surprisingly also changed kit, choosing black and white stripes. When the City team emerged, the roar which greeted them was 'something to remember'.

The game itself was a thriller and City were unfortunate not to get a draw which would have earned a Roker Park replay. Patsy Gallacher put the First Division side ahead after nineteen minutes, and City's equaliser was controversial. Loughlin's header was scooped out by the Sunderland keeper but the referee and linesman adjudged the ball to have crossed the line. A dreadful error seven minutes from time cost City a replay. A harmless-looking cross into their penalty area was almost out of play beyond the far post when goalkeeper Tommy 'Shadow' Allen and Bell went for the ball together. In the mix-up the ball rolled slowly back across the empty goalmouth. Gurney 'arrived on the scene' and tapped in.

The crowd of 31,673 was smaller than the 35,000 anticipated. It was, however, a new ground record which would stand until 1936. Receipts added up to £1,854 14 shillings.

City's good home form continued after the Cup exit – they won ten and drew one at home between November and April, with Billy Lake and Loughlin regular scorers, but in the same period they lost ten consecutive away games, culminating in a 2-10 hammering at Norwich – the first and only time the club have conceded double figures in a Football League game.

City ended the season in 6th place with 47 points, 21 behind champions Plymouth, but easily their best since entry into the League in 1919. A settled forward line of Richards, Widdowson, Loughlin, Lake and Pick helped themselves to a club record 84 League goals with Jimmy Loughlin, in his first full season, netting 28 goals in all competitions – another club record. Despite these plusses, the average gate was down 2,000 at 12,985 and the *MDT* reported that the gates were netting City around £500 per home match. With a further £100 coming from reserve games, this meant the club had to survive on £600 a fortnight.

The following season, **1930-31**, it was back to 14th. A bad injury to Loughlin restricted him to eleven games. This, coupled with the loss of Norman Dinsdale to Bristol Rovers, were blows McIntyre was unable to overcome. With the club's finances in a parlous state quality replacements could not be afforded. In February 1931, a majority of the board voted for the dismissal of McIntyre. It was common knowledge that chairman (Brandish) and manager had been at loggerheads for some time, and the club's poor form was an excuse to remove the latter. McIntyre responded: 'My reasons for resigning are consequent upon the intolerable attitude of Walter Brandish and under no account could I carry on under his Chairmanship.' McIntyre became manager of Fulham and the following season, as if to prove a point, led the London club to the Third Division (South) championship.

Director Bill Slade took over as caretaker until the directors appointed Harry Storer on 11 April. Billy Lake shone through the gloomy season and netted 23 League and Cup goals, including four in the 5-1 home win over Bristol Rovers in March. Poor home form saw crowds slip by over 2,500, reducing the average to 10,327.

Son of a famous England and Liverpool goalkeeper and nephew of a Derbyshire and England cricketer, Harry Storer was, at 33, ready to end his playing career with Burnley and step into management at Highfield Road. He had excelled as a wing-half with Derby and won two England caps before moving to Turf Moor in 1929. His arrival would launch a period of unprecedented success at Highfield Road. Many supporters believe that, but for the Second World War, the club would have been promoted to Division One 30 years before they finally did.

They finished 12th in **1931-32**, Storer's first season. Behind that modest statistic, however, lies a story of spectacular goalscoring. The team scored 108 goals, bettered only by divisional champions Everton, Wolves and Fulham. City's centre-forward Clarrie Bourton was the Football League's top scorer with an amazing 49 League goals – the third highest total in the history of the League (after Dixie Dean's 60 in 1928 and George Camsell's 59 in 1927).

Storer had spotted Bourton playing for Blackburn and persuaded the board to pay £750 for the Rovers reserve. It was a superb investment, as the Bristol-born centre-forward went on to notch 182 goals in 241 games for the Bantams in the thrilling period between 1931-37. Another shrewd signing from Lancashire was Scot Jock Lauderdale, who arrived for £270 from Blackpool shortly after Bourton. The two struck up a fine partnership, with Lauderdale's artistry on the ball creating many of Bourton's deluge of goals during the golden era.

City won seventeen out of 21 home games, scoring 74 goals and conceding only 28. The biggest was a League record 8-0 over Crystal Palace. A week later Gillingham were beaten 6-4. Bournemouth were also thrashed 6-1, Watford 5-0, Mansfield and Reading 5-1. Another five were notched against champions Fulham, although the Cottagers replied with five of their own in the highest scoring draw ever seen at the ground. City scored five so often it revived the old nickname of Foleshill Great Heath – 'the Old Five'. Bourton scored seven hat-tricks, six of them at Highfield Road. They included a five against Bournemouth, and four against Mansfield (he netted three in the return at Field Mill). Between 19 September and 28 November, Clarrie netted in all eleven League games, an achievement unlikely to be ever beaten. Lauderdale chipped in with nineteen goals and Billy Lake, who would continue to represent the club up to the Second World War, contributed fourteen in only 27 games. In the 1980s, supporter Les Raven reminisced about Bourton's nap-hand against Bournemouth: 'City were losing 0-1 at half-time – from a penal-ty. Then came the Bourton specials, each scored from a different angle with each foot. Each hit the back of the net like a bullet, giving the goal-keeper no chance. In those days, remember, they played with a leather ball.'

Bourton's hat-trick at Mansfield in the penultimate away game took his season's tally to 46, one goal behind the divisional record held by Abe Morris of Swindon. The following Saturday, in the final home game against Watford, needing two goals for the record, he netted his seventh hat-trick in a 5-0 win. On scoring his second to create the new record 'the crowd cheered for a full minute or more, and Bourton's colleagues crowded round him and embraced him'. Watford's players patted him on the back and one 'over-enthusiastic fellow' jumped over the fence at the covered end and raced to shake Clarrie's hand. At the final whistle sup-porters raced onto the pitch and carried Clarrie 'shoulder-high' to the dressing room. Many of the crowd were 'so completely lost' in the heat of the occasion that they headed for the nearest exit, across the pitch and police had to step in 'and remind them that such a procedure could not be encouraged'.

Although the average attendance at 12,235 was up from the previous season it was still well below the figures from the early 1920s. Only dis-mal away form – they won only once – cost City a higher final position. Curiously, it was reported that Storer only saw the team play four times all season, so busy was he scouting for new players.

In February 1932 long-time club benefactor David Cooke died. In his will he cancelled all debts to him (around £7,500), which enabled the club to have a new share issue with the capital increased to £5,000. Earlier that month the supporters club opened new premises at the back of the New Stand in Thackhall Street. Previously they had used the Sydenham Palace for their meetings, but now had a base at the ground they could call their own. At the opening ceremony, chairman Walter Brandish paid tribute to 'the spirit of co-operation that exists between the two organisations'.

In **1932-33** Bourton, despite close and often heavy marking, contin-ued where he had left off and topped the League's scorers again with 41 goals. Lake (18) and Lauderdale (14) again supported him as City notched

106 goals, a total only bettered by League champions Arsenal. Modest away form kept the team down to 6th, eighteen points adrift of champions Brentford. In the modern-day game that would have been good enough to qualify for the play-offs.

The club's training conditions in those days were pretty spartan. In 1972 George Mason reminisced about the facilities: 'We used to hang our clothes on the nearest nail when we changed; we had one pair of football boots which we wore whatever the playing conditions and tracksuits were unheard of. We trained in any old pair of flannels and jerseys we could lay our hands on. Before a practice match the trainer used to walk into the dressing-room and tip a great pile of old jerseys and socks on to the floor. It was then a free-for-all to find something suitable to wear. For a kickabout there were two footballs – one at each end of the pitch. There would be 18 or 20 professionals trying to get a kick at each ball.'

Attendances increased just slightly to an average of 12,479, only bettered by Brentford in the division. The most exciting match, a Thursday afternoon February clash with Norwich which ended 5-3 to the visitors, was watched by the smallest crowd, 6,016.

The performance of that 1932-33 season was probably the 7-0 home win over QPR, with all the goals in the last half-hour. A goalkeeping error opened the floodgates. Billy Lake scored a nine-minute hat-trick, Bourton added two more, with Lauderdale also scoring. The *CET* noted that in eight home games since Christmas the team had scored 38 goals, an average of almost five a game.

That season Storer introduced several young players who would form the team that ultimately won promotion. Amongst them were goalkeeper Bill Morgan, wing-halves Harry Boileau and Billy Frith, and a young commanding centre-half from Birmingham called George Mason. In January 1933 Bourton scored in nine successive games. Only a blank day at Gillingham spoiled a record which saw him score in fourteen out of fifteen games.

A year later, **1933-34**, the Bantams progressed to runners-up, seven points behind Norwich. In those days only the champions were promoted from the Third Division and City would have to wait two more years to achieve their ambition of returning to Division Two. In December 1933 Bourton suffered a knee injury which kept him out for two months. The fans had no need to fear his absence – his deputy Arthur 'Rasher' Bacon scored sixteen goals in fourteen games, including five in a 7-3 win at Gillingham. Sadly Bacon suffered a serious eye injury soon afterwards and had to retire from professional football. Bourton returned, and on 28 April in the final home game netted four goals as Bristol City were demolished 9-0, the club's record League victory at Highfield Road. The club had reached 100 League goals for the third successive year but had missed out on the top prize. The biggest home crowd was on Christmas Day when a League record 27,589 saw City win 4-1. The season's average, 14,093, was the highest in the section and better than two First Division clubs, Blackburn and Middlesbrough.

The summer of 1934 saw the construction of terracing at the covered west end, thanks to the fund-raising activities of the supporters club. The cost of the concrete terracing and crush barriers was almost £900. It would take three years to complete and to pay off. The supporters club helped out in many ways, such as assisting supporters to buy season tickets and repay the supporters club in instalments – one local factory had 320 employees enrolled in the scheme. When completed, 13,000 spectators could be accommodated under the roof on the new terraces. Before the **1934-35** season started, a new concrete wall, 3ft 6ins high, was erected at the same end, with the supporters club again chipping in by demolishing the old wooden perimeter fence.

The Spion Kop was still a shale bank and the late Bert Woodfield remembered his early trips to the ground. 'There were four turnstiles in Swan Lane and Dad used to lift me over the turnstile and didn't have to pay for me. Then you came up a ramp that circled round and came out at the top of the Kop. There were also steps down the incline from the centre of the Kop – I think they were railway sleepers knocked into the shale bank. Later they made the steps concrete. There was a refreshment bar at the top of the Kop where you could buy tea and food. You could buy pies and hot drinks (tea and Bovril) and crisps or biscuits and a small bottle of home-made pop like Dandelion and burdock. Later you could get small bottles of R Whites pop. Invariably my Dad would take a sandwich in his pocket because we were very poor.

'We always stood in the same position, just to the right of the goal about three quarters way back – the same place every game. Lots of people stood in the same place every game. When I was a lad I used to sit on the wooden crash barrier – all me legs used to get red from sitting there through the game. In the left-hand far corner (the corner adjacent to the Main Stand) halfway up the bank there was a stable with the horses.

'The horse – I think he was called Ginger – was there to pull the heavy roller over the pitch, before they had tractors or petrol-driven mowers. Before the match my Dad used to lift me up at the stalls and show me the horse. You could walk from the Covered End to the Kop and some supporters, especially kids, would walk round at half-time to be behind the goal that city were attacking. There were four policemen, one at each corner of the pitch, and they used to sit on a little seat. The band used to play at half-time, walking on the pitch. I remember the Bulkington Silver Band playing.'

Storer was building a promotion team and in January 1934 he made another astute signing by paying Cardiff £2,000 for Welsh international inside-forward Leslie Jones. Jones blended well with Lauderdale and Bourton and proved to be the catalyst for promotion. In 1934-35 Jones, not renowned for his goalscoring, even outscored Bourton with 27 goals to Clarrie's 26. As Storer realised he had to play a tighter game, especially away from home, George Mason finally assumed the pivot role, and a tightened defence conceded just 50 goals – City's best record in sixteen seasons of League football. City only finished 3rd, ten points behind champions Charlton, but the average crowd of 15,060 was the best since 1928-29. The biggest win was reserved for the FA Cup, when Midland Leaguers Scunthorpe and Lindsay United were dumped 7-0, a record FA Cup score at Highfield Road.

Exclusive access to the club's minute books from the 1930s gives a curious insight into the running of a professional football club. In 1934 Oswald Mosley's British Union of Fascists (BUF) asked to stage a political meeting at the ground. The minutes record: 'the board agreed that while they were not prejudiced against this kind of thing, they did not think it wise for the club to be involved with any political parties and it was left to Director Mr Jones to send a reply to this effect.' The board meeting took place just five days after an infamous BUF rally at London's Olympia, when 500 anti-fascist infiltrators were roughed up by 1,000 'black shirts'. Within five months Mosley's organisation had adopted anti-Semitism as party policy.

That same month the minutes reveal that Mr TW Page was granted sole rights to sell newspapers on the ground, a privilege for which he paid £15 per annum. At the same board meeting a request to put on an exhibition of Open Air Boxing was rejected.

In November 1934 the board discussed the practice of boys being lifted over the turnstiles and avoiding payment. They determined that this practice must stop and all boys had in future to pay. A request by the family of a Mr Crossley to scatter his ashes on Highfield Road was rejected, and a quote of £135 from a Mr Clifford to re-roof the new stand was accepted.

In early 1935, following Italy's invasion of Ethiopia, pacifists of the League of Nations Union campaigned for a Peace Ballot. The club rejected a Union request to send sandwich men round the ground advertising the ballot. Eleven million people participated, expressing an unmistakable desire for peaceful negotiation of international quarrels. The results of the Peace Ballot were publicised worldwide, to little avail.

In January 1935 the board received a letter from the City's Sanitary Officer regarding a complaint about spectators 'committing a nuisance at the Swan Lane end', presumably urinating on the bank. It was agreed that a notice be posted regarding this.

The club's trainer, Sid Kimpton, was in demand. In 1934 he had been 'coach' to the French national team in the World Cup finals in Italy, and in March 1935, according to the board minutes, the club agreed to release him that summer for a week to train the French team. In May, however, it was decided to replace Kimpton and assistant Jesse Bennett. Kimpton wrote to the chairman seeking an explanation which received a blunt riposte: 'a more efficient trainer could be obtained.' A former England player, Dick Hill, was appointed soon afterwards.

In 1996 Ron Patten recalled the Tuesday afternoon visit of Reading in April 1935. He was ten at the time and attended Holbrook Lane Junior School. He had gone to school in the morning but developed a convenient headache and went home at lunchtime. 'Mother thought it would be a good idea to get some fresh air and where better than Highfield Road?' Reading's goalkeeper, Harry Wildman, wore a bright red jersey and his acrobatics prevented the Bantams scoring a hatful.

The board discussed the fate of a Miss Rogers who worked in the Highfield Road offices. The previous Christmas she had been deemed good enough to receive a '£1 Christmas box for extra work put in for the Cup tickets', but five months later she was discharged with a fortnight's wages, according to the board minutes because, 'a man would be more suitable for football business.' If today's Employment Law had been in place, it would surely have led to a claim for unfair dismissal on the grounds of sexual discrimination.

May 1935 saw the country celebrate the 25th anniversary of the accession to the throne of King George V. Every town and village held pageants or other events, and Coventry chose Highfield Road as the venue. The programme started at 11.30am to coincide with a national thanksgiving service at St Pauls Cathedral, with the Highfield Road crowd estimated at 40,000! Among the spectacles, 2,000 local schoolgirls with veils of red, white and blue muslin formed a giant human Union Jack on the pitch. The Coventry Silver Band accompanied community singing before a speech from the city's mayor. The occasion finished with a 'rousing' performance of the National Anthem.

The huge crowd constituted a 'ground' record and with temperatures in the high 70s there were many cases of fainting, with the dressing rooms being taken over as treatment areas by the St John Ambulance Brigade. By 3pm the crowd had dwindled to 3,000 and the Bantams lined up for an exhibition game against Leicester City. The game ended 3-3 with Jones (2) and Bourton netting for the home side.

The summer of 1935 saw more ground developments. Mr M Briscoe was 'engaged' to draw up plans and a few weeks later terrace improvements and 'ground equipment' (crush barriers) was approved. The first work carried out by FG Robinson – a local builder based in Swan Lane – was the building of a concrete wall in front of the covered end terracing. The minutes of August 1935 discussed a proposal from John Elwell & Company (believed to be steel erectors from Oldbury) 're Terrace Covering'. The directors agreed that 'we cannot proceed at the moment' with what was probably a proposal to cover the Spion Kop.

Terracing steps were repaired with railway sleepers but some months later the board discussed 'unsatisfactory' work on the terraces, and it was agreed that Robinsons be contacted to 'send a man up'. There were still unterraced areas under the covered end, while the Spion Kop was a largely unterraced shale bank which on wet days became a quagmire.

Regarding the team, promotion talk was in the air – third time lucky. The board backed Storer's judgement by rejecting a £6,000 bid for Les Jones from Tottenham, but signing two experienced wingers, George McNestry from Bristol Rovers and Arthur Fitton from Preston.

Two months into the **1935-36** season chairman Walter Brandish died aged 58. He had been taken ill the previous December, on the coach home from a Cup-tie at Hartlepool, and the illness reoccurred during a cruise. Brandish had been instrumental in bringing Storer to Highfield Road and the club's revival in his seven years as chairman was phenomenal. He died just six months before his ambition – of seeing City win promotion – was realised, and his loss was a potential body blow. Having been invited to take charge during the 1928 crisis, he gathered around him men in whom he had the greatest confidence, and the board evolved into one trusted by supporters and local people alike.

The chairmanship passed to Fred Stringer, and Brandish's eldest son Walter junior joined the board. In July Brandish and the board had rejected the offer of an interest-free loan of £3,000 from the *Midland Daily Telegraph* to 'assist the club building for promotion'. In February 1936 when City were knocked off the top with a 0-5 defeat at Watford, the directors did a U-turn and accepted the offer. Storer was given the go-ahead to sign full-back Jack Astley from Brentford and centre-forward Tommy Crawley from Preston, after which the team lost only two of their final fifteen games to clinch promotion.

As the climax to the momentous season approached, City were locked together with Luton Town, who they had to play twice in their last three games. The 1-1 draw at Luton was watched by a record Kenilworth Road crowd of 23,112. For the return two days later, City's officials anticipated a new record gate and Storer announced that an expert 'packer' had been employed to 'ensure that no standing space on the terrace and popular side will be wasted'. The game kicked off at 6.15 – too late, according to the night-shift workers who would have to leave the match before the end to 'clock-on' at 8pm – and the gates were opened at 5pm.

A crowd of 42,809 – 11,000 more than the Sunderland record set six years previously – crammed in to see a goalless draw. Despite the knowledge that the game would attract a capacity crowd, the club did not issue a full sixteen-page match programme, which were reserved for Saturday fixtures. Instead, just 2,500 copies of the team sheet were printed.

The following day the *Midland Daily Telegraph*, under the headline 'A Scene Of Chaos', described the aftermath: 'Highfield Road looked this morning as though it had been struck by a tornado last night. Cartloads of paper and other rubbish was left behind by the record crowd … while the condition of the barriers smashed to match-wood on the Swan Lane side, near to the corner of the old stand, provided ample evidence of the crush.'

A rare football-orientated editorial in the *Telegraph* summed up one of the most memorable nights in the club's history: 'Coventry has never witnessed such a spectacle before – an attendance nearly equal to a quarter of Coventry's entire population lined the ground, perched on the top of stands, clung to advertising signs, fences and posts. Hundreds sat on the grass close to the touchline; humanity was packed as close as it could be within the capacious Highfield Road enclosure, and yet thousands who went to see the match had perforce to remain outside.'

It was reported that frustrated fans 'gate-crashed' one entrance, and a Nuneaton 'enthusiast' sent a postal order for one shilling in lieu of his admission. He admitted walking in through the broken gate but evidently thought the game and the occasion was so worthwhile that he paid his 'honest-bob' for the privilege.

Amazingly no one was hurt, despite some madcap jinks by some spectators to get a better view. On the top of the Spion Kop 'rows of stones' were piled up as stools by supporters in order to get a better view. The *MDT* speculated that 'many tons of packing from the back of the banks must have been pulled up' to form a makeshift grandstand. A major disaster must have been narrowly averted. Spectators climbed advertising hoardings, the wooden scoreboard on the Kop, and onto the roof of the covered end, as well as being forced from uncomfortably packed terraces onto the perimeter of the pitch. This anticipated the scenes 31 years later, when 51,452 were shoe-horned in for the famous Wolves game. The newspaper hypothesised that to enable a capacity for 60,000 would 'not entail much alteration to existing conditions'.

The two draws with Luton left City with what looked like the easy task of beating Torquay in their final game five days later to clinch promotion. But they would have to do so without Mason, injured in the first Luton game. A full match programme was issued, but again only 2,500 copies were printed.

The programme had few words, but 'From The Board Room' spoke of the momentous occasion: 'Today, in our last game, we play the most vital match of the season, probably the most vital game in the history of the Club. A win to-day definitely gives us second division status next season, a dream all interested in the affairs of our Club have had since that tragic year when we were relegated to the third division. Assuming our dream comes true, it has taken a long time, much anxiety and strenuous effort to achieve this, and the heroic way our team, often with several reserves owing to the unusual crop of injuries from which we have suffered this season, have fought in the interests of this is difficult to describe in words.'

'Topical Notes by Supporter' discussed the Luton game: 'Monday evening's gate of 43,000 has settled many past arguments as to the holding capacity at Highfield Road.'

The supporters club Notes by the 'Sec' read: 'I am desired by Arthur Bacon to express his thanks to all who contributed to the fund organised on his behalf. The sum of £69 14s 0d was collected, which is in itself a remarkable demonstration of the sympathy our crowd holds for anyone who meets with misfortune. May good fortune be with you, Arthur.'

The gates were opened at 1pm, two hours before the kick-off, with several hundred already queuing impatiently outside. By 2, when the band started up, it was estimated that there were already 12,000 in the ground, many of whom had come straight from work – the majority of Coventry factories worked a 5½-day week in those days – and were 'enjoying an alfresco meal'.

The frightening scenes from the previous Monday were not repeated, and the queues at turnstiles were tiny compared to the Luton game. The longer than usual music programme kept the spectators entertained and a bandsman arriving late caused the biggest cheer of the pre-match activity. The 'tardy' bandsman was cheered every step he made until he was ready for action.

As the teams ran out, hundreds of young boys poured over the barriers to squat on the edge of the pitch, and the police had to ensure they stayed back away from the touchlines. After a nervous and goalless first hour, City were awarded a penalty with twenty minutes left. McNestry, normally deadly from the spot, drove the ball straight at the goalkeeper and minutes later Torquay broke away and scored. Luton were drawing, which meant promotion was slipping away. City piled on the pressure and were awarded another penalty. This time stand-in skipper Ernie Curtis converted, and with three minutes remaining Fred Liddle dribbled along the by-line and slid a pass to Clarrie Bourton, who netted the winning goal.

At the final whistle the jubilant City fans in the 30,614 crowd stormed onto the pitch. The players, sensing what was about to happen, 'made a dive for the player's exit.' The Torquay men managed to escape and one or two City players as well, but the rest 'were swallowed up in the avalanche of people'. Bourton, Curtis, Elliott, Frith and McNestry were 'hauled into the air' and carried by excited fans. 'Hundreds of hands' sought to pat the players on the back or shake their hands – 'anything to touch these idols'. At one stage, matters seemed to be getting out of hand, but the crowd carefully 'chaired' their heroes to the entrance to the dressing room.

With the players safely inside the dressing room the crowd turned their attention to the directors box, where Alderman Fred Lee, the club president, stood with a microphone installed especially for the occasion. Before speeches could start, however, the crowd set up a chant: 'We want Mason.' Soon afterwards the players, led by the injured Mason – who had spent the second half pacing around Gosford Green, too nervous to watch the game – and Leslie Jones, who also missed the game, entered the box to 'deafening' cheers. When they subsided Alderman Lee spoke: 'What a happy moment we live in. After years of toil we have just achieved the greatest success in the history of Coventry City FC.'

Mason stepped up to the microphone to renewed cheers. He was too overcome with emotion to make a sensible contribution but thanked the supporters for the reception. Similarly Bourton, called to the microphone by an incessant 'We want Bourton', thanked the crowd in a short but emotional speech. Finally manager Storer was pushed to the mike and said: 'You have done as much to win promotion as we have. We could not have done it without your loyal and continued support.'

The huge crowds for the last two games lifted the average to 19,232, the highest in the club's history and the best in the Third Division again. The team dropped only three home points all season – Aldershot ruining the Christmas morning game by triumphing 2-0. City finished on 57 points, one point ahead of Luton, who would follow them up the following season.

Another trophy found its way into the club's boardroom that season. On 2 April the club lifted the Division Three (South) Cup, a midweek afternoon knockout tournament that attracted little interest. Some 2,000 watched the second leg of the final at Highfield Road. A City team comprising half a dozen first-teamers and a smattering of fringe players beat Swindon Town 3-2 to clinch a 5-2 aggregate victory. In the absence of captain George Mason, Harry Boileau was presented with the trophy by Mrs Darbyshire, wife of the secretary of the Division Three Southern Section.

Since the Canadian club Hillhurst in 1911, no foreign team had visited Highfield Road, but in the summer of 1935 City were approached by Austria Vienna FC regarding an autumn tour of England. At the time, the Austrian national 'Wunderteam', managed by the legendary Hugo Meisl, was recognised as one of the strongest in the world and had reached the World Cup semi-finals the previous year. Several of the Wunderteam played for Austria Vienna, including Matthias Sindelar, a tall, thin, pale, blond centre-forward nicknamed 'the man of paper', who compensated for his fragility with superb technique. He is considered one of the greatest Austrian footballers of all time and in the modern game would have been a highly paid superstar. In 2006 Brian Glanville placed him in his top twenty all-time world stars.

Such a 'big-name' team wanted to be paid for their services and a fee of £150 was agreed upon. The sides met on a wet Thursday afternoon and even with Sindelar in the team (few City supporters would have heard of him) only 3,000 turned out to see City win 4-2. Storer selected a side composed mainly of reserves – four days previously the team had been held to a draw in the Cup by non-league Scunthorpe. They faced a League fixture on the Saturday and the replay in Lincolnshire the following Monday. Press reports describe the City and Vienna teams exchanging 'beautiful banners'.

Sindelar's impact on the small crowd went unreported, but two years later – after the German invasion of Austria and the Anschluss – his career was thrown into crisis. He refused to play for a 'greater' Germany team in the 1938 World Cup and in 1939 mysteriously died in a gas-filled room. But in May 1936, six of the Vienna side who appeared at Highfield Road were in the Austrian team that defeated England 2-1 in Vienna.

The Vienna FC game initiated Highfield Road's first ever sound system. A company called BJH Limited installed 'sound apparatus' and probably used it for primitive loudspeaker announcements. Whether the trial was a success or not is not known, but the following summer proposals were sought from Lee Beesleys (a local electrical company based in Queens Road) and Hansons (a music shop in Hertford Street) for 'sound equipment'. During the 1936-37 season Hansons' advertisement in the match programme boasted that 'the amplifying equipment on this football ground for your pleasure has been supplied and is operated by Hansons, the entertainment specialists'.

With promotion to Division Two accomplished, many urged the club to invest in better-quality players and, following the chaos attending the Luton game, stadium improvements. Shortly after the Torquay game 'Supporter' penned a succinct letter to the *MDT*: 'May I suggest it is time some of our shillings were spent on ground improvements? We all know the old stand is an eye-sore and standing on the Swan Lane bank is no rest for the legs.' The *MDT* reported receiving many letters 'almost begging for the opportunity to contribute to a fund to make Coventry City's ground worthy of the club's higher football sphere'. 'Nemo' added his weight to the clamour and the seeds of a fund were sown.

On 23 May 1936 the *MDT* reported that a public subscription fund should raise £5,000 to finance a new main stand, on the King Richard Street side to replace the 1899 John Bull stand. The club did not have the funds both for team strengthening and ground improvements. The appeal fund was to be supervised by William Erle Shanks, the owner of a local timber merchant and joinery firm. Shanks, a public spirited supporter who no doubt saw an opportunity of some substantial work for his company, would administer the 'Stand Fund' and organise a system of 'district collecting agents'. A donation of 500 guineas by the football club inaugurated the appeal fund and Shanks' open letter in the *MDT* urged local businesses and individual supporters to make generous donations. In the same edition Storer confirmed the club's financial donation and revealed that Shanks had recently turned down an offer to join the board, on the grounds that it would take up too much of his time. By August he had changed his mind and became a key member of the board, heading the ground sub-committee and becoming involved in negotiations with the Mercers Company over the ground lease.

On 30 May the *MDT* reproduced a sketch of the proposed new stand that 'will accommodate 3,000 spectators and feature tip-up seats with a terrace enclosure situated in front, holding a further 2,000 supporters'. This design by Mr CH Beney, a local architect, would cost the greater part of £5,000 but if more money was raised the development would extend to phase two and include club offices, a gymnasium and baths.

In late June the board gave the scheme the go-ahead and tenders were dispatched. On 4 July the successful bidders were declared as builders A Hall & Son, whose tender for £12,400 included the broader scheme with offices, gymnasiums and baths. Work had commenced that day. The *MDT* waxed lyrically: 'The shapeless forlorn old stand has long since disappeared, and this morning a start was made on the new structure.'

It is notable that new stands were erected at fifteen Football League grounds that summer, including Preston, Middlesbrough and Sunderland, the latter two designed by the eminent football stadium engineer Archibald Leitch.

With **1936-37**'s opening Division Two home game on 31 August, only eight weeks were available for the new stand to be erected and fitted out – a tight schedule. The fund-raising had stalled at just over £2,000 and it was becoming obvious that other sources would have to be sought.

On 14 July the *MDT* described the site as 'many huge holes', which would take the steel structure of the stand, and 'heaps of excavated soil'. The paper also reported that a bantam hen had been found at the ground, nesting in a mechanical excavator and laying eggs in the cabin.

Two weeks later the *MDT* photographer was granted access to the building site and painted a disconcerting picture. The steelwork was only half assembled and it looked unlikely that the stand would be ready in five weeks for the big kick-off. A photograph shows no roof and workmen fixing the last section of steelwork.

On 15 August the club held its first public trial. Although far from ready, hundreds of supporters 'promenaded along the front of the stand to inspect the handsome addition to the ground'. At kick-off the workers downed tools and 'settled themselves down on one of the highest girders' to watch. The completed terraces under the covered end were 'packed' by the 6,500 crowd who saw the stripes (the first team) beat the whites (the reserves) 6-5. Football fever had taken hold of Coventry, with the club reporting season ticket sales up 100 per cent from the previous campaign.

City's opening game in Division Two was at Doncaster, whilst on the same day the reserves kicked off at home to Arsenal. The day before, season ticket holders were advised that the tip-up seats were not installed and their allocated seats would not necessarily be used. A crowd of 11,700 attended the Arsenal game, three thousand more than the previous record for the 'stiffs', and were kept in touch with first-team happenings from Belle Vue – a 1-1 draw.

Two days later there was a buzz of anticipation for City's return to Division Two after an eleven-year absence. Swansea were the visitors and

26,245 saw Coventry take up where they had left off with a 2-1 victory. Photographs in the *MDT* clearly show the stand incomplete. The wing section nearest the covered end was not finished. The front of the stand was also incomplete, so no advertisements were displayed. Over the next few days grumbles surfaced over duplicate season ticket numbers and problems transferring from the ground to the new enclosure.

It was becoming clear that the stand fund had fallen short – the last total given was just short of £2,600. Shanks was scathing about the poor response to the appeal 'The ordinary supporter has done his bit with alacrity but some of the big business people have been very tardy in replying to the hundreds of invitations I have sent out.'

More money was also required to complete phase two, the installation of offices, dressing rooms and a gymnasium. Since 1899 the club had been tenants of the landlords, the Mercers Company. A new lease on Highfield Road had recently been negotiated, but Shanks had other ideas. He proposed that the club exercise an option to purchase the freehold. It would mean taking out a mortgage for £20,000 but with ongoing developments there was plenty of security to reassure lenders. The board gave Shanks a mandate to enter negotiations on this and any other financial issues.

First stop was the *MDT*, which had lent money earlier that year. Shanks, however, soon reported no luck on the newspaper lending more. In the interim, he arranged a £2,000 overdraft with Midland Bank in Foleshill Road. In November 1936 the club announced 'the most important business deal in their history', when Sir John Siddeley, Chairman of Armstrong-Siddeley, the world renowned Coventry-based aircraft manufacturer, invested £20,000 to purchase the freehold from the Mercers company. The club would repay a minimum £1,100 a year, inclusive of interest at 4 per cent per annum, with a repayment period of 32 years. Any sums over and above the interest would be deducted from the capital sum. At the next board meeting Mr Jones proposed a vote of thanks to Shanks for 'arranging and completing all matters connected with the new stand'. Erle Shanks had arrived.

The supporters club, too, wanted to do their bit and set up a 'shilling fund' to provide more concrete terracing. They raised 300 shillings (£15) overnight and this, with other donations, meant work commenced immediately on the 24 unfinished steps under the covered end. On 3 August 1936 the supporters club inspected the work done by Farsley Limited and announced the new concrete terracing with metal barriers ready for the new season. In the final reckoning, the supporters club paid £856 for the work.

The board minutes reported niggles with the new stand. Supporters in the wing stand complained of wet seats, so it was agreed to cover them with tarpaulins between matches – not a satisfactory long-term solution. A few weeks later there were similar problems with the front seats.

On the pitch, life in Division Two held no fears and the team finished 8th, only ten points behind second-placed Blackpool. A tight defence pretty much picked itself, with Mason the pivot and new signing Jack Archer slotting in at left-half. Up front, Bourton's touch deserted him. He only scored nine goals but still ended up as joint top scorer. Lauderdale, like Bourton, 28 years old, struggled in the higher league and left the club after only a handful of games in the higher division.

Crowds were up again, averaging 23,342. Many 'big' teams visited Highfield Road for the first time that season, including Aston Villa (in their first ever season outside of Division One after 44 seasons in the top flight), Sheffield United, Newcastle and Burnley. In the FA Cup, City knocked out League leaders Charlton in round three and, after beating Chester in round four, were drawn against West Brom. The board minutes report that the Charlton match would be filmed by Gaumont British Films, presumably for showing at cinemas nationwide the following week before the main feature film. This is probably the first instance of a City home game being filmed. An unprecedented 5,000 programmes were printed for the Charlton tie, and the players prepared at Margate for two weeks. In the event, the crowd was only 29,118, well below expectations.

The visit of Villa in February attracted the season's best League crowd of 39,828. City won 1-0, but that gate was trumped two weeks later when West Brom arrived in the Cup. This time the board sanctioned a 6,000 print run for the programme.

It was estimated that 14,000 Baggies supporters poured into Coventry by bus, motor car and train. Traffic on the Birmingham to Coventry road was so heavy that vehicles passed at the rate of more than twenty a minute! The slightest hold up resulted in 'a complete wall of vehicles stretching half a mile and sometimes almost a mile'.

Four thousand arrived by train and made a bee-line for Highfield Road with 'rattles, trumpets, bugles and all manner of noise-makers'. Restaurants, cafes, sandwich shops and public houses did a 'roaring trade' with thousands of 'visitors' who had left work hurriedly needing 'square meals' on arriving in the city. In many cases supplies of food ran out. It was quickly obvious the ground record would be smashed again. Long queues snaked around Highfield Road before the gates were opened at 1.30pm. Half an hour before kick-off long queues still threaded down Thackhall Street but the ground looked 'as though it would not hold another single person'. Soon afterwards the gates were closed with several thousand still outside. Youngsters were allowed on to the cinder track behind the goals but no foolhardy persons climbed the advertising hoarding this time. One press photographer got an excellent view on top of the new stand, leaving his colleagues to squeeze around the perimeter of the pitch shoulder to shoulder with the young fans.

The weather was 'kind for the occasion' although the pitch was so muddy that when City captain George Mason tossed for ends the coin stuck upright. It needed a third attempt, on a grassy patch yards from the centre-circle, for Mason to win the toss. With both teams' normally wearing blue and white, both changed. Albion appeared in white shorts with black shorts, and City in 'smart scarlet jerseys'. City survived a first-half penalty but lost 2-3. The crowd of 44,492 was a new record and generated receipts of £2,798.

The summer of 1937 saw more concrete terracing on the Spion Kop. Many of the metal crush barriers were acquired from the Gaumont cinema for £5. Glass panels at each end of the main stand solved the 'wet seat' problem. Internal telephones were installed for the first time, and the pitch had its first drainage system. Phase two of the main stand facilities were completed. These included dressing rooms, gymnasium and a new secretary's office. Harry Barratt, reminiscing in 1986, described the new facilities: 'Heated dressing rooms with large tiled baths to replace the old tin soft water tank type of bath. Gone too were the old coke stoves which had been in both dressing rooms.'

Later that season the players took possession of a recreation room with a bar and sports facilities. Meanwhile, Robinsons tarmaced the area behind the main stand at a cost of £232 and a new club flag was purchased. After many complaints new urinals and WCs were installed under the old stand by A Ward & Co at a cost of £68 15s.

The Standard Electric Company came up with a novel proposal for the loudspeaker system. They offered to install the equipment free of charge provided that they could advertise Co-op tea, and make it the exclusive tea at refreshment outlets. The only expense incurred by the club would be gramophone records played over the system and performing rights charges. The club also received 75lbs of Co-op tea!

It is probable that Ginger, the old nag who used to haul the roller and grass-cutter across the Highfield Road pitch, passed away in the summer of 1937. The minutes reported in September that a petrol-driven roller, weighing 17½ hundredweight, was ordered on approval from Wallis & Steevens of Long Eaton, and in March 1938 the club bought a Ransome gang mower.

A new kit was introduced after many letters to the *MDT* complained about the 'scruffy' faded shirts. Storer was not impressed: 'Our players go onto the field to win matches, not to look like matinee idols.' Out went the blue and white halved shirts to be replaced by a new shirt with three broad vertical panels. The central white panel was flanked by two light blue panels. The V-neck was fashionably laced with white string and the dark blue shorts were switched to white. The team photo taken in August 1937 shows a dapper team surrounding a scowling Storer.

To strengthen his squad Storer signed forward Magnus McPhee from Bradford Park Avenue for £2,000 and uncompromising defender Walter Metcalf from Brentford for £1,500. The club resisted bids from First Division clubs, including Bolton, for star players George Mason and Leslie Jones.

1937-38 started with fifteen games before the team lost at home to Sheffield Wednesday in November. Their 0-0 draw at Villa Park in front of 67,271 was a Division Two attendance record at that time. Coventry was becoming football crazy and home gates under 25,000 were rare. City led the table until Christmas Day, and two days later 40,746 saw them toss away a two-goal lead in the last two minutes against new leaders Sheffield United.

Promotion still looked likely before the final home game with Fulham, but an early injury to Bobby Davidson contributed to a shock 0-1 defeat. City finished 4th, a point behind second-placed Manchester United, who were promoted with Aston Villa. Villa's visit again attracted Highfield Road's biggest crowd, with a record 44,930 present to watch the Villains' 1-0 victory. The average crowd was an all-time high of 27,159, a figure not surpassed until the 1966-67 promotion season.

After Les Jones was finally sold to Arsenal in November 1937, many supporters claimed the directors didn't want promotion. City didn't quite play with same zing after Jones left, his replacement Bobby Davidson was injured, and Arsenal lifted the Division One title with Jones a major influence. The legendary Bourton had also left, joining Plymouth after scoring 182 goals for City. Storer brought in several experienced players and put his faith in talented youngsters like Ted Roberts, Harry Barratt and Leslie Warner. All of these would become post-war legends at Highfield Road.

In those halcyon days, most players would travel to the ground by foot – or by bus or bicycle if they lived beyond walking distance. A lucky few, like Ashall and Billy McDonald, were known to own motor cars. The club owned one car and in December 1937 this was replaced by a brand new Vauxhall 10-horse power from Brandish's, the motor-car dealer owned by the director. The car would have been used by Storer and his assistant Dick Bayliss, the 'chief scout', who spent a lot of time 'on the road' looking at potential players and scouting on future opponents.

In April 1938 the minutes reported an 'unattended lorry had caused extensive damage to the Swan lane terracing on Good Friday'. Temporary repairs were carried out, but the incident was not mentioned again and a crowd of 30,000 got in to watch the Easter Tuesday game with Barnsley.

Ground upgrades in the close-season of 1938 included building the Crow's Nest on the Spion Kop terracing. This upward extension of the banked terracing consisted of timber boards in a lattice-like structure supported by steel. It offered a 'lofty vantage point' for standing spectators and probably increased the capacity by a couple of thousand. The work was carried out by George Robinson & Co and cost £400, with the majority coming from the supporters club 'shilling fund'. A new flagpole was erected on the new structure.

It is unclear whether the Crow's Nest was in use for the start of the season: the minutes of 20 September 1938 reported 'attempts to be made to speed up the delivery of the iron fencing for the back of the Crow's Nest'. By November, however, it was reported that Robinson's had 'knocked £7 3s 4d off the final account and agreed to rent an advertising sign on the Crow's Nest for five years at a cost of £9 per annum'. The wooden scoreboard on the Spion Kop was demolished and the half-time scores thereafter displayed on the concrete perimeter wall. Tip-up seats were installed around the perimeter wall for the use of patrolling policemen.

With the political climate in Europe worsening, evidence of a forces recruitment campaign appeared in the board's minutes of August 1938, when the club agreed to a request from the Naval Recruiting Office to post recruiting notices around the ground.

Brighter news came when the Football Association requested the use of Highfield Road for a Junior International with Scotland in April 1939. The fixture, between a Birmingham County FA XI and a Scottish Juniors XI went ahead and ended 0-0 in front of 9,000 spectators.

For the **1938-39** season the club increased season ticket prices. A ground ticket now cost £1 3s 6d, with stand tickets varying from £2 10s to £3 10s for the centre seats in the new stand. Despite finishing 4th again, there was a negative ring in the air. Impatient fans demanded money invested in players, but prudent directors were reluctant to saddle the club with more debt, having cleared the liabilities stemming from 1920s' mismanagement. Two transfers that did take place were the sale to Birmingham, for £3,000, of winger Jackie Brown – who had allegedly

disgraced himself in a hushed-up incident in the toilets of a local ball-
room – and the arrival of his replacement, George Ashall, at £3,500 a
record signing from Wolves. Ashall had been selected for England the
previous season, but injury denied him his cap.

Training for footballers in those days was very different than in the
modern day. In 1986, former City player Harry Barratt described the pre-
season routine in the 1930s: 'The first two weeks of training consisted
mainly of track lapping at Highfield Road [running around the perimeter
of the pitch] with an occasional break for physical jerks. After a lunch
break it was back for a repeat of the morning's programme. Road work
was sometimes introduced, with the players running through Gosford
Green, along the Binley Road, St James Lane, London Road, Humber
Road and back to Highfield Road. Sprinting on Fridays was introduced
after the first two weeks training had been completed.'

Ball-work was not much in evidence. Another former 50s player, Lol
Harvey, recalled that until Jesse Carver and George Raynor arrived in the
summer of 1955 it was rare for City players to kick a ball in training –
other than a practice game. The British attitude was 'if you starve the
players of the ball in the week, the more hungry they will be for it on a
Saturday afternoon'.

After a poor start to 1938-39, eighteen games with only three defeats
took the team to 3rd in February. The club had announced a profit of
£4,907 for the year to 31 December 1938 – the seventh successive year
of profits – and paid their first ever dividend to shareholders. The club
owed John Siddeley over £19,000 on the mortgage and the *MDT* £1,780
from the 1936 loan, but assets in the form of the new stand and the freehold on Highfield Road more than outweighed these liabilities.

Following a 4-0 win at Newcastle in February, City were three points
behind the top two with two games in hand. The club had cash balances
of £7,000 and when goalscoring sensation Tommy Crawley's goals dried
up Storer signed West Ham's centre-forward Tommy Green to fill the
gap. For once Storer's judgement failed, Green failed to deliver the goals,
and promotion was missed by four points. Many fans felt City should
have spent more to help the promotion push.

Also in February the board had discussed extensions at either end of
the main stand, increasing the seating capacity by a further 2,000 and
offering covered accommodation for 20,000. The plan, estimated to cost
£10,000, would be implemented only if City won promotion to Division
One in 1939. When promotion failed to materialise, so too did the extension plans. Further major ground developments would have to wait for
another 25 years.

Gates dropped by 6,500 as the novelty of Second Division football wore off, although 38,163 turned up for the only Midlands derby, against West Brom in February.

The club received many requests to use Highfield Road during this era, most of which were turned down. Among those refused were a professional tennis tournament in the summer of 1939, a display by Cossack horseriders, a request to stage professional wrestling, and another from a Reverend Griffiths to play a football match between 'a team of parsons and some other body'. The club did, however, normally allow local junior clubs to play finals at the ground, and the *Midland Daily Telegraph* and subsequently the *Coventry Telegraph* staged their Cup finals there. In 1939 the Girls Night Shelter played their Cup final on the ground. Storer was behind many of the refusals on the grounds that the pitch was already overburdened, and he had a point. Match reports from the era are littered with references to ankle-deep mud and puddle-strewn pitches. Reports of a reserve game against Southend in January 1939 describe horrendous conditions: 'the pitch so soft that there was scarcely a square foot where the players did not sink in up to their ankles.'

In April 1939 a circular arrived from the Football Association encouraging players to join the Territorial Army and hoping 'they would display a patriotic example to the youth of the country'. Many joined up to spend their leisure hours preparing for the seemingly inevitable. Liverpool joined the Territorials as a club, including the manager and secretary, and special Footballer units were formed, including a famous one for Bolton Wanderers. But not all clubs shared this collective urge to volunteer. City's directors discussed it at length and concluded that 'the club should not in any way influence players to join up, but the circular [should] simply be read out to them without any comment'.

Despite the mounting threat of war, the summer of 1939 saw the construction of a canopy at the front of the main stand. It extended nine feet and ensured that standing spectators in the paddock in front of the stand were protected from the elements, likewise the front rows in the stand. The work cost £1,300 and was again largely funded by the supporters club. A water spraying system for the pitch cost £86 from Bowyer & Johnson and the broadcasting equipment supplied by Standard Electric Company (remember the tea deal?) was purchased for £100. Owing to the poor state of the Highfield Road cover, an order was placed with Matterson, Huxley & Watson for the repair of the roof and guttering at a cost of £249, which would be financed by the supporters club.

Days before the start of the **1939-40** season, with the country on the brink of war, the board incredibly discussed the possibility of an

Argentina XI playing a friendly at Highfield Road in February 1940. A charity game with Aston Villa on 25 September 1939 in aid of Coventry and Warwickshire Hospital was also planned.

The season commenced on 12 August with the traditional public trial, and 4,058 watched the stripes beat the reds 6-5, with nineteen-year-old George Lowrie, a £1,750 signing from Preston, scoring a hat-trick for the first team. This game saw the first appearance of numbers on players' shirts, 'an experiment found to be of considerable value.' After almost twenty years of lobbying by certain clubs, the Football League had agreed to introduce the numbering of players in League games. Numbers had been used in the 1933 FA Cup final when Everton played Manchester City (the players were numbered 1 to 22 and rugby union had used shirt numbers for at least ten years). A week after the trial match, Lowrie scored the winner as City beat Birmingham 3-2 in the Football League Jubilee Fund friendly in front of 7,979.

City opened the League campaign with a 1-1 draw at Burnley. On Monday, 28 August only 18,500 turned up for the first home game, against West Brom. Tommy Green scored twice as the Bantams threw away a 3-0 lead to draw 3-3. Many supporters, their minds set on war, stayed away. On Friday, 1 September the evacuation of children from London got under way but fixtures for the following day went ahead. City defeated Barnsley 4-2 at home with Lowrie marking his debut with a goal in front of only 11,611. On the following day, Sunday, 3 September, war was declared on Hitler's Germany and competitive League football was suspended.

The board did not waste time in reacting to the outbreak of hostilities. Two days after Neville Chamberlain's fateful radio broadcast, all playing contracts were cancelled and the players and the majority of the staff were given a week's money. Only three staff were retained: manager Harry Storer, secretary Bernard Hitchiner, and groundsman W Austin – all three accepted a 50 per cent cut in wages. Amongst the staff paid off were chief scout Dick Bayliss and trainers Dick Hill, Leslie Bruton and Arthur Fitton.

War could not have come at a worse time for the club. Despite a healthy bank balance in the spring of 1939, summer wages of £3,000 had been paid out, in addition to £1,750 for the signing of Lowrie and £1,300 on ground improvements. There was a £1,000 tax bill due in early 1940, and normally the takings from three home games would cover that sum. The low crowds for the first two put a spoke in those wheels and the club were in dire trouble. The club wrote to John Siddeley asking if interest payments on the debt might lapse for the duration of war. Subsequent discussions resulted in a two-year suspension of capital payments with the deeds of the ground being held by Siddeley. Storer was instructed to discuss the postponement of repayments of the loan from the *MDT* for the duration.

With no income, and fixed costs to bear, City were in serious financial difficulty. The club owed money on pre-war purchases of George Lowrie and Tommy Green and had to inform the Football League that it could not meet its commitments.

On 14 September the FA announced that regional (within 50 miles) friendly matches could be played but no player could be paid, as contracts had been cancelled. Any receipts from these games had to be donated to charity. City played Stoke City two days later at the Victoria Ground and subsequently played five more friendlies on successive Saturdays. Crowds were restricted by the Home Office to 8,000 and City played two home friendlies against Leicester (a 3-3 draw watched by 3,236) and Wolves (a 0-4 defeat watched by 6,558).

In early October plans were drawn up for a regional competition involving all but six Football League clubs. Clubs could now pay players 30 shillings (£1.50) per game. City were in a group with seven other Midland clubs: Wolves, Birmingham and Leicester (all Division One teams), West Brom and Luton (Division Two) and Northampton and Walsall (Division Three). Aston Villa did not enter. Season ticket holders were given the choice of using their tickets for the wartime competition or returning them with a guarantee that when normal football resumed they would get a free ticket.

City's first game in the new competition on 21 October was a 1-1 draw at Northampton, and in the first home game the following Saturday they trounced West Brom 6-3. Several first-team players had gone off to war, but only twice did City have to 'hire' guest players: veteran Jock Lauderdale played four games and D Murray, an unknown guest, scored five goals in four games. The club normally issued team sheets for their home games with a typical print run of 1,000.

Between October 1939 and the final game on 8 June 1940, City played 28 League games, finishing 3rd in their section, and five Cup games. The public's reaction to these quasi-friendly games was apathetic, with home gates ranging from 1,212 versus Leicester on a foggy Saturday before Christmas, to 8,713 who watched a 5-2 win over Wolves in May. The winter was severe, which did nothing to encourage venturing out to watch football, and 27 January saw the coldest recorded temperature in the city since 1894. The highlight of that first wartime campaign was a 10-2 win over Luton Town on Easter Monday. Tom Crawley scored eight goals, a club record, including three in three minutes shortly before half-time. The final four games were played in front of crowds of under 1,500. The low gates are not surprising considering that the British Army was being evacuated from Dunkirk as Hitler's army forced them to retreat to the French coast.

CHAPTER FIVE

The 1940s

The evacuation from Dunkirk was a catastrophic defeat trussed up as a glorious victory. Paris had fallen and an invasion seemed imminent. The Battle of Britain was set to begin. The outlook for football looked similarly bleak.

At the Football League's AGM on 29 July 1940 it was decided to carry on with however many clubs could muster teams. For the **1940-41** season they would be divided into two groups, North and South. There would be no professionalism, trophies or medals. Clubs could choose their own opponents, but First and Second Division clubs must play at least two Third Division clubs. Matches would be localised and sanctioned by local regional commissioners. There would be no points for wins or draws. Instead the league tables would be compiled purely on goal-average, so as not to disadvantage clubs playing fewer matches. Fixtures would only be compiled up to the end of the year, when the situation for the second half of the season would be reviewed. Only 68 clubs chose to carry on, with Aston Villa, Wolves, Sunderland and Derby amongst those turning their backs. The City directors were initially undecided, but then took the plunge.

Finances were so bad that the club was struggling to pay the interest on John Siddeley's £20,000 debenture. In June the club wrote to him asking if interest payments could be suspended, but the reply was not promising; that quarter's interest had been earmarked for charitable purposes and must be paid. The club paid up but advised that they could not commit to paying the interest regularly but would endeavour to pay as much as possible.

Cost-cutting exercises were rife. Coventry Corporation helped out by reducing the club's rates from £585 to £250 per annum. The board discussed Storer and asked him to seek employment elsewhere while carrying on his football duties with the club 'supplementing his wages to the amount he now draws'. He subsequently took a managerial job at Rootes Humber motor works. Simultaneously, Austin the groundsman had his wages inexplicably increased by 10 shillings a week. The club drew the line at some fund-raising activities; in May they rejected a proposal from a Mr Incley to hold boxing shows at the ground on summer Sundays.

In July the secretary reported that Highfield Road had been requisitioned by the military authorities for 'an indefinite period'. The club would benefit from £200 rent per annum and a portion of the rates, leaving the club full use of the ground, boardroom, and general office.

Several players had joined the armed forces, including Jack Astley, Les 'Plum' Warner, Jack Snape and Ted Roberts, but the Bantams were still able to put out a strong side. They lost only two of their first ten games, with big wins over Reading (7-3) and Cardiff (5-2), in which George Lowrie and Tom Crawley scored seven goals apiece.

Coventry was, of course, a major centre of manufacturing and at the outset of war Coventry companies Daimler, Dunlop, GEC, Humber and Armstrong Whitworth produced a whole range of manufactured products from bomber aircraft to scout cars. Much of this work was quickly transferred to 'shadow' factories built on the outskirts of the city to reduce the threat of aerial attack and to take the threat of bombing away from residential areas.

The first recorded bombs to be dropped in the area were on 25 June 1940, when five fell on the Ansty Aerodrome. This was soon followed by a string of bombs on the Hillfields area, close to Highfield Road, which resulted in sixteen deaths. On the evening of 25 August a short sharp raid left more dead and the city's prestigious cinema, the Rex, in ruins. The next day the cinema was scheduled to play *Gone with the Wind*.

October 1940 witnessed many small but intense night-time raids, leaving 176 dead. At the board meeting on 15 October Storer reported to the directors that a bomb had hit the ground and there was bomb damage to the terraces at the covered end. The next game, scheduled for 26 October was postponed, but the home game with Northampton on 2 November went ahead but attracted a crowd of only 307. The following Saturday the side won 4-1 at West Brom in what would be the last City game for over two years.

On the evening of Thursday, 14 November 1940 Coventry was subjected to the single most concentrated attack on a British city in the war. On a clear moonlit night the Luftwaffe dropped 500 tons of high explosive, 30,000 incendiaries and 50 land mines on the city. There were 4,330 homes destroyed and three-quarters of the city's factories were damaged. The next morning amongst the rubble lay the sometimes unidentifiable remains of 554 men, women and children. Another 865 were injured. The city described twenty years previously as one of the 'finest preserved medieval cities in Europe' had been ravaged.

Football, as you can imagine, was not high on the list of public priorities that autumn. At Highfield Road it was reported that two high explosive bombs had landed on the ground, causing substantial damage to the terraces and a hole in the new stand. On 23 November the *MDT* noted:

'There will be no football at Highfield Road for a long time, Hitler having done a spot of ploughing up the playing space with a series of bombs, besides knocking a large-sized hole in the new stand. In addition to that, nobody knows the exact whereabouts of the players. It is thought they are all safe, but at the moment it would be impossible to guarantee the raising of a team.' The club's directors had no alternative but to suspend operations. The Football League and Football Association wrote expressing sympathy with City's plight, hoping that the club could carry on in the New Year. Messrs Breeze and Burdett surveyed the damage and prepared estimates for insurance claims.

From a financial point of view, the suspension of football was almost the last straw, and Erle Shanks made a far-reaching proposal that aimed to keep the club afloat and prepare for the cessation of hostilities at some time in the future. The main points of his plan were:

'The suspension of football for the duration of the war, but the club to maintain the structure of the organisation, to enable football to be resumed with the least possible delay at the conclusion of hostilities.

'The retention of Harry Storer, at £3 per week on condition that the club had first option of his services on the resumption.

'The books and accounts to be placed in the hands of Messrs Daffern & Co who would collect outstanding amounts and pay bills when they became due and deal with all financial matters in the future.

'The retention of the groundsman at his present salary. He would be instructed to maintain the ground and stands in the best possible manner for the resumption of football when required.

These were positive and pro-active proposals from Shanks, who was emerging as the most dynamic of the club's directors, and at a board meeting on 18 December they were accepted. The club's accountants, Daffern & Co, were basically put in charge of everything financial and were asked to draw up a full resume of the current state of affairs. Storer was relieved of financial responsibilities so as to give more of his time to his job at Rootes.

Phil Mead, a young partner of Daffern & Co, started attending board meetings and preparing the minutes. By March he had been appointed Acting Secretary. He soon reported that the club had lost £429 in the year ended 31 December 1940, and with no football there was no income. In an attempt to generate revenue the club agreed to lease the new stand to John Anslow Limited, a local furniture company who used it for storing furniture for £4 per week. The car park was let to Coventry Corporation, and this brought in a further £4 a week. Coventry & North Warwickshire Cricket Club's hire of the football club's roller brought in another £1 5s a week in the summer months. In another income-generating project, the Leamington football ground acquired before the war as a training ground and venue for A-team matches was let to the Lockheed Brake Company for £7 per week.

A clerical error at the Football Association resulted in City being included in the draw for the 1940-41 War Cup. The club hastily issued a statement confirming that there was no chance of football at the ground in the near future. The bomb craters in the pitch had been filled, but the terracing and stand repairs (estimated at £1,800) were impossible in the financial climate and would require a war damage insurance claim.

The air raids on Coventry continued, although they were generally lighter than the November blitz. Two, however, were heavy. The Easter raids of 8 and 10 April 1941 lasted between six and eight hours and inflicted serious damage to the roof of the new stand. Heavy rainfall caused substantial damage to the seats before tarpaulins were spread over the offending areas, but it was noted that the furniture stored there had sustained damage. In June the directors agreed that the 'expense and difficulties of repairing the ground were too great to be undertaken'. Erle Shanks was tasked with investigating other options, including the feasibility of using Coundon Road, the ground of the rugby club, and the Leamington ground. He concluded that although the rugby club were happy to accommodate the team, substantial amounts would need to be spent on fences and turnstiles for it to be used regularly. Leamington was out of the question from a financial point of view.

The conclusion reached was that a resumption of play was impossible for a variety of reasons, including a financial one, and that it would be hard to obtain the release of players from munition factories on Saturday afternoons. Additionally, Storer himself would be needed to administer the club and even if Rootes were prepared to release him he would still require a part-time job to supplement his income.

In August 1941 Mead's report on the financial position of the club made uncomfortable reading. City had £43 in its current account and £427 in a building society deposit account. It owed £123 to various tradesmen for ground repairs and the Corporation in rent. More importantly, there was over £1,000 owed to the Inland Revenue, £420 to John Siddeley in Debenture interest, and £1,280 was still outstanding to the *MDT*. The tax man was threatening to send in the bailiffs, and some careful negotiating was necessary to avoid distraint action. The directors also recognised that, when hostilities ceased, funds would be needed to pay players until competitive football recommenced. They were therefore reluctant to use their small deposits on repaying these liabilities.

Further problems arose in early 1942 when groundsman Austin was called into the services. The solution was to let the ground to the Humber-Hillman Social and Athletic Club, of which conveniently Harry Storer was the secretary. They would pay a rental of £250 per annum and provide a groundsman to maintain the ground. On 21 February 1942 Coundon Road provided the venue for a friendly match in aid of Warship Week. Storer constructed a team from players still living and working in the area and put out City's first team since November 1940. They faced an exiled team representing the Czech Army, which had a large contingent of men based around South Warwickshire. City won 4-1 with two goals from Jock Lauderdale and further goals from Vic O'Brien, an ex-City player attached to Watford, and Tom Crawley.

Six weeks later Highfield Road staged its first game for eighteen months. On 6 April the club were persuaded to host the final of the *MDT* Challenge Cup between local teams Morris Motors and AWA (Baginton). AWA were Armstrong Whitworth Aircraft Limited, a major employer in the city. A crowd of 6,582 saw the morning kick-off, which Morris won 4-1. The gate receipts of £271 4s 3d were given to local charities. The pitch was reported to be in excellent condition but parts of the terraces were 'out of bounds' because of the bomb damage.

On 18 April 1942 City's George Mason played for England against Scotland in a War International at Hampden Park – the first City player to play for England, albeit in a game for which no caps were awarded. The regular England centre-half was Wolves' Stan Cullis. Mason's chance came when Cullis – who rarely missed a wartime international – was injured. Mason was barely fit himself, as he had played little football in the previous twelve months. He was up against Jock Dodds of Blackpool, one of the best centre-forwards of the war years, who scored a hat-trick in Scotland's 5-4 win. Mason might have been overwhelmed by a 75,000 crowd at Glasgow's enormous stadium, but at least he had the satisfaction of playing in the same side as such luminaries as Stan Matthews, Eddie Hapgood, Joe Mercer and Tommy Lawton. Mason was an 'essential worker' during the war, inspecting parts in an aircraft factory.

Three weeks later Mason kept his place against Wales at Ninian Park. England lost 0-1 and by October, when the next international was played, Cullis was fit and able to reclaim his position. Against Wales, Mason faced club-mate George Lowrie, making his international debut. Lowrie, proving just how wrong Preston had been to free him before the war, went on to make eight wartime appearances in the Welsh side.

City returned to Highfield Road on 25 May 1942 when a friendly was arranged with Birmingham. A crowd of 5,491 watched the Bantams defeat the Blues 4-2 with two goals apiece from Welsh international Leslie Jones, guesting, and Tom Crawley. City's team included many pre-war stars, such as Mason, Morgan, Lowrie and Boileau, as well as guests Jones and Australian Frank Mitchell, who had been on Birmingham's books before the war. Morgan, Harry Barratt and Billy Frith had all guested for Leicester City on a fairly regular basis.

Prospects of a return to regional war football were boosted in July when the club received around £350 from the War Damages commission and plans were set in motion to repair the new stand roof and the terrace damage to the enclosure. On 1 August chairman Stringer told the *CET*: 'Within the limits placed upon us by a variety of reasons we aim to give our public the best football possible under war-time conditions, in as comfortable circumstances as possible'. The club were admitted to the Midlands section of the War League, which would commence on 29 August, with the first home game a week later against Walsall. No programmes would be issued and the terrace entrance charge was 1s 6d.

Meanwhile, the Inland Revenue were pursuing the club's debts and threatening High Court action, presumably to put the club into liquidation. They were persuaded to hold off for four months, at which time the club anticipated having some liquid funds to start repaying a debt which now stood at £1,244.

City lost their opening match of **1942-43** at Walsall 0-1, but on 5 September reversed that score in front of 6,356. For the scorer, Walsall-born 36-year-old George Taylor, it was a bitter-sweet final game in a City shirt. Signed for a large £2,250 fee in 1937, he had not been at his best before the war, and now injury would end his career. Spectators were allowed into three sides of the ground. The profit after expenses from the first home game was £140, and the board agreed to let servicemen in for half price at future games.

A week later the crowd doubled to welcome Aston Villa. Villa had not previously competed in the Wartime Football League, and their fans were desperate for action. Their team included pre-war internationals such as Frank Broome and Ronnie Starling, but two Crawley goals won the game for City in front of 14,720, generating a profit of £360. Shortly afterwards Storer was allowed to re-employ Dick Bayliss as a scout on a salary of £1 per week, and his own salary was increased to £5 per week for the season.

By Christmas Day, City had only lost one more game out of fifteen. Injuries, work commitments and service duty meant Storer had to rely increasingly on young local players from works football and guests from other clubs who were stationed in the Midlands and could get clearance.

Stalwarts like Mason, Lowrie, Billy Frith, Crawley and Harry Boileau were joined by local youths such as Dennis Simpson, Alf Wood and Alf Setchell. Fifty players were used in 38 league and cup games that season.

The Wartime League set-up was complicated. City only faced other Midland sides, including Villa, Birmingham, Wolves, Leicester, West Brom, Walsall and Northampton, but their results went towards a League North Championship. On Christmas Day 1942, after eighteen games, the championship concluded with City 7th out of 48 teams. There then followed ten games for a Cup qualifying competition, of which City won seven and lost three to qualify for the knockout stages. Paired with West Brom in a two-legged tie, City drew 1-1 at home but lost 0-3 at the Hawthorns to bow out. The last six weeks reverted to league games, with the results since Boxing Day (including the cup games) counting towards a North Second Championship. City finished 18th out of 48.

Attendances averaged 8,094 but the Villa crowd of 14,720 was never bettered. Gates tailed off after the Cup exit and the lowest was 4,188 for a 3-1 win over Leicester. Lowrie's goals were crucial – 23 in 33 games including three hat-tricks.

By the summer of 1943 the club's finances were healthier, due to the efforts of the directors, manager and the financial acumen of Daffern & Co's Phil Mead. Storer and Mead were each awarded £50; Storer's was a bonus, whilst the unpaid Mead's was classed as an honorarium. A second War Damage Claim of £586 was paid to the club, and with the tax arrears now settled and debenture interest paid up to date, the club was back in the black.

In 1984, shortly before his death in a road accident, 77-year-old Mead looked back to the club during the war: 'There was an administration problem. After every home match Bernard Hitchener, Reg Johnson and I, together with a friend of mine, Cecil Jones of the Halifax Building Society, would gather together at Highfield Road to count the money and fill out the league match returns, which had to be despatched the day after the match. I would take the money home on Saturday after the match in the leather bags and put them under the bed. On Sunday morning I loaded the bags into the car and took them down to Highfield Road. After the counting ceremony I took them back home and slept on them again until I could take the money to the bank on Monday morning. It was a result of these antics and the fact that I had undertaken the whole of the accountancy for the club that I was invited to become a director in March 1945.'

The **1943-44** Wartime League season operated on the same basis as the previous one, but the Bantams were no longer a power in it. George

Lowrie was in the armed services and missed half the games, but still managed thirteen goals in nineteen games. Tom Crawley netted twenty in 34 games, but goals from others were scarce. Constant team changes were forced on Storer and 47 players were utilised, including many local amateurs. The first half of the campaign ended with an 8-0 drubbing of West Brom on Christmas Day, with Crawley netted five in front of a poor 7,398 crowd. In the second stage of the season City earned enough points to qualify for the knockout War Cup and were drawn to face Derby in the two-legged first round. Over 12,000 watched the Bantams overturn a 1-2 deficit at Highfield Road from the first leg and set up a plum second round tie with Aston Villa. A week later Villa won 2-1 at Highfield Road in front of 23,664, the biggest home crowd for five years. In the second leg, Villa won by the same margin to progress to the quarter finals of a competition they would ultimately win.

City's attendances tailed off, and only 1,775 turned out for the last home game, against Notts County, in May 1944. The stay-aways missed a 8-2 home win. County turned up minus a goalkeeper and an 'obviously unfit' Bill Morgan offered to deputise. He had, however, failed to recover from shoulder problems and it would be his final competitive game. Six months later he was advised to retire and later became City's trainer.

Whilst Allied forces were preparing for the Normandy landings City's directors were looking ahead to the resumption of peace-time football. A reserve team was reconstituted and entered the Coventry and North Warwickshire League as Coventry City 'A'. Another team called Coventry Tile was fashioned as a nursery club. The reserves played at the Butts Football Ground (later to become the Butts Stadium) which the club rented for 30 shillings per week and charged spectators 3d a game.

After complaints from Customs & Excise about mispriced tickets – apparently the club were using pre-war tickets showing incorrect prices – new ticket rolls were ordered with up-to-date prices.

With club finances looking more healthy, the club hoped to pay accrued benefits due to players from before the war. Almost £3,000 was earmarked for this purpose before the Football League intervened to demand settlement of a pre-war transfer debt of £400 with Preston relating to the signing of Lowrie. The debt was soon settled and the pre-war players got a welcome bonus.

By December 1944, with the end of the war in sight, the directors started planning ground repairs to Highfield Road. Erle Shanks was tasked with obtaining a building licence for 'fairly extensive repairs to the ground, including repairs to the Highfield Road cover'. It was expected that any expenditure would be covered by the War Damage Claims.

That month the ground hosted another new sport, when an American Football game took place in aid of Coventry and Warwickshire Hospital. Over 8,000 watched the US Army beat the US Navy 7-0 and raise over £1,000 for the rebuilding work on the hospital.

The quality of the Coventry City team suffered during **1944-45**, with many called-up players posted overseas as the war in Europe reached its climax. Of the pre-war Second Division side, only George Mason and Tom Crawley played regularly, although City benefited from having Birmingham's George Edwards, a Welsh international and one of the best left-wingers around. With goalkeeper Bill Morgan retiring through injury, and his deputy Alf Wood overseas, City used five different custodians and shipped 95 goals in 38 games. Ron Garner conceded eight at Northampton, and Sid King, a guest from Birmingham, let in nine at Villa Park in May.

The team failed to qualify for the War Cup and won only twelve games all season to finish 41st out of 54 in the North Championship and 42nd in the North Second Championship.

On Saturday, 20 January 1945 Highfield Road hosted a charity representative game between the RAF and an FA XI, with all the proceeds being divided between the Red Cross and St John Fund and the RAF Benevolent Fund. The game gave local supporters the opportunity to see top stars of the day and the England and Scotland selectors a chance to size up players for their international at Villa Park in two weeks time. The four-page programme listed many players who had become regulars in the England wartime team and become post-war stars. The RAF team included Middlesbrough's George Hardwick, Blackpool's Stan Mortensen and Brentford's Leslie Smith. The FA XI, if anything, were stronger, with Everton's extraordinary centre-forward Tommy Lawton, a young inside-forward from Bradford by the name of Len Shackleton, and pre-war England captain Joe Mercer. The programme listed Stanley Matthews in the RAF team but he pulled out when his father died. Local fans were massively disappointed as Matthews was considered to be the top English player of his day. He would never get the opportunity to play at Highfield Road again.

On a snowbound pitch the RAF team won 6-4, with Mortensen playing his way into the England team with a hat-trick for the RAF and Jock Dodds – his partner who grabbed two goals – being called into the Scottish team. A 12,000 crowd saw the game and raised £2,485 for the charities. The *CET* reporter was impressed: 'It was plainly demonstrated that given star artists, football can be grand entertainment – in spite of the snowbound ground that threatened to ruin the show.'

On 2 April 1945 City played host to the Polish Air Force team. The Polish Air Force had been based in Britain since the fall of their country in 1939 and played a major role in the Battle of Britain in 1940. Their football team was based at RAF Newton in Nottinghamshire, which was a training school for the Polish Air Force from 1941 and became known as Little Poland to locals. Three of their players caught the eye: Gerard Wodarz, formerly of Ruch Chorzow, was a left-winger who was capped more than twenty times before the war and played in the 1938 World Cup in France. His career would end in November 1945 when he broke an ankle playing for Fraserburgh in the Scottish Highland League. Mieczyslaw Pawlow played wartime football for Notts County, Lincoln City and Peterborough, and goalkeeper Bishek Stankowski for Notts County, Brighton and Peterborough. The gate proceeds were split between the Polish Red Cross and a local charity.

The teams drew 2-2 in front of just 2,892. Tom Crawley scored City's goals with Wozny and Majeran replying. Following the Poles' game at Watford, a local newspaper reported: 'The Poles' greatest asset was their speed, for they were an exceptionally light team and in the early stages relied on complicated strategic moves.' The *CET* however thought 'the Poles depended on big kicking and speed'.

The final event staged Highfield Road that season was baseball. The American sport got its second airing at the ground, following the game in 1918, when teams from US convalescent centres at Packington and Stoneleigh fought out a close game with Packington winning. There are no records of the attendance or details of the game.

In May 1945, two weeks after VE Day had marked the end of the war in Europe, it was announced that manager Harry Storer was leaving the club to join Birmingham, taking up his duties in July, in time for the transitional season. His departure was a shock to Coventry fans, who believed that Storer was the club and could not imagine life without the great man. He had been manager for fourteen years, all but six of them in peacetime, and had transformed the club from perennial strugglers who staggered from boom to bust, to a side which, but for the war, could have been promoted to Division One.

Boardroom discussions with Storer had been ongoing for months. In April the chairman had asked him to resume full-time employment 'with an increase in salary to an amount equal to the salary he was paid at Humber'. The minutes indicate that Storer was happy with this, and that Humber were happy to release him, but needed to find a replacement. Looking back at those austere times it is hard to fathom Storer's mind. Perhaps he felt he should have been better rewarded for the loyalty he had shown the club during the dark years. Maybe he was ripe for a new challenge and felt that the potential at St Andrews was greater than at Highfield Road. In retrospect, Birmingham seemed to have prepared better for the return of peacetime football.

Storer's loyal assistant since 1931, Dick Bayliss, was appointed in his place, with Bernard Hitchener becoming secretary (on £7 a week) and ending the dual role of secretary-manager which had existed since professional football was forged back in the 19th Century. Meanwhile, groundsman Austin rejoined the football club from the armed services at £6 per week.

On Monday, 7 May plans for the transitional season of **1945-46** were drawn up. The clubs, led by Arsenal, vetoed the League's Management Committee's idea to restart league football immediately. There were still many players in the services and problems with travel and accommodation persisted. Instead, the 44 First and Second Division clubs were split into North and South sections. City were in the South, giving them games against First Division giants Arsenal, Villa and Chelsea. The FA agreed to reinstate the FA Cup, but to have first round ties onwards played over two legs. Guest players were still allowed for league games but limited to six per team, and further reduced to three in November.

City announced that the admission prices would be unchanged from 1939, apart from boys, who would now pay 9d, an increase recommended by the Football League. Match programmes would recommence but only for first-team fixtures.

The war in Asia ended soon after the Bomb was dropped, first on Hiroshima, then Nagasaki in early August. Six years of war saw no casualties among City's playing staff, but of the club's 31 professionals, 21 were still in the services. Players who had been away for years – like Ted Roberts, George Ashall, Lawrie Coen and Jack Snape – were still away. Others, such as Ellis Lager, Jack Astley and Tommy Green would be forced to retire through injury. Guests would therefore be essential for the coming months.

City's opening game in 1945-46 brought the first ever visit of mighty Arsenal, and attracted the biggest league crowd of the season, 20,943. Goals from Fred Gardner and Lowrie won the game for City, who were helped by former hero, Les Jones, now guesting from Arsenal.

The team finished 13th out of 22 clubs in the Football League South, which was won by Storer's new team, Birmingham. Derby County won the FA Cup, beating Charlton in the final 4-1 after extra-time. City, however, lowered the Rams' colours at Highfield Road in March with a 3-1 league win.

City had bowed out of the Cup when defeated by Aston Villa over two legs. Coventry won the first leg 2-1 at Highfield Road in front of 27,197. Three days later 30,000 fans saw Villa sneak through courtesy of a 2-0 win against ten-man City, Bob Ward having been ordered off for dangerous play.

With Lowrie still in the services and not available every week, Harry Barratt was transformed into a goalscorer and top-scored with 26 in 44 games. Lowrie managed eleven in 21. Barratt's highlight came in the 7-2 home win over Millwall, when he netted four of City's goals. Spanish refugees Emilio Aldecoa and Jose Bilbao also found the net.

City used 41 players, including fourteen guests, none of whom played more than a handful of games. At the season's end the team were rewarded for their efforts with a week-long trip to Denmark, where they played four matches against some of that country's top sides (all amateurs). City won three and drew one.

The **1946-47** fixture list was identical to that for the aborted 1939-40 season, so City kicked off with a trip to Burnley, followed by home games with West Brom and Barnsley. City's first post-war League goalscorer was Fred Bett, an inside-forward signed that summer from Sunderland. He scored in his first three games for City as the team replicated their 1939 points total of four. At Burnley, Bett was the only City player not on the club's books in 1939. Back then, Warner, Barratt, Wood, Coen, Snape, Frith and Roberts were promising young fringe players. Seven years on, they formed the backbone of the side, even though they were in their late twenties with their best years behind them.

City's good home record (they lost only to Burnley) meant they finished 8th, overcoming patchy away form. George Lowrie was back to his best, ending the season with 29 goals in League and Cup.

The major event of the season was the sudden death of manager Dick Bayliss. Never the healthiest of men, Bayliss's wellbeing became cause for concern around the turn of the year. In February, during the worst winter in memory, he had driven to Scotland on a scouting mission. On his return he became stranded on the Yorkshire moor and was later confined to bed with a chill. Kidney problems left him prostrate, and he died on 5 April at his home in the city. That afternoon, for the visit of Sheffield Wednesday, the flag flew at half-mast and a minute's silence was observed. Fans and players alike had been stunned by the news but the players responded with a 5-1 win.

In December 1946 the club hosted a neutral FA Cup-tie for the first time. Northampton and non-league Peterborough United had drawn twice and in those days of unlimited replays a third game had to be played at a neutral ground. Over 13,000 turned up to watch the Cobblers thump their county upstarts 8-1.

The dreadful winter played havoc with the fixture list, and City went seven weeks through February and most of March without a home game. When the thaw eventually arrived, the authorities banned midweek games in order to safeguard vital industrial production, which meant rearranged games had to be played on Saturdays. As a result, the season dragged into mid-June, with the League Championship not decided, in Liverpool's favour, until the 14th of that month. City's final game was at Chesterfield on 26 May, a month later than planned, and the reserves' last home game was on 7 June.

Gates soared across the country in that first proper post-war season, with Second Division Newcastle topping the lists with an average of 49,379, a record high. Six First Division clubs topped 40,000. City's increase was modest, their average of 19,975 being just 450 more than in 1938-39. This was not surprising really, as City had been serious promotion contenders in the last post-war season.

The match programme for the opening game of **1947-48**, against Luton, reported that the summer had been glorious, weather-wise, but not so good for City's new pitch: 'Although no one grumbles at such weather, it has rather retarded progress on our playing pitch, on which much time and money have been spent since our last match on June 7th. Much of the drainage was destroyed by bombs during the war raids. This damage has now been repaired, but owing to the short close season and the dry weather, the turf has not recovered to the extent we had hoped. However we think a great improvement will be noticed as the season advances. The damage to the Highfield Road cover has been repaired and a licence obtained for completing the roof, which still shows many war scars. A licence has also been obtained for improving lavatory accommodation, and this work will be carried out shortly.'

City, under the managership of former player Billy Frith, opened the new season in style, beating Luton 4-1 with George Lowrie netting all four. By the turn of the year the Welsh centre-forward had netted seventeen goals in eighteen games and was a wanted man. When he netted goal No 18 in the 1-1 draw with promotion favourites Newcastle in February, it convinced the St James' Park club that he was the man to clinch promotion. Two weeks later they paid £18,500 to get him, and ushered in another era of Coventry again being a selling club.

Other changes to the playing squad that season saw the final appearances of pre-war players Charlie Elliott, Bobby Davidson and George Ashall. Among the newcomers, Birmingham-born Peter Murphy and

Norman Lockhart from Northern Ireland formed an excellent left-wing partnership. The side were in mid-table all season and finished 10th with crowds averaging 22,288.

Bert Woodfield recalled that team: 'Jack Snape, Harry Boileau and George Mason were the characters that I loved. Snape was reputed to have 3-4 pints before a game. Boileau was always told to go on and rough up the opposition's star man. Mason was a very nice man even though he looked tough and was as hard as nails on the pitch. Alf Wood was a tough goalkeeper – he was still aggressive in his old age and allegedly got turned out of his residential home for fighting when he was over 80.'

Tom Dentith recalls the Bury home game that season: 'George Lowrie was my hero. He had a tremendous shot and that day he burst the ball. It looked a certain goal when he hit it but the old-fashioned ball went high up in the air like a pigeon being shot, then gently fluttered to the ground. The crowd were all looking for the ball in the back of the net and it went straight up in the air as it burst.'

Two unusual events took place at Highfield Road in the spring of 1948. On 10 April the ground hosted for the first time a schoolboy international, between England and Wales. Over 25,000 turned out to see England win 2-1.

At centre-half in the England team was a Welsh-born youngster called Brian Nicholas, who would later play for Coventry. Although born in South Wales, his family moved to Slough when he was four years old and thus qualified for England. Nicholas later played for QPR and Chelsea before joining City in 1958.

The following month another 25,000 crowd watched professional boxing at Highfield Road. The Turpin family from Warwick were famous in fight circles, with three brothers – Dick, Jackie and Randolph (Randy) – vying for the spotlight. Dick, the first black man to fight for a British boxing title, topped the bill on 18 May 1948 for a British Empire Middleweight title fight against New Zealander Bos Murphy. Turpin despatched the champion within 2 minutes and 55 seconds of the first round, to set himself up for the British title fight a month later at Villa Park against Vince Hawkins, which he duly won. Dick, aged 27, held the Commonwealth title for twelve months before losing to Australian Dave Sands. His grasp on the British title lasted two years, but by that time younger brother Randy was emerging as an even greater force and would, for a short time, become World Middleweight champion in 1951 by beating the legendary Sugar Ray Robinson at Earls Court.

The middle brother Jackie was also on the bill at Highfield Road but lost to Ben Duffy, whilst future British heavyweight champion Don

Cockell defeated Johnny Williams from Rugby. There were seven bouts in all, and the whole event was promoted by local entrepreneur Jimmy Gough.

1948-49 started badly for the Bantams and by early November, with the team languishing in the bottom two, manager Frith was sacked. At the same time, chairman Fred Stringer stepped down and was replaced by HG Jones who took temporary control of team affairs. Three weeks later Harry Storer returned from Birmingham City, saying: 'Coventry is my club. I made the mistake of leaving it once and have regretted it ever since.' Allegedly when he heard of Frith's departure he rang Jones and said: 'Dust the chair. I'm coming back.'

Whilst at St Andrews, Storer's record had been impressive. Following their League South success in 1945-46, the Blues had missed out on promotion in 1946-47, but Storer led them to the title the following season. Their first season back in the top flight had started with only one defeat in eleven games, but Birmingham had dropped back to mid-table when Storer dropped the bombshell that he was returning to Coventry.

His impact at Highfield Road was immediate; the team won five games in a row and gates soared from 20,000 to 32,000 for the Christmas game with Bury. He barely tampered with the side he inherited – just giving the team some self-belief and confidence. A final position of 16th meant relegation fears were forgotten. A massive 39,480 crowd for the visit of First Division-bound West Brom at Easter ensured the average again topped 22,000.

Meanwhile, the supporters club had reformed following its hibernation through the war years. Controversy arose in December 1948, however, when an article in the *Coventry Standard* claimed the supporters club was run by Nazis and Fascists! The hullabaloo was soon dismissed as a misunderstanding arising from a supporters club meeting in which they discussed organised chanting by younger fans. Such chants seemed to work well at Tottenham and Bury, and should be considered at Highfield Road. A reporter submitted an inaccurate account of these proceedings and soon had to go cap in hand with apologies.

1949-50 saw a revamp of the club's match-day programme. Shortage of paper after the war necessitated a much reduced programme for the last three campaigns. Two folded foolscap sheets made an eight-page publication, but with the centre-page spread taken up by team-sheets, and adverts inside the front and back covers, that left only two pages for 'club news' and fixtures and league tables. The new programme was printed on superior paper, had an extra sheet, making twelve pages, and allowed for players' appearances and goalscorers, plus visitors news.

On the field, Storer's tricks, however, did not seem to work. The side won only once in the first twelve games and drastic action was needed. Storer persuaded the board to dig deep into their pockets to strengthen the team.

George Mason was slowing down and Storer spent £12,000 on Martin McDonnell – his former centre-half from Birmingham – and Welsh inside-forward Bryn Allen. These signings, plus the return from injury of Harry Barratt and a change of tactics, saw City end the season with six wins and two draws to finish 12th.

The tactical switch was suggested by Barratt, and involved wing-half Noel Simpson pushing up more. Despite the team's mediocre form, attendances held up well, the average increasing by several hundred to 22,822. Large crowds were seen for the visits of Leicester at Christmas (36,981) and promotion-bound Spurs (36,320), but both games were lost. In the Cup, Bolton became the first top-flight visitors since West Brom in 1937.

With England centre-forward Nat Lofthouse in their ranks, Wanderers won 2-1 in front of 29,350. Long-suffering fan Robert Ward remembers the game: 'Alf Wood was a tough goalkeeper but Lofthouse barged Woody over the goal line and knocked him out.' Eight years later Lofthouse would cause a controversy by barging Manchester United's goalkeeper Harry Gregg over the goal-line to score Bolton's second goal in their FA Cup final victory.

Wood was a fixture in the Coventry City goal throughout those early post-war years. The Staffordshire-born keeper had adopted the City of Coventry and after being understudy to the great Bill Morgan before the war, and despite contracting meningitis and being told by doctors that he would never play again, he claimed the green jersey as soon as war ended. From August 1945 until April 1951 he did not miss a single game, and was considered by Bob Dennison – Coventry's chief scout in the 1970s and Wood's manager at Northampton in the 1950s – to be the best uncapped English goalkeeper in his heyday.

The supporters had a soft spot for Alf, as Alan Tyrell fondly recalls: 'My cousins and I got a good spot leaning over the wall at the Kop. Alf Wood came out for the warm up, peeled an orange and gave each one of us kids a segment. This was the first orange I had ever seen, and of course, tasted.'

Peter Murphy topped the club's scoring chart that season with fifteen. That summer, when the board needed to balance the books, it was the Birmingham-born Murphy who was sold to Tottenham Hotspur for £20,000.

The 1940s therefore ended with the club further away from Division One than they had been on the eve of the Second World War, but the next season would rekindle dreams of playing top-flight football.

CHAPTER SIX

The 1950s

The **1950-51** season started brightly, so by the end of October City were top with only three defeats in fifteen games. The form of Ken Chisholm, signed the previous March, had meant that Murphy had not been missed – 'Chizzy', a nomadic and burly Scottish forward had already notched ten goals and a virtually unchanged City team looked capable of winning almost every game.

On 14 October, City overwhelmed Blackburn 6-1 in front of 35,000 in what is considered one of the finest games of the decade. Norman Lockhart put City ahead after only twenty seconds and Blackburn equalised 40 seconds later. The final score could have been 7-7, so many chances were created. The best goal was City's sixth, scored five minutes from the end by Lockhart, following a dazzling run. It had even the normally unemotional Harry Storer jumping off the pitchside bench.

By the end of the year, with promotion in sight, Storer believed he had strengthened the side by paying out £30,000 on two players. A club record £20,000 went on Grimsby centre-forward Tommy Briggs. Briggs had scored prolifically for the Mariners and would continue to score heavily throughout the 1950s, but at Highfield Road he was a flop. His arrival sparked dressing room unrest, team spirit collapsed, and form suffered. Full-back Terry Springthorpe was signed from Wolves, but three months later decided to quit the game and emigrate to America.

September had seen the arrival of Turkish side Galatasaray for a friendly. It was a gala occasion with flowers presented to the crowd by the Turkish players, and City captain Harry Barratt was kissed by the Turkish captain before they spun the coin. City won 2-1 in front of 9,350.

In early February 1951 the club were honoured by staging an Amateur international between England and Ireland. The Irish team were all based in Northern Ireland and were outclassed – 6-3. England's centre-forward, Jack Lewis, who later starred for Chelsea, scored four goals, whilst on the left wing Ireland were tormented by Finchley's George Robb, who rejected overtures from Italian club Padua in order to continue his teaching studies at Loughborough University. Robb later turned professional and won one full cap for England – in the infamous 3-6 defeat to Hungary in 1953. Amateur football was enjoying a golden period, with the FA Amateur Cup finals at Wembley attracting full houses, and teams like Bishop Auckland, Crook Town and Pegasus were household names.

The match programme regretted the timing of the match as it clashed with City's derby at Leicester. The programme even advertised a football excursion train to Leicester that day! For 4 shillings and 6d (22p) (or 3s 6d from Bedworth) you could travel to Leicester, returning that evening at 8.15 (presumably allowing time for a pint or two after the match).

Attendances averaged 26,694, a 20 per cent increase. City eventually finished 7th and their chance of promotion to Division One was gone for many years. Few could have foreseen however the disaster that lurked around the corner.

The team that kicked-off the **1951-52** season had an average age of 31, the oldest in the club's history. Six of the team were over 30 and some had played before the war. The supporters kept faith in Harry Storer, but a 1-7 defeat at Swansea in late August set the alarm bells ringing. Injuries, loss of form and bad luck turned the season into a disaster. The team never recovered from an eleven-game winless run in the autumn. Club legends Alf Wood and George Mason were dropped, with Wood moving to Northampton. Old favourite George Lowrie was signed for a second time, then the sale of Chisholm freed up cash to sign defender Roy Kirk from Leeds and centre-forward Eddie Brown from Southampton. Results improved a bit and hopes of survival were raised. The final home game, against promotion-chasing Sheffield Wednesday, became crucial. A crowd of 36,337 turned up to witness Derek Dooley, Wednesday's 46-goal centre-forward, score two goals past City's third-choice goalkeeper Derek Spencer, who only played because of injuries to the senior keepers. City travelled to Leeds for their last game with only a faint chance of survival but lost 1-3 and were relegated. In all, 34 different players were used by Storer but the new signings came too late to prevent the almost inevitable, and after ten seasons in Division Two the Bantams were back in Division Three (South).

There were few highlights that season, but at least City had the pleasure of knocking Leicester out of the FA Cup. After a 1-1 draw at Filbert Street, the Bantams won 4-1 on a miserably wet Monday afternoon, only to go down 0-2 at First Division Burnley in the fourth round. The average attendance was down by over 4,000 to 22,548. It would be the last time attendances topped 20,000 until the Jimmy Hill era.

On the afternoon of Wednesday, 16 January 1952 Highfield Road played host to Rugby Union again, when the touring South Africans (the Springboks) met a Midland Counties XV. Since the last visit of an international side – the New Zealand All-Blacks of 1924 – the Midlands' games against touring sides had been either at Villa Park or Coundon Road. The Midland Counties team was selected from an area stretching from the Wash to the Severn, and from Stoke to South Warwickshire. They included six Coventry RFC players, including internationals Ivor Preece and Ernie Robinson. The Springboks were nearing the end of a successful tour, having beaten all four home nations and suffered only one reverse, to London Counties. The match programme noted that the Midland Counties had never beaten a touring international side, and they failed to halt the Springboks that day, losing 8-19. Photos in the *Coventry Evening Telegraph* show a very muddy pitch. A crowd of 21,326, boosted by thousands of schoolboys from all around the Midlands, paid receipts of over £4,000.

Like today, relegation in the 1950s had serious financial consequences on football clubs. Fortunately, in those days clubs were not hampered by a wage-bill more fitting for a higher-division club. Clubs operated renewable one-year contracts and a maximum wage, but supporters were much less likely to watch lower-status football. Although 18,000 turned up for the first home game of **1952-53**, against Swindon, gates quickly tumbled when a quick return to Division Two was ruled out, and by Christmas the club had recorded a gate under 10,000. A seasonal drop of 9,000 spoke for itself. The impact on the club's coffers was catastrophic.

To compensate for the slashed income, Irish international winger Norman Lockhart was sold to Aston Villa for £15,500. Storer had to rely on the home-developed youngsters who he had chosen carefully and nurtured as Modern Machines FC in the Coventry Works leagues. Until 1952 there had been no formalised competition between league team's youth sides, but City had a host of promising youngsters on their books who were now given their chance in Third Division football. Goalkeeper Reg Matthews, defenders Frank Austin, Lol Harvey, and forwards Gordon Nutt, Ronnie Waldock and Peter and Jimmy Hill were all handed their chance. Yesterday's heroes – George Lowrie, George Mason, Plum Warner and Bryn Allen – were quietly leaving.

The **1953-54** season was tumultuous for Coventry City. An inconsistent start heaped pressure on manager Storer, but it was still a shock in November when it was announced that he had 'resigned'. A bitter Storer was quick to point out that he had been sacked, a scapegoat for the general mismanagement of the club, and had been hamstrung by a lack of financial support. Club president Erle Shanks, a staunch backer of Storer, resigned in protest, and at a stormy AGM in April 1954 the five-man board also resigned. Soon afterwards a new board was installed, with Shanks becoming chairman again, replacing Jones. One of the two new directors was a 36-year-old concrete garage manufacturer by the name of Derrick Robins.

In October 1953 the club unveiled their first floodlight system. It consisted of wooden poles, each topped with a pair of large bulbs, and pairs of similar bulbs attached to the roof of the two stands parallel with the touchlines. In total, approximately 48 lights illuminated the pitch. According to the club's accounts, published in April 1954, the system cost £3,967. Floodlights were all the craze, and City were one of the first clubs outside London to install them. In the same month several other clubs inaugurated their lights, among them Manchester City, Luton, Wolves and Bury. For their first floodlit game, City invited Scottish club Queen of the South to Highfield Road.

The programme makes quaint reading: 'Opinions differ regarding the permanency of floodlight football, but we believe there is a great future in this type of entertainment. And why not? Does it not give us the opportunity of allowing our supporters to see the best teams, not only in Great Britain, but also Continental teams of repute. We realise that only the best will continue to attract, and it will be our endeavour to bring teams that under normal circumstances would not be seen in Coventry. What a start we have made! Queen of the South, Wolverhampton Wanderers and East Fife.'

Such opponents would not inspire awe today, but back then all three were attractive teams. Wolves led the First Division at the time. Queen of the South had been fixtures in the Scottish First Division (the top division) for almost twenty years and were current League leaders. East Fife had finished third in the Scottish League two years running and recently lifted the Scottish League Cup.

For both teams it was their first experience of playing under artificial lights. In his match report in the *Coventry Evening Telegraph*, 'Nemo' wrote: 'the players had no difficulty in following the flight of the ball under the artificial lighting, and the spectators found it equally easy to follow the play.' Queens manager, however, said his goalkeeper had occasional difficulty with high crosses. A crowd of 16,923 paid to watch. The game ended 1-1, with a fourth-minute Don Dorman header being the first goal under the lights, and a Scottish equaliser three minutes later.

A week later 18,680 attended the second floodlit match, against Wolves. The First Division leaders, playing in their famous old gold shirts, fielded eight of their previous Saturday's First Division side, but the three absent were their England international stars, captain Billy Wright and wingers Jimmy Mullen and Johnny Hancocks. Wright was no doubt resting ahead of the forthcoming international with Hungary. Wolves took things gently but City wanted a big scalp and won through Iain Jamieson's penalty.

The programme for the Wolves game gave City a self-congratulatory pat on the back for the success of the floodlights: 'This new venture was one which has required courage on our part ... the best teams in the land ... Arsenal, Celtic and Glasgow Rangers have already been approached with a view to bringing them here under floodlight.' The programme thanked British Thomson Houston Company and the East Midlands Electricity Board, who had made the games possible.

Two weeks later the third floodlit game, with East Fife, ended 2-2 and was by general consent the best of the three, but the attraction of flood-lit games was already waning, with only 12,644 spectators present. Only Arsenal of those big clubs mentioned ever did play under the Highfield Road lights, and that was in the First Division fourteen years later.

Floodlit friendlies were the flavour of the season and in January 1954 the first continental visitors were Yugoslav side Hajduk Split. Boasting top internationals in goalkeeper Beara and centre-forward Vukas, Hajduk were too good for the Bantams and won 3-2 in front of 4,214 fans. It was a bitterly cold night and on a pitch that was severely frozen many players lost their footing.

Evening floodlit friendlies were staged against all kinds of opposition, including Southern League Nuneaton Borough (won 4-0), Scottish club Hamilton Academical (won 5-0), First Division Portsmouth (won 5-2) and Second Division Leeds United (won 4-1). Against Leeds, City fans got a chance to see emerging star John Charles, who netted 42 League goals that season. He scored Leeds' goal from a twice-taken penalty, but only after City had hit two in the first 40 seconds through Eddie Brown and Ronnie Waldock. Leeds' manager, the famous Raich Carter, also appeared, despite having retired three years previously. None of the four above games attracted more than 6,000 spectators.

In the meantime, Storer's successor had been named. Jack Fairbrother, a former Newcastle goalkeeper who played in their 1951 FA Cup-winning team, had been successful in his first managerial job with non-league Peterborough, and took up his duties in January. Within weeks his wife Belle died after falling down the stairs at home and fracturing her skull, leaving Jack a widower with two young children.

By the season's end apathy amongst supporters was rife. For the visit of QPR in April there were only 4,785 present, the lowest home crowd since 1928. The season's average was 10,505, down almost 3,000, and this was reflected in the slashing of gate receipts from £39,000 to £29,000 in the club's accounts published that month. The club finished 14th, with the only bright spot being the goalscoring form of Eddie Brown – twenty goals in 33 games.

It was rumoured that the new board paid off a large slice of the club's £23,000 debt. Scouting and coaching systems were reshaped; a sports-room and restaurant were provided for the players; the club's gymnasium was re-equipped. More money was spent on the Highfield Road facilities than at any time since the war. The **1954-55** season dawned with the aim that was virtually to become the club motto for nearly the next ten years: 'Promotion this season.'

In the alleged 'brown and cream' manager's office, Jack Fairbrother plotted the new season. Despite the financial constraints, a new left-wing pairing of Tommy Capel and Colin Collindridge arrived for a £10,000 fee from Nottingham Forest. The season started well and 'the team that Jack built', as they were dubbed by the press, won six out of the first seven games. Eddie Brown scored eight goals in those seven games, including the fastest goal ever at the ground, against Leyton Orient, timed at twelve seconds.

October was one of the most traumatic months in the club's history. Brown was dropped after a defeat at Leyton Orient and ten days later was sold to Birmingham City for £10,000. Home-grown winger Gordon Nutt also had a transfer request accepted, although he did not move until two months later, when First Division Cardiff paid £16,000 for him. All was not well between chairman and manager. The next match programme's 'From the Boardroom' notes contained outspoken criticism of some of the playing staff: 'We will not tolerate any player playing for Coventry City who is not giving us 100 per cent effort for 90 minutes.'

Fairbrother said nothing publicly, but eleven days later resigned, according to the club's official statement, 'through health reasons'. In the programme for the following home game he described the pressure he had felt since his wife's death – 'I should have had a holiday' – and thanked the club's directors for their support and help. The real story has never been revealed, but it is likely that Fairbrother resented Shanks' dressing-room interference and objected to selling Brown. Ironically, City were up to 4th when Jack decided to go.

On the night of Fairbrother's resignation, City's reserves were at home to Millwall. Watching from the stands in his capacity as Aston Villa scout was former boss Harry Storer. It was Storer's former first lieutenant and cricketing buddy, Charlie Elliott, who was asked to step up from chief scout to be caretaker-manager until a replacement was found.

The proceeds from the sales of Brown and Nutt were frittered on mediocre replacements. The only bright star in a dull season was the form of young goalkeeper Reg Matthews. Having started the season as under-study to Peter Taylor, Reg grabbed his opportunity when it came and within four months was playing for the England Under-23 side. An England 'B' cap followed soon afterwards.

In January 1955, Erle Shanks pulled off a coup when he persuaded AS Roma's English coach Jesse Carver to become City manager in the summer. The waiting was bound to be an anticlimax, and gates tailed off in the spring. Newport County on a wet Monday (5.30 kick-off) attracted only 3,974, a gate that still stands as City's lowest since 1928. A final position of 9th flattered the team, as they finished 23 points adrift of the promoted champions Bristol City. In the FA Cup, City reached the third round, where they faced First Division Huddersfield. The draw brought the agility and bravery of Matthews to a wider audience. Over 23,000 paid £3,308 and braved bitter weather to watch the Thursday afternoon replay, which City lost 1-2 after extra-time.

A 1-1 floodlit draw with Raith Rovers in March was watched by just 6,000. Despite lobbying from many clubs, neither the FA nor the Football League yet permitted floodlight competitive games. This explains why the Huddersfield Cup replay was an afternoon kick-off, and why City preferred to rearrange League games for April – after the clocks had been put forward – to avoid low crowds for afternoon kick-offs in the darker months. It would be another twelve months before the football authorities allowed competitive floodlight games.

In March 1955, in an effort to lure spectators to Highfield Road on Grand National day, the club made plans to broadcast a race commentary over the tannoy. The *CET* described this as a stunt, but dreadful weather put paid to the game against Southend, so it was impossible to assess the plan's success.

The match programme for the Millwall game in April spotlighted the club's oldest employee, Fred Rhodes. He had been employed as a gateman since 1918 and been head gateman from 1926 until 1954. He was now in charge of stewards, and although his age is not mentioned, his employment history – he retired from Morris in 1946 – indicated that he was 70-plus.

Excitement was high in Coventry in the summer of 1955. The build up to Carver's arrival on 1 July 'would have done justice to a Hollywood star'. The 43-year-old Carver's *curriculum vitae* was outstanding. Although never a top player himself, he had coached extensively on the Continent since the war and was an innovator, at the forefront in improving the skills, athleticism and theoretical knowledge of players. He had coached Juventus to the Scudetto (League championship) in 1950 and although he had not repeated that feat at Lazio, Torino and Roma, he had a fine reputation. It was rumoured that his salary at Roma was £5,000 a year; he and his wife had an apartment in the exclusive Via Archimedes in the Parioli district in the north of the city, where his neighbours included the exiled ex-King Farouk of Egypt and actress Ingrid Bergman.

Carver's first appointment at Highfield Road was another coup, making Lazio's English-born coach George Raynor his assistant. Raynor was a folk-hero in Sweden after leading that nation to the gold medal at the 1948 Olympic Games in London, and third place in the 1950 World Cup in Brazil. Like Carver, he had then coached in Italy. He would be the tracksuited training-ground man to Carver's smooth-talking suited front man. The money was attractive, the two men were supposedly paid £70/100 per week at Highfield Road, but both had a nagging desire to prove themselves in their own country.

Carver arrived with a tan that complemented his man-about-town persona, and with his tailored light grey suits and camel coat he looked more of a Hollywood film mogul than football manager. He warned supporters not too expect too much, but his words went unheeded – promotion talk was, as always, in the air.

One ground innovation that summer was the erection of its first clock. The large timepiece on steel stilts appeared at the rear of the Spion Kop and was donated by the *Coventry Evening Telegraph*. A match programme from the previous season described what to expect: 'An eminent Architect has been employed, and one of the best clock makers in the country have now built the clock in readiness for erection.'

The Carver-Raynor partnership introduced radical new training methods to Coventry. These included wooden clogs and bathrobes to prevent players catching cold while walking to and from the showers, as well as personal lightweight continental boots. Every player had his own football for the rigorous ball-playing routines which formed the main part of the new bosses' blueprint for success.

The first home game of **1955-56** – a 3-1 win over Bournemouth – pulled in a crowd of 24,000. City were big news in the Third Division and opposing crowds flocked to watch them when they visited. Home form was outstanding – the team stayed unbeaten well into 1956 – and the players' extra fitness usually ensured a thrilling final fifteen minutes. Away from home it was a different story, with goals and points hard to come by. It was soon apparent that the type of football played by the top Serie 'A' teams or by the Swedish national side would not get City out of Division Three.

Press-talk of Carver's discontent and approaches from Italian clubs first surfaced in November. They were denied, but in mid-December 1955 Carver asked to be released from his contract. On 30 December, after a three-win Christmas programme had hoisted the team into 5th place, Shanks announced that the club were releasing Carver because of his wife's health problems. When a local reporter asked if Shanks had had any offers from foreign clubs, he gave a 'wry smile' and replied: 'No, none at all.' Carver agreed not to undertake any position in English football for the next two and a half years. Within days of leaving Coventry he joined Internazionale of Milan on a reputed £130 per week.

Raynor was elevated to the manager's post, but the team could not sustain their Christmas form and eventually finished 8th. Try as they might, the club could not keep out of the headlines. The next back-page news related to the San Lorenzo 'friendly' which ended in wild scenes. San Lorenzo were one of Argentina's top sides and in January 1956 were touring Britain. They arrived in Coventry on the back of a 1-5 hammering at Wolves, complaining about the muddy state of English pitches. Top international referee Arthur Ellis was in charge and near the end of a tetchy first half awarded City a penalty when Dennis Uphill was pushed off the ball as he was about to score.

The Argentine team went wild. Inside-left Sanfilippo kicked Ellis, and when the player was ordered off there followed five minutes of mayhem. There was pushing and mauling from the Argentine players, with the 5ft 4ins Sanfilippo shaking his fists and stamping his foot as he refused to go. According to *CET* reports, 'police were called on to the pitch to give Ellis protection and San Filippo was dragged from the pitch by his team's reserve players and trainer, kicking and struggling like a wild tiger cat.'

Ellis meanwhile had walked off the pitch, where he told officials of both clubs that he was abandoning the game, refusing to continue under 'impossible conditions': 'The player kicked at my legs and I collared him, although all the Argentine players mingled in so that I could not get at the offender. They formed a screen, jeering and gesticulating. I told him to get off but he refused to leave the field. I will not tolerate this sort of conduct from any club. This has never happened to me before and I think it is about time that these Argentinians were taught sportsmanship. Perhaps now English clubs will think twice before they invite South American clubs over here for matches.'

After half an hour of appeals for Ellis to reconsider, chairman Erle Shanks told the crowd of 17,357 that the game was abandoned. Under FA rules a substitute referee was not permitted. The crowd, which previously had been whistling and slow-handclapping, received the decision quietly, and quickly dispersed.

Afterwards, Coventry officials and players mingled with their visitors in the boardroom, where drinks and sandwiches were served and Shanks presented the chairman of San Lorenzo, Senor Luis Traverso, with a plaque. Club badges were exchanged, and Traverso, through an interpreter, expressed his deep regret for the incident. Sanfilippo would be sent back to Argentina on the first available plane as a punishment and the rest of the team would be severely censured. Additionally, he offered to bring the team back to Coventry, free of charge, to replay the game. This gesture was later rejected by the Coventry board anxious to avoid another debacle.

The following morning San Lorenzo left for Southampton for the final match of the British leg of the tour, but Sanfilippo didn't fly home until the team got to Paris a few days later.

Jose Sanfilippo went on to become a San Lorenzo legend, and his 200 goals is a club record that stands today. He won his first cap for Argentina later that year and won 29 caps, scoring 21 goals, a national record at the time. His final international was against England in the 1962 World Cup finals in Chile, and he scored in Argentina's 1-3 defeat.

Two days prior to the San Lorenzo fiasco, England winger Tom Finney had dazzled 13,000 rain-soaked spectators as his Preston team beat City 4-1 in a friendly. Finney bamboozled City's left-back Charlie Timmins so much that Timmins pleaded at half-time for Raynor to switch him to right-back. Raynor obliged, and Frank Austin faced 45 minutes of torment from Finney.

The San Lorenzo fiasco did not deter City from friendlies with foreign teams, and in February a game was arranged with Spartak Subotica of Yugoslavia. At the last minute, however, the Yugoslav authorities denied the team permission to travel and the game was called off.

At long last, competitive matches under floodlights were now permitted, so midweek Cup replays and rearranged League fixtures could be played under lights and therefore kick off later. City's first such game was in March 1956 when Southend were entertained on a Monday evening. Over 12,000 – probably 3,000 more than if the game had kicked off at 5.30 – watched a 0-0 draw.

Reg Matthews' meteoric rise continued through the season. Following two more impressive displays for the Under-23s and many outstanding displays for City, he was selected for his first full England cap in April at Hampden Park. He was the first Coventry City player to play for England and gave an excellent display in a 1-1 draw that earned him further caps against Brazil at Wembley and Sweden and West Germany on the end-of-season tour. Reg was never on the losing side for his country and looked set for a long international career. Of course, rumours abounded regarding Reg's future at Coventry, and Shanks admitted that several big clubs had made offers, but the board were determined to hold on to him. Shanks employed Matthews as a salesman for his timber business for the summer, a move which ensured that Reg could be paid more money for probably minimal effort.

International honours were soon awarded to another City man, when sixteen-year-old Kent-born George Curtis was selected for the England youth team. Curtis, still on the groundstaff, had played the final three games of the season – the start of a memorable career.

That roller-coaster 1955-56 season ended with City seventeen points behind champions Leyton Orient. Only three sides lowered City's colours at Highfield Road, but the team won only four away games. The 'Carver' effect ensured gates averaged 17,658 – easily the club's highest since the relegation year and the highest in their division.

The next, **1956-57** season was equally traumatic, with the club seemingly staggering from one crisis to another. Shanks set the ball rolling in June when he appointed Harry Warren as team manager. Warren had managed Southend United for sixteen years and was almost an institution at the Essex club. Shanks' powers of persuasion worked like a charm and Warren gave up the comfort zone for what was becoming one of the most precarious jobs in football. George Raynor was demoted to trainer-coach but his continental methods were jettisoned by Warren who insisted on traditional 'kick and rush' tactics. Raynor was informed that the club would not stand in his way if another offer came his way.

In July 1956 a grand plan was proposed by the supporters club, which now boasted 3,500 members. They mooted the idea of covering the Spion Kop end – a plan promulgated several times over the next 40 years. They envisaged a three-year project costing £20,000 which would be funded by a football pool which had been successfully launched earlier that year.

Jack Patience, chairman of the supporters club said: 'We think that a cover over the Spion Kop would be a great asset and would prevent gates falling when the weather is bad.' Erle Shanks' response was, on the face of it, positive: 'I have long been in favour of covering Spion Kop. If the Supporters Club can raise the money I think it would be a very good thing. After all it is the chap who pays his two-shillings who matters and we must consider his comfort.' Strangely it would take 40 years and the Taylor Report on football grounds for the Kop to be covered.

That summer, players assisted in the concreting of terrace steps in the corners of the covered end. When finished, the last of the shale banks had gone. It's hard to imagine players from the modern era mucking in, in the same way.

The 1956-57 season saw later kick-off times for early season midweek games. With the rules relaxed on using floodlights, City wanted to shift kick-offs from 5.30 or 6pm to 7 and later 7.30 and finish the games under lights. This would allow more fans to get home from work, eat and get to the game. The club's initiative was rewarded with higher gates for the first three midweek fixtures than for Saturday games.

Warren's team were unbeaten in their first five games. Gates were high – 20,000 gates were recorded four times in the first two months – but all was not well in the camp. Heavy defeats at Norwich, Northampton and Ipswich prompted rumours, denied by Shanks, that he, Shanks, was on the verge of resigning.

In October, against Millwall, City gave a debut to their first black player, South African 'wonderkid' Steve Mokone. He had paid for his own passage to trial with City, and the club gave him a one-year contract after witnessing his skills. Stunning performances for the reserves saw him promoted to the first team, but after four games Warren refused to play him. Against Millwall, Rod Dean also remembers seeing hooliganism for the first time. Twenty or so Millwall 'fans' were pushing and shoving in the midst of the Kop and using foul language.

City staged another representative game in November 1956. The annual fixture between teams from Division Three South and North came to Highfield Road. The South team was 'managed' by Harry Warren and included Reg Matthews, whereas the North was 'managed' by Harry Storer – now in charge at Derby County. A crowd of 14,156 saw the South win 2-1.

George Raynor threw in the towel in early November, complaining that he 'no longer had any say in coaching and merely carried out orders'. A few months later he became coach to the Swedish national team for the second time and started preparing them for the 1958 World Cup, to be staged in their country. He would lead the Swedes to the final, where they lost to Brazil.

In early October Reg Matthews won his fifth England cap in Belfast, but a few weeks later was dropped for the next international. Matthews, who despite all the rumours of big-club interest had not previously asked for a move, now started to believe newspaper pundits who advised him to leave. Hoping that playing for a First Division club would help restore his England place, he put in a transfer request. In November he moved to Chelsea for £22,000, a world record fee for a goalkeeper. In retrospect his move was not a good one; he was never selected for England again and because of the maximum wage he earned no more at Stamford Bridge than at Highfield Road.

It was a miserable autumn for City. The early promise had dissipated and the team won only one game between mid-September and Christmas. Matthews, so often the saviour, was badly missed and as the goals poured in so the fans poured out. On the Saturday before Christmas barely 8,000 saw City play Crystal Palace. It was goalless when, six minutes into the second half a partial floodlight failure forced the referee had to abandon the game. Three days later even fewer were present for the Christmas Day clash with Newport. That was also abandoned goalless, this time because a blizzard made conditions unplayable.

The Palace abandonment sparked angry scenes outside the directors entrance, with fans blaming Shanks for the floodlight farce and demanding his resignation. The club blamed the East Midland Electricity Board, whose response was to blame the club for not testing the lights and not having an engineer on site. When the dust settled the true story emerged and Shanks was vindicated: it was a technical fault caused by a cable defect that the club could not be blamed for. In consequence the club planned to replace the whole light system with a pylon system 'of the most up to date character', and took no more chances by bringing forward the kick-off times for Saturday afternoon games from 3pm to 2.30 to avoid the use of lights for afternoon games.

By the time Palace returned for the rearranged game in April, City were third from bottom. With the bottom two having to seek re-election, the situation was desperate. A late rally, with five wins out of six, pushed City up to 16th, their lowest placing since 1928. But the problems went deeper. Nine players wanted away, among them the latest home-grown starlet Ray Sambrook. Players were barred from speaking to the press, the club was said to be haemmorhaging £250 a week and could not afford the £6,000 summer wages bill. It was reported that the Matthews payments were spread over two years. Shareholders were up in arms over what they felt was a collapse in the club's fortunes since Shanks & Co took over. Attendances, generally a bell-weather to the club's health, averaged 13,686, down four thousand in a year.

Light relief arrived in the shape of a players' benefit in March 1957, when City played an All-Star Managers XI. A team comprising such luminaries as Bill Shankly, Jimmy Hagan, Peter Doherty and Jack Rowley – most of whom were the wrong side of 40 – 'outspeeded and outwitted' City's first team, winning 2-1, in front of 6,036.

The summer of 1957 was miserable at Highfield Road. Erle Shanks and the board survived shareholder pressure at an Extraordinary General Meeting in June, but their lack of co-operation frustrated supporters. When manager Warren was asked whether he had 'complete control' over team affairs, he declined to answer. Ominously, no directors rose to defend the manager.

In September 1957 the club began broadcasting match commentaries to three local hospitals. Once again the supporters club were instrumental and raised the £1,500 needed to get the plan off the ground. They also lobbied for the hospitals to be kitted out with the necessary wiring and headphones for patients.

Spice was injected into the **1957-58** season with the planned reconstruction of the two Third Divisions into Divisions Three and Four. The top twelve from South and North would form the new Third Division, whilst the bottom twelve would constitute the Fourth Division. Third Division was demeaning enough, and City were determined never to be a Fourth Division side.

The drama started almost at once. Only one of the first eight games was won and nineteen different players pulled on the blue and white shirt. A 2-1 win over Torquay failed to stop the axe falling on Warren. The man appointed to replace him, Billy Frith, had nine years previously been sacked unceremoniously by City. Warren, who with hindsight had lost the directors' support at least six months previously, was believed by many to be the scapegoat for an increasingly inept boardroom. The players, however, had lost faith with a disorganised and clueless manager. Warren did, however, later fight a successful legal claim over his dismissal.

Frith steadied the ship, but he had inherited a hotch-potch of a squad with no leader on the pitch and no regular goalscorer. By the season's end he had solved both problems. The switch of boy-wonder George Curtis to centre-half was the making of the young colossus, and acquiring centre-forward Ray Straw from Derby guaranteed goals. Other players came and went, and Frith put the emphasis on youth, but by February it was obvious that a top-twelve finish was beyond the team and relegation was inevitable.

October 1957 saw the baptism of the new floodlights. Erecting and commissioning them took three months. The new system consisted of four pylons, one in each corner of the ground, each carrying a bank of 24 x 1,500-watt lamps. The *CET* described the system as 'similar to that on the Stoke City ground and will employ the same basic principles as those incorporated in the floodlighting at Wembley, St Andrews, Hillsborough and Old Trafford'.

Each pylon measured 100ft 'from the base to the bottom of the lights frame' and were described in the programme as being 'neat, sturdy and light, and in our opinion quite attractive'. The 'state of the art' installation incorporated a 'booster' system which allowed the lights to be turned up just before kick-off. The manufacturers were GEC and the lights were installed by Lee Beesley & Co, a Coventry-based electrical company. The whole project cost £15,000, which was funded solely by the supporters club and to be paid for over the next four years. Funds earmarked for the Spion Kop cover were diverted to this project – a decision 'not taken lightly but it was felt that lights were the top priority'.

GEC's engineers said that 'there will be no glare and visibility will be perfect from every part of the ground'. A control room for the lights was erected in the south-east corner of the ground, on top of the terraces, which offered an excellent view across the whole ground and was later used by the police in the 1960s and 1970s to monitor hooliganism. The lighting system was controlled by four press-button switches mounted on a panel. The old lights were sold for a 'nominal sum' to Crewe Alexandra, and some were still doing duty in 1995.

In July the club had hoped to attract First Division or continental opposition to inaugurate the new lights, but the cost of top foreign opposition was prohibited by large financial guarantees. Ultimately, Scottish First Division club Third Lanark were invited for the first game, with further friendlies under lights planned with Partick Thistle and Manchester City. Frith used the opportunity to blood promising reserves, including Jimmy Knox, Ron Sheppard and Mick Walters. Knox, who would leave the club after just two first-team games and become a successful manager at Lockheed Leamington and V S Rugby, scored twice in a 2-2 draw. Walters and Sheppard were not up to scratch. The crowd was just 9,018 and referee Arthur Ellis had no repeat of the shenanigans encountered when he had officiated at the San Lorenzo friendly.

Two weeks later the next Scottish visitors, Partick Thistle were beaten 3-2 in atrocious conditions. Over 7,500 brave souls braved pouring rain and saw 'plenty of laughs as the hapless players slithered and sloshed about in the quagmire'. Peter Hill scored two goals and Ken McPherson netted the third. The third and final floodlight friendly produced the best result, a 3-1 win over First Division Manchester City, who fielded a full first team including German goalkeeper Bert Trautmann, Footballer of the Year in 1956. Coventry's star was left-winger Ray Sambrook, who scored twice and virtually clinched a £15,000 transfer to Maine Road on the strength of his display. A good but inconsistent winger, Sambrook found it hard to settle at Maine Road, but his departure was another blow for the Coventry fans who saw the sale of another home-grown talent as a lack of ambition by their club.

League gates, which had started the season as high as 16,000, slipped after Christmas and were down to 5,846 in March when City put on their best display of the season to beat Aldershot 6-0. For the first time, two City players, Jimmy Rogers and Peter Hill, scored hat-tricks in the same match. The final average attendance was 11,907, over 10 per cent down.

Three weeks later chairman Shanks resigned after four stormy years in the chair. According to the *CET* his resignation came after an incident following an April home defeat by Swindon. Shanks had stormed into the home dressing room and in front of the manager and several other directors launched a tirade against the players. Lol Harvey, who played that night, remembers it well: 'Erle was known to have a short fuse but all the players liked him because he cared so much about the club. That night we had been dreadful but were shocked when he came into the dressing room – he never came in there – and started ripping into the players in general. He didn't criticise me though, I remember he turned to me and said, "well played Lol".'

Shanks' resignation was accompanied by a club statement, which said lack of success on the playing field had caused Mr Shanks 'bitter disappointment' and has been poor reward for his ceaseless and untiring efforts. Like directors before and after him, Shanks' hard work and financial backing was taken for granted by many fans. They didn't appreciate what Shanks had done, especially in 1936 when his involvement and funding of the ground improvements was crucial to the club's development. His Herculean efforts to bring success to the club was displayed by his coup in bringing Carver and Raynor to Coventry and his invaluable committee work. Walter Brandish, son of the City chairman of the same name in the 1930s, took over as chairman.

A final position of 19th guaranteed Fourth Division football, the club having slipped to its lowest position since entering the Football League in 1919. City's travelling fans now looked forward to trips to places such as Workington, Barrow and Gateshead. One positive thing to emerge from the reorganisation of the League was that forthwith four clubs would be promoted from Division Four. At the League's AGM in June, the maximum wage was increased from £17 per week to £20, with a similar increase for summer wages to £17.

In February 1958 rugby union returned to the ground, when the touring Australian team were defeated 3-8 by a Midland Counties XV. Around 8,000 spectators watched the game on a pitch with 'very little grass but well rolled'. Coventry Rugby Club were the top club side in the country and the Warwickshire team, comprising mainly Coventry players, would win the county championship – the premier domestic competition in those days – in seven out of the next eight years. That day there were ten 'Cov' players in the Midland team and their 'star' winger, Peter Jackson, who had scored England's winning try against the Wallabies two weeks previously, made the only try of the game for captain Fenwick Allison. A few weeks later it was suggested that Warwickshire play the county championship final at Highfield Road. Their opponents, Cornwall, planned to bring 4,000 fans and it was doubtful that Coundon Road could accommodate everyone who wanted to see the game. After some discussion it was decided Highfield Road was impractical and the game went ahead at Coundon Road.

City opened the **1958-59** season with a new kit. The fashion trend in football shirts was to dispense with collars in favour of a v-neck, collarless shirt. City retained the three-panelled blue and white shirts, which had been introduced in 1953, but in a collarless 'v-neck' version. The opening home game, a 0-0 draw with Darlington, attracted 15,143. It was the lowest opening-day crowd at the ground since 1931 but still the highest gate in the division, demonstrating City's elite rating in the new division and the fans' expectations of instant promotion. After three games City, with just one point, were next to bottom – 91st in the Football League. They did not stay there long.

Frith signed veteran Northern Ireland international Reg (Paddy) Ryan and made him captain. City lost only three games out of 24 until the end of January, at which time they were top of the table and promotion probables. Not that there weren't any hiccups on the way.

In September, City's new goalkeeper, 38-year-old Jim Sanders, broke a leg in a 7-1 home win over Aldershot. Defender Roy Kirk pulled on the green jersey twenty minutes from time with City coasting 6-0. Jimmy Rogers completed his hat-trick (to add to Straw's earlier threesome) with ten minutes left before Aldershot scored a minute later. With five minutes remaining, City's regular spot-kicker Kirk raced upfield to blast a penalty over the bar.

Initially, Frith passed the keeper's jersey to Alf Wood, the first-team trainer who had 'retired' two years previously. Wood, 41 years old according to newspaper reports at the time, was in fact 43 and the oldest first-team player in the club's history. It was an inspired decision by Frith. Wood played ten games, only one of which was lost, and in five of them he kept a clean sheet.

Frith also made shrewd signings. Alan 'Digger' Daley and George Stewart helped the promotion push, but of greater significance was the signing of wing-half Ron Farmer and goalkeeper Arthur Lightening. Farmer would become a key player for the next nine years and the club's penalty expert, whilst the acrobatic and popular Lightening thrilled City's fans over the next four years.

Gates improved throughout the season, and crowds at Highfield Road were always the highest in the division and invariably better than many Third Division and a few in the Second. For the October visit of Millwall, 21,000 turned up, then two weeks later 22,000 against Northampton. York pulled in 24,000 and in December 27,000 came for the Plymouth Cup-tie and the Torquay game on Boxing Day. Winning at home helped matters. City lost only once in the League, to Carlisle early in the season, and won eighteen out of 23 games at home. The final average crowd was 16,330, bettered by only three Third Division clubs and higher than nine Second Division clubs.

Strangely, the Coventry public still shunned three floodlight friendlies. Second Division Derby for Peter Hill's testimonial (lost 0-1), First Division Luton (0-0) and Sunderland (1-3) attracted less than 7,000. The club concluded that non-competitive fixtures were no longer what the public wanted. Other clubs felt likewise. Although a new national flood-light competition had been discussed, many top clubs objected. Southern teams already had the Southern Professional Floodlight Cup, and in 1958 City entered the knockout competition for the first time. The first game was a disaster, with City – fielding five reserves – losing 1-6 at Millwall.

The League season saw many highlights, none better than the Monday evening visit in March of leaders Port Vale. A crowd of 28,429 – the biggest at the ground for over three years, with a large Potteries follow-ing – saw Ray Straw grab the winning goal. It left City just two points behind Vale and five ahead of their nearest rivals. A shaky run of five games with neither a win nor a goal had the fans biting their nails, but the team regrouped and clinched promotion on a Monday night at Millwall with a 1-1 draw. The team won many plaudits for their attacking style: Leyton Orient manager Alec Stock described City's display at Millwall as 'some of the best football I have seen all season anywhere'.

Celebrations at the final home game with Watford (a 1-0 win) were muted on a miserably wet day which kept the crowd down to under 14,000, but the players and their wives joined the directors and all the club's staff for a cocktail party afterwards. The final table showed City second, two points behind Port Vale. York and Exeter also went up.

The 1959 close season was quiet, although the club made waves by attempting to increase admission charges. At the Football League's AGM in June a restriction setting aside a certain proportion of each ground at a minimum of two shillings (10p) was lifted. City, who had charged only two shillings at the Spion Kop end the previous season, took the oppor-tunity to increase prices there to 2s 6d (13p). In July, however, after much negative reaction, the club reversed the decision and the 2 shilling charge was restored at the Kop. The club did, however, increase the charge for the covered end of the ground from 2s 6d to 3 shillings.

One innovation was to send 100 free season tickets to the Old Age Pensioners Association, and all pensioners were given a 6d concession at the turnstiles on production of a token. Watching football then was a rather different experience than today. Barbara Hill, wife of 1950s star Peter, remembers going to Highfield Road to watch her young husband in the 1950s: 'Sometimes I went to matches with my neighbour and stood on the Kop even though I had a seat in the stand. I liked it there – you could say exactly what you thought about the opposition and be standing next to a supporter of that team and nobody batted an eyelid. It was great! I remember when there were no police cars, no police horses, a few policemen outside the ground and that was it.'

Another new kit with a far more radical look was introduced in 1959. The light blue and white stripes were abandoned for the first time in living memory and replaced with an all-white kit. The continental-style shirt, however, showed a large bantam badge and a round collarless neck with a blue solid V at the front and short sleeves with blue trim. The change strip was the reverse – blue shirt with a white v-neck. The thinking behind the new kit is unknown but at the time Real Madrid, in their all-white kit, were the most revered team in world football. Whatever the reason, it was popular with the fans, who did not seem too upset about what was a radical change. Over the next decade there would be more than just shirts being changed.

The new **1959-60** season in the higher division started well. In late September Czech club Banik Ostrava were guests as part of 'Meet Czechoslovakia week' in the city. The idea was to provide the people of Coventry with some concept of how the Czechoslovak people filled their leisure hours. According to the match programme, the Banik team had four internationals, including Pospichal, Ondracka and Kosnovsky. A crowd of 9,350 were lured as much by City's 'mystery' goalkeeper as by their visitors from behind the Iron Curtain. City's goalkeeper turned out to be Blackpool's Brian Caine, who City hoped to sign as a deputy for Lightening. Caine was not on the First Division club's transfer list and according to the *CET* 'if he remains "Mr X" until the match, there is a greater chance of City signing him without opposition from other clubs'. As it turned out, most of the crowd went home none the wiser as to his identity: the loudspeaker announcement before the kick-off merely said Lightening was not in goal for City.

Despite financial pressures, City were in the top four for most of the 1959-60 season. At the AGM in October, chairman Brandish announced a loss of over £10,000 during the promotion season and outlined the club's budget proposals. Income was estimated at £58,000 for the season, whilst expenditure of £53,000 (£30,000 on the wage bill) allowed a surplus of £5,000 – 'a sum totally inadequate to provide funds for transfer fees which must necessarily be paid if we are to attain, and preserve Second Division status.' Donations from the supporters club had dwindled and been used to pay for the floodlights. Brandish hoped that his 'frank disclosure' would help supporters realise the seriousness of the club's plight and back the fund-raising activities of the club and the supporters club.

Christmas 1959 saw the last instance of Christmas Day football at Highfield Road. Wrexham were the visitors for the morning kick-off and a four-goal blast from Ken Satchwell helped City to a 5-3 victory which maintained their excellent recent yuletide record – they had dropped only one point in five Christmases. An attendance of 17,526, though higher than average, was not the bumper crowd expected on 25 December. There was increasingly less public transport on Christmas Day and fewer teams chose to play on that day. The year ended with City 3rd, but only ten points separated the top fifteen clubs.

City had again entered the Southern Professional Floodlight Cup, and although Chelsea and Tottenham turned their backs, all the other London First and Second Division clubs were in. Southend were overcome after a replay, then First Division Fulham likewise. Fulham had entered even though Craven Cottage lacked floodlights, so the tie was switched to Highfield Road. A 15,000 crowd saw City dominate their 'seven-international' opponents, but fall victim to a late penalty equaliser. England captain Johnny Haynes graced Highfield Road for the first time and future England stars George Cohen and Alan Mullery were given a hard time by their opponents. The Cottagers refused to travel back Coventry for a replay and insisted on a London venue. Brentford was chosen and Ken Satchwell's goal won the tie.

By the time of the March semi-final, City had shot their bolt in the promotion race. Despite home wins over promoted Southampton (4-1) and Norwich (2-1), three defeats over Easter dashed their hopes. City finished 5th, seven points behind runners-up Norwich.

Southampton returned for the Floodlight semi-final and were beaten again, 2-1. City were drawn at home in the final against First Division West Ham, and 16,921 roared the Bantams to victory. The Hammers included future England captain Bobby Moore and future City manager Noel Cantwell. Two goals from recent signing Ron Hewitt meant he became the first City captain to lift a trophy since 1936.

A minor incident at Highfield Road in April 1960 should have high-lighted the serious fire risks in the main stand. In what was eerily similar to the fire which consumed the same stand eight years later, firemen were called to the ground to deal with a 'smouldering' four-foot-square portion of ceiling in the manager's office. According to newspaper reports a cigarette end had fallen through a gap in the floorboards of the directors box during a schoolboys match and smouldered on the asbestos ceiling through the night. It was speculated that if the butt had fallen onto one of the wooden supporting beams just inches away it could have started a more serious fire. One club official flippantly described it as 'the fire that never was' and no one foresaw the disaster waiting to happen.

Despite the disappointment of missing a second successive promotion, the board rewarded manager Frith with a new four-year contract.

CHAPTER SEVEN

The 1960s

What in retrospect was the most exciting decade in the club's history started with a miserable and desolate **1960-61** season. City went backwards after two good years in Division Three and finished 15th, only six points clear of the drop. Manager Frith started the season with an experimental 4-2-4 formation, which was a disaster, with nineteen goals conceded in six games. By the time he had abandoned the new 'continental' system in September, City were in the bottom six and never recovered. Average gates were 11,996, 4,500 down.

The summer of 1960 saw the central portion of the main stand enlarged and 480 extra tip-up seats fitted, replacing the existing bench-type seats. The new seats would cost 5s 6d, 6d less than the old centre seats, but the larger area would increase the club's overall income.

A new competition was with us, the Football League Cup, a knockout competition played in midweek and specifically geared to the growing craze for floodlit football. There was the usual resistance from bigger clubs who foresaw fixture congestion, six of whom – including Wolves and West Brom – declined to take part in the first season. The new trophy meant the end of the Southern Professional Floodlight Cup, and City were left as its last winners. According to press reports, they were supposed to return the trophy, a silver rosebowl, to the FA at the conclusion of the 1960-61 season but evidence suggests it was still at Highfield Road at the time of the 1968 fire.

City's first League Cup-tie was at home to Fourth Division Barrow on Monday, 10 October, in front of 6,643. City scored four, then ran out of steam on a 'pitch in which players often sank ankle-deep in the mud' and allowed Barrow to pull two goals back. Crowds for the new competition were low everywhere and the Cup had little credibility. In round two there were only 4,500 at Portsmouth's Fratton Park to see City knocked out by their Second Division hosts.

In the boardroom, Walter Brandish stood down as chairman and was replaced by Derrick Robins. Robins, who had been on the board since 1954, spoke of the club's financial difficulties, exacerbated again by poor crowds, and was prepared to 'bridge the gap' – presumably he was lending the club money or guaranteeing an overdraft. The Kent-born Robins had moved to Coventry in 1939 and after serving in the army as a major in the war had established a successful building firm, Portable Concrete

Buildings, which later became Banbury Buildings. He had also been a prominent cricketer in local circles and in his first interview with the local newspaper heaped praise on Billy Frith: 'I am absolutely convinced he is among the best six managers in the country.'

Robins outlined his ambitious but vague plans for improvement in the supporters club handbook that autumn. He mentioned 'many things we have to do, the chief of which is to improve the accommodation for the spectators, level the playing pitch, which could well include underground heating, cover Spion Kop and, indeed, more cover generally'. He went on to say that the old stand would not last for ever but prefixed the whole piece with the 'fundamental' aim – to put the club's finances on a sounder basis 'than has been the case in the past'.

The club was losing £250 per week, which put all the pipedreams for the stadium and team strengthening into perspective. One positive step he announced was the establishment of a Bantams Fighting Fund, a weekly pool, in addition to the supporters club lottery, which would generate extra income. Retiring club captain Paddy Ryan would run this scheme.

In the same publication Jack Patience, chairman of the supporters club, announced that the floodlight fund had been paid off. Regarding covering the Kop, a pet project of the supporters club, he suggested it would have to wait until the club was on a firmer footing.

A wet summer and autumn saw a rapid deterioration in the Highfield Road pitch. Between July and November more than 740 millimetres of rain fell in the Coventry area, more than in a typical year, with a record-breaking 211mm in October, the wettest month since November 1940. The pitch was pretty bad in early October for the Barrow match, but a month later 'Nemo' in the *CET* described it as 'quite the worst Football League pitch I have seen in my experience'. One quarter of the playing surface was 'nothing more than a bog' and 'Nemo' sank to his ankles in 'oozing mud'. Two Youth Cup replays and a Football Combination game had already been postponed, and several first-team games were in jeopardy. The match report for the Tranmere game in November describes a surface 'more suited to a hippopotamus'. 'Nemo' questioned the sense in playing: 'Spectators pay to see football, not 22 grown men floundering like helpless ducks in a farmyard morass.'

Highfield Road hosted a Friday night game for the first time. The fixture with Brentford in early December was brought forward to avoid a clash with an international rugby trial at Coventry Rugby Club's Coundon Road and the live televising of the Wales v South Africa rugby international in Cardiff. City's directors saw this as an opportunity not only to assist their rugby-playing friends, who without floodlights could not stage evening games, but also to assess fans' interest in Friday night football. City won 2-0 and the attendance of 13,589 was the biggest since early September and 3,500 higher than the previous Saturday game. Once again, however, the state of the pitch was blasted by 'Nemo' – 'an embarrassment to the club' and 'an apology of a playing surface'. In the spring the club successfully applied to play three further Friday night games and attracted reasonable crowds. In the run-up to the League's AGM in June 1961, City debated staging all but two home games the following season on Fridays, but with some opponents uneasy it was agreed to stick to Saturdays between 1 November and 1 March.

In January 1961 Jimmy Hill's influence was first felt at Highfield Road when the Professional Footballers Association (PFA), of which Hill was chairman, threatened strike action over wages and freedom of contract. As a club chairman, Robins was against a strike, describing the players' threats as 'crass stupidity'. After Southern clubs had voted for action he tried to stop the Midland vote going the same way: 'I gather the impression that the majority of the players at yesterday's meeting didn't want to strike but were swayed by one man. It may suit that one man to have a strike but the vast majority of footballers know that a strike is not in the best interests of themselves or their clubs.' The 'one man' Robins was referring to was Hill, whose performance in pursuit of his union's aims must have impressed the chairman as much as it alarmed him. In less than a year he would be offering Hill the manager's job. The bulk of the Coventry first team, addressed by Ron Hewitt, the PFA representative, affirmed its support for Hill's cause. Strike action was averted at the eleventh hour and many of the players' demands were met, including the removal of the maximum wage of £20 per week.

The 1960-61 season petered out, with home gates below 10,000 and apathy everywhere. The club hosted a Schoolboy international between England and Eire in April, which attracted 9,108, a thousand more than the League game the previous Saturday. The captain of Coventry boys team, Graham Parker, played right-half for England, and one future full international, Peter Storey – later a key member of Arsenal's 1971 double team – won his first cap at centre-half. City missed out on Parker: he went on to join Aston Villa as an apprentice, but played only a dozen first team games. England's star in the 8-0 victory was Prosser from Aston schools, who helped himself to four goals but never made the grade in League football.

Robins was anxious to give Highfield Road a facelift. Years later he was quoted: 'It had a terrible entrance to it and the whole place seemed to cry out "Don't come in". I felt we needed a smart entrance to make people feel welcome, plus a decent manager's office and boardroom. So I told the other directors: "You put in what you can afford and I'll make up the rest." From then on we were pulling together. I also said that no director must charge a farthing to the club.'

During the summer of 1961 a new façade was built behind the main stand, incorporating a new directors entrance and modern offices, including a dedicated office for the pools set-up. In the *CET* Robins said: 'The old offices have no ventilation and are quite impossible to work in. The new offices will have a proper ventilation system. It won't cost the club a penny. The directors are paying for it all.' The work was carried out between May and July and at least one player, Scot Stewart Imlach, a joiner by trade, signed on with the company carrying out the work, probably Shanks' joinery company.

When the fixture list for **1961-62** was published, City had fixed thirteen home games for evening kick-offs, with nine on Friday evenings – continuing the experiment from last season. Robins insisted this was purely financial – the club could make more at the gate when there were fewer competing attractions on a Friday night. Likewise, all reserve team games would be played on midweek evenings instead of the traditional Saturday afternoons.

The directors increased entrance charges by 6d, with the Spion Kop now costing 3 shillings and the covered end 3s 6d. A 'Bantam' season ticket covering all first team and reserve games could be bought for £3. The news from the money-raising pools was positive; weekly profit had increased from £180 to £700 during the season and the supporters club handed over a cheque for £7,000 in August. Their donation was allocated to ground improvements, whilst the other pool, the Bantam Fighting Fund, gave direct help to the club.

The club certainly needed financial help. The first home gate was under 14,000, below the 'break-even' figure of 16,000. When the club's accounts were published they disclosed that the club had lost £40,000 in four years. Robins repeated his determination to run the club on a firm financial basis and announced that Leamington-based travel agent and former journalist John Camkin had joined the board as the club's first press liaison officer. Another board change saw Walter Brandish resign after 26 years as a director. He was made president of the club, a position which had been vacant since Lord Kenilworth relinquished the role earlier that year.

On the pitch, things were going from bad to worse, and a League Cup exit at Fourth Division Workington did not help Billy Frith's cause. By

October gates were down further and Friday nights didn't pull in many more. Team morale was low, but the FA Cup seemed to offer a lifeline to a season rapidly going downhill, not to mention a financial boost. After a first round win over Gillingham, Frith greeted the home draw with Southern League King's Lynn with confidence: 'It looks as though our luck with the draw has changed.' His confidence was misplaced.

The youth team made an early exit from the Youth Cup with a club record home defeat, 1-9 to Aston Villa who featured a young George Graham, the ex-Coventry schoolboy Parker, and four players who had appeared in the First Division. City's team featured future stars Dietmar Bruck and fifteen-year-old Bobby Gould.

A 0-2 Friday night home defeat to Crystal Palace the week before the King's Lynn tie sparked a rare event of hooliganism. As the Palace team coach was pulling away down King Richard Street a brick smashed one of the windows.

A week later, the Cup defeat by King's Lynn put paid to Frith's second spell in charge. 'Nemo' in the *CET* described it as Black Saturday and 'probably the most grim page in City's modern history'. Only captain George Curtis was exempted from scathing criticism: 'City's strolling attitude to this whole tie was not just dangerously complacent, it was sheer folly.'

Despite City scoring first through an own-goal, the Linnets bounced back with two goals. 'Wait until the second half, class will tell' was the cry at half-time. But City's pathetic efforts proved fruitless and Lynn, bottom of the Southern League, progressed to the third round. Lynn manager Len Richley thrust the dagger deeper: 'It wasn't as hard a fight as we expected.' At the final whistle the ground was virtually empty.

Legend has it that Jimmy Hill was watching from the back row of the old stand, because four days later he had been appointed City's tenth post-war manager. In his autobiography Hill says he was offered the job over lunch at Derrick Robins' house in Leamington a week earlier but deferred any decision until after he had seen the side against King's Lynn. On the following day Hill telephoned a shell-shocked Robins to tell him he would accept. Robins had assumed the disastrous performance would have dissuaded Hill. Thus began a partnership that would take Coventry City from Third Division strugglers to the First Division in five exhilarating seasons.

Hill wanted his own coaching staff so, in addition to Frith, his coaches Alf Wood and Ted Roberts, and scout Arthur Jepson all left the club. It was Hill's first job in management following his retirement as a player earlier that year – a retirement that meant relinquishing the chairmanship of the PFA. Having been on opposite sides of the fence during the players' dispute, manager and chairman now had a common agenda, and a potent relationship was born.

Most City fans didn't get too excited by the new boss, and for Hill's first game, against Northampton, the crowd of 13,000 was swelled by 4,000 Cobblers fans. City's 1-0 victory was the first of four wins in Hill's first month and bought him some breathing space, but the first dramatic change was the club's PR profile. A ten-year ban on players talking to the press was lifted and every night the *CET* seemed to carry a story as Hill strove to keep the club in the public consciousness. After the Boxing Day game with Grimsby the club invited young fans to have 'pop and crisps' and get the players' autographs. The club anticipated 100 youngsters but over 500 turned up and the players patiently signed for over two hours. This inexpensive idea generated much goodwill amongst the future fans of the club, and many of City's over-50 supporters still remember the occasion with affection.

In January Hill invited the Pathe News cameras to Highfield Road for three days to film a documentary 'A Day in the Life of a Manager'. The cameras were still whirring when the home game with Southend United kicked off. Bizarrely, the referee stopped the game after three minutes to make City change from their white shirts with blue sleeves because it clashed with Southend's blue shirts with white stripes. City changed into their red away kit but the referee was wrong – he should have made Southend change, as they were the away team.

Hill arranged several friendlies in an effort to improve teamwork. Top Czech side Slovan Bratislava included five internationals, one of whom, Jan Populhar, would captain his country to the World Cup finals the following June. Watched by 8,000 fans, and wearing their change red shirts again, City won 2-1. Hill's first signing, Roy Dwight (cousin of Elton John), scored one of the goals. Two weeks later West German First Division club TSV Aachen, with former Yugoslav legend Branko Zebec, were hammered 5-3. In between, City played the British Army, a team packed full of League players. They included City's own Mick Kearns, completing his National Service at the time.

As the consecration approached of the city's revolutionary and much-discussed new cathedral in May 1962, plans were hatched for a celebration game at Highfield Road. Benfica, the European Cup-winners, were tipped to come, but their extortionate match fee of £8,000 made it unfeasible. Instead Burnley, who lost the FA Cup final to Spurs days earlier, gave a thrilling display to win 4-2. Over 7,000 watched the game, in which City featured England centre-forward Johnny Byrne as a guest.

In the League the honeymoon was soon over and Hill sensed the team needed an overhaul. Despite beating the leaders Portsmouth in April and a satisfying win at Peterborough, results were patchy and the side finished 14th. The average attendance was 10,256, the lowest since 1928. The Friday-night experiment had proved inconclusive but Hill made it clear that he wanted to revert to traditional Saturday afternoons.

His new team was taking shape and, with several senior pros eased out before the season ended, some youngsters got a chance. Robins, apparently flush with cash from a share issue by his company, gave £30,000 to the club. Hill was entrusted with spending it, an enormous amount at the time (the club's record fee was only £20,000), on the players he wanted. Hill opted for a complete new forward line.

The largest fee, £12,000, was spent on Peterborough's prolific scorer Terry Bly, with the balance used to sign Willie Humphries and Hugh Barr from Northern Ireland, Jimmy Whitehouse (Reading), Bobby Laverick (Brighton), and defender John Sillett (Chelsea). All bar Laverick would play a significant part in the rebirth of the club.

Hill was out to change for ever the trouble-scarred image of Coventry City. The white strip was discarded in favour of a new continental-looking all sky blue. It was unlike anything seen in England before, and preceded Liverpool's all red or Chelsea's all blue. The programme got a revamp, and when the *CET* described the team as 'the Sky Blues' a new nickname, in line with the new image, was born.

The fans responded to the publicity about their new-look team and over 22,000 turned up for the opening game of **1962-63**. They saw goals from new men Bly and Barr launch the Sky Blue era with a 2-0 win over Notts County.

The new team had teething problems, losing 3-4 at home to Southend and being thrashed 1-6 at Watford. Goalkeeper Lightening was sold to Middlesbrough following a court appearance for handling stolen goods. Laverick was jettisoned after four League games and replaced by a lean, whippet-like eighteen-year-old groundstaff boy named Ronnie Rees. South Wales-born Rees was an instant hit and would be an influential figure in the next few years. Hill's treatment of Laverick was an abrupt message to other players: if you didn't shape up to Hill's standards you were out.

Robins was not deterred by the modest start and at the October AGM he said: 'I honestly feel that we have turned the last corner of this dreary old lane – a lane which has been with us for at least ten years.' He urged patience whilst being prophetic: 'Please remember the revolution has only begun to take place.' The club's accounts showed another deficit, but with £11,000 generated by the supporters club and the Fighting Fund, the loss was the lowest for five years.

In mid-October the side started an unbeaten run which would last 23 matches and only be terminated by mighty Manchester United. It was the worst winter Britain had seen since 1740, and the first signs of the dreadful weather came at Highfield Road at the end of November when the England v Switzerland youth international was abandoned after only nine minutes because of fog. Despite enhanced floodlight bulbs, paid for by the supporters club, the grey blanket did not disperse and the few hundred spectators were given a cash refund.

The club's innovations continued with the opening of the Sky Blue Club in October. Designed as a place where the fans could 'rub shoulders with the players after the game', it was officially opened by famous former cricketer Dennis Compton. That same month the club flew by aeroplane to a match for the first time – a testimonial at Windsor Park, Belfast against Linfield. Then in December for the visit of Colchester, the club launched the Sky Blue Song. With lyrics by Jimmy Hill and director John Camkin and sung to the tune of the Eton Boating Song it went thus:

Let's all sing together,
    Play up Sky Blues,
While we sing together,
    We will never lose.

Proud Posh or Cobblers,
    Oysters or anyone,
They can't defeat us,
    We'll fight till the game is won.

The idea was to insert the day's opponents into the second line of the second verse. 'Oysters' was in fact an old nickname for Colchester but suited the song better than the 'Us'. The club hoped the fans would sing along, but also planned to have it recorded by the players. The Colchester game, on the Saturday before Christmas, was affected by fog. At halftime, with City leading 2-0, the referee had to abandon the game but not before rousing renditions of the new song filled Highfield Road.

The fog was just a prelude to the icy spell. The Christmas doubleheader with leaders Peterborough would be the last games for almost two months. After City had won 3-0 on a white pitch at London Road, 25,000 – the biggest home crowd for three years, paying record receipts of £3,960 – saw a thrilling 3-3 draw on a carpet of snow. City's groundsman

Ellick Smith and an army of City fans helped remove much of it, and persuaded the referee to let the game go ahead. City's ten-game unbeaten run put them 4th, poised for a promotion challenge.

From Boxing Day to early March, much of Britain was blanketed under snow and very little football was played anywhere. City's third round Cup-tie at Lincoln would be the first of fifteen postponements. Groundsman Smith, desperate for anything to unfreeze his pitch, slipped on the ice and broke his leg. The snow lay thick on the ground until the first week in March, but two home games were possible in late February when the club invested £250 in de-icing pellets and bales of straw to protect the pitch. Two hundred volunteers, mainly schoolboys, who helped clear the pitch of straw and snow, were thanked by Jimmy Hill over the tannoy system.

Always keen on publicity, Hill had realised Ireland was far less badly affected by the weather and organised eye-catching friendlies there with Wolves and Manchester United, who scraped a 2-2 draw in Dublin with a late goal. Wolves beat City 3-0 in Cork and 6-3 in Belfast. The experiment earned the club several hundred pounds in gate money.

A famous FA Cup run had started inauspiciously in November with a 1-0 home win over Bournemouth. A 0-0 draw at Millwall in the second round attracted over 22,000 to the replay, paying record Cup receipts of £3,816. The frequently postponed Lincoln tie finally took place at the sixteenth attempt on 6 March, 60 days late, and was won 5-1. With massive fixture congestion facing all clubs, City were forced to play three ties with Second Division Portsmouth in the space of six days – drawing 1-1 at Fratton Park, 2-2 at Coventry in front of another 25,000 crowd, before winning 2-1 in the second replay at neutral Tottenham. The home replay marked one of the first examples of crowd segregation at Highfield Road. Visiting fans were hoarded into the enclosure in front of the main stand, in that part closest to the covered end.

Plans were drawn up for pitch levelling, and when the thaw arrived in March City rapidly rearranged all their home games to ensure the contractors could start work as early in May as possible. It was still anticipated that the work would not be completed in time for the start of the following season and the club provisionally requested starting the new campaign with two away fixtures. The pitch had always had a slope – it fell by fifteen feet from the corner flag in the north-west corner to the opposite corner at the Spion Kop end. At a cost of £15,000 it was not cheap, but thoughts of under-soil heating would have to wait for another day.

Previously, City's League games, like those of their rivals for promotion, were postponed because of weather. Now it was Cup commitments causing postponements, and in March the team played six Cup-ties and only three League games. Six days after defeating Portsmouth, City faced Sunderland on a Monday night in the biggest post-war home game, with the prize at stake a home quarter-final tie with Manchester United. The Football Association had continued to make the Cup draws on the due dates, as if the 'big freeze' had not existed. Sunderland were poised for promotion to Division One, averaging 40,000 crowds, and a week earlier had hit seven past Norwich.

Over 50,000 fans converged on Highfield Road that night and half an hour before the kick-off the turnstiles were closed with thousands locked out. Three gates were broken by frustrated fans and hundreds rushed in without paying. The terraces could not cope. There were fans up the floodlight pylons, on the stand roofs, and hundreds on the running track. The official attendance was 40,487 but it was hopelessly wide of the mark – there must have been some 48,000 inside the ground.

Those who witnessed it will never forget the suspense as Sunderland led through a 33rd-minute goal from Johnny Crossan. Three thousand Rokerite fans roared the Blaydon Races. With eight minutes left, City levelled when a shot-cum-cross by Dietmar Bruck flew in off the upright and prompted a mass pitch invasion. Three minutes later the Iron Man George Curtis bulldozed his way into the penalty area to meet John Sillett's cross with his massive forehead to score with a thunderous header and provoke a second, even bigger pitch invasion. The tannoy system warned that referee George McCabe would abandon the game if there was any further encroachment, but Curtis's goal was the last of the night and the ecstatic youngsters waited until the final whistle before launching a third invasion. The Sky Blue song finally drowned out the Blaydon Races, and the result earned Coventry City pride of place with the country's sports media.

Eric Howell recalls the night: 'The official attendance was 40,000, but in reality it was many, many more. A while before the kick-off the gate in the corner between the main stand and the Covered End – the one the tractor came through – burst open and thousands of fans poured into the ground, all looking a bit bewildered and wondering what to do next. Officials rapidly did the sensible thing and, realising it was impossible to remove them or integrate them into the crowd, asked them to sit around the edge of the pitch.'

George Ling also remembers the Sunderland tie: 'I was 17 at the time and my dad had made me an old-fashioned rotating rattle for the match, and being an engineer of Victorian methods it was built to last. It did not. When Bruck scored, my over-enthusiastic rattling caused the head to fly off, sending a rather heavy projectile across a swathe of delirious fans. It must have hurt a few but no one complained, or threatened me, and smilingly the head was returned to me. Victory dulls all pain.'

Rod Dean, sixteen in 1963, retains vivid memories: 'As we left Long Itchington, extra early on that sunny Monday evening, our collective excitement was intense. Due to the cars heading into Coventry and the speculation of "a big gate", we parked twice as far away than we normally did, next to "The Humber" in Stoke. Even at 6pm there were people everywhere and I will never forget the site of the Kop as we turned into Swan Lane – it was packed. Our walking turned into a desperate run and we arrived at the turnstiles – the "boys" turnstile had long queues. We eventually got in and made our way to a vantage point behind the goal and halfway up – it was not too full there, but soon the crushes in all four corners of the ground were intense – a mass of swaying heads. The first crush barriers of a flimsy aluminium tubular construction collapsed and were passed over the heads of the crowd. Children were allowed over the wall and soon fans started to climb up the floodlight pylons and onto the covered end roof at the other end of the ground. I remember my father saying it was like this against Luton in 1936, when he had stood on the Kop. The game got under way but it was far too tense to really have much flow to it – the huge crowd dominated everything. The gates had been shut but a couple were broken down and the 40,400 crowd was certainly a gross underestimate. The last ten minutes were pure delirium and the feeling after the match was the most exciting of my life – more so than the FA Cup final. It was to be the first of many, many exciting times at Highfield Road – we had finally arrived.'

The quarter-final tie with Manchester United was scheduled for the following Saturday, and after the mayhem of Monday night was made all-ticket. Cup fever had hit the city and everyone was jumping on the bandwagon. The club planned to issue tickets for sale on Wednesday evening but some supporters queued from 5.30 in the morning and by mid-afternoon, with the rain pouring down, queues estimated at 17,000 stretched all around the ground. The police, concerned about the welfare of the supporters, requested that the club start selling them early, and at 3.20pm a roar went up when the ticket kiosks opened. In just three hours most of City's 30,000 allocation of the 44,000 total was sold. An estimated 15,000 went home disappointed without a ticket.

Rod Dean again: 'I skived off school and caught the bus to Coventry at 8.15am. It was wet, very wet and even by 9.15 there were large queues at the ground. I stood by the Co-op in Mowbray Street for five hours before they started selling tickets and got my two precious tickets. My father arrived at 3.30 and he managed to get a couple as well. I hardly slept in the period up to the match – such was the level of expectation.'

George Ling again: 'I bunked off school to queue with half the population of Coventry trying to get a ticket. I met my dad but he was way back in the line as he had been to work. He failed to get a ticket but the proverbial man down the pub came up trumps. After the scenes at the Sunderland game we wanted to get there early and find a reasonable viewpoint. Unfortunately we had to leave a family wedding early, resulting a long-running family feud. I never understood why the wedding was not cancelled for an event of this magnitude.'

The rain barely abated all week, and on the morning of the big day pools of water dotted the pitch. Referee Ernie Crawford arrived early from his Doncaster home and expressed doubts about the surface. Hill and Robins were at the Hotel Leofric for lunch when they learned of Crawford's fears. They raced back to the ground and complied with the referee's demands that the pitch be forked. The pools slowly disappeared and the referee gave the go-ahead.

The omens looked good when Dick Knight, a Midland radio journalist picked City to win on lunchtime radio. Hill, always on the look-out for unusual pre-match entertainment, persuaded Ken Dodd – who was appearing at Coventry Theatre – to go on to the pitch in a Sky Blue shirt. The City fans roared with glee, but roars turned to boos as he reached the centre-circle and peeled off his shirt to reveal a red United one underneath. The Radio Sky Blue DJ aptly played the Cascades' *Rhythm of the Rain*, a top-ten hit of the time. BBC's television cameras were on hand to record the action and the highlights were shown later that evening with Kenneth Wolstenholme commentating.

City stunned the Reds by going a goal up within five minutes. Terry Bly, who with 27 goals had been a key man in the club's revival, scored from a Willie Humphries cross at the Kop end. Rees hit an upright when a second goal may have possibly ended United's hopes. Bobby Charlton, out of form in the League, put on a super show, scoring twice to give United a 3-1 victory. Matt Busby's team would go on to win the FA Cup, beating Leicester City 3-1 in the final, with future Coventry manager Noel Cantwell lifting the trophy at Wembley.

Ling remembers the game as a bit of an anticlimax: 'The atmosphere wasn't as emotional as for the Sunderland match, which was under lights and had an enthusiastic and bigger crowd that really wanted to be there. That made the difference. Even after Bly's goal we never looked like winning against Man Utd. Afterwards I remember not being too disappointed, as I thought we'd still go up.'

There was honour in defeat for the Sky Blues – they had converted the fickle Coventry footballing public and put the club on the back pages of the nation's press. Receipts from the Sunderland and Manchester United games neared £19,000, erasing the club's debts at a stroke. Hill was in no mood to sit still. With sixteen League games to play and with City pushing for promotion, he paid a record £21,000 for Peterborough's prolific scorer George Hudson. That meant no place for Bly.

In retrospect, Hudson was an inspired buy, but to City fans at the time it was impossible to fathom why Hill would shun a player scoring virtually a goal a game. Even though Hudson scored a hat-trick on his debut against Halifax, Hill faced a barrage of criticism for weeks afterwards. In the long term, the ball-skills of Hudson won over the sceptics and he became a club hero. Bly moved on to Notts County (with City making a profit) but his career was on the down slope and he was playing in non-league circles in less than eighteen months.

After the Cup exertions the team derailed in the League. The 22-game unbeaten run ended spectacularly, 1-5 at Wrexham, and a shaky Easter programme culminated in a 1-2 home loss to Bournemouth in front of 30,289 – the biggest home League crowd since 1952. Form fluctuated wildly and fans' emotions likewise. With seven games left, promotion was still possible, but ultimately the Cup run had drained the players and the team finished 4th, five points behind second-placed Swindon. The final attendance figures showed a 70 per cent rise to 17,098, the best in the division and better than two First Division clubs.

Even before the season ran its course the club had unveiled plans for ground improvements. In addition to pitch levelling, the dressing rooms, referee's room and treatment room would be upgraded and the main stand seats would all be tip-ups. The biggest change, however, would see a new stand built on the north side to replace the 1910 'Atkinsons' stand. Built of reinforced concrete, when completed it would comprise six sections and, at 360 feet, would stretch almost the length of the pitch. Phase one, that summer, would see the erection of two separate wing sections either side of the old stand – allowing the continued use for one last season of the original 1910 version. Phase two, planned for the summer of 1964, would see the demolition of the old stand and the construction of the four middle sections.

Phase one would add 1,700 extra seats, all tip-ups, and after phase two there would be 5,100 seats in the new stand, taking the club's overall seating accommodation to 7,700. The total cost was budgeted at £80,000 and the *CET* reported that 'much of the money for this huge project will be raised by the Supporters Club'.

The architect, Philip Skelcher of Solihull, explained that the cantilever principle – used to good effect for the first time at football grounds at Scunthorpe and Hillsborough – was ruled out at Highfield Road as there was insufficient space. Instead, to minimise obstructions for spectators, five slim posts would support the roof, which would project beyond the front row of seats allowing better than usual protection from the weather. The effect, said Skelcher, would be 'slick, clean and modern' and as the material was concrete, maintenance costs would be low as there would be no need to paint it.

The roof would consist of ultra-light aluminium 'barrel' sheets spanning the main roof beams. Robins' own company, Banbury Grandstands, would be the contractors, using quick-build methods which would prove enormously successful over the next five years as the face of Highfield Road changed for ever.

Season ticket prices and match-day admission prices rose to help fund the largest development ever carried out at the stadium. The dearest season tickets were increased to £7 10 shillings, but to ease the burden the club introduced a scheme by which fans could pay a 10 shillings deposit and the remainder in fortnightly instalments before the start of the new season. Within a week secretary Paul Oliver announced that they had sold 1,750 season tickets, 50 per cent up on the total for 1962-63, and worth around £10,000 to the club – and the season had not even started. When it did, the number had exceeded 3,000, generating £21,000, almost five times the income from the previous season.

The pitch levelling was undertaken by BMF Sports Ground Contractors from Knowle. It was completed by the end of June at a cost of £15,000. BMF employed City's Roy Dwight and former international goalkeeper Reg Matthews to help with the relaying. At the first home game of **1963-64** supporters gasped when they saw the change. The excavations had exposed the terrace wall at the north, west, and east corners, which was now some ten feet tall. The new pitch looked immaculate and would, it was hoped, now be well drained. In addition, new refreshment bars were erected at each corner of the ground.

In July the club acquired an eleven-year lease on a site at Ryton, which would become its training ground. An all-weather pitch and floodlights would be installed, but in the short term players would continue to train at pitches at the GEC Sports Ground at Walsgrave and Shilton.

The new pitch got its first airing in a 'private' friendly with Derby, which City won 5-3. A week later the Sky Blues opened the season with another 'old five', slamming Crystal Palace 5-1. Wing-half Ron Farmer netted a hat-trick. City soared to the top of the table with a string of wins and the fans responded. Over 26,000 saw the Palace game and in mid-September almost 30,000 saw the visit of Crewe (another 5-1 win). Only once did the crowd fall below 20,000 and that for Luton on the Saturday before Christmas. City's away following was one of the best in all four divisions, with 5,000 travelling to Walsall and 7,000 to Luton.

The club's accounts showed a profit for the first time in five years. The big crowds ensured that the coffers continued to swell, and the club's receipts record was broken twice in November – the £4,600 takings from the Peterborough game was topped by £5,200 at the Bristol Rovers FA Cup-tie.

The next innovation was the introduction of Radio Sky Blue. Director John Camkin, with his journalistic background and experience of commentating on televised football, became the 'anchor', combining interviews with pop records for 45 minutes before kick-off. Later, former England wicket-keeper Godfrey Evans and Charles Harrold took the microphone. It may not sound innovative today, but then there was little or no pre-match entertainment, save for the occasional marching band. Other entertainments, on the pitch, included netball games, gymnastic displays from the Butlin Girls, trampolining, the Royal Signals motorcycle display team and Coventry's own 'pop' group – the Mighty Avengers. Soon showbiz stars, many of whom were appearing at Coventry Theatre came 'on the air'. Jimmy Tarbuck, Frankie Vaughan and Frankie Howerd all popped over to Highfield Road. In another twist, Hill had a telephone installed by his seat in the directors box to communicate with the trainer's bench and Radio Sky Blue.

Bert Woodfield had wonderful memories of the 1960s: 'My son Richard was the mascot in the Jimmy Hill era. He was picked because he was captain of the school football team. He wore a Sky Blue bantam head, with sky blue tracksuit bottoms, and would parade twice round the pitch before the game. The crowd used to roar at him as he ran round. Then, as the game kicked off I used to look in the stand and there was Rich sat next to JH. I used to curse on wet days – I was getting soaked on the terraces and he was warm and dry in the Main Stand. I used to take him up to the gate and the gateman would take him off my hands and take him to Hill's office where all the gear was stored. The first couple of times I went in with him and on Hill's desk was his baby in a carrycot with his wife sat there – she never watched the matches, she just sat in his office. I saw JH at the Sky Blue Heaven exhibition a couple of years ago and he remembered Richard well.'

In October, City mauled Shrewsbury 8-1, their biggest win since the Clarrie Bourton days of the early 1930s, to cement the top spot. Eleven unbeaten games later, on 3 January 1964, City stood nine points clear and looked near-certainties for promotion. Cup defeats by Rotherham (League Cup) and Bristol Rovers (FA Cup) were shrugged off – Cup runs would distract the team from the main aim of promotion. November was a golden month for George Hudson, with the striker netting thirteen goals. These included three hat-tricks in ten days – at Trowbridge in the FA Cup, in an 8-0 friendly over German club Kaiserslautern, and at QPR in a 6-3 victory which convinced the London press that the Sky Blues were going places. The 4-2 League win over Bristol Rovers was preceded by a minute's silence for the death of US President John F Kennedy, assassinated in Dallas the previous day.

Another foreign side, Hungary's Ferencvaros, were guests for a friendly in December. Over 12,000, including Alf Ramsey and the England squad – preparing at Birmingham for an international – saw City triumph 3-1. The Hungarian champions boasted four players who would represent their country in the 1966 World Cup, among them stylish centre-forward Florian Albert. On Radio Sky-Blue, announcer Godfrey Evans interviewed Jimmy Greaves.

The new 'Sky Blue' stand was taking shape. By October the two wing stands were complete and towered over the still-in-use old stand. It was impossible to sell tickets for all seats in the new wings because the back rows had a restricted view, but the usable seats added around 1,200 to the seating capacity. Work on the centre sections would have to wait, but at no time did the building affect the terraces in front of the stand. With gates averaging 25,000, that terrace room was needed. The club, however, had still not committed to the completion of phase two in the summer of 1964.

The New Year however brought a shuddering halt to City's progress. From 3 January until 28 March the Sky Blues failed to win in eleven games. Home games were generally drawn, but even that comfort was shattered on Friday, 13 March when Southend destroyed the team's fragile confidence by winning 5-2. It was the first time a Coventry side had conceded five at home since the war. Hill reacted quickly, paying £12,500 for much-travelled centre-forward George Kirby – to replace Hudson, out of touch since a groin injury in January – and £11,000 on Spurs' inside-forward John Smith, to fill the place of Ernie Machin, out with a knee injury since the autumn.

City had lost top spot to Palace and trailed by four points but the signings steadied the nerves, with Kirby netting a hat-trick on his debut in a 4-1 win over Oldham. As the season neared its climax City, without the dropped Hudson, staggered towards the finishing line. For the last two away games City's fans almost became an extra man. There were 8,000 to watch a 0-0 draw at Millwall then, two days later 12,000 made the trip to Peterborough, only to see City slump 0-2.

The final game was at home to Colchester and the promotion situation was on a knife edge. Palace were already up with 60 points, while City were second with 58, ahead of Watford on goal-average. Victory over Colchester was essential and Hudson was recalled as part of a double strike-force with Kirby.

Hill's tactical gamble paid off, with Hudson and Humphries carving gaps in the visitors' defence before Hudson netted after 24 minutes from a Rees cross. After half-time the attention of the 36,901 crowd switched to news from the two other vital games. With City kicking off later at 3.15 the other games finished first and Godfrey Evans read the scores over the tannoy. Watford had led Luton for most of the game but conceded two late goals to ensure City's promotion. Palace amazingly lost at home to Oldham, meaning City would be champions by a better goal-average of 0.17 – provided they hung on! On the pitch, the last ten minutes seemed to drag until the referee blew the whistle to spark a pitch invasion. The players disappeared under a mass of young fans in scenes reminiscent of those the previous season against Sunderland.

In due course the players emerged in the main stand, high above the sea of fans, to milk the applause. There was no trophy to present to the track-suited heroes (it was at previous year's champions Northampton and would not be presented to City until the League's AGM). Derrick Robins' attempts to make himself heard long enough to present George Curtis with the Midland Footballer of the Year trophy ended in noisy farce as the fans clamoured for Jimmy Hill.

Hill, Robins and the players had reclaimed the club's Second Division status after twelve years. For the third time in one season the club's receipts record was broken, with £5,846 being taken at the turnstiles. The final average attendance was 26,017, the club's highest since 1950-51, and the highest by any Third Division club since the golden post-war years. The figure topped those of First Division neighbours Aston Villa, Leicester, Wolves, Birmingham and West Brom. For the first time, City were the best-supported club in the Midlands and would continue to be for the next seven years.

The following day Hill revealed two secrets behind the team's preparation for the big game. Firstly, he had instructed the players to take sleeping pills on Thursday and Friday nights and they had 'worked like a charm'. The players were more relaxed than they had been in weeks. Secondly, Hill had invited the comedian Jimmy Tarbuck into the dressing room for 25 minutes before the match. Hill explained: 'I asked Jimmy to crack a few jokes and keep the lads' minds off the game. It helped them to relax in the worst time – just before the game.'

After a celebration dinner at the Leofric the players faced a hectic week, with friendlies in Dublin (Monday), at home to Spurs (Tuesday), at Bedworth Town (Wednesday), home to America FC of Brazil (Thursday) and at Eastbourne (Friday).

The Tottenham game, arranged at short notice after the FA refused to sanction the Brazilian team's visit, gave the fans a chance to applaud their heroes one by one in the centre-circle. The players were then joined in the main stand by the manager, chairman and Hill's management team – Pat Saward, Alan Dicks and Peter Hill. Robins thanked the crowd for their wonderful support and led the players in a rendition of 'three cheers' for the fans. Spurs, missing only Jimmy Greaves and Maurice Norman from their first team, won 6-5 in front of 15,638, with Les Allen scoring an eleven-minute hat-trick. Their Welsh international winger Cliff Jones later said: 'It was a bit of an experience to see a crowd of 15,000 turn out so quickly for a friendly match. I don't think I've heard a crowd shout so much at a friendly match.'

By Thursday night the players were on their knees. The Brazilians turned on the style to win 5-2, with their international Zezinho scoring a hat-trick.

City's players and wives were treated to a two-week holiday in the Spanish resort of Gandia, where Hill organised a friendly against Spanish Second Division club Onteniente.

Back at Highfield Road work resumed on completing the Sky Blue Stand. In January 1964 Derrick Robins and vice-chairman Phil Mead went to the City of London to get financial backing for various plans. A six-hour board meeting ensued at which Hill decided on a priority list. At a press conference the following day he outlined exciting developments. Firstly, the board gave the go-ahead for the completion of the Sky Blue Stand, including the provision of bars, new toilets, a pools office and supporters club facilities underneath. The terracing in front of the new stand would be remodelled with a new wall constructed, under which 120 spectators could be seated in the dry. This pitch-side area was used by invalid cars whose owners were allowed to park their vehicles around the pitch and watch the game in the comfort of their cars.

The opposite, main stand-side of the ground would also be updated. At a cost of £10,000, a covered promenade at the rear would be built that summer enabling ticket-holders to file in from either end instead of through entrances along the front. Underneath the promenade a new ticket office was planned, as well as a club shop. Inside the 30-year-old building the boardroom would be expanded and toilet facilities improved throughout the stadium. A private bar – the Viking Room – would be opened for a new Vice-Presidents Club, with its own entrance.

The most exciting news related to the Kop. This was more of a long-term idea and involved, at a potential cost of £150,000 a double-decker stand providing a further 5,000 seats, with the possibility of a dance hall, shops, and petrol filling station underneath. Hill was keen to stress that nothing was set in stone, but: 'We hope to get it off the floor within two years – and by that I mean not get it built, but get it approved.' The most optimistic start date would be the summer of 1966. Future under-turf heating and multi-storey car parking was also discussed.

It was extraordinary to see how far the club's ambitions had changed in less than eighteen months. Success on the pitch had given the directors the confidence to act bold. Any supporter returning from two years overseas would have had to pinch himself to believe what was happening. The role of the supporters club during this period should not be under-estimated either. Between 1957 and 1971 it had raised over £117,000, which equates to £1.2 million at today's prices. The two clubs were in almost complete accord, with Hill and Robins perhaps the only officials to fully appreciate the importance of harmony with supporters superbly led by Jack Patience.

Demolition of the 1910 stand began within hours of the Colchester game and took ten days to complete. The four centre blocks of the Sky Blue Stand started going up, and the club announced the sale of every seat in the ground – bar 250 for emergencies. Season tickets netted the club over £60,000, three times the previous season, in advance sales. 7,200 seats in all were sold and ground season tickets bumped up the final figure.

Fans awaited the **1964-65** Second Division fixture list with excitement and trepidation. Some pundits tipped City to win promotion to Division One at the first attempt. When City won their first five games, that did not look so far-fetched.

The new Sky Blue Stand was ready for the first home game – a 2-0 win over Malcolm Allison's Plymouth. In the match programme Hill listed twenty projects undertaken during the close season and each one was completed on time. Never before or since has there been such a hectic summer at the ground.

Wins at both relegated clubs – Ipswich and Bolton – took City top, and further home wins over Ipswich (5-3) and Middlesbrough (3-0) kept them there. Almost 38,000 watched a home thriller with Ipswich, in what was considered one of the finest displays of attacking football in memory. Visiting Wolves directors told Hill they had not experienced such an atmosphere since their club's famous battles with Honved and Spartak Moscow in the 1950s. Two weeks later that attendance was topped for the visit of Derby, when 38,278 paid record receipts of £5,959 to see the Rams inflict City's third defeat in a row. The opening five-win burst was followed by five defeats, whereafter the season settled into mini-bursts of wins and losses. The side was unchanged for the first seven games, but through the winter Hill made subtle changes.

The most dramatic signing was Bill Glazier's for £35,000, a world record fee for a goalkeeper and one of Hill's shrewdest purchases. Within a month England manager Alf Ramsey picked Glazier for the Under-23 team against Romania for the first such international at Highfield Road. Glazier's appearance boosted the crowd to 27,000. They witnessed a 5-0 England win with young Alan Ball taking the eye. It was soon revealed that Glazier had been given a five-year contract, supposedly the longest contract ever awarded to a British footballer. His signing was only possible because of the strong financial position the club now found itself in. Profits for the year to May 1964 were a record £11,231, and with the supporters club undertaking to defray the whole £120,000 cost of the Sky Blue Stand, money was available for good players.

For Derby's visit in September the country's first electronic scoreboard was unveiled. Donated by the *Coventry Evening Telegraph*, it stood at the top of the Spion Kop. Operated by the same small power-unit which controlled the floodlights, it displayed the names of City's opponents in bold orange letters, plus the running score and the shirt numbers of individual goalscorers. In the top-left-hand corner was a clock; in the right-hand corner was the name of City's next opponents, giving the date and time of kick-off.

In early October City entertained a local leagues XI to raise money for Coventry Schools FA, running in nine goals without reply. By the end the 2,500 crowd were more preoccupied with seeing whether City could fill all ten goalscorers' places on the new scoreboard.

City endured a miserable November and December. They sank 0-5 at Bury and on 1 December suffered the biggest home defeat in the club's history – 1-8 to First Division Leicester in the quarter-final of the League Cup. The absence of an injured George Curtis for half the match did not help matters. Two raw full-backs – Bill Tedds and John Burckitt – were badly exposed, and every time Leicester attacked they seemed to score. The result was pounced upon by the cynics who said it was evidence that the team were well short of top-flight quality.

Days later Rotherham took City to the cleaners at Highfield Road, winning 5-3 with debutant John Galley capitalising on Curtis's absence by scoring a hat-trick. In an effort to shore up the defence, Hill signed Allan Harris, brother of Chelsea hard-man Ron, spending another £35,000. The introduction of David Clements, a cheap buy from Wolves, and the return from injury of Ernie Machin sparked an upturn, although a 0-3 FA Cup defeat at Villa Park again illustrated the gulf between the top two divisions.

The team's upturn started with the Christmas visit of Preston, one of the strongest sides in the section. On a freezing night George Hudson mastered the conditions to give a virtuoso display. In the 3-0 victory he scored with a nonchalant chip, made another goal, and generally led the visitors' defence a merry dance. Two weeks later another classic saw City beat leaders Newcastle 5-4, but only after a nervous last twenty minutes as City threw away a 5-1 lead.

In late January, with City out of the Cup, Hill arranged a friendly with his old club Fulham. It was the day of Winston Churchill's funeral and a trophy commemorating the great man was donated by Derrick Robins. First Division Fulham, boasting former England captain Johnny Haynes, sneaked a 2-1 win to become the first holders of the Winston Churchill Remembrance Trophy. On a bitterly cold day a crowd of 10,881 observed a minute's silence, which was followed by the *Last Post* played by the buglers of the Warwickshire Regiment.

By Easter the season was petering out when Glazier broke his leg in a collision with Glyn Pardoe at Manchester City. His form since joining the Sky Blues had been so good that a place in the 1966 World Cup squad was predicted. He would have found it hard to displace Gordon Banks but was strongly tipped as Banks' heir apparent. The bad break ended those dreams.

The first team's inconsistency turned the spotlight on the reserves, who won promotion to Division One of the Football Combination. Crowds for the 'stiffs' averaged an improbable 4,820, with 12,132 attending the 1-0 win over QPR that virtually clinched promotion. That was a Highfield Road record for a reserve game, topping the 11,700 who had watched Arsenal in August 1936. To put the figure into perspective, there were just 10,800 at Maine Road four days later to see City's first team.

The season ended with Coventry sealing the relegation of Swansea, who had signed City's Willy Humphries and George Kirby in an effort to avoid the drop. Then, in a repeat of twelve months previously, they entertained Tottenham, who this time won 3-0 in front of 14,000. The final average home League gate was 26,621.

The **1965-66** season saw Coventry get as close to Division One as they had ever done. They finished third, a point behind Southampton, who were promoted as runners-up to Manchester City. The Sky Blues were rarely out of the top three and led the division several times, but they were chiefly undone by two away defeats over Easter.

The major surprise was the fall from grace of crowd favourite George Hudson. In August he could do nothing wrong, notching all four goals in the 4-3 pre-season friendly with First Division Nottingham Forest and scoring both in the League opener at home to Wolves – and a unique goal in the 5-1 win over Southampton. 'The Hud' had reached twelve goals by the end of October, but managed only five in the next eighteen games. He appeared listless, and after City failed to win in February Hill accepted First Division Northampton's £29,000 bid for the player. The fans were shocked to such an extent that several coachloads travelled to the County Ground to see Hudson's scoring debut against Leeds rather than travel to Goodison Park to support City in the FA Cup.

Hill justified the shock sale: 'With every player, there is a time to sell and a time to buy. I give the fans this assurance – I would never do anything against the interests of Coventry City.' It was a virtual re-run of the Terry Bly scenario, and Hill had been proved spot-on in his judgment of Bly. Considered in retrospect, despite scoring a few goals, Hudson failed to keep Northampton in the top flight and within a year was sold to Tranmere for £15,000. Other than help dump City from the FA Cup in 1968, he never again set the football world alight. His golden days were undoubtedly at Highfield Road, City got an inflated fee, and that helped towards team-strengthening that a year later was rewarded with promotion. In local youngster Bobby Gould, Hill had a ready-made replacement centre-forward who, while never the charismatic star that Hudson was, would score the goals that took City up.

In September 1965 Dietmar Bruck became the club's first ever substitute. The rule enabling the use of one substitute restricted it to injury – tactical substitutions were permitted a year later – and the City sub wore a shirt with no number (the No 12 shirt was also introduced the following season). It would take a further 22 years before two substitutes were allowed in League games. Bruck came on at half-time in the 3-3 home draw with Manchester City, after Ron Farmer fractured his cheekbone and was unable to carry on. In total City used only nine substitutes in that first season.

Off the field, the latest innovation – in October – was a club train, the 'Sky Blue Special', with the rolling stock hired from British Railways and manned by their own stewards. This came in response to British Railways suspending 'football specials' the previous season after well-published damage caused by Stoke, Manchester United and Everton yobs. City decided to undertake the commercial as well as the damage risk and run their own trains. Radio Sky Blue was piped through the carriages and Sky Blue catering and bingo kept the fans occupied. The first trip was to Preston in October and was an unqualified success with tickets priced at a competitive 24 shillings (£1.20). Sky Blues' administration manager Charles Harrold commented: 'We are confident that this move will stamp out hooliganism. After all, anybody who causes damage will be hitting at Coventry City, and not at British Railways.' The trip to Preston was a 600-seat sell-out and for the trip to Middlesbrough in December a local pop group, the Midnights, provided entertainment and dancing in a special converted carriage. In the four years of the 'special' there were no reported incidents of hooliganism.

City had already experimented with closed-circuit television when the game at Cardiff was relayed back to Highfield Road and watched by 10,295 on four giant screens on the pitch. Earlier requests seeking permission from the Football League were rejected on spurious grounds, but in September the club got approval to relay the game at Ninian Park. In view of the high costs and threats of technical difficulties, the risk was borne by Viewsport Limited, who purchased the necessary equipment on the understanding that they would take any profit but also, more importantly, shoulder any losses.

The screens, three in front of the Sky Blue Stand and a fourth in front of the main stand (for VIPs), were erected following a reserve game the previous evening. The workmen, hampered by fog, toiled all night long and a dummy-run of the projectionists had to be cancelled. More fog on match-day meant the team had to cancel their chartered plane to south Wales and go by coach, but at Highfield Road the whole experiment was at risk. The fog thankfully lifted and the crowd were treated to pre-match entertainment in the shape of interviews with players and images of the players warming up at Ninian Park. City wore red and white stripes, borrowed from Stoke City (and used in Jimmy Hill's football 'soap', *United*), to avoid confusion on the black and white transmission. Former Spurs and Northern Ireland star Danny Blanchflower gave his views at half-time and the evening ended with a late goal to clinch a 2-1 away win, sending the City fans delirious at both venues.

The pictures were clear and all agreed that the experiment was a success and the way football would go in the future. City repeated the experiment when they played at Charlton. This time the 'gate' at Coventry was higher, 11,321, while 15,000 watched the live action at the Valley. With the lighter evenings, kick-off had to be put back to 8.30. This time, however, City lost 0-2, which all but ended their thin promotion hopes, and the crowd were more subdued. Viewsport again took on the risk and said they had broken even, but Hill was not convinced: 'It is a matter of finding the right time to relay.' The following season Manchester United relayed a game from Highbury to 28,000 at Old Trafford, and Liverpool's Cup-tie at Goodison was relayed across Stanley Park to 41,000 fans at Anfield – both financially more successful than City's efforts.

For home games, the crowds poured through the turnstiles. The club's receipts record was broken again in November for the League Cup-tie with West Brom. The game was made all-ticket, with 40,000 tickets initially for sale. On the night 38,476 turned up, the second highest figure in the competition at that time, and only 1,300 below the record. The game ended 1-1 draw and earned £9,572. The Baggies, riding high in Division One, brought 8,000 travelling fans. In the replay, West Brom romped home 6-1, with Jeff Astle unstoppable.

In early December, Huddersfield – one of City's key rivals in the promotion chase – wrecked their unbeaten home record with a 3-0 win and knocked the Sky Blues off the top. The game was the first ever to see a reigning British Prime Minister: Harold Wilson was born and bred in Huddersfield and a keen Town fan.

City continued with evening friendlies in the autumn of 1965 but poor crowds made them less attractive. First Division Stoke were beaten 5-1, Second Division Manchester City – standing in at short notice when Swiss club FC Biel pulled out – lost 4-2, and French club Stade Francais were beaten 4-1 before just 3,000 spectators, which meant it was time to call a halt.

Despite staying on the fringe of the promotion race, City were not playing particularly well. This did not dissuade 15,000 fans cheering them to a 1-0 win at Molineux, or the enormous away followings which witnessed defeat at Manchester City and in the FA Cup at Everton. Average home attendances were 25,370, down by around 1,200.

By 1966 George Curtis and Mick Kearns had given ten years' service and the club agreed to a testimonial. It is unlikely that any club had ever before organised testimonials on such a grand scale as for these two loyal servants. It was set up over a two-year period with an ambitious £15,000 target. All manner of activities were staged – dinners, cricket matches and even a competition which had a house as the main prize. On the pitch the club arranged two eye-catching games. The first in May 1966 was against Northampton for the Winston Churchill Trophy. Hudson played. A crowd of 13,576 contributed £3,000 to the fund. They watched a game without tackles that ended 2-2. A year later 25,000 watched the second testimonial game, a 2-1 victory over Liverpool.

As the nation prepared for the World Cup, being held in England for the first time, Hill and Robins prepared to strengthen the City team. Despite the excellent gates and a raft of other money-making enterprises, another major source of funding was needed if City were to secure promotion to the big league. That summer a new Sky Blue Pool was launched with the aim of generating £100,000 a year. Launched as 'Rocket The Sky Blues into Europe', Robins donated £10,000 to kick-off the competition, which boasted it would offer a £1,000 weekly first prize by Christmas. The aim was recruit 250,000 members from the city and the surrounding areas.

There was plenty of transfer activity. Allan Harris returned to Chelsea for £45,000, John Sillett left for Plymouth, and John Key – a former playing colleague of Hill's – arrived from Fulham. Speculation linked City with various midfielders, including Spurs' international Alan Mullery and Preston's Howard Kendall, but the big signing was Ian Gibson, a £55,000 buy from Middlesbrough. 'Gibbo' was a ball-playing inside-forward who would quickly assume the mantle of Hudson as the fans' favourite. With Glazier fully fit following his broken leg, the scene was set for a renewed assault on the promotion summit.

In what would be the club's finest season, **1966-67**, the team started poorly, especially away, where four of the first six games were lost and goals hard to come by. The new signings might as well have not been there: Key was injured on his debut and Gibson's form was patchy. Matters came to a head after defeat at Carlisle. A dressing room slanging match saw Gibson dropped and demand a transfer. Hill's response was vague: 'We just don't seem to see eye to eye on the way he should play in the team.' Third Division Brighton then piled on the agony by winning at Highfield Road in the League Cup.

Despite good news on the financial side – the club announced record profits of £49,000 – the promotion dream was fading fast, and over the next month, with Gibson in the reserves, there were few signs of resurgence. On 19 November City lost 1-3 at Huddersfield, seven days after Crystal Palace had inflicted their first and only home defeat, leaving the Sky Blues 7th in the table. Following the Palace defeat 'Nemo' in the *CET* identified the problem as 'puny firepower': 'City really have been living on borrowed time. Most of their results this season have been based on defensive effectiveness, particularly at home.'

For the following game Gibson was recalled, Key was back after injury, and City turned on their best performance to beat Cardiff 3-2 at home. Gibson scored two and did much else besides. December was the crucial month, and the Sky Blues started with two dazzling victories in six days. Leaders Wolves were beaten 3-1 at Molineux, and on a Friday night Ipswich, who had taken over at the top, were put to the sword. City's attacking display was described by 'Nemo': 'probably their best performance in the Second Division and on a par for skill and excitement with the great victory over Sunderland in 1963.' Despite Bobby Gould's hat-trick, the goal of the night was from cheeky Gibson who chipped the ball over seven defenders to find the top of the net. The goal guaranteed himself enduring cult status with City fans.

The goals continued to flow, with home wins over Rotherham (4-2) and Portsmouth (5-1), and by the turn of the year the Sky Blues were second behind Wolves on goal-average. The Boxing Day encounter with Rotherham was soured when a City fan climbed over the terrace wall at the covered end and attacked the Millers' stand-in goalkeeper John Galley and their trainer. Police quickly dealt with the situation but the club's reputation for well-behaved supporters was tarnished.

The Sky Blues and Wolves proved themselves by far the best sides in the division and by early March it was obvious that, barring a disaster, the two Midland rivals would be dicing for the championship. Just to ensure there were no Cup distractions, City fell at the first hurdle, but only after a Highfield Road classic against First Division Newcastle. Despite being in the relegation zone, the Magpies brought 8,000 fans to Coventry and exposed some of the deficiencies in the Sky Blues' defence. Wyn Davies, a perennial thorn in George Curtis's side, scored a hat-trick in Newcastle's 4-3 win. One consolation for City was the attendance of 35,748 who paid club record receipts of £9,724.

In the League, City's unbeaten run needed close shaves and late goals to preserve it against Rotherham, Norwich and Preston. Visiting sides usually defended in depth and provided a stern physical test. One such club was Carlisle, who refused to buckle under extreme attacking pressure despite the dismissal of goalkeeper Alan Ross for pole-axing Gould with a left hook early in the second half. It needed a late Ernie Machin goal to seal the points.

In early March Jimmy Hill got another chance to test his men against top-class opponents when West Ham arrived for the Winston Churchill Memorial game. It was 3-3 at the end, and by prior agreement the match was settled by a penalty shoot-out, the first ever at the ground. Each side had ten attempts and West Ham won 9-7 against City's young reserve keeper Martin Clamp. An excellent crowd of over 18,500 watched two of West Ham's World Cup heroes, Geoff Hurst and Bobby Moore.

Two weeks later BBC's *Match of the Day* cameras came to Highfield Road for the first time. In those days the programme showed highlights of only one game. It had been running since August 1964 and had featured City at Huddersfield the previous season on BBC2. Since England's World Cup victory, the programme had moved to BBC1 and millions of armchair fans got their first view of Hill's Sky Blues. The 1-1 draw was not one of City's better performances. Bolton grabbed a late equaliser but City's goal would have won 'Goal of the Month' if such a thing had existed in those days. Ronnie Rees's jinking run from halfway was reminiscent of great wingers of the past, leaving defenders in his wake as he crossed for Gould to nudge the ball home. Kenneth Wolstenholme, the top commentator of the day, was perched on a temporary gantry high in the Sky Blue Stand. A month later the visit of Huddersfield also featured on *Match of the Day* and although the 1-0 victory virtually clinched promotion, the Sky Blues once again appeared somewhat camera-shy.

In February 1967, Highfield Road hosted an FA Cup second replay between Hull and Portsmouth. Pompey, cheered on by many of their fans in the 18,500 crowd, won 3-1 thanks to two goals from Albert McCann, an ex-City inside-forward jettisoned by Jimmy Hill in 1962. Hull's consolation was scored by Chris Chilton, a player coveted by more than one Coventry manager during his high-scoring days at Boothferry Park. In 1971 Noel Cantwell would finally spend £90,000 on the burly striker, but his best days were behind him and a back injury ended his football career after only 29 games in a Sky Blue shirt.

Easter was crucial for City, and a 1-0 win at Blackburn – one of the teams frantically trying to catch the Sky Blues – was followed by the Tuesday evening visit of Northampton. The poor Cobblers were heading for their second successive relegation. A crowd of 38,560 roared City to a 2-0 win, with goals from Ernie Machin and, inevitably Gould – his seventh in seven games. The attendance was the biggest in the League at Highfield Road since 1949.

The next home game, a 2-2 draw with Derby, witnessed obscene chanting for the first time at the ground. Referee Roy Harper was the target of jeers questioning his parentage after decisions went against City. A loudspeaker announcement asked the miscreants to desist, offering to 'refund their entrance money if they would leave the ground'.

City clinched promotion to Division One on Tuesday, 25 April when closest challengers Blackburn only drew with Bolton. Celebrations started in Coventry that night, and everybody focused on the visit of Wolves four days later. Hill described it as the Midlands Match of the Century. With both clubs assured of promotion, the title was at stake.

A week before that crunch Wolves game, City hosted a schoolboy international, in which England Under-18 Schoolboys beat Wales in front of 8,465 and won 3-0 (Lappage 2, Partridge). One England player, Alan Gowling of Stockport Grammar School, would progress to a successful professional career with Manchester United and Newcastle, and earn Under-23 and Amateur caps.

The club had already decided against the Wolves game being all-ticket, fearing that if the weather turned bad, many – knowing their entry was assured – would arrive late and cause congestion. With 10,000 Wolves fans expected, crowd packers were employed to assist in breaking the ground record of 44,930 set in 1938.

City's unbeaten run stretched back 22 games, whilst Wolves, under the management of Ronnie Allen, had gone fourteen games without defeat. As far as the title was concerned, Wolves were in the driving seat, having a two-point advantage and better goal-average.

On the day, thousands were turned away and the turnstiles closed fifteen minutes before kick-off. Hundreds gained admittance illegally and the club reckoned 53,000 actually saw the game. Many complained of being unable to get a view of the pitch and the terraces at both ends overflowed. Children were manhandled out of the seething mass and allowed to stand on the running track, so that by the time the teams came out the youngsters were four or five deep around the perimeter. Dozens more perched precariously on the base of the floodlight pylons, and at one stage 50 or so were squatting on the roof of the covered end. Despite loudspeaker warnings that the tea-bar rooves were unsafe, desperate fans paid no heed. One roof collapsed at the covered end and four people fell through, but no one was seriously injured.

The greatest day in Highfield Road's long history had arrived, and City blessed it with one of their finest displays. They shrugged off a Peter Knowles goal on 41 minutes to blast the Wolves defence in an unrelenting second half. Kicking towards the Kop end, Ernie Machin equalised and four minutes later – in scenes reminiscent of the Sunderland game four years previously – Ian Gibson put the Sky Blues ahead. After each goal youngsters spilled onto the pitch, and referee Norman Callender used the tannoy to warn that further invasions would make him abandon the game. Knowles hit a post for Wolves, but with five minutes left City broke away for Rees to score a third. The fans on the perimeter seemed to pause for a second, but none encroached in an admirable display of self-discipline. The final whistle, however, sparked a massive invasion. 'Nemo's' match report said: 'Those who were there will never forget it. Nor perhaps will they ever be able to convince those who were not of the unforgettable drama and electricity of the greatest day in Highfield Road's history.'

The official crowd was 51,452, the receipts topped £12,000, a record. £10,000 was taken on the day and 20,000 programmes sold, but many fans complained that they couldn't see because of the crush – some even claimed to have left the ground before kick-off. There were sad stories too – of two boys who got in at one o'clock, eventually jumped over the perimeter wall because they were worried about the congestion on the terraces and then being told by police – they claimed – that they had to go back on the terrace or leave the ground. They left without seeing the game. On a happier note, the police reported only four ejections, amazing when one considers the size of the crowd.

Chairman Robins promised to review all areas of the ground to determine how to control large gates in the future – promotion meant big crowds were expected to be the norm. Plans to build the west stand were well advanced and the ground would be a hive of activity during the close season. The decision to proceed with the new stand, estimated to cost £80,000, had been taken by the board in February. It would be of a cantilever design, with 3,200 seats, and built by Banbury Grandstands, a subsidiary of Derrick Robins' company Banbury Buildings. The extra seats would raise the total seating in the ground to 10,500 – one of the largest seated capacities in the League – and the terracing underneath would remain unaffected. The design would ensure an excellent view for all with each row of seats fifteen inches above the one in front. The plan was for demolition of the old covered end to commence after the final league game against Millwall on 13 May and for the new stand to be ready for the opening First Division home game in August. With extra season ticket revenue being generated, it was hoped the stand would be paid off within three years.

Highfield Road had a special night before the final League game when Liverpool came for the second Curtis/Kearns testimonial. Bill Shankly's side were at virtually full strength, with future City personalities Gordon Milne and Ian St John, but were beaten 2-1. Before kick-off Robins and Hill made an unusual lap of honour; Robins driving the kitted-out Curtis and Kearns in one of his fleet of Rolls Royces, a convertible with personalised number plates DHR2 (at one stage he owned four DHR1-4), and Hill in full hunting gear on horseback. The crowd, still euphoric after the Wolves game, could not get enough of it. Ronnie Rees scored the goal of the night, capping a 50-yard run with a bullet shot. Over 25,000 raised £6,000 for George and Mick's testimonial fund. The acerbic Shankly declined to assess the Sky Blues: 'I never discuss performances in friendlies.' Never one for over-statement, he added: 'I was impressed with the whole atmosphere here.' Not so impressed that night was Scottish international forward Ian St John, later to be City's assistant manager briefly under Noel Cantwell. He recalled: 'Within minutes of the kick-off George Curtis performed a crunching tackle on me. I woke up being carried off on a stretcher. When I tackled George about it later he said: "It's a man's game, Saint." And that for a man we were down trying to make a few bob for.'

There was still the Second Division championship to be won. Despite beating Wolves, the Sky Blues still trailed their rivals on goal-average. The following Saturday, in their penultimate games, City drew at Ipswich – to extend the unbeaten run to 24 games – while Wolves beat Norwich 4-1. On the final day, Wolves travelled to Crystal Palace, needing a point for the title, whilst City entertained Millwall. Jimmy Hill was quoted: 'The odds must be on Wolves to get a point,' whilst Derek Henderson in the *CET* stuck by his earlier prediction that Wolves would land the top prize. Both were left to eat their words following another afternoon of high drama, as City won 3-1 and Wolves crashed 1-4.

Not for the first or last time, the late kick-off at Highfield Road added to the intrigue. Just before the teams came out for the 3.15 start the crowd were told that Wolves were already trailing. George Curtis led his players out to a thundering chant of 'Champions, champions'. By half-time City led Millwall 2-0, and during the second half as Wolves' embarrassment at Selhurst Park deepened, the mood of City's fans turned from nervous nail-biting to euphoria. With fifteen minutes to play, a steward raced out of the players tunnel and raised four fingers, and a minute later the tannoy confirmed that Wolves had lost 1-4. The Sky Blues, 3-1 ahead, were champions.

Following the final whistle the players emerged in their tracksuit tops in the directors box. For the second time in two weeks Hill led the crowd and the players in an emotional rendition of the Sky Blue Song. One of the most vociferous was Bobby Gould, dressed in a lounge suit and crisp white shirt. City's top scorer had been forced to miss the last three games through injury.

No sooner had the last of the 32,000 spectators drifted away than the demolition squad (GW Hilditch, whose sign hung from the covered end that afternoon) moved in. With the aid of floodlights, that end was flattened by Monday and the building of the new stand could commence. The covered end had become the spiritual home for City's 'choir' during the 1960s. It is difficult to pinpoint when organised singing or chanting began at Highfield Road, but it had become an important part of the City scene during the 1962-63 FA Cup run, after the club launched the Sky Blue Song in December 1962. Several hundred fans would chant the songs of the day and generally bellow their approval.

City's average crowd for this momentous season was 28,269, the highest in the division, fourteenth highest in the country, and a club record. The reserves, who had a good season in the Football Combination, averaged 5,428 at home.

Celebrations continued for weeks. On the following Monday the team travelled to Nuneaton Borough for a testimonial and won 7-3. The following night the club were guests of honour at a civic reception at the Hotel Leofric, at which the Second Division trophy and medals were presented. Then the team was toasted by a Sky Blue cocktail – a mix of white rum, cointreau and blue curacao, invented by Ray Rastall, the Leofric's bartender, who had recently won the UK cocktail championship. A week later all City's first-team players had signed new contracts. Before the month was out they flew to the West Indies for a three-week 'break' in which they had to play six friendlies.

Ground developments continued apace during June and July. On 8 July, Derek Henderson reported that work on the west stand was a week ahead of schedule. He described the new stand thus: 'it rises, with its stark white concrete, over the terraces.' He detailed a new, ground-level bar on the corner of the main stand, an extension to the Vice-Presidents club, a new 50-seat press box to handle the demands of a larger press corps for the First Division, and an entrance block to the west stand from Nicholls Street. With the ticket office working at full stretch to meet the massive demand, the whole stadium fairly buzzed that summer.

All non-standing season tickets were sold within a fortnight of being on sale. This left only 1,000 unreserved seats available for each game, for visiting supporters or casual spectators. City would be assured of a good away following as the newly formed Sky Blue Travellers Club quickly sold all 500 places, designed to guarantee seats on the Sky Blue Special. The, train, which could take 600, was almost sure to be a sell-out for every away game. On 18 July the **1967-68** fixture list was published. As requested, the first two games were away from home, giving the club an extra week to put the finishing touches to the new stand.

A bombshell then exploded. Forty-eight hours before the club's first Division One game, at Burnley, Hill resigned. Rumours had been circulating for much of the summer, and behind the scenes the board had tried to persuade their in-demand young manager to stay. A huge salary of £10,000 was mentioned. Hill broke the news to Derek Henderson of the *CET* and made it clear that he would stay until the club appointed a successor, however long that took. Derrick Robins was holidaying in Venice when the story broke, and the Bridge of Sighs must have caused him an ironic smile.

It soon became clear that Hill was not going to another club but to TV, although it transpired that one reason for his decision to leave was the denial of the ten-year contract he had demanded – he felt he needed that time to build a side capable of challenging for the top prizes. He also probably wanted to try something new, and sensed that the First Division was going to be a hard struggle. Many blamed him for his apparent greed and the bad timing of his departure. In 1998, in his autobiography, Hill confirmed he had delayed his announcement in the hope of the club agreeing to his requests.

Robins returned from Venice to pay glowing tributes to Hill, adding that bad news was not necessarily disastrous: 'We have put our foot on the first rung of the ladder, and are determined to climb to the top.'

Seven thousand City fans travelled to Turf Moor to see their team end their 25-game unbeaten run with a 1-2 defeat. Three days later even more travelled to Nottingham Forest to see how City would fare against the League runners-up. After four minutes George Curtis was stretchered off with a broken leg following a clash with Frank Wignall. City's reshuffled side led three times but had to settle for 3-3 draw. Hill described it as: 'the finest performance in 5½ years.'

City's first home game in the top flight, which also opened the new west stand, was against Sheffield United. Little did the 33,000 crowd realise that the Sky Blues and the Blades would be bitter relegation rivals to the end of the season. Twice the Blades led and twice the Sky Blues bounced back, with John Key scoring the club's first home goal in Division One, a powerful header at the Kop end. Dietmar Bruck saved the point after a Glazier howler. All eyes were on Tony Knapp, a veteran centre-half signed the previous day by Hill after it became apparent that iron-man Curtis's serious break would keep him out for most of the season. Three days later Forest arrived and won 3-1 against a side already hit badly by injuries.

As the season unfurled the Sky Blues struggled to make an impact, and spent virtually the whole time in the two relegation places. The first win came in September, 2-1 against old rivals Southampton, in the full debut of red-haired seventeen-year-old Willie Carr. By mid-December City had won only once more, 4-2 over West Brom, a side they had the Indian Sign over in the early years of life in Division One.

The search for a fresh manager alighted on any number of top names. Brian Clough dillied and dallied too long, having been made what was described as an 'unbelievable offer'. He preferred instead to sign a new contract with Derby. Malcolm Allison, Manchester City's young coach, announced publicly that he had accepted the Coventry job, a mindless breach of confidence that cost him the job there and then. Finally, on 12 October, former Manchester United captain Noel Cantwell was appointed. Two days later Jimmy Hill formally handed over the managerial reigns, whereupon Coventry promptly lost 2-3 to Tottenham, for whom Jimmy Greaves scored a chipped goal out of nothing. A 0-3 home loss to Fulham plunged City to the foot of the table. Not until his tenth game did Cantwell's team taste victory, 5-1 over Burnley.

Cantwell signed veteran Maurice Setters from Stoke for £25,000 to add steel to the centre of defence, Tony Knapp having manfully but inadequately tried to plug the gap. Forwards Gerry Baker (£25,000) and Ernie Hannigan (£55,000) also arrived.

Despite the poor results the crowds poured into Highfield Road in record numbers. Football's TV exposure was in its infancy, with BBC's *Match of the Day* showing highlights of one game on Saturdays and ITV a regional game on Sundays. With so little TV coverage, there was a great mystique about the stars of the day and a need to see them 'in the flesh'. West Ham paraded their three World Cup stars – Moore, Hurst, Peters – on a Friday night to avoid a December Saturday when Christmas shopping was at its peak. On a bitterly cold evening the three luminaries wore gloves and were given 'stick' by the home fans. Hurst's response was to score in the 1-1 draw. On Boxing Day 42,000 watched the 1-1 draw with mighty Liverpool, with the Reds reduced to ten men after Ian St John's perfect left hook downed City's Brian Lewis.

Sad to say, the large crowds often failed to spur the team when they were in trouble – five years' near-invincibility at home had left many supporters blasé. They expected the Sky Blues to win every home game and a string of home losses was hard to take. In January Derek Henderson of the *CET* stoked the fires by writing: 'I have been appalled at the meagre vocal backing given the Sky Blues,' and compared the City crowd unfavourably with Nottingham Forest's. He urged City fans to get behind the team and help them to avoid the drop.

Crashing 1-4 at home to Newcastle left the Sky Blues bottom, with just sixteen points from 25 games. Cantwell had to buy, but first Bobby Gould had to be sold. Arsenal paid an inflated £90,000 for City's 'local hero', the money immediately spent on Sunderland's elegant striker Neil Martin.

On 3 February a 1-0 victory at West Brom signalled a turnaround, and home wins over Chelsea and Sheffield Wednesday followed. Punctuating these victories was an inglorious FA Cup exit at Third Division Tranmere, which in other circumstances would have been calamitous. Now it came almost as a relief, for survival in the top division excluded all other considerations. Against Chelsea, the photographers captured an unprecedented image: a City forward line comprising five Scots. Strictly it wasn't truly accurate – Gerry Baker was born in New York – but he had a broad Scots accent and it suited the editor's story. The other four were Hannigan, Martin, Gibson and Carr. That day also witnessed Highfield Road's worst football violence, when angry Chelsea fans carried on the destruction they had started in the west end after the game. Hundreds of booted skinheads wreaked havoc from Far Gosford Street to the railway station. Many glass shop-fronts were shattered. It was to be the first of many cases of football violence inside and outside the ground over the next few years.

One crisis followed another. On the morning of 6 March, Highfield Road's main stand, built in 1936, was gutted by fire, with most of the club's administration block underneath destroyed. Amongst the cinders were the club's trophy cabinet and most of the club's archives. Over 50 firemen and ten engines from Coventry and Warwickshire fought the blaze, which was spotted by a woman passing the ground at 7am. The fire quickly spread through the offices, the press box and a large section of the roof. Coventry's Chief Fire Officer, Mr A Leece, said his men found the fire particularly difficult to fight because the stand was 'like a rabbit warren with dozens of rooms and passages.'

Harry Green of Wyken was there that morning. He and a mate were passing Highfield Road and found it surrounded by fire engines. Somehow the friends got onto the pitch to view the smouldering remains of the stand:

'We watched as a fireman emerged from the smoking remains with a number of trophies. We wandered over to the perimeter wall in front of the stand and we identified two of the mangled molten silver trophies. One was the Second Division championship trophy and the other the Southern Professional Floodlight Cup.'

Both trophies were irreparable and in Harry's words 'knackered'. The following day the *Coventry Evening Telegraph* printed a photo of Bill Glazier and Mick Kearns holding the melted Second Division trophy. It was insured by the Football League but a few weeks later a search revealed an almost identical trophy in Goldsmith's Hall in London. The trophy was acquired and was presented to the new holders, Ipswich.

Takings from the reserve game the previous evening were saved in an office safe, as was £1,000 worth of medical equipment in the treatment room, but many records were lost as the majority of the offices were gutted. The boardroom, ticket office and the club shop were also damaged beyond repair, but firemen managed to save all the players' kit and boots, and the dressing rooms were untouched. It was later concluded that the fire was caused by a cigarette falling through a gap in the wooden floorboards and igniting years of accumulated rubbish underneath. The warnings highlighted in 'the fire that never was' in 1960 had been ignored and a high price was paid. Rumours abounded that it was 'an insurance job'.

The stand was patched up sufficiently to enable the match of the season, against Manchester United, to go ahead ten days later. The wing stands were undamaged and experts declared them safe. The centre section, however, required temporary scaffolding to make it usable. Director John Camkin was given the task of ensuring every season ticket holder was found a seat for the United game, and workmen worked around the clock to get the ground ready. A temporary press-box and VIP area was installed and the club placed an advertisement in the *CET* telling affected season ticket holders where they would be sitting. Camkin admitted it would be 'impossible to erect a new stand for next season'.

Within days, however, chairman Robins was talking about a replacement stand to be built that summer and be ready for the 1968-69 season. It would hold 5,500 seats and increase the seating capacity to around 14,000. Nothing, it seemed, could faze the club's benefactor and figurehead.

Manchester United flew back from a European Cup quarter-final success in Poland to face their old chum Cantwell's desperate team. The gate of 47,111, the second biggest in the club's history, witnessed a famous victory, secured by goals from Machin and new skipper Setters, another ex-United man. Once again the huge crowd necessitated the use of the running track for young fans, and they duly raced on when the first goal went in. After a tannoy warning, they controlled themselves until the final whistle when they had the freedom of the park. Two more new players, signed the previous day on transfer-deadline day, made their debuts – Ernie Hunt, another forward, from Everton for £65,000, and full-back Chris Cattlin from Huddersfield for £70,000. Cattlin had the task of marking George Best, then at the peak of his career, and the lanky young defender did well to contain Best and disappoint those who had come to feast on his talent. With the press room destroyed, Matt Busby and Noel Cantwell held the post-match press conference in a nearby garden shed.

As the season neared its climax, City won home games against two of their relegation rivals, Wolves and Stoke, but slipped up at home to Leeds and Leicester. In the final weeks the Sky Blues found themselves locked in their fight with Fulham and Sheffield United, any two of whom would be doomed. Fulham were the first to perish. With two games left, City led the Blades by one point. Both of City's games were away, at West Ham and Southampton. They drew the first 0-0, but Sheffield won at Burnley, leaving the two clubs tied on points going into the final game. On a nervy occasion at the Dell, 7,000 City fans roared their team to another backs-to-the-wall goalless draw. When the final whistle blew, ecstatic supporters invaded the pitch, knowing that Chelsea had won at Bramall Lane to send the Blades into Division Two.

In their way, City's performances during 1967-68 were as heroic as any in the ensuing decades and it is a testament to the spirit of players and supporters alike that the average home gate of 34,705 has never been bettered. That figure was the tenth highest in the country, better than 'big' clubs such as Arsenal, Sunderland and Sheffield Wednesday, and almost 15,000 higher than the average at Villa Park.

City's youth policy was beginning to prosper and the youth team reached two Cup finals that season. They lost to Burnley in a two-legged FA Youth Cup final. A crowd of 14,836 saw City win the first leg 2-1 at Highfield Road, but Burnley snatched the Cup with a 2-0 second leg victory against a Sky Blues team without star man Willie Carr who was needed for the first team's relegation fight, and who lost goalkeeper Dickie Dighton early on with concussion. Consolation came with a 4-1 aggregate victory over Arsenal in the Southern Junior Floodlight Cup.

One abiding memory from that era is of Wal's Catering. Frank Wood recalls 'a chap with a massive tea urn on his back wandering the empty terraces or on the running track with his cry of "Any more for tea".'

Work commenced on the demolition of the old stand before the end of April. Once again Robins' company, Banbury Grandstands, were the contractors and work progressed at an astonishing rate, which of course was essential if the stand was to be ready for the new season. The deadline was the third Saturday in August, and that relied on the club playing their first two games away from home. In **1968-69**, for the first time, the Football League's fixtures were compiled by a computer and there must have been a glitch. City's officials requested two away games but when the fixture list was published at the end of May, City were down to play Chelsea at home on 10 August and receive Tottenham three days later. Frantic phone calls were needed to get the two London clubs to postpone the games to midweek in September, leaving the Sky Blues to start the season with two away games. The first home game, against West Ham, would take place on 24 August, when the new stand would, it was hoped, be complete.

In early August it was reported that the stand was ahead of schedule and would be in operation on 24 August but not fully functional until Christmas. Robins declared the view from the stand to be 'the finest from any stand in the country'. The final cost would be £150,000. The club had exceeded the previous season's record season ticket sales of £124,000 (10,500 seats) and expected the final figure to be around £130,000, a figure believed to be the highest in the country, although some top clubs limited their season ticket sales. The new stand would give the ground a capacity of 52,000.

The new stand had the same lightweight, metal-vaulted, wave-like roof as the Sky Blue stand opposite, and had a clean, uncluttered look. Unlike the Sky Blue stand, it had no pillars to obstruct the view. In the days before executive boxes, the area in front of the stand could accommodate a few hundred standing supporters either side of the players tunnel. The team dugouts were unusual, little huts resembling bird-watching hides, perched above the tunnel. The facings in the stand were dark, polished wood. Inside the stand could be found offices, modern dressing rooms, and a top-quality restaurant. The Grandstand Restaurant was used by the Vice-Presidents Club on match-days but was open to the public for weekday lunches. It accommodated 80 diners and could be hired for banqueting and wedding receptions. In addition there were two cocktail bars, two 'more usual' bars, a snug bar and four tea bars. On the 'street side' of the stand were the Sky Blue Shop, a Sky Blue Buttery, for snacks, the ticket office and the club's main reception. Neil Solman, a former project manager with Garlicks, became the first stadium manager in July 1968.

This, the third new stand in four years, made Highfield Road arguably the most modern stadium in the land. Visitors to the first two reserve games got a glimpse of the new main stand before the official opening. The reserves had switched from the Football Combination to the Central League for the 1968-69 season and the first two home games attracted good crowds. Over 7,000 saw the visit of Sheffield Wednesday, and 10,302 were present four nights later to see the stiffs draw 1-1 with Manchester United, but the new grandstand was not in use.

The first team opened with two away defeats, then lost the third game, at home to West Ham, leaving them at the foot of the table. Ian Gibson, the fans' hero, was omitted from the opening game and caused a stir by suggesting it might be in everyone's interests if he moved on. But Gibson returned with a bang for the visit of West Brom, being the architect of a 4-2 victory. Cantwell afterwards raved about Gibson's display, declaring it to be 'as good an inside-forward performance as I have ever seen. No club in the country would want to sell a man playing like this.' Gibson helped forge good results against Burnley, Newcastle and Portsmouth, scoring in each match.

The two rearranged midweek games turned sour on the Sky Blues. Against Chelsea over 36,000 braved a deluge to see City lose 0-1 after giving what Derek Henderson in the *CET* described as 'the best display of football I have seen City give'. A week later, 40,000 packed in to witness a virtual replica: this time it was Spurs who snatched an unlikely win. Unmerited defeats have a way of draining the spirits, and in Coventry's case they sparked a ten-match winless run. The signing of Tony Hateley, the only signing Cantwell was allowed, couldn't avert a miserable autumn. The new season looked a carbon copy of the last.

It was a cold winter – not as bad as 1963 – but it denied City a home League game for ten weeks. By the end of February 1969 City had earned a miserly fourteen points from 25 games and had not picked up two home points since September. Yet to general astonishment they again staged a dramatic recovery, remaining unbeaten in their last nine home games. These included another famous win over Manchester United, watched by a 45,000 crowd.

The most significant result, however, was the 1-0 home victory over Leicester on 1 April. In the final reckoning City finished two points ahead of the Foxes, and that was the difference between heaven and hell. The result bucked history, which showed Coventry as having vanquished their opponents only twice at home in the League since 1945, and never since 1950. The result hinged on a moment seven minutes from time. Leicester substitute Brian Greenhalgh raced into the penalty box and in the act of shooting had his legs whipped away by George Curtis. It was an obvious penalty and the referee blew, then noticed a lineman's flag raised for offside. After a brief confab between them, Coventry restarted play with a free-kick. Leicester were further aggrieved when Mick Coop crossed to the far post. Peter Shilton, for once, was caught in two minds whether to come or to stay and did neither. Martin hurled himself forward to volley the only goal. Its worth to Coventry was immeasurable.

In a further echo of 1967-68, the season concluded with three battling draws, the last – 0-0 with Liverpool – being contested in an atmosphere the like of which Highfield Road has rarely seen. At half-time Radio Sky Blue DJ Joe Stainer came on the air: 'I want you all to cheer the lads on so loud that they can hear you over in Leicester.' All around the ground the fans responded with almost continuous chanting. Even the Liverpool fans joined in, as their team had no chance of winning the League. Derek Henderson in the *CET* was full of praise: 'Never in all my years of reporting events at Highfield Road have I heard a City crowd so behind its team in such volume as it was last night. The spontaneous sympathy for City's cause was reflected in every throbbing shout of "Coventry, Coventry" as Liverpool had to fight every inch of the way to keep a point.' Fans were now getting used to roaring on their team in backs-to-the-wall situations. The game's flashpoint came when Maurice Setters and Liverpool's young striker Alun Evans exchanged a flurry of punches and were ordered off by referee Vince James. In so doing, Setters became the first City player dismissed on the ground since Billy Myerscough almost nine years previously.

In those days there was no rule obliging all teams to play their final game concurrently – which has put a thankful stop to tacit match-fixing – and City had to endure a tortuous wait as Leicester played out five outstanding fixtures, a product of the inclement weather and a protracted FA Cup run, which carried Leicester to Wembley. With City's programme complete, all eyes turned to Leicester. First, they suffered the colossal disappointment of losing the Cup final to Manchester City, after which they had to pick themselves up to cram five games into two weeks. Their target to overhaul the Sky Blues was seven points. Home wins over Spurs and Sunderland harvested four, but Leicester lost narrowly at Ipswich, then drew at home to Everton, leaving them having to win at Manchester United – of all places – to ensure survival. In view of Noel Cantwell's Old Trafford connections, rumours of dirty deeds were rife. With three minutes gone Leicester were in front. They hit the woodwork twice, too, but United had reasons of their own to put on a show. It was Matt Busby's final game in charge, and his boys eventually triumphed 3-2. Leicester were down.

That 1968-69 season saw a sad increase in hooliganism in general and at Highfield Road. One letter to the programme summarised the situation: 'when other rival supporters were wrecking trains and football fans were being vilified for their atrocious behaviour we found that City fans were welcomed everywhere. They were held up as a splendid example and praised by the press and on TV … The young man who asked his group to spell out the name COVENTRY was always answered and we learned to recognise his voice and to admire his enthusiasm. Now I regret to say that though the caller and his group are still with us and still urge the players on, they have allowed 'another element' to join them and to mar the splendid example they used to set.' (The writer is referring to the legendary Reg, who under the old covered end and later the west end, was hoisted onto the shoulders of others to lead the fans in their chants. He would shout to the massed ranks: 'Gi' me a C' and the crowd would respond with a C, 'Gi' me an O' and again the choir would roar back O.

Having gone through all eight letters he would then yell: 'What have we got?' and the fans would reply 'Coventry'.)

'Another element' referred to a group, who whilst ardent supporters, wanted to fight opposing supporters, although in many cases this was a retaliatory action to the visiting fans 'invading' the west end terrace. City's protective attitude to 'their end' caused numerous pitched battles in the early years in the First Division, a situation exacerbated by the lack of segregation. Away fans could pay at the west end turnstiles and enter what at times resembled a war zone. In the first two seasons the London clubs, especially Chelsea, Arsenal and Tottenham, gave a pasting to the naïve home fans, both inside and outside the ground, and there was serious fighting at home games with Wolves and Nottingham Forest.

Those fans who were teenagers in the 60s recall other war-cries emanating from the west end. Pete Lea recalls Reg leading 'Zigger Zagger, Zigger Zagger, Oy Oy Oy', a popular rallying call at many grounds and the basis of a hit play by Peter Terson. A more tuneful chant was sung to the 1950s hit tune, 'You, Me & Us'. The choir sang: 'Aye, Aye, Aye, Aye, Glazier's better than Yashin, and Bobby Gould's better than Eusebio and Wolves [or whoever City were playing] are in for a thrashing.'

During George Hudson's time the fans used to sing – to the chorus of the Christmas carol *The First Noel* – 'Hudson, Hudson, Hudson, Hudson, born is the king of Coventry'. The arrival of Noel Cantwell enabled to fans to resurrect this chant and use almost the original words. Other than the Sky Blue Song, most of the terrace songs were copied and adapted from the chants of rival supporters. Like most choirs, City fans could do the Liverpool anthem *You'll Never Walk Alone* and a passable impression of the London clubs' *Knees Up Mother Brown*, whilst the 1964 Jim Reeves hit record *Distant Drums* got the terrace treatment with: 'I hear the sound of distant bums, over there, over there.'

Despite the early poor home form, attendances held up well and only once fell below 25,000 – against Southampton. The final average, boosted by the final four large gates, was 33,223, easily the top Midland crowd. City's away following was lower, however, sometimes just a few hundred, and in November the club had to cancel the Sky Blue Special train to Liverpool because of insufficient demand. For the second year running, the Sky Blues programme was voted best in the country, deserved recognition for Ian Willars, the club's Public Relations Officer, who edited the ground-breaking programme.

There were more honours in April when City staged not one international but two. England's Schoolboys beat Holland's 5-2, with goals from Chris Guthrie (2), Terry Spinner (2) and Ronnie Goodlass in front of

6,000 spectators. It was the first ever schools international between the countries. Eleven days later it was the turn of the Under-23s, who beat Portugal's 4-0 in front of a disappointing 13,600 crowd. England's goals came from Allan Clarke (2), John Sissons and 'Pop' Robson. No City players took part, although Chris Cattlin had been called up earlier in the season, but future full-back Wilf Smith – then of Sheffield Wednesday – played. The game was originally scheduled for Filbert Street, but the poor state of its pitch necessitated a switch. At the post-match banquet, England manager Alf Ramsey praised City's Ryton training facilities and FA officials noted that City's hospitality 'exceeded anything he had known before at an international match'. Derrick Robins asked about the chances of the ground staging a full international and was jocularly told: 'You'll have to work hard for that.'

The season ended with a 1-1 draw with Brian Clough's Second Division champions Derby in a testimonial for Brian Hill. A crowd of 10,190 benefited Hill to the tune of £2,600.

In the 1969 close-season work was completed on the offices and the other facilities, like a new buttery bar and club shop under the new main stand. Remedial work was undertaken on the pitch after the severe winter had left it a virtual mudheap for the last two months. The club also pioneered executive facilities by offering access to a plush 50-seat lounge on a match-by-match basis at 25 guineas (£26.25) with a block of adjacent main stand seats.

Not surprisingly, City were installed as bookmakers' favourites for the drop in **1969-70**. This was a situation supporters subsequently became accustomed to, and even – perversely – relished, for there are few greater pleasures in life than thumbing your noses at those who are invariably proved wrong.

It was no surprise that the club announced record profits of £119,000 for the year to 31 May 1969. £135,000 of the turnover came from the season ticket sales and a further £57,000 from the highly successful Sky Blue Pool. The accounts also revealed that the new main stand had cost just under £300,000, whilst a cheque for £177,000 was received from the insurers following the destruction of the old stand. At the AGM in November, Robins outlined the next stage in the ground's development. There would be a double-decker stand at the Swan Lane end with 10,000 seats in the top tier and standing room underneath, and a club room underneath the stand. They would prove to be the first of Robins' ground plans not to come to fruition.

It soon became apparent that the seasons of struggle were over – at least for now. For many supporters 8 October 1969 announced the arrival of City as a *bone fide* member of the top flight. That was the day City visited Brian Clough's all-conquering Derby at the Baseball Ground. Unbeaten in 25 home games, Derby had conceded only five goals in thirteen games since their promotion, but City won 3-1. It was the Sky Blues' fourth away win of the season. Clough acknowledged City as 'brilliant'. Two months earlier Derby's visit to Highfield Road had attracted 41,036, a massive crowd but disappointing for the club who had expected 50,000. Over 37,000 had seen Willie Carr – playing as emergency striker – score a dramatic hat-trick to bury West Brom, and 38,000 were there two weeks later to see Wolves beaten 1-0.

Hooliganism raised its ugly head in October when an eighteen-year-old West Ham fan, Barry Hedges, was hospitalised with a blood clot on the brain after being attacked by Coventry fans outside the city's fire station after the 2-2 draw. Ugly scenes were the norm at home games and the police were struggling to contain it. During the visit of Manchester United in November, the Red hordes took over the city and the west end with barely a sky blue scarf to be scene. On the pitch, United gave a good account of themselves and inspired by Best won 2-1. Reporting on the game, Derek Henderson in the *CET* said: 'there were occasions in the second half when 40,000 City followers watched in near-silence. All that could be heard was the shouting of the players on the field, and the taunting cries of United fans.' He criticised some City fans for 'always wanting an excuse to give the side the support it needs'.

The healthy financial position allowed Cantwell to make two shrewd buys in November 1969. Striker John O'Rourke joined from Ipswich for £80,000 and central defender Roy Barry from Dunfermline for half as much. Barry was a player whose historical significance is disproportionate to the number of games he played. He made only fourteen appearances in 1969-70 yet, as that rarity, a creative central defender, he became the fulcrum of the side and gave supporters the sight of a true great.

Barry's arrival launched a run of eight wins and a draw in ten games, at the end of which City stood 4th. Wins at Palace, Hillsborough and Upton Park established City – briefly – as a member of the First Division elite, but the finest result was a 0-0 draw at Goodison, where the champions-elect, boasting the much-vaunted Ball-Kendall-Harvey midfield, had hitherto proved invincible. In March, Barry broke his leg during the visit of Sheffield Wednesday, but by then City were in unchartered waters. They entered the final straight needing three points from three away games, not for survival, but for a place in Europe.

Barry's arrival marked the end of George Curtis's 534-game City career. In December he joined Villa for £30,000. Other experienced men from the Hill era were also nearing the end, and by the end of the season Brian Hill, Dietmar Bruck and Maurice Setters had moved to other clubs. The new breed coming through was led by Willie Carr and Jeff Blockley. Others like Dennis Mortimer and Bobby Parker were also given their chance.

Another strong youth team emerged, coached by former player Ron Farmer. They reached the FA Youth Cup final, where they faced Spurs over two legs. The sides – with Mortimer and Spurs' Steve Perryman and Graeme Souness outstanding – were so closely matched that the tie went to four games. In the second leg, at Highfield Road, 9,968 watched Spurs' keeper Barry Daines keep the Londoners in the game. After City won the toss of a coin, the third game attracted 14,926 to see a 2-2 draw. Souness, sent off in game three, scored the only goal in game four to lift the trophy for Spurs.

It was City's away form – ten wins on their travels – that was the key factor in their final position of 6th, a massive achievement in light of the two previous seasons of struggle. The home form frustrated many fans who didn't travel – City won only nine and lost six games, and the average attendance slipped by 1,200 to average 32,043. Robins believed some fans stayed away 'because we are not in a survival battle' and reckoned a good Cup run would excite fans and boost crowds.

Another representative game came to Highfield Road in March, when 26,000 watched the Football League play the Scottish League. Until the early 1960s these games were an opportunity for in-form or sometimes long-serving players to be rewarded, and occasionally non-English players would be selected.

On Alf Ramsey's accession to the England manager's role in 1963, however, he had insisted on using inter-league games to field England hopefuls in a competitive environment. With the World Cup looming in Mexico in June, his original squad of fourteen for the Scotland game included key players, including Martin Peters, Keith Newton, and Emlyn Hughes. There were also places for fringe players hoping to be on the plane to Mexico – Jeff Astle, Peter Osgood, and goalkeepers Jim Montgomery and Alex Stepney.

Derrick Robins appeared to fire a broadside at Ramsey for not selecting Bill Glazier, but later retracted his comments. As it turned out, the squad was racked by withdrawals. Glazier got a belated call-up and sat on the bench alongside Chris Cattlin, which probably helped to increase the gate.

Glazier saw 45 minutes' action, had little to do, but ended up conceding two soft goals. The star of the Football League's 3-2 win was Burnley midfielder Ralph Coates, who staked his World Cup claim by creating two goals for Astle. Astle made Ramsey's final 22 for Mexico but Coates did not and never became an England regular. In the Scottish team were the Rangers and Scotland captain John Greig and teammate Willie Johnston, who would become notorious at the 1978 World Cup, expelled for drug-taking.

A week before Christmas, City hosted the third replay of an FA Cup second round tie between Brighton and Walsall, which Walsall won 2-1. In April, Highfield Road was on stand-by for an FA Cup final replay. The finalists, Chelsea and Leeds, had drawn at Wembley 2-2 with the replay scheduled for Old Trafford. The Football Association decided that in the event of a second draw, then a second replay would come to Coventry. A 50,000 all-ticket crowd was planned, and it is believed tickets were printed. As it turned out, David Webb's extra-time goal gave Chelsea a 2-1 victory and the plans were scrapped.

Three months earlier, City's third round FA Cup-tie with Liverpool was made a 48,000 all-ticket affair. Secretary Eddie Plumley explained that since the ground record of 51,000 three years previously there had been substantial development, much of which had increased the seating capacity but some had eaten into the terracing. He believed the capacity to be around 56,000 but: 'by setting a limit of 48,000 we have arrived at a figure which should satisfy the police, and allow everyone to see the tie in comfort. It will also give us a valuable guide as to how many the ground can hold.' Liverpool, who initially had taken their 12,000 allocation, then returned 4,000. City, who had sold 36,000 tickets, expected a 40,000 crowd. On the eve of the tie, snow forced a postponement. The attendance the following Wednesday on a cold January night was only 33,000 – with many Merseyside fans not making the trip. City's increased capacity was not tested, nor would it ever be.

With the season ending early to help Ramsey's World Cup preparations, the bad weather in January and February was unwelcome. City suffered several postponements, although one match that did go ahead was Chelsea.

Noel Cantwell was presented with the Manager of the Month award before kick-off, whereupon Chelsea won 3-0. They were arguably the best side in the land at the time and in eighteen-year-old Alan Hudson had the find of the season. He took his goal, the third: 'with the aplomb of a man of many more years experience.'

In May, the club's place in the European Fairs Cup was confirmed by virtue of their 6th-place finish, and the club could start planning their European adventure.

It had been a long, hard road, but after three seasons the Sky Blues had proved that the optimists knew best. Jimmy Hill's proud vision looked like materialising. Chairman Derrick Robins pronounced with justified pride: 'we can now look forward to a new era.'

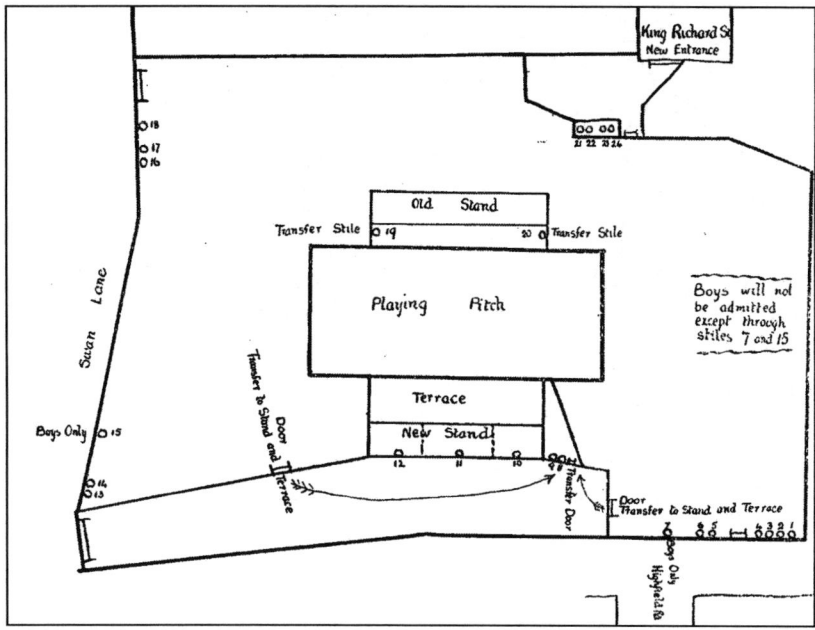

A plan of the ground, reproduced from the club handbook of 1919. The Thackhall Street side of the ground would remain virtually unchanged until 1963

A motorcycle football match between Coventry and Wolverhampton in May 1929

A team photo from the 1912-13 season. Captain Eli Bradley has the ball at his feet, and is flanked by Chairman David Cooke and Secretary Robert Wallace

Opposing supporters in the Spion Kop away area in the 1970s

Work being carried out on the Spion Kop in the summer of 1936 to convert the old shale bank to concrete terracing

David Speedie, one of City's cult heroes of the late 1980s, takes on an Aston Villa defender in November 1988. This was City's first win over Villa since 1937

Danny Thomas, one of the finest products of the club's youth system, demonstrates his athleticism. He is wearing the controversial Talbot kit of 1981-82

A training session from Highfield Road in the 1950s.
Trainer Alf Wood keeps a watchful eye on stretching exercises

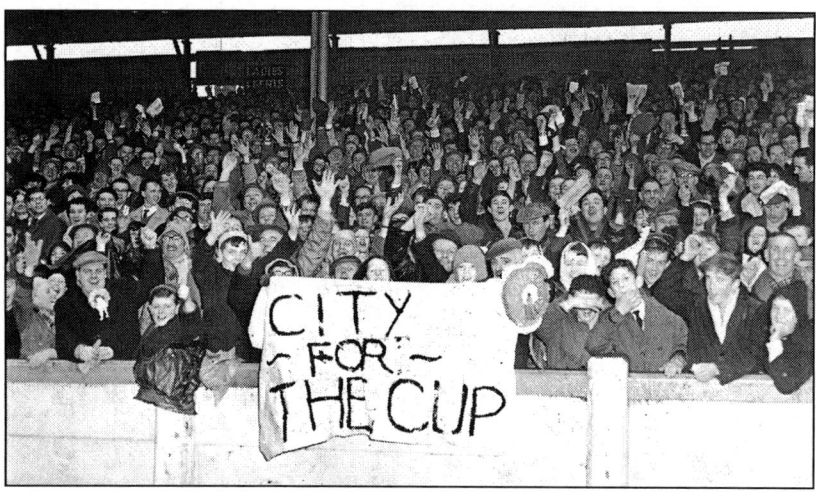

A packed covered end during the 1963 FA Cup run

29 April 1967. Fans get a better view of the Wolves game by climbing up the floodlight pylon

A 1948 programme from the biggest boxing event held at Highfield Road

Highfield Road fans watch the closed-circuit television pictures of City's game at Cardiff in 1966

Dick, Kerr's Ladies XI. A picture taken around the time they played
in front of 25,000 at Highfield Road

23 November 1974. Alan Green shoots for goal against Arsenal in the 3-0 home win

29 April 1967 v Wolves. Ian Gibson has shredded the Wolves defence and scored City's second goal, prompting a pitch invasion by the young fans massed behind the goal

October 1950. A scene from the memorable 6-1 victory over League leaders Blackburn

A pre-season photo from 1937 as Walter Metcalf, Bill Morgan, Clarrie Bourton and
Billy McDonald share a joke on the pitch

9 February 1952. City and West Ham players observe a minute's silence
for the death of King George VI who had died three days earlier

December 1964. The legendary George Hudson scores City's first goal in a shock 3-5 home defeat by Rotherham.

19 October 1968. Big signing Tony Hateley scores his first League goal for the Sky Blues in his sixth game, a 1-1 draw with League champions Manchester City

April 1972. Willie Carr and Chris Cattlin (right) combine to thwart Manchester United's George Best, in his final appearance at Highfield Road. United won 3-2

Cyrille Regis, one of the FA Cup-winning team, takes on Everton's Kevin Sheedy in the opening game of the 1988-89 season at Highfield Road

A partially completed West Stand pictured in the summer of 1967.
The new stand took only twelve weeks from start to finish
and was ready for the City's first home game in the First Division

Tommy Hutchison, regularly voted the fans' favourite player of the modern era,
celebrates his 250th game for the club

November 1958. Weight-training under the Main Stand.
Messrs Harvey, Hill, Kirk, Nicholas, Curtis and Sanders

Happy fans on an early Sky Blue special train in the mid-1960s

13 May 1967. Ernie Machin (hidden) scores City's third goal in the 3-1 win over Millwall. It confirms City as Second Division champions

August 1966. The Sky Blues warm up for the new season with a 1-1 draw against Bulgarian side Varna. Bill Glazier collects a cross

August 1937. Coventry City show off their new kit for the pre-season photo call

The players pose before boarding the coach behind the old Main Stand.
They are off to Sheffield Wednesday in February 1949

The team parade through the streets of Coventry in an open-top bus to celebrate their
Third Division championship in 1964

30 March 1963. City's FA Cup run ends in a 1-3 home defeat by Manchester United.
Denis Law (10) turns to celebrate Albert Quixall's goal which made it 1-3

January 1966. On a snow-bound pitch City thrash Plymouth 5-1. Goalkeeper Leiper can
do nothing to stop a sliced shot from one of his defenders going into the net.
Ray Pointer follows up just in case

A 1930s photograph of a Highfield Road training session

August 1994. A short-lived experiment to introduce a Continental-style fans' flag

August 1966. Chairman Derrick Robins pulls the first pint at the Sky Blue pub in Coundon,
watched by Dietmar Bruck, John Tudor, George Curtis, Bobby Gould,
Ray Pointer, Ron Farmer and manager Jimmy Hill

29 April 1967 v Wolves. The ball hits the net for Gibson's goal
and the young fans cannot contain themselves

Christmas 1966 and the Sky Blue players sign autographs for the young fans
at the annual 'Pop 'n Crisps' session

The players' lounge under the Main Stand in the late 1930s

May 1977 v Bristol City. Tommy Hutchison puts the Sky Blues ahead.
The game ended 2-2 in controversial circumstances and both sides avoided relegation

2 May 1936. Amazing crowd scenes as City beat Torquay 2-1
to clinch the Third Division (South) championship.
Ecstatic supporters crowd around the 1910 stand to cheer their heroes

29 April 1967 v Wolves. The referee clears the young supporters from
the pitch perimeter before allowing the game to start

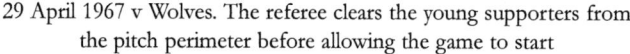

The team line-up for a pre-season photograph at Highfield Road in 1956.
A young George Curtis is fourth from the left in the front row

A photo of the first refreshment bar at the ground, taken around 1906. It was operated
by John Tipping, landlord of the Vauxhall Tavern, and is believed to have been situated
on the south-west corner. The gentleman on the left is believed to be Tipping

17 May 1987. The successful FA Cup-winning team parade the trophy on an open-top
bus through the streets of Coventry, cheered on by an estimated 250,000

An aerial view of Highfield Road in the late 1990s

25 April 1964 v Colchester. The fans salute their heroes following a 1-0 win which clinched the Third Division championship. Note the wing section of the partially built Sky Blue stand

May 1993. The demolition of the Spion Kop is under way, preparing the way for the new East Stand

6 March 1968. The Main Stand burns as firemen vainly try to save some of the structure

Police monitor young fans entering the ground at the Thackhall Street terraces in the early 1970s

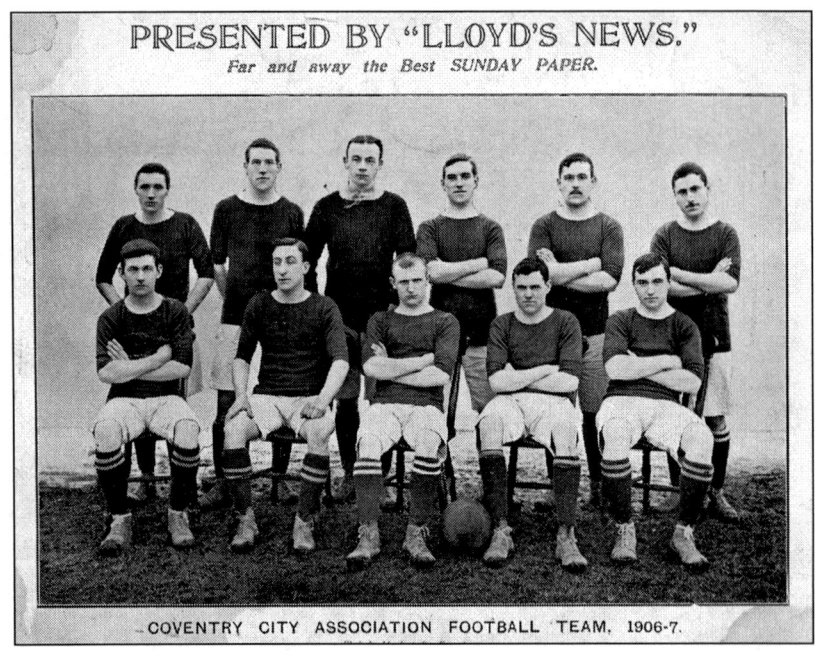

A team photo five away by *Lloyd's News* in 1906

Highfield Road was of the country's top grounds in the late 1970s.
This photo was taken before the ground became all-seater in 1981

The uninterrupted view from the Crows Nest on the Spion Kop.
This photo was taken soon after the Main Stand was rebuilt in 1968

A team picture from 1908-09, the club's first season in the Southern League

City's first post-war manager, Dick Bayliss, gives a pep-talk to George Mason, Charlie Elliott, Harry Barratt, and Emilio Aldecoa

Highfield Road gets a new drainage system in the early 1960s

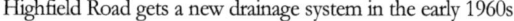

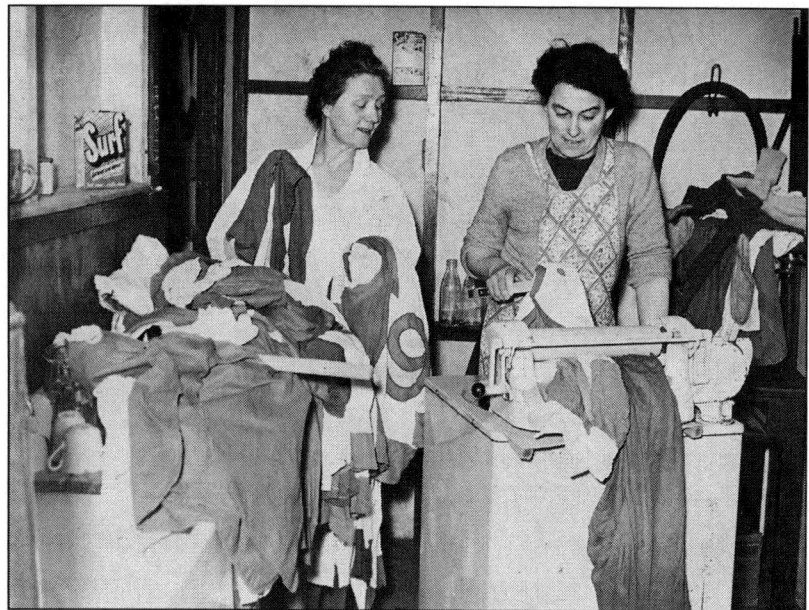

It's wash day and the two Mrs Bradshaws put the kit through the mangle

13 May 1967. Manager Jimmy Hill leads the fans in a rendition of The Sky Blue Song following City's 3-1 win over Millwall which sealed the Second Division championship

Mick Kean nets a penalty in the 1-0 victory over Bristol City in September 1966

A scene from a reserve game against West Ham in 1937.
The photo was taken before the Crows Nest was built on the Spion Kop

In the bath at Highfield Road after a training session, around 1956.
The wooden sandals lining the bath were introduced by manager Jesse Carver

April 1987. The Cup final squad record their song 'Go for It'

March 1968. The first electronic scoreboard at Highfield Road records a 3-0 victory
with a hat-trick for No 9, Neil Martin

13 May 1967 v Millwall. John Key scores the first goal in City's 3-1 victory

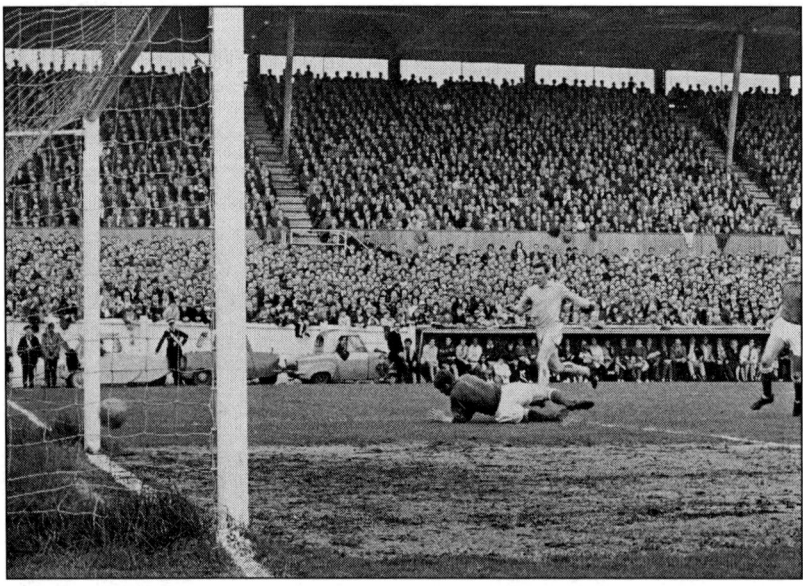

CHAPTER EIGHT

The 1970s

As Coventry City fans awaited the European Fairs Cup draw in the summer of 1970, chairman Robins announced more plans for Highfield Road. The *CET* reported that planning for the Swan Lane end (the Spion Kop) was at 'an advanced' stage. Talks had been held with Coventry Council and architects regarding a double-decker stand incorporating a sports complex. No firm dates had been mentioned, but in the club's handbook Robins wrote: 'We are going to become the Real Madrid of England. In five or six years we shall have without doubt the finest and most revolutionary stadium in this country both for spectator facilities and social amenities.' He added: 'within three years it is proposed to build an eight to ten thousand seater double-decker stand with standing room for 18,000 beneath it.'

The plan was for the new stand to adjoin the existing main and Sky Blue stands, and although not specifically mentioned by Robins, presumably ultimately to the west stand to create a bowl. The sports centre facilities would include indoor tennis courts, five-a-side soccer hall, squash courts and sauna baths, with local clubs and schools able to use them. On the first floor would be a club-room for supporters with a capacity of 2,000, with bars, lounges and a restaurant – open every night of the week. A new floodlighting system would be installed and, when completed, the stadium's capacity would be 60,000 – with more than one third seated.

These plans were the most ambitious to date and would require more funding (around £1 million was mooted) than for the three stands already built over seven years. The supporters club had limited fund-raising capability and the Sky Blue Pool, whilst successful, was never going to generate that kind of money. Nor were the plans universally approved. Director John Camkin resigned from the board over 'a matter of club policy' in August 1970. A key player in the Sky Blue Revolution, his departure signalled that all was not well internally – he believed the club needed to invest in players and hold fire on everything else.

Ironically, shortly after Camkin's departure City paid a club record fee of £100,000 for Sheffield Wednesday's Wilf Smith, fighting off a strong challenge from Chelsea for the England Under-23 full-back. In the club's annual report published in October, the chairman stressed the need for finances to be watched 'most carefully' before 'embarking on further capital expenditure'. He stressed the need for 'a period of consolidation'.

The Swan Lane plans were not raised again and it looked like common-sense had prevailed.

Despite the lure of European competition, there were early signs that the great tide of support was beginning to ebb – this probably influenced Robins' decision to hedge on his ground plans. Of the first six home games in **1970-71**, only Wolves attracted over 30,000, and that was 7,000 down on the previous season. When Bulgarian side Trakia Plovdiv arrived for the very first European game, only 20,000 bothered to watch and Highfield Road's European baptism was unexpectedly tepid. Admittedly City had the tie in the bag by winning the first leg 4-1, but there were other factors – not least lack of goals and lack of quality in the team. Mind you, crowds were down everywhere as the 1966 World Cup glow wore off, but City's retreat was bigger than most. Derek Henderson in the *CET* felt City's attendances were going through 're-alignment' but sensed that cup success would cause them to surge again.

The second round pitted City against Bayern Munich, whose stars – Beckenbauer, Maier and Muller – were the core of the West German side which beat England in Mexico. Bayern were poised to become one of the top European sides of the 1970s. Minus the injured Glazier in goal (he was replaced by Eric McManus) City were thrashed 1-6 on a boggy pitch in Bavaria, so that the home leg, originally a likely 50,000 all-ticket extrav-aganza, was watched by just half that number. The crowd, who roared the team on as though it wasn't a lost cause, saw the Sky Blues regain some of their lost pride with a 2-1 victory. For 30 minutes they pum-melled the Germans. Dave Clements had an inspired game, making goals for Neil Martin and John O'Rourke.

League form was patchy, but in October the *Match of the Day* cameras recorded City's 3-1 home win over champions Everton. The highlight was an extraordinary free-kick goal by Ernie Hunt. Practised on the train-ing ground at Ryton and attempted at Blackpool in a pre-season friendly, Willie Carr stood over the ball at the west end. With Hunt lurking, Carr flicked the ball up between his heels and Hunt volleyed the dropping ball over Everton's bemused wall and past Andy Rankin in goal. The 'donkey-kick', as it became known, remains one of the most remarkable goals ever seen at Highfield Road, perfect TV, with the images repeated for years as part of the programme's opening credits.

In the League Cup, City had a faint whiff of Wembley after home wins over West Ham and Derby, but were sunk on a wet night at White Hart Lane by a hat-trick from the striker of the season, Martin Chivers. Any thoughts of FA Cup glory were rudely quashed on a Monday after-noon at Third Division Rochdale. After a postponement the previous

Saturday, when Cantwell, in a rare display of assertiveness, refused to play under Rochdale's candle-powered floodlights, City were humbled 1-2 in a game which ranks as one of their worst humiliations.

Defeat at Rochdale was something of a watershed. Before the season was over, Neil Martin had left for Nottingham Forest and other senior players were under threat from youngsters Brian Alderson, Billy Rafferty, Bobby Parker and the increasingly impressive Dennis Mortimer. The final tally of 37 goals was the lowest for over 50 years. The team failed to score on nineteen occasions.

The unattractive fayre had its impact on crowds, and although 40,000 welcomed Leeds on a Friday night in February, the slide continued. For the penultimate game, against Burnley, there were only 18,000 present. The average fell by 6,000 to 26,039 – below Midland rivals Wolves and Aston Villa, and the lowest for five seasons. Looking back, it is therefore something of a relief to find the Sky Blues finished a comfortable 10th in Division One.

Highfield Road was twice chosen for 'big games' which never happened. Had the League Cup final between Tottenham and Aston Villa in March been drawn it would have been replayed at Coventry, and similarly the FA Cup quarter-final second replay between Arsenal and Leicester. A mooted pre-season friendly with Athletico Madrid or Argentina's San Lorenzo (presumably 1956 was forgotten) never materialised, owing to extortionate guarantees demanded. One friendly that did go ahead was Aberdeen in March, when 8,000 saw Roy Barry's return after a year's absence with his broken leg in a 1-0 win.

Away from the spotlight, City's youth policy was generating a wealth of talent under Ron Farmer, so it came as a shock when the youth team were knocked out of the FA Youth Cup by Arsenal. The youngsters mauled Brentford 13-0 on the way to lifting the Southern Junior Floodlit Cup, and the kids even perfected the 'donkey-kick'. Cantwell promoted several into the reserve team, which finished in the top six of the Central league and scored 50 goals in 21 home games. City's young starlets, Mick McGuire and Alan Dugdale, joined Bobby Parker in England's winning team in the Little World Cup, whilst others – Jimmy Holmes, Colin Randell and Alan Green – all showed great potential. Despite the bright future the fans were not prepared to sit idly by and wait. They demanded jam today.

From the first match it was clear that **1971-72** would be Cantwell's make or break season. Rumblings from terraces and boardroom were becoming louder. A poor opening game reminded everyone of the previous season, while a crowd of less than 21,000 illustrated the apathy that was pervading the club. In September, after just one win in the first seven games, Robins sanctioned what would be Cantwell's last big signing – Chris Chilton, a £92,000 buy from Hull. The big striker, who had an outstanding scoring record for Hull, was a disappointment, scoring only four goals in 29 outings and was forced to retire with back problems just over a year later.

The arrival of Chilton and former Liverpool and Scottish international Ian St John briefly livened up proceedings. The team won three games in a row, their scalps including a first top-flight victory over Don Revie's Leeds. A crowd of 37,000 saw Quintin Young, a tricky Scottish winger, tease England full-back Terry Cooper and lay on two goals. Derek Henderson in the *CET* described it as 'the Sky Blues' best result in the First Division'.

Things were picking up and by late autumn it looked as though City were in for what is euphemistically called a 'transitional season', but then things began to deteriorate. From early November until April, City mustered only one win in nineteen games and found themselves sucked into a relegation battle.

Less than a month after the Leeds win, only 16,000 saw the 2-1 win over Huddersfield. The average was down another 3,000 at 23,724, but that figure was dwarfed by neighbours Birmingham City and Aston Villa, who both averaged 31,000 in the lower divisions. The experiment with Friday night football was not a success. The three fixtures – with Crystal Palace, Chelsea and West Brom – failed to attract bigger crowds and two other planned games were rearranged for Saturday afternoons.

By February, Cantwell was under pressure, and when City were eliminated from the FA Cup, 0-1 at home to Second Division Hull, there was no way back. He lingered on, a lame-duck manager, for another month, and ironically the game which probably sealed his fate does not feature in official records. On 4 March Sheffield United were 2-0 up at Highfield Road during a snowstorm when the referee Peter Walters controversially abandoned the game. Torrential rain had turned the pitch into a paddy-field and when the rain turned to snow early in the second half he called a halt. City fans were relieved but the Blades were fuming.

Cantwell's time had come, and gone, and he was sacked by Robins on Sunday, 12 March. The board's press statement was blunt: 'Results have not come up to the expectations or necessary standard required for Coventry City.' Bob Dennison, the chief scout, became acting-manager until the end of the season. The pressures on Dennison were onerous: with no top flight managerial experience to call upon he was now given a few weeks to rescue City from the drop. The question on supporters' minds was, 'would Coventry be better without Cantwell or worse?' The answer was decisive. For the final month it was as if a dead-weight had been lifted from the team. They responded with three wins, enough to ensure safety and restore some pride.

The final judgement on Cantwell's five-year tenure is best summed up in his own words: 'the ghost of Jimmy Hill followed me around the dressing room.' Set in the context of the previous 32 years, he deserves a more favourable judgment. Circumstances, at times, dictated a functional, muscular and defensive approach, but that was in keeping with much football everywhere – Cantwell loved his team being described the 'new Leeds'. More to the point, any side put out by Cantwell carried greater threat than those of some of his successors – Terry Butcher, Don Howe and Phil Neal to name but three. Cantwell also bore too much of the blame for the collapse in support after 1970. Viewed with hindsight, gates of 30,000 were improbably high, a quirk of history perhaps, and even a winning side would have struggled to sustain such figures.

Hooliganism was rife that season and reached new depths during the Easter visit of Manchester United when a thunderflash exploded in the packed west end. With ten minutes of the game left, the percussion reverberated round the ground and caused the players to stop momentarily before carrying on. At first it was believed a firework was to blame, but the police said later a thunderflash was more likely. Some fans were heard chanting 'IRA, IRA'. Coming six weeks after an IRA bomb killed six people at Aldershot Barracks this was not a particularly subtle chant.

In 1971-72 City also entered a new competition, the Texaco Cup – launched the previous season for top English and Scottish clubs missing out on European Competitions. City's first opponents were Falkirk, which the Sky Blues survived despite losing the first leg 0-1 in Scotland. They needed two extra-time goals in the second leg to win 3-1 on aggregate. The home crowd of 14,283 was heartening, whilst Falkirk's attack was led by an elbowy striker named Alex Ferguson, later manager of Aberdeen and Manchester United. In round two City drew 1-1 with Newcastle at home in front of 12,311 but crumbled to a 1-5 defeat at St James' Park.

In December the club hosted a friendly with Polish side Gornik Zabrze. To try and boost the attendance City fielded two guests from Third Division Bournemouth. At the time, the goalscoring feats of Ted McDougall and Phil Boyer were the talk of football: McDougall had already scored 28, including nine in an 11-0 FA Cup win over Margate, and both were destined for the First Division before too long. Gornik, boasting three Poles who would help remove England from the World

Cup a year later, had too much skill and won 2-0 with the centre-forward
Wlodzimierz Lubanski netting the second goal. A cold night kept the
crowd down to a disappointing 6,838.

In April the ground hosted a testimonial for long-serving defender
Dietmar Bruck who had joined Charlton a year earlier. In a double header, an Old City XI met Jimmy Hill's Internationals in a 40-minute warm
up, Hill's team prevailing 1-0. Then City's first team played Bruck's
Charlton, the Londoners winning 4-3 in front of a poor 4,381 crowd.
The biggest cheer of the night came when referee Roger Kirkpatrick, one
of the most eccentric officials of the era, decided to show off his footballing skills. He took a pot shot at the City goal and then awarded
Charlton a penalty for his own handball, which a delighted Dietmar netted for a rare goal.

The season ended with the youth team again lifting the Southern
Junior Floodlit Cup. They beat Chelsea 3-2 over two legs, with future
first-team players Mick Ferguson, Jimmy Holmes and Donal Murphy
(who scored the winning goal) all impressing.

During the three-month hiatus during which Bob Dennison was caretaker manager, the club buzzed with speculation over the identity of the
new manager. The job, on paper, looked enticing. It offered a reasonable
squad of players, one of the most modern stadiums in the country with
state-of-the-art training facilities, not to mention the backing of the
Robins' family's financial resources. Many of the game's 'great and the
good' were reputedly linked with the job. Brian Clough was approached,
but decided to stay at the Baseball Ground, where he had just won the
League Championship. Much later Clough admitted that he had been
very tempted by City's offer.

At Highfield Road the floodlight system was enhanced to comply with
the new higher standards demanded by UEFA for European competition. A new system of lights was installed on the existing pylons and
necessitated considerable re-wiring. The cost, £16,000, was met by the
supporters club. Also during the summer of 1972 a new roof was put on
the Sky Blue Stand. The new flat roof replaced the eye-catching undulat-
ing roof which had been in place since the stand was erected in 1963-64
but was found to have defects. The pitch, too, benefited from a major
overhaul, with improvements to the drainage system in front of the main
stand where the pitch was often shaded from the sun. All three projects
were completed before the start of the **1972-73** season. After a decade of
kicking off at 3.15pm on Saturdays, the club reverted to 3pm, and also
unveiled a new kit – retaining the Sky Blue format but introducing black
shorts and a black collar on the shirts.

The search for a new manager ended on 15 June 1972 with the news that Gordon Milne, non-league Wigan Athletic's 35-year-old player-manager and Joe Mercer, Manchester City's 57-year-old general supremo were to be jointly appointed. There would be no early splash into the transfer market, as the duo needed to take stock of the players available. But when the first six games came and went without a win, the stocktaking process had to be accelerated. After eleven games, by which time the Sky Blues had clocked up their first two wins, the dealing started in earnest. Jeff Blockley was sold to Arsenal for a club record £200,000. He earned an England cap soon afterwards, but that marked the peak of a career that tailed off rather quickly. With hindsight, therefore, the fee proved to be good business for City. The money enabled the club to pull off two master strokes that would kick-start the season into life. Tommy Hutchison and Colin Stein, players of proven pedigree, were signed from Blackpool and Glasgow Rangers respectively.

The arrival of the two Scots sparked an irresistible period in the club's First Division history. The team suffered only five defeats in 24 League and cup games from October to mid-March. Although there were too many draws to make a major impact, relegation thoughts were banished. The season also offered many individual highlights – Hutchison's goal at Highbury, for example, and an FA Cup run which ended tamely at Molineux in the quarter-finals. Only twice before had Coventry progressed so far on the road to Wembley, in 1910 and 1963.

Hutchison's debut sparked a scintillating 3-2 victory over Manchester City and some of his early performances were the stuff of legend. The ability to beat a man once, then again, and again, and then send a perfect centre onto Stein's head, provided a rare treat. Hutch's tussles with the likes of Billy Bonds and Mick Mills would sow the seeds for man-to-man confrontation that would last throughout the 1970s.

Fast-flowing, attacking football brought the fans flooding back and in January the visit of relegation-haunted Manchester United yet again pulled the season's best crowd, 42,911, the biggest at the ground for three years. Tommy Docherty had fashioned an ugly United that besmirched their reputation for stylish football. An estimated 5,000 United fans came down and there was trouble all day. A police task force of 200 officers arrested 32, half of them under seventeen. Shop windows were smashed in Far Gosford Street, house windows smashed in Wren Street, and cars damaged in Fairfax Street car park. Inside the ground police had to deal with yobs climbing the floodlight pylons, children crushed in the Spion Kop, and intruders climbing walls to access the west end. The United mob rampaged after the game and staged running battles with police through the Precinct and back to the train station. Chief Superintendent John Ridley said: 'While professional football is attracting this type of hooligan fan in the numbers it is, no police force can do much about it.' He estimated that three-quarters of the arrests were Manchester United supporters, although none was from Manchester.

The following week 38,000 turned out to see City progress to the fifth round of the FA Cup with a 1-0 win over Grimsby. One of the largest away followings ever seen, estimated at 10,000, saw the Mariners hold out for 86 minutes until conceding a dubious penalty which Mick Coop converted at the Kop end in front of the baying Grimsby hordes. The United visit earned the club record receipts of £22,102, whilst the Grimsby game raked in £20,904 – a record for a Cup game at the stadium.

Hull were thrashed in round five to avenge the previous year's reverse with two trademark Stein goals. On hearing that Colin had joined City, one Scottish journalist said 'he will run through brick walls for you', and Coventry fans loved the Scot for his bravado. For probably the first time, supporters thought City had a realistic chance of reaching Wembley and many pundits tipped them to go all the way. Fifteen thousand fans descended on Molineux for the quarter-final, but they were to be disappointed. City never really got going, and exited the competition in deflated circumstances.

The aftermath was anticlimactic: anyone surveying the season overall would have deduced that it was a poor one. It had not, however, been short on thrills, and had given the fans something to cheer after years of dull defensive soccer. That said, the seven consecutive defeats to round off the League was unprecedented, and an injury to Carr was a further blow to the longer-term prospects. No doubt the final fade-out would be forgotten come the new season in August, by which time the autopsy results on 1972-73 would have given Milne and Mercer the benefit of the doubt.

Early season attendances had continued to slide, but in September the crowd for the visit of Stoke was given as just 14,317 – 2,000 below their previous First Division low. Three days later the club admitting misreading one block of turnstiles, the actual attendance being 16,391. But there were under 9,000 to see City beat Hartlepool in the League Cup, the first time the gate had dipped under 10,000 in that competition since 1960. The resurgence in form boosted attendances to such an extent that the overall League average was 24,623, up 902 (3.8 per cent) – the first rise in gates for five years.

On 28 March 1973 the ground staged its first full international when Northern Ireland faced Portugal in a World Cup qualifier. Civil unrest in

Northern Ireland at the time forced the Irish Football Association to seek alternative venues for home games. This was, in fact, the first game played outside the province. The Irish team featured Tottenham's classy goalkeeper Pat Jennings, former City midfielder Dave Clements – who eighteen months earlier had joined Sheffield Wednesday – and Martin O'Neill of Nottingham Forest, who later would be manager at Leicester, Celtic, and Aston Villa. George Best had announced his international retirement and did not play. The Portuguese, whilst not the force they had been in 1966, were favourites to qualify from a group that also included Bulgaria and Cyprus, who had severely dented Irish chances by beating them in Cyprus a month earlier. Two stars from the 1966 Portugal team were still around, Eusebio, the star striker, and winger Simoes. Eusebio's penalty equalised O'Neill's earlier goal and the game, watched by 11,273, ended 1-1. Later, the Irish played internationals at Fulham, Hillsborough, Anfield, and Goodison Park.

As for City's reserves, only 412 saw the game with Everton, then the club's lowest ever Central League gate, but a week later that fell to 299 to welcome Stoke's reserves. City's stiffs were in contention at the top, and the sudden drop in attendances was a mystery. When City's young reserve team, supported by veteran Ernie Hunt, beat Blackpool 3-2 on 30 April they went top, but were pipped into second place by Liverpool's strong second string.

Earlier in March, Highfield Road had hosted an FA Amateur Cup semi-final tie for the first time. Highgate United, from Birmingham, faced Walton & Hersham, from leafy Surrey, and 4,440 watched a tedious 0-0 draw. The Surrey side later won the Selhurst Park replay to reach their first ever amateur final at Wembley where they defeated Slough Town.

On 1 April 1973 the Government introduced Value Added Tax (VAT) at a rate of 8 per cent. City's secretary announced that the club, which had lobbied hard for exemption from the new tax, would have to swallow it for the last few games of the season, but warned that new season ticket prices would have to rise.

In the last week of the season, Ernie Machin – who had earlier joined Plymouth – had his testimonial against Aston Villa. One of the first players signed by Jimmy Hill, Machin scored in a 1-1 draw watched by a dismal 4,181. The game was overshadowed by an emergency board meeting at which chairman Derrick Robins' resigned for 'health reasons'. His 30-year-old son Peter, a board member for six years, took the chair, with former player Iain Jamieson, 44, a director of Courtaulds, joining the board. Robins' parting shot was directed at televised football: 'At first I fought for more money from the television company … now I am certain I was wrong and that TV should be banned except for the Cup final and inter-nationals.' Was this the great innovator turning Luddite, or more likely the far-sighted chairman seeing the game he loved selling its soul for money?

Robins snr also revealed the club was pressing ahead with plans for a double-decker stand at the Swan Lane end, but surprisingly the 'plan' was not raised for many years. Over the summer of 1973 twelve luxury boxes were installed in front of the main stand. The boxes, which cost £1,000 a year to hire, accommodated a dozen people and came with three car-parking spaces. By the end of May only one box was unclaimed.

Gordon Milne continued his team rebuilding. In came his former Blackpool teammate John Craven, a tough midfielder from Crystal Palace for a modest £42,500. Roy Barry moved soon afterwards to Palace, hav-ing never re-established the eye-catching form shown before he broke his leg in 1970. He was another case of 'if only'. Ernie Hunt would follow, joining Bristol City, before Christmas.

Willie Carr's time at Coventry was coming to an end. We did not know it at the time, but the knee injury suffered at home to Liverpool in April 1973 would signal his demise at the top level. City agreed to sell him to Wolves in mid-season for £240,000, only for Carr to fail a medical. The Molineux club got their man a year later but for a much-reduced fee. Carr played on for many years, winning a League Cup winners medal with Wolves in 1980.

The **1973-74** season started brightly, and for the first ten games City were handily placed in the top five. Following a 2-0 win at Leicester they even went second. Hutchison's form earned him a call-up for Scotland and, later, a place in Willie Ormond's squad for the 1974 World Cup finals in Germany. Home crowds too, were up, averaging 25,000, and a good season seemed to be in prospect. Even a place in Europe did not seem too fanciful.

As summer turned into autumn everything started to turn sour. An injury to Craven, coupled with other enforced changes, disrupted the flow of the team. Goals, always pretty scarce, evaporated, and six suc-cessive goalless games expunged hopes of a successful League season. It took a plunge into the transfer market to help arrest the slide. David Cross, the Norwich striker, was signed for £150,000.

The winter of 1973-74 is remembered in political terms as the Winter of Discontent, when the Conservative Prime Minister Edward Heath took on the coal-miners in an industrial dispute that forced an early 1974 election. The impact on life in Britain that winter is still vividly recalled by those old enough to have lived through it. Football at large was heav-ily disrupted for three months by the miners' strike, which saw Heath's

Government implement the 'three-day week'. In early November, a State of Emergency came into force, banning display advertising and flood-lighting. The Football League declared that Saturday games would kick-off at 2.15, 45 minutes early. League Cup-ties would move from evenings to midweek afternoons. These problems coincided with City's compelling run in the League Cup. Following victories over Darlington and Bristol City, the home tie with Stoke in November went ahead only with the help of generators borrowed from the local Massey Ferguson factory. Even then, only three floodlight towers were active. Despite a blown fuse just before kick-off, City negotiated the gloom to progress to the next round, 17,000 watching a 2-1 win. Secretary Eddie Plumley said: 'The generators made a big difference. If we had played in the afternoon, then we expect-ed no more than 6,000 fans.' Days later the Government banned the use of generators unless they were actually owned by the club.

Needless to say, all this had an adverse effect on attendances, with cup replays attracting only half the usual gate. The match programme suf-fered too with several issues – including that for the Leicester game on the Saturday before Christmas – reduced from 24 pages to sixteen and stacked with adverts. For the League Cup-tie with Stoke and the FA Cup replay with Sheffield Wednesday, the club only issued a single-sheet 'reserve-type' programme.

Though all clubs faced the same difficulties, City negotiated the twin roads to Wembley with pluck, stumbling in unfortunate circumstances on both journeys. The League Cup march to the quarter-finals equalled their longest ever run in the competition, but their reward for beating Stoke in round four was a home tie with the eventual winners Manchester City. Power-cuts necessitated the tie to be played on a Wednesday afternoon in December in front of a predictably low crowd of 12,000. Eddie Plumley gloomily noted that receipts were only £7,000, of which the Sky Blues' share was £2,000: 'If we had won the game the size of the players' bonus for this stage of the competition would have meant the club lost money.'

The tie ended 2-2, despite the normally placid Jimmy Holmes being sent off early on. Brian Alderson was City's hero, scoring twice in reply to Tommy Booth and Dennis Leman. In the replay, two more Alderson goals carried the team to within twelve minutes of that first elusive semi-final, but three Manchester goals in ten minutes turned the tables. It was a finish that drained the players of emotion and left 25,000 travelling fans stunned and incredulous.

One unexpected consequence of the three-day week and power cuts was that the Football League finally agreed to permit Sunday football. Cambridge United led the way with an FA Cup-tie in early January 1974 and two weeks later Millwall staged the first Sunday League game. Later that month City staged their first ever Sunday game, a fourth round FA Cup-tie with Derby, which attracted 41,000 – the last occasion such a figure would ever be associated with Highfield Road – with some 15,000 from Derby. The law prohibited charging a Sunday entrance fee, so City instead charged 50p (the ground admittance fee at the time) for a single-page team-sheet to circumvent the law. Derrick Robins, now club president, wrote in the sixteen-page programme: 'We've got our match on Sunday at last and today we have the first rewards of four to five years of hard work ... to allow these experiments to take place.'

The tie ended 0-0, but City pulled off one of their best Cup results of the era by winning the Baseball Ground replay 1-0 after extra-time under generator-powered floodlights. City were also destined for another late show with surprise team of the season QPR in round five. After a 1-1 home draw, the gates were closed at a packed Loftus Road for City's fifth cup replay of the season. The Sky Blues were seconds from extra-time when Stan Bowles' free-kick sent them out.

The three-day week ended after the beleaguered Ted Heath called a General Election and lost. The next day, all the strikes were off. The rest of the League season was anticlimax, with the final placing of 16th not really doing justice to the early performances. This was the first season of three up, three down, and was the most fiercely fought First Division for years. Although relegation was never a threat for City, Highfield Road crowds slipped by 5 per cent (averaging 23,280) – much in line with the national trend.

Hooliganism was an ever-present problem. On the opening day of the season 2,000 visiting Spurs fans arrived by train at Coventry to be met by a new special task force of 250 police. The verdict from Superintendent Gerry Whittaker was depressing: 'There was no sign of any improvement on Saturday – it was exactly as I expected. There is still a minority of fans who are intent on causing trouble.' Most of the sixteen arrests were sixteen or seventeen-year-olds who appeared in Coventry court the following week and were fined between £40/60. At the time, the IRA were waging a war of terror around mainland Britain and the police's valuable resources were already stretched. Whittaker noted that things could be worse – at Derby and Arsenal there had been battles between rival fans on the pitch. At Highfield Road the police had installed closed-circuit TV cameras, with some in the small building originally constructed as a control room for the floodlights, at the corner of the Spion Kop and main stand. The police hoped the cameras would help them spot and record trouble-makers.

At that Tottenham game, the crowd were welcomed by an innovative pitch design. Groundsman Eddie Hartley had abandoned the traditional up and down cutting and rolling treatment, and gone about it in a circular fashion, leaving the pitch looking like a giant dartboard. It got a mention on *Match of the Day* when their cameras took in the Southampton game in early September.

City's third and final Texaco Cup got no further than the first hurdle, when they tumbled 2-4 on aggregate to Motherwell for the second season running. Over 9,000 watched the first leg at home and jeered City's players off, soundly beaten by a team containing ex-City player Bobby Graham and managed by another, Ian St John.

A Friday evening in April saw Highfield Road play host to an amateur international between England and Scotland. It would be the final amateur international ever played by England. It ended 1-1 and was watched by a pitifully low crowd of 1,221. Dave Bassett's name stands out from the England squad listed in the programme. Bassett, a midfielder with Walton & Hersham, did not play, but he would soon join Wimbledon and steer that club to the pinnacle of domestic football.

During the summer of 1974 English football's spotlight fell briefly on City and the club's general manager Joe Mercer, who agreed to act as England's caretaker manager for what turned out to be seven internationals, winning four and drawing three. During those carefree few weeks England played soccer in the old way, eschewing the defensive tactics practised by Alf Ramsey in his later years. Mercer even utilised some of the game's mavericks, such as Frank Worthington, whom Ramsey had spurned.

Back at Highfield Road, there were more pressing problems to contend with. The defence had sprung a few leaks and a dominant stopper was high on Gordon Milne's shopping list. As ever, it seems, in the history of Coventry City, a financial crisis was brewing. The free-spending days were over and money to buy could only be acquired by agreeing to sell. Liverpool's Larry Lloyd was City's target, for whom a club record fee of £240,000 was agreed. Lloyd duly signed, but the other half of the deal – the sale of Mick McGuire and Alan Dugdale to Spurs for £200,000 – fell through when manager Bill Nicholson lost his job. Having in consequence gone substantially into the red, it would be some years before City would again be in a position to trade freely in the transfer market.

At the November AGM, Peter Robins announced debts of £250,000, which needed a break-even crowd of 28,000 and the club had to sell. Just over a year after his father had stepped aside, the Sky Blues were in the mire, reminiscent of the bad old 1950s. A few months later Peter came out with a quote from that bygone era: 'we will never again have to sell star players to balance the books.' After years of frankness and relative openness in its dealings with supporters, worthless football clichés were back in fashion at Highfield Road.

City were many pundits' favourites for relegation in **1974-75**, and once the curtain went up it was clear that this was going to be a long hard season. Winless after the first nine matches, the club quickly settled to the bottom of the pack and manager Milne was under pressure.

One familiar face was missing from those early matches. Goalkeeper Bill Glazier, a regular for over ten years, was granted a testimonial in November against the England 1966 World Cup XI. A crowd of 15,205, just a few hundred less than had watched the previous League game with Arsenal, earned Glazier a cheque of around £10,000. It was a night of nostalgia with lots of football and nine members of the 1966 team made an appearance (Preston's Nobby Stiles and Bobby Charlton were involved in a Cup-tie), as well as City boss Gordon Milne, who had been a member of the squad in 1966. In a light-hearted game the scores ended 6-6, with Glazier netting a last-minute penalty after being blatantly tripped by somebody five yards away. Jimmy Hill ran Radio Sky Blue that evening, and Glazier's former teammates George Curtis, Bobby Gould and Dave Clements made cameo substitute appearances for England. Glazier played just a handful of games after that, the last of which, at Wolves in December, brought the curtain down on an outstanding career.

That season also welcomed a new scoreboard, replacing the one erected in 1964. Like its predecessor it was paid for by the *Coventry Evening Telegraph*, at a cost of £25,000.

On 21 November 1974, 21 people were killed by an IRA bomb in a Birmingham city-centre pub. Two days later security was heightened at Highfield Road when Arsenal were the visitors. Extra police were on duty and stringent checks were made on spectators entering the ground. After an hour, with the Sky Blues leading 2-0, the game came to a halt when over the tannoy came an announcement that a bomb warning had been received from an anonymous phone-caller. The game was stopped for several minutes but only a few people made for the exits. There was a brief consultation on the pitch between the managers and the referee and then to a round of applause the game restarted.

There would be no cup runs this season: City were knocked out of the League Cup at the first stage at home to Ipswich (0-1), and out of the FA Cup at Arsenal in a fourth round replay, following a torrid 1-1 draw at Highfield Road. The brightest memory of that short-lived Cup campaign was Larry Lloyd's goal in the 2-0 third round victory over Norwich, when from deep in his own half he hoisted a sky-bound shot which swirled over the outstretched arms of Kevin Keelan. For older supporters, that goal was reminiscent of a Roy Kirk strike at Northampton twenty years previously.

League results were too uneven to reveal any pattern, but a splendid spurt at home saw the Sky Blues lose only once in fifteen games between November and the end of the season. Although a final position of 14th might be considered satisfactory, the club's financial problems overshadowed everything else. Boot-sales were the order of the day as Mick McGuire, Carr and Colin Stein were sold for what the fans considered to be derisory fees. The three outgoing players brought in around £240,000, with Carr's sale to Wolves raising only a third of what Wolves had agreed to pay before his medical, and the sales did little to ease the pressure on the club's cashiers. Lloyd was not the player for Coventry that he had been for Liverpool, looking overweight, unfit and displaying an attitude that did not endear him to many supporters. It could hardly be said that he was over the hill: three years later he would help Nottingham Forest to a League championship and the European Cup. In Forest's shirt he even earned a recall to the England team.

Finances were not helped by the April announcement that Derrick Robins, for so long the club's main benefactor, was to settle in South Africa. Robins had been actively involved with the club for over twenty years, fourteen as chairman, and his wealth and generosity would be greatly missed. From the perspective of the boardroom, it was the end of an era. Sir Jack Scamp, more famous for his industrial relations expertise than anything else, replaced Peter Robins, who resigned because of heavy business commitments. Joe Mercer was also appointed to the board, where his many years of experience in the game would supplement Scamp's undoubted business acumen.

Another, even bigger shock came at the end of that 1974-75 season with the news that Jimmy Hill was returning to the club. He became soccer's first managing director, an unpaid role. Football was changing fast both on and off the pitch, but it was not yet clear what function the 'bearded wonder' would perform. It had been eight years since his departure to the world of television – he was by now the *Match of the Day* anchorman. He was returning in a more cynical time – the 60s were now a distant memory.

Two home-grown youngsters had broken through to the first team. Full-back Graham Oakey made such an impression he was voted Player of the Year by the supporters, and Mick Ferguson, a lanky Geordie striker, did enough in twelve games to demonstrate that he had a big future.

Other changes in the backroom staff saw youth-team coach Ritchie Norman sacked as part of cost-cutting. First-team coach Tommy Casey left to take up the manager's job at Grimsby and was replaced by former Aston Villa coach Ron Wylie.

Average gates plummeted by 4,000 to just over 19,000 – the lowest since 1962-63 – with the largest League crowd just 25,460 for the visit of Leeds in November (35,000 had turned out the previous season for the same game). City's season ticket holders were down too – only 4,500 compared to 12,000 at the peak in 1968.

After a relatively trouble-free season hooligan-wise, the last home game against Middlesbrough exploded with violence. Fighting between rival fans turned the west end terrace into a battleground. Police waded in to separate fans as the trouble flared twenty minutes from the end of the game. Seventeen were arrested inside and outside the ground as running fights carried on for more than an hour after the final whistle.

At the end of the season the Birmingham Senior Cup final was played at Highfield Road with local sides AP Leamington and Atherstone Town competing for the trophy. It was the 100th anniversary of the foundation of the Birmingham County FA and the two Southern League sides pulled in 1,844 to see Atherstone prevail 1-0 thanks to a first-half penalty earned by ex-City striker Ernie Hunt and scored by Barry Franklin.

Jimmy Hill threw himself into his new role with vigour and the ideas came pouring out in true Hill-style. Reserve games, which had been switched to Saturday when the club joined the Central League in 1968 to comply with league regulations, were moved where possible to Tuesday evenings. Manager Milne saw the benefits, as he would be able to see the club's younger players in competitive games more often.

The fanfare which signalled the second coming of Jimmy Hill was less triumphal than that which greeted his original arrival in late 1961. Derrick Robins was no longer there to bear the burden of expenditure that was required if the club was to make further progress. The selling that had begun the previous season continued as players were traded to ensure the books were balanced. Out went goalkeepers Bill Glazier and his expected successor, Neil Ramsbottom, and striker Brian Alderson made the short journey up the A46 to Leicester. Coventry banked £110,000.

In the close season, veteran Celtic full-back Jim Brogan arrived on a free transfer, and Bryan King, the long-serving Millwall goalkeeper, arrived for £57,000. Soon after the season was under way, Barry Powell, Wolves' England Under-23 midfielder, was signed for a bargain £75,000. Of these three, only Powell, a regular for the next four years, would make any real impact at Highfield Road.

As usual, City played a number of away pre-season friendlies, but then staged a rare pre-season game at Highfield Road. The game, more an event, was to raise money for the Lord Mayor's Christmas Appeal. It featured a first half between a Sky Blues Past XI and the current first team, then after half-time the old timers were replaced by the club's youth team. The first team won both halves, beating the Past team 5-0 and the Future team 3-1. Jimmy Hill presented the teams on Sky Blue Radio as well as introducing many older former City players such as George Mason, Bill Morgan, Jack Snape and Alf Wood. A crowd of 3,377 watched an entertaining evening, the highlights of which were ex-England goalkeeper Reg Matthews playing at right-back and trying to contain Tommy Hutchison, and the first sight of Garry Thompson, a precocious fifteen-year-old centre-forward from Birmingham, who scored a fine goal.

The **1975-76** season began with City facing insolvency and, according to the bookmakers, relegation. All told, it was therefore a welcome surprise to the fans when the team started off so well. The stunning opening-day win at Goodison was followed by a pleasing draw at Old Trafford – against Tommy Docherty's exciting, newly promoted young side – and a home win over a star-studded Manchester City. After eight games the Sky Blues, boasting a new Admiral egg-timer kit, had lost only once and the critics were eating their proverbial hats.

The new kit was controversial – it was the first time the club had struck a 'kit deal', receiving a payment from Admiral, who then had a patent on the design to stop other manufacturers from producing cheap replicas. Local sports shops warned that the cost of a child's full kit would, at £6.75, be double the price from the previous season. Former player Ernie Hunt, who ran a sports shop in the city, said: 'the Admiral kit is a bit pricey but I will definitely be stocking it because the kids want it.' In a sign of the times, the *Coventry Evening Telegraph* criticised Admiral, arguing: 'it is debatable … whether youngsters really need top quality sports goods.'

The impressive early form was soon confined to memory, in the wake of consecutive home defeats by Stoke, Middlesbrough and Burnley. The slide accelerated with an early exit from the League Cup at Mansfield – another black cup exit to add to a long and growing list.

Though the fans might turn a blind eye to the club's finances, the directors could not. Despite Peter Robins' naïve comments the previous spring, the wolf was inching closer to the door. The club were desperate for funds and £175,000 came in by selling star player Dennis Mortimer to arch-rivals Aston Villa. The loss of such a jewel, not to mention the timing of the sale – a week before Christmas – stretched supporters' patience to breaking point. Mortimer had played over 200 games for City and had blossomed into a much-coveted England Under-23 performer who was strongly tipped to win full caps. But still labouring under a £250,000 overdraft (puny by today's standards), as well as owing Derrick Robins £88,500, albeit on an interest-free basis, and losing £4/5,000 per week, City were hardly in a position to keep him, no matter how bitter a pill it was to swallow.

In the wider context, of course, Mortimer's sale provided further evidence of Coventry's parlous financial state and its inability to compete on a level playing field with bigger clubs. Jimmy Hill dressed up the sale 'as in the long term interests of the club and building a stronger position for the future'. But these words were to ring hollow when City slumped out of the FA Cup, 0-5 at Newcastle. The only consolation was that the first game at Highfield Road, a 1-1 draw, was watched by over 32,000, paying record receipts of £29,672.

The team were capable of fine performances – notably wins over West Ham, Manchester City, and two draws with Manchester United. These kept City in the comfort zone, but the 1975-76 season was hardly one to shout about. Attendances averaged 19,288, slightly up, with Manchester United, rejuvenated after a season in Division Two, attracting the biggest (33,922). Following the sale of Mortimer, attendances dipped as low as 13,000 against Sheffield United and Arsenal, the lowest for more than thirteen years. If ever City needed Jimmy Hill to weave his old magic, this was the time.

Striker David Cross scored sixteen League and cup goals, the best seasonal haul by a City player in the First Division. They included the unusual feat of hat-tricks on the first and the last day of the season. Tommy Hutchison was again ever present (he had missed just one League match in four seasons with the club) and was fast becoming a City legend in his own lifetime. Whenever the going got tough, he could always be relied upon to turn on a bit of magic, to bring a smile and a cheer to the fans on the dullest winter days.

Early in the season City led the way in becoming the first club to video every home first-team game. Using state of the art equipment supplied by Midlands company Focus, the facility allowed Gordon Milne to use recordings to improve team performances, and also enable Jimmy Hill to receive recordings of the weekly action. He was unable to get to Saturday games because of his *Match of the Day* commitments.

There was chaos at Highfield Road for the opening League game with champions Derby. A dozen turnstile operators failed to turn up and hundreds of fans did not get into the ground until twenty minutes after the kick-off. Many gave up and went home. The club apologised profusely and promised it would not be repeated.

In November 1975 the Sky Blues were briefly pushed off the local football pages as Coventry's other club, Coventry Sporting, took the limelight with a thrilling FA Cup run. The West Midlands League side, who played their home games at Kirby Corner at Canley, stunned the non-league scene by reaching the first round of the FA Cup. Their tiny ground, which had packed in 485 for their fourth qualifying round victory, could not cope with any sizeable crowd, so City offered them Highfield Road. On 22 November Coventry Sporting beat Tranmere Rovers, a top three side in Division Four, 2-0 in front of an enthusiastic 4,500 crowd, both goals coming from teenager Stuart Gallagher. There were no former City players in the Sporting side but ex-keeper Reg Matthews assisted manager David Kite on the coaching side. The victory earned them another home tie, with Peterborough United, then managed by former City boss Noel Cantwell. Posh were made of sterner stuff than Tranmere Rovers and ran out easy 4-0 winners in front of a Highfield Road crowd of 8,556, the majority of whom supported the local team vocally from the west end.

Sporting returned to Highfield Road the following August as guests of City in a pre-season friendly but were on the wrong end of a 8-0 result. Despite the driest summer on record and no localised rain for months, the Highfield Road pitch was in superb condition. Like everyone else that summer the club had made efforts to reduce their consumption of water; in fact the club were industrially metered. The lush pitch was a tribute to groundsman Eddie Hartley and his staff. Hartley, who had been at the club for three years said: 'When I came to City I said it would take about five years to make the pitch one of the best in the country and I would like to feel that it is now among the top 10.'

The close season of 1976 was unusually quiet, both on and off the field. There was only one incoming transfer, the QPR midfielder John Beck, and at just £40,000 he was a low-key signing. Long-serving, popular full-back Chris Cattlin was given a free transfer and joined Brighton, despite a concerted campaign from supporters who collected 3,500 signatures on a petition for him to stay. The bookmakers again installed City as favourites for relegation and that judgment also reflected the views of many supporters. The team's start to **1976-77** did little to alleviate their pessimism, as Middlesbrough and Manchester United both recorded comfortable victories – the latter match was also disgraced by the dismissal of Larry Lloyd for any number of nasty fouls. It was an indisciplined performance that would hasten his departure from the club; he was to play only three more games for City before joining Brian Clough's revolution at Nottingham Forest.

Clearly, drastic action was needed to stabilise the club, and it arrived quicker than expected. Out of the blue, on 27 August, Milne made three signings – Terry Yorath (captain of Wales) from Leeds for £145,000, Ian Wallace, a young striker from Dumbarton for £75,000, and Bobby McDonald, a full-back from Villa for £40,000. All three were introduced before the home game against Leeds on a wet Saturday afternoon and their appearance seemed to spur the rest of the team to a much-needed victory. That match also marked the coming of age of young Mick Ferguson, who scored a fine goal in the 4-2 win. Better times had arrived, but they came at a price. The ritual 'balancing of the books' meant that David Cross was sold to West Brom. The silver lining came in the form of Ferguson, which softened the blow of Cross's departure.

Better results and brighter play went hand in hand. Ian Wallace seized his chance and looked every bit a Division One player. He scored the first of many Sky Blue goals in a 4-2 home win over big-spending Everton in front of the *Match of the Day* cameras, and manager Milne compared him to Francis Lee as a goal-poacher. Just as the corner seemed to have turned, Mick Ferguson injured his ankle and was sidelined for almost two months. Soon afterwards Ian Wallace suffered facial injuries when his car lost control on an icy road, forcing him to miss six matches. Then severe weather damaged the Highfield Road pitch which ruled out all home games between 22 January and 2 April. The lack of income had a serious impact on the club's cashflow and in March Jimmy Holmes was sold to Tottenham for £120,000. After thirteen winless matches, relegation again stared City in the face.

Speculation about Gordon Milne's future intensified, especially as his contract expired in the summer. In April, however, as City looked down the barrel he was given a new two-year contract, with Hill publicly praising his ability. First Division survival rested largely with the new strike-force of Ferguson and Wallace. They had been scoring quite freely, though without regularly swinging matches City's way. Home wins over Derby (2-0) and Stoke (5-2) – the latter witnessing a Wallace hat-trick past England keeper Peter Shilton – eased the situation, but with the final three games at home City's First Division life still hung by a thread. First up were Liverpool, *en route* to their first European Cup success. A 0-0 draw virtually clinched the championship for the Reds and prompted a Borussia Moenchengladbach spy to ask in wonderment why Coventry were in such a low position. A crowd of 38,160, the biggest League attendance for six years, saw City stretch Liverpool to the limit.

Four days later City lost 0-1 to runners-up Manchester City, a setback which meant victory seemed imperative in the final match the following Thursday, against Bristol City.

At kick-off, the foot of Division One looked incredibly congested. Spurs and Stoke had completed their fixtures and were down, leaving any one of the three clubs above them to join them. A draw would suit Bristol City, since that would keep them above Coventry. Likewise a draw for Sunderland at Everton that same night would keep them above one or other of the teams slugging it out at Coventry. The Sky Blues could ensure safety only by winning. The only other combination of results that could rescue them was to draw with Bristol City while Sunderland lost at Goodison.

A huge, almost capacity crowd of 36,892 had assembled, but severe traffic congestion delayed large numbers of Bristol fans. Not for the last time, a late start for a vital City game would provoke charges of gamesmanship. Whether responsibility for the delay fell at the feet of the club or the police cannot be known. Either way, the start was put back by five minutes. Any possible repercussions seemed academic as the Sky Blues took an early lead. John Shaw could only palm away a cross and Tommy Hutchison scored only his second goal of the season.

At the start of the season Hutch had almost joined Norwich. Now, on 52 minutes, he put Coventry two up, shooting in off the bar after Powell's shot had hit a post. Within a minute, though, Bristol pulled one back through Gerry Gow. The visitors, roared on by their massive following, pressed hard, and with eleven minutes left full-back Don Gillies squeezed in an angled shot at the near post.

A draw, of course, was all Bristol needed. Depending on Sunderland's score, Coventry might or might not have to conjure a winning goal in the time remaining. Whatever the logic of the situation, the Sky Blues looked dead on their feet. Their composure vanished and they could do little more than boot the ball upfield in desperation. Bristol, meanwhile, coolly went for the jugular. It looked bad for Coventry, but then there was a commotion in the directors box, and news of Sunderland's 0-2 defeat was flashed on to the scoreboard. Provided there was no change to the score at Highfield Road, both teams were safe. Without going so far as to sign a truce, the teams simply stopped playing. For several minutes the ball was tapped this way and that, aimlessly from one side of the field to the other and back again. It was an extraordinary sight for those who witnessed it, almost unprecedented in competitive English football. The referee was probably as embarrassed as anyone, and in the circumstances injury-time would have been an irrelevance. When he finally called a halt to the farce, both sets of fans celebrated with mutual embraces. Bristol fans invaded the pitch and crowded in front of the main stand chanting for manager Alan Dicks. Dozens clambered on to the executive boxes, and the crowds only dispersed twenty minutes after the final whistle when some of the Bristol players appeared and threw their shirts to the crowd. Outside the ground fans of both clubs were too ecstatic to cause trouble and made their way to the city's pubs to celebrate.

Sunderland lodged a complaint to the Football League, and an inquiry was conducted, which wisely drew a veil over the whole thing. But then, what was the alternative?

As a result of the huge crowds against Liverpool and Bristol City, the club's average rose almost 2,000 to 21,242. This was despite an increase in hooliganism. In November 1976 Coventry magistrates even withdrew the licence from Highfield Road for a period. It meant that there was no alcohol for sale at the ground and was hoped to have an effect on crowd disturbances. Serious trouble always simmered under the surface. At the games with Tottenham and Aston Villa there were multiple arrests (45 alone at the latter) and the courts were busy for days afterwards dishing out small, useless fines. In total there were almost 350 arrests at the ground during that 1976-77 season and the club knew they had to take action.

As the season came to an end the club announced a novel plan to fight troublemakers, abolishing reduced price admission through the turnstiles for juveniles. Instead they offered half-price season tickets for young fans incorporating a type of identity card, which would be withdrawn in the event of any breach of the peace connected with football. Under-sixteens would pay £10 for their season ticket. But there was a flaw in the plan – the identity of youngsters appearing before juvenile courts was protected by law. So the club would never know the identity of those juvenile 'passport' holders who got into trouble.

Inside the ground, the police request for a 'no-mans land' between rival fans was implemented in the west end, where most trouble occurred. The following season the police made it a City-fans only area, removing the barriers down the centre of the terracing. Visiting supporters were accommodated in one half of the Spion Kop, but surrounded by high metal fences and a five-foot dry moat down the terraces.

As regards the team, in spite of the close shave which averted relegation, a relatively optimistic atmosphere pervaded the club and its supporters in the run up to **1977-78**. The consensus was that the squad was better than their final position indicated, and that better times might be just around the corner.

The only notable signing was Aston Villa's right-winger Ray Graydon for a modest £40,000 fee. Graydon's arrival was, however, indicative of an attacking tactical emphasis. The team would line up 4-2-4 with two wingers to nourish the goalscoring potential of Wallace and Ferguson.

Pre-season friendlies gave little indication that things were improving, and the first half of the opening match against Derby was no better. The match was transformed via Wallace's boot and Ferguson's head, and that pattern was to be sustained more or less throughout the season – which turned out to be the most exciting since the Second Division championship year.

Goals flowed freely at both ends, with the dynamic duo of Ferguson and Wallace establishing themselves as a feared strike-force. The two-man midfield – Terry Yorath and Barry Powell – were called upon to work like Trojans to compensate for their numerical deficit.

Many of the stay-away fans of recent years were lured back by the excitement. Coventry netted 75 goals during that 1977-78 season, their most since 1963-64, and provided thrills to match. Several home games would be contenders for the best of recent times, notably Manchester City, Norwich, Chelsea and Everton.

Many City players were performing at their peak – Yorath and Powell certainly, Ferguson and Wallace probably, and Jim Blyth and Bobby McDonald possibly. Full international honours were won by Wallace, Yorath, Donato Nardiello of Wales, and Blyth – who was named in Ally McLeod's ill-fated Argentina World Cup expedition – although the form of McDonald, Ferguson and Hutchison merited international recognition too.

City's League Cup run acquired a head of steam with a win at Spurs. This was followed by a breathtaking 2-2 draw at Anfield, where it looked for long periods as if a famous first victory was on the cards, with 8,000 City fans shouting themselves hoarse. The replay at Highfield Road had to be delayed three weeks on account of Liverpool's other commitments. By that time, a run of five matches without a win had blunted City's edge, and they ended up beaten 0-2 in front of 36,105 spectators. Many fans, with their heads in the clouds, had been convinced that City's name was on the cup that year. They crashed to earth with a bump.

It wasn't long before City entertained Liverpool again, this time in the League, but the 1-0 victory was scant revenge for the cup defeat. That League encounter is fondly remembered for a bruising battle between Yorath and Souness, and was part of City' six-match winning streak at Highfield Road. Among City's other victims in that purple patch were Manchester United, beaten 3-0.

Away from Highfield Road it was a different tale. The FA Cup exit at Middlesbrough was typical of City's spluttering expeditions. It was this travel sickness that finally dashed hopes of qualifying for Europe. One win in the last eight League games was hardly European form, but had Ipswich not confounded expectations by beating Arsenal in the FA Cup final, Coventry would have claimed a UEFA Cup place.

Finances were on a surer footing and the debts of two years previously had been erased. Chairman Sir Jack Scamp, who with Hill had steered the club through the difficult period, passed away in November 1977. The healthier financial state enabled the club to dip a toe into the transfer market. The mid-season signing of Keith Osgood from Spurs bolstered the defence, before he faded. Garry Thompson was given his chance near the end of the season and earned rave reviews, illustrating that competition for first-team places was hotting up.

Two matches stand out among many as contenders for match of the season. In terms of goal-avalanches, nothing could compare with the extraordinary happenings when Norwich City were beaten 5-4 on 27 December. City led 2-0 after 21 minutes, thanks to a Barry Powell penalty (his first for the club) and a spectacular bicycle-kick from Wallace. Three Norwich goals in the space of thirteen minutes turned the tables – a John Ryan penalty and two goals from future £1 million striker Kevin Reeves. In addition, Norwich's Martin Peters had a goal disallowed for offside. In the second half Gooding's thunderbolt, his first ever City goal, made it 3-3. Ten minutes later Bobby McDonald curled a shot around Keelan, and but for two disallowed Coventry goals the outcome would have been sealed. But Norwich bounced back again, Peters heading an equaliser and then hitting a post with a free-kick. The ninth and winning goal came after 81 minutes, when Graydon headed over Keelan, but Norwich had the chance to make it 5-5 when, with 90 seconds left they were awarded their third penalty of the match. Blyth's save extended Norwich's dismal record at Highfield Road to seventeen successive defeats.

It takes something special to relegate such a goal-feast to the also-rans, but that is the case in 1977-78. During the second half of the game with Manchester City the Sky Blues touched heights seldom equalled before or since, scoring three times in the final seventeen minutes to turn probable defeat into exhilarating triumph. During the 1960s and 70s the Maine Road club produced some dazzling teams, none better than that which descended on Highfield Road in October 1977 as unbeaten League leaders. Coventry, too, had started the season promisingly, and prior to a home defeat by West Brom on the previous Saturday had lost only at Old

Trafford and Anfield. The Manchester club, also playing 4-2-4, took an early lead and wingers Peter Barnes and Tueart gave Coventry's full-backs a torrid time. The Sky Blues levelled through Ferguson on the half-hour, only for Barnes to restore the visitors' lead on the stroke of half-time, latching onto a long punt over Coventry's static defence before shooting past Sealey. Throughout the second half Coventry camped in the visitors' half, attacking relentlessly and creating chances galore. In the 73rd minute the dam broke: Beck flicked on Oakey's cross and Fergie lobbed Corrigan to make it 2-2. Six minutes later Yorath, architect of many attacks, swung over a cross, Ferguson glided a header into Wallace's path, and the Scot beat Corrigan with ease. Manchester hit back. Barnes climaxed a dazzling run with a shot that flew narrowly wide, leaving Coventry fans baying for the final whistle. In the final minute Ferguson completed his hat-trick with a classic goal. Hutch crossed from the left and the big man took the ball on his chest and drove it past Corrigan. That goal brought the crowd to their feet, where they stayed to the final whistle. The Sky Blues came off to a standing ovation. The following day managing director Jimmy Hill told City's 'floating' supporters: 'Something exciting is now happening at Highfield Road. Don't miss it.'

The final home game saw City entertain Brian Clough's Nottingham Forest, the undisputed team of the season. Forest needed just one point to clinch their first ever championship and the game was made all-ticket with a capacity of 39,000. On the day there were 36,894 inside the ground to witness a classic, in which Peter Shilton was the outstanding figure. One save, from a Ferguson header, had fans comparing it to Gordon Banks' from Pele in the 1970 World Cup.

Coventry's bold attacking football boosted crowds, which rose for the third season running. The average was up 2,000 to 23,353.

In November 1977 City awarded a testimonial to long-serving defender Mick Coop. Coop, who had made his debut in City's Second Division promotion season, captained a Coventry City Great Britain XI against a Scottish international XI. City's first-teamers were scattered between the two sides and supplemented by current internationals, including Roy McFarland, Colin Todd, Laurie Cunningham, Mick Channon and Willie Johnston. Also appearing were a few former City stars who got warm welcomes from the 7,883 crowd. They included Colin Stein, Willie Carr and David Cross. Coop's team won 7-5, thanks to a hat-trick from David Cross, but the biggest cheer of the night was reserved for Stein when he scored the opponents' fifth goal.

In May 1978 the ground again hosted the Birmingham Senior Cup final, this time between Nuneaton Borough and Redditch United, but watched by just 913, Borough, boasting future City players Trevor Peake and Kirk Stephens, won 1-0.

After the previous season's success, expectations were high in **1978-79** that City could repeat and even improve upon their 7th place. The season saw the introduction of perimeter fencing at the ground – to meet UEFA regulations and the Safety of Sports Grounds Act. If the club had qualified for Europe much of this work would have been compulsory but they decided to carry it out in anticipation of achieving European qualification. Other safety measures were completed, including the building of an away supporters' 'pen' at the Kop end, and the official capacity was set at 40,000 – ironically this figure was never reached again at the stadium. In all, around £200,000 was spent on ground alterations and improvements, much of which was recouped from grants from the Football Grounds Improvement Trust.

Injuries would play a big part in what was by comparison a disappointing campaign. Key players Yorath and Ferguson played in fewer than half the games and they were missed. Wonder-kid Wallace was never likely to startle opposing defences second time round. It is to his credit that, though marked more tightly, he still reached fifteen goals, including a hat-trick against Southampton. What consistency the side possessed, was attributable to Bobby McDonald and Tommy Hutchison, both of whom were ever present.

City's strength, once again, was at home. Only three games were lost – all in a three-week spell at the end of winter, and although the quality of play was not up to the previous campaign's standards, City still scored 41 goals at home and four times scored four. Away from home things were not so bright, and there were a few disasters – the League Cup exit at Third Division Chester and a 1-7 embarrassment at the Hawthorns, fast becoming a bogey ground, were followed by heavy defeats at the Dell (0-4) and Ashton Gate (0-5).

At home there was a thrilling 4-2 victory over Derby, when the team scored three goals in the last eleven minutes, and a pre-Christmas 3-2 win to terminate Everton's twenty-match unbeaten run, but the winter freeze then mothballed Highfield Road for seven weeks. When the snows finally melted, City's form melted with it. Having been impregnable at home for sixteen matches over almost a year, City suffered three reverses in a row before a thumping win over FA Cup finalists Manchester United. That sparked a productive run-in, with City losing only one of their last nine games to finish 10th.

The FA Cup draw was harsh, pitching City against their bogeymen of West Brom. The Baggies, under Ron Atkinson, had a potent side with the 'three degrees' Cyrille Regis, Laurie Cunningham and Brendan Batson at the peak of their powers, and destined for their highest League finish for almost 30 years. City missed chances in the first game for which they were punished in the Hawthorns replay, their only consolation being a share of the £51,500 gate receipts over the two games – those from the 37,928 crowd at Highfield Road constituted a City record.

City's conveyor belt of gifted youngsters showed no signs of slackening. In Yorath's absence Andy Blair seized his chance. Teenagers Paul Dyson, Gary Bannister, Jim Hagan and Mark Hateley also made encouraging debuts at one time or other. The fine crop of teenagers was reflected in some free-scoring reserve games at the ground that season. Preston were beaten 6-4, Bury 7-2, and the games with Bolton saw City win 6-4 at Burnden Park but lose 5-6 at home. In the FA Youth Cup the team marched to the last eight before losing 1-6 at home to Everton. Garry Thompson was an able deputy for Ferguson and cemented his England Under-21 claims by his domination of Manchester United's Scottish international Gordon McQueen in City's 4-3 League win in March. Two weeks later Thompson broke his leg in training.

Two bargain buys were to prove excellent long-term investments. Defender Gary Gillespie, snapped up for £75,000 from Falkirk the previous March, made an impressive start and after a handful of games was called up to the Scottish Under-21s. At eighteen he would blossom into one of the finest defenders of the era. In the summer, Steve Hunt had signed for £40,000 from New York Cosmos. Hunt, once of Villa, was a star in America, where he had partnered Pele in two successive NASL championships, but he was determined to succeed in England and scored on his debut in a 2-0 win at Derby.

Off the pitch, that 1978-79 season was dominated by two transfers that never were. In November City accepted a mammoth £440,000 bid from Manchester United for goalkeeper Jim Blyth. Blyth, a £20,000 buy from Preston in 1972, had suffered back problems which City thought had been solved, but United thought otherwise. Then in January, City bid £1 million for England striker Trevor Francis from Birmingham. For a club that had only recently been up to its eyes in debt, it seemed extraordinary bold – or foolhardy – for low-lights like Coventry to be the first British club to offer £1 million for a player. But Francis preferred to join Brian Clough at Nottingham Forest. City also tried to buy Kevin Beattie from Ipswich for £450,000, but fears about the player's underlying fitness proved well founded and the deal feel through.

The confidence to make bold moves like this stemmed from the club's healthy finances. At the AGM, Scamp's successor as chairman, Phil

Mead, the man who had been instrumental in saving the club during the war, announced a profit of £50,000 and told the shareholders that by Christmas 1978 they would have paid off all the club's debts, including the loan from Derrick Robins.

In a rare home pre-season friendly the Sky Blues entertained the Japan National XI and in front of 5,000 won 2-0. In October there was a match with a difference when, in a game to raise funds for the Textile Benefit Association – the major charity for the UK's textile industry – a combined Coventry/Derby County XI took on a combination representing Forest and Leicester players. The game came about because Coventry-based Courtaulds had responsibility that year for organising the fund-raising, and City director Iain Jamieson was also a Courtaulds director. The 1,154 crowd saw a low-key game which ended 3-1 in favour of the Forest/Leicester team.

Earlier that month the ground hosted a League Cup second replay between Aston Villa and Crystal Palace, which was decided in Villa's favour 3-0. Any City fans in the 25,445 crowd saw not only their former hero Dennis Mortimer, but also Terry Venables' Palace, unbeaten in Division Two, on their way to promotion.

New security measures were introduced early in the season, enabling police to pinpoint regular trouble-makers in the crowd and eject them or turn them away at the entrances. Since the introduction of the away fans' 'pen' they had been taunted by a hard core of Coventry fans, and the new powers enabled the police to identify and banish the offenders.

In March 1979 Jimmy Hill announced the installation of a £40,000 under-pitch heating system, following the disruption of so many home games because of the weather.

He also announced the building of new executive boxes at the back of the main stand and talked about his long-term vision of covering the Spion Kop end: 'At the moment we have more seats than we have people filling them. When we do turn our attention to the Kop end it will be to provide a covered all-seater stand … not just a cover for the terraces … but there is no point in spending £2/3 million until the demand is there.' The average attendance slipped slightly, by around 700, to 22,638. The biggest League crowd was 28,585 for the visit of reigning champions Nottingham Forest back in August. What Hill and his directors did not realise was that the average gate would not reach 20,000 again for twenty years, and in consequence the Spion Kop would not be redeveloped until 1994.

The heating system comprised 22 miles of piping to circulate hot water eight inches below the surface. The pipes were laid in just four days in May 1979, using a tractor-pulled machine designed to cause very little disturbance to the pitch. Two gas-fired boilers controlled by thermostats fed the pipes and were designed to cater for frost removal, maintaining a clear pitch during falling snow and melting any settled snow.

As the 1978-79 season drew to a close it witnesed an unprecedented achievement. In the space of five days three City players scored hat-tricks at Highfield Road. On 17 April the reserves beat Manchester United 4-0 with three goals from Clive Haywood; two days later the reserves beat Bury 7-2 and Tommy English netted four times; two days later, on the Saturday, Ian Wallace netted a hat-trick for the first team in the 4-0 win over Southampton. Quite a week.

1979-80 was a season of experiment and laying foundations for the future, but fans found themselves disappointed by the team's inconsistency, impatient at its shortcomings, and in the end disenchanted with everything. After five years of relative transfer prudence, when (Trevor Francis aside) City declined to compete with the 'big boys', the chequebook was suddenly brandished.

Gary Collier had been no more than an average centre-half with Bristol City but in June 1979 he became the first out-of-contract player to negotiate his own transfer when walking out on Ashton Gate to join Coventry. The fee of £325,000 was determined by a tribunal and, coupled with Everton's England Under-21 defender David Jones signing for £250,000, City announced their arrival as big spenders. Someone had to go to balance the books, and on the eve of the season Terry Yorath joined Tottenham for £300,000. Two months into the season Barry Powell and Keith Osgood left for Derby, and City collected £500,000 for the pair.

The opening match, at Stoke, proved calamitous. City's defence – with new men Collier and Jones – were all at sea and shipped three goals within the first 55 minutes. Collier and Gooding were publicly blamed and were dropped forthwith. A week later the axe fell on Jones and Blyth, following further humiliation at Nottingham Forest.

Milne's plans lay in tatters and it was clear to everyone that the season ahead would be long and arduous. The away form was depressing, but mercifully the vultures were kept at bay by virtue of City's home performances, which harvested eleven points from the first six games. Wallace returned from injury in September and the clouds began to lift. He and Ferguson resumed their partnership, only for Ferguson to get crocked again a week later and sidelined for six weeks.

There was drama during the visit of Norwich in September, when eighteen-year-old youth-team goalkeeper Steve Murcott was hurriedly forced into making his debut after regular keeper Jim Blyth hurt his back during the warm-up. Murcott, who had played for the youth team at Ryton in the morning, kept a clean sheet and at the final whistle was given a standing ovation. The team lined up to clap him off the field. City won 2-0 but Murcott never appeared for the first team again.

In November, City surrendered their thirteen-game unbeaten home record to Stoke. Coventry looked a shambles but were not helped by individual errors by David Jones, precipitating the end of his City career. He was substituted at half-time and barely got another look in. Suddenly, everything about the club was put under the microscope – tactics, transfers, ambition (or lack of it).

But football is as fickle as everything else in life. Within a week, with Ferguson back from injury, the team embarked on their most productive spell of the season, four games, no defeats, ten goals scored, eight by the bearded striker.

What was the match of the season was also Ferguson's crowning glory, a four-goal blitz to demolish Bobby Robson's Ipswich, who had themselves just tried to pick him up for a bargain. Ferguson, the first City player to score four goals in a game for twenty years, was now a wanted man. Within weeks he came close to making a £900,000 move to Forest, with Martin O'Neill coming in part-exchange. Forest manager Brian Clough, however, had second thoughts.

The New Year brought an FA Cup win at Oldham and a fourth-round tie at Third Division Blackburn. Expectations were further raised with a victory over the leaders Liverpool before the *Match of the Day* cameras. Jimmy Hill positively glowed on the Beeb that night as the nation saw the array of young talent at City's disposal.

On a bitingly cold day it was the only fixture to survive in the Midlands thanks to the under-soil heating which created a fine surface. Paul Dyson's early header ended Liverpool's nineteen-match unbeaten run in front of the biggest crowd of the season, 31,644. It was the second time the new heating system had come into its own – on New Year's Day, after the coldest night of the winter, the Middlesbrough home game went ahead on a soft surface.

Perhaps the Liverpool victory went to City's heads. At an icy Ewood Park the team bowed out of the FA Cup, miserably losing 0-1. Several of City's young bucks froze in their minds as well as their boots. Wallace's wretched luck in front of goal continued, and before many weeks had passed he was dropped and had slapped in a transfer request.

Milne persisted with the youngsters and the Sky Blues team that completed a 0-0 home draw with Manchester City was one of the youngest in the club's history, with an average age of 21. Milne also signed City's first serious foreigner, paying FC Cologne £250,000 for 29-year-old Belgian winger Roger Van Gool. As always, the books had to be balanced, but the sale of Ferguson to Aston Villa for £750,000 fell through.

Garry Thompson returned from his year out with a broken leg and scored twice against Southampton. But that was City's only win in the seven games without the dropped Wallace. Following a shameful home defeat by Wolves, Milne was forced to recall the flame-haired Scot for the trip to Middlesbrough.

By this time 'Milne out' chants were increasing in intensity, and Wallace responded by scoring both goals in a 2-1 win. His overall performance, however, did little to convince supporters that his heart was really with the club. At least Wallace brightened up the last few weeks of a dull season by getting sent off, along with Crystal Palace's Kenny Sansom – City's first red card at home for three years. The attendance for Palace, 14,310, was the lowest at home for three years and the average had slipped by over 3,000 to 19,315.

Away from the first team, the quality of young talent was reflected in the runners-up spot in the Central League. The stiffs scored 96 goals with Hateley (16) and Gary Bannister (15) leading the way. Despite having three internationals, plus the precocious Danny Thomas, the youth team failed to make a mark in the FA Youth Cup, losing at the first hurdle to Walsall.

August 1979 saw a night of nostalgia when 1,808 fans braved lashing rain to help raise money for the Sparks children's charity. The first team were pitted against a City past team, and despite the old 'uns having their goals count double, the current team ran out 8-2 (8-4) winners. Many players from the 1960s were on show, among them Willie Humphries, Ronnie Rees and Jimmy Whitehouse.

The spring of 1980 saw four 'non-City' games at the stadium, which was now recognised as one of the country's top venues. In February England's Under-21's met Scotland's in a European Championship quarter-final first leg. The top brasses at the FA made clear that the under-soil heating had a major bearing on their choice of ground. England, managed by Manchester United boss Dave Sexton, included several 'stars' of the future, including West Brom's Cyrille Regis and Bryan Robson, and Tottenham's Glen Hoddle.

Robson and his clubmate Gary Owen scored the goals in England's 2-1 victory, with Aberdeen's Steve Archibald scoring for the Scots. Coventry youngsters Andy Blair and Gary Gillespie impressed for Scotland, who also featured future City player Alan Brazil. The attendance was a healthy 15,354. Three weeks later England went through by virtue of a 0-0 draw in the second leg.

A month later the ground was chosen to host England's Youth game with Denmark – the second leg of a qualifying tie for a European Youth International Tournament to be played that summer. City's blossoming youth policy was rewarded with places for three players – strikers Mark Hateley and Tommy English and full-back David Barnes. Hateley who at that point had failed to score for City in six appearances, hit all four goals in a stunning individual display. English, already a first-team regular, set up two of them with crosses. England coach John Cartwright predicted a great future for Hateley. Also in the England side was Spurs' diminutive striker Terry Gibson – destined to replace Hateley in City's team three years later – and Gary Mabbutt, later to become a Coventry hero for other reasons. In the Danish squad were future stars Michael Laudrup and Jan Molby. The crowd was just 2,464. That summer Hateley, English and Barnes emulated Parker, Dugdale and McGuire from 1971 by helping England to win the 'Little World Cup', as the European Youth tournament was known.

On Saturday, 12 April Highfield Road again hosted the Birmingham Senior Cup. Nuneaton Borough beat Lye Town 2-0 to lift the trophy for the sixth time. Borough, who had that season become founder members of the new Alliance Premier League – the first national league outside the Football League – included former City youth player Bob Stockley. Only 970 bothered to turn up.

A far bigger game was staged on Thursday, 1 May when the ground staged its first FA Cup semi-final. Arsenal and Liverpool had drawn three times – in the days before penalty shoot-outs – at Hillsborough and twice at Villa Park, in what had become a five-and-a-half-hour marathon. A crowd of 35,632 paying receipts of £115,556 were at Highfield Road to see Brian Talbot's twelfth-minute goal carry the Gunners to a Wembley final with West Ham, which they lost 0-1. Two days after the semi-final, Arsenal – playing six reserves – returned to Highfield Road to win the final League game of the season 1-0.

In May 1980 chairman Phil Mead retired, severing a connection with the club dating back almost 40 years. Jimmy Hill, by now a major shareholder, took his place.

Almost Hill's first act was to sanction the sale of Wallace to Nottingham Forest for a mammoth £1,250,000. Hill's explanation to the largely resigned City fans was that 'Ian Wallace doesn't own the word ambition, we are ambitious too'. The fee went some way to financing the impressive 'Sky Blue Connexion' at the club's Ryton training ground. It also meant that in five years City had sold nearly £4 million worth of players, while spending only half that sum on new ones.

CHAPTER NINE

The 1980s

Despite the pressures on manager Gordon Milne to quit, he started the **1980-81** season still in charge. Ian Wallace was not the only player to leave in the summer, Gary Collier had been transferred to Portland Timbers in the NASL for the astonishing fee of £365,000, more than he cost in the first place. Considering he only played two first-team games for Coventry, the club were fortunate to recoup the money. New chairman Hill negotiated the club's first sponsorship deal, with Coventry-based car manufacturer Talbot. This provided another welcome injection of cash, although the FA rejected an application to rename the club Coventry Talbot. At this time, sponsor's names were only allowed on players' shirts in untelevised games.

The young side showed promise but, with an average age of just 21, lacked the discipline that can only be gained with experience. Milne signed Derby's Irish Republic midfielder Gerry Daly in August, mainly just to add experience, but it proved much more than that.

Controversy attended one of Daly's early games, the televised visit of Crystal Palace. Early in the second half, with City leading 2-1, Palace's Clive Allen shot past Jim Blyth. The ball struck the far stanchion and flew back into play. The referee consulted his linesman and disallowed the goal, believing the ball to have struck the junction of bar and post. Television replays clearly confirmed a goal, and that Palace were victims of a miscarriage of justice. To rub salt in their wounds, City scored a third before the end.

In the League it was to be an erratic season, and there seemed little hope of pleasant diversion in the League Cup when City were paired with Manchester United at the first hurdle, but 1-0 wins home and away sparked one of the finest cup runs in the club's history. In the third round they were sent to Brighton and, with Hutchison returning from his summer sojourn with Seattle Sounders, Coventry's midfield had enough to see them through 2-1. Four days later Everton inflicted Coventry's worst home League defeat since 1919, winning 5-0 and wrecking City's goal-difference with a vengeance.

By the time of the next round of the League Cup, storm clouds were gathering. Feeble Norwich had won at Highfield Road, Bobby McDonald and Hutchison had controversially been sold to Manchester City, and gates had slipped under 12,000. When City only scraped a home draw with Second Division Cambridge the fans were chanting for Milne's head. But a determined display in the rain-swept replay yielded a 1-0 win and the fans began to see Wembley on the horizon. The quarter-finals paired City with Second Division Watford. In a tense game at Vicarage Road, City drew 2-2, but they made no mistake in the replay. On a night to remember, the club reached their first-ever major Cup semi-final by beating Graham Taylor's side 5-0. Considering the youthfulness of the side it was an amazing feat. Nineteen-year-old Peter Bodak scored a stunner before Hateley – yet to score a League goal – added two more. The result had an uplifting effect on a city depressed by industrial closures and unemployment, and the semi-final with West Ham was anticipated with relish.

Good form in the Cup spilled over into the League, at least at home. From mid-October to the end of February the only side to lower City's colours at Highfield Road were the old bogey side Aston Villa, who were destined to lift the Championship. By now, an FA Cup run was starting to take shape, thanks to a hard-fought third round tie with Leeds, which was won after a replay, followed by a 3-2 fourth round win over neighbours Birmingham.

Both legs of the semi-final were enthralling. A Highfield Road packed with an all-ticket crowd of 35,411, including 7,000 Hammers fans, saw the first leg. With only eighteen minutes left West Ham appeared to be cruising to their second successive Wembley final. Les Sealey had allowed Bonds' weak header to squirm from his grasp, then Thompson, chasing back to dispossess Devonshire, poked the ball past the outrushing keeper 'like trains on different tracks'. The big striker sank to the turf and had to be consoled by Steve Hunt before he could continue. Hunt, who had emerged as one of the best midfielders around, raised a clenched fist to the west end, demanding the fans get behind the team. At half-time the wavering fans asked: 'What do you expect with a bunch of kids?'

As the minutes ticked away, Thompson steered Andy Blair's weighted pass beyond Phil Parkes, and four minutes later Daly equalised when the West Ham keeper could only parry Danny Thomas's fierce shot. With five minutes to go West Ham's David Cross netted, but Allen was given offside. With seconds remaining, Thompson bamboozled Alvin Martin and let fly into the left-hand corner of the net – 3-2. After one of the greatest fight-backs in the history of Highfield Road, City had a vital advantage to take into the second leg.

Alas, the Sky Blues' one-goal lead was overturned at Upton Park. None disputed that West Ham were the better side, though the tie was seconds from extra-time when substitute Jimmy Neighbour, perhaps offside, got on the end of a free-kick to put the Hammers through 4-3 on aggregate.

Four days later Spurs ended City's FA Cup hopes, after errors – both tactical and individual –– left the Sky Blues with a mountain to climb and the team's season was as good as over.

The effect of these twin blows on a young side was little short of catastrophic. The team nose-dived into seven defeats in eight games, the consequence of which was to pitch City once again into the jaws of relegation. Two wins and a draw in the last three games averted the danger; but it had been a close enough shave to convince some members of the board that the team needed a new steersman at the helm.

On 13 May 1981, after nine seasons in charge, Milne, in what seemed an amicable move, was shunted sideways to the post of general manager, and his assistant manager Ron Wylie was released. A week later, Dave Sexton, recently sacked by Manchester United, took charge of Coventry's team affairs. His appointment was a break from City's tradition of going for young untried managers. Sexton was as experienced as they came, having guided Chelsea and Manchester United to FA Cup triumphs and taken unfashionable QPR to within a whisker of the championship in 1976. He was also a member of Ron Greenwood's England coaching staff, with responsibility for the Under-21 side. He had first-hand knowledge of several City players, who he had selected for the Under-21s, including Thomas, Dyson and Thompson.

Jimmy Hill caused a stir at the reserve game with Huddersfield in October when, after a miserable first half, he ordered the Sky Blue Radio DJ to tell the fans: 'If the game does not improve please feel free to show your disapproval.' Hill later explained: 'I felt sorry for the fans … on a cold night the football was just not up to the standards we expect.' Things did improve and the reserves won 1-0.

In November Steve Hunt scored a stunning goal to beat Birmingham City. Hunt collected the ball in midfield, surged past Alan Curbishley, played a one-two with Garry Thompson, and then bent a left-foot shot wide of the Blues goalkeeper Jeff Wealands. At the season's end it was voted London Weekend Television's 'Goal of the Season', worthy recognition for a player converted from a winger to a midfield play-maker a year earlier, who had forced his way on to the fringe of the England squad.

Coventry's investment in North American football came in the form of a stake in Detroit Express, costing £280,000. In March 1981 the owners decided to move the club from recession-hit Detroit to Washington and rename the team Washington Diplomats. City stumped up a further

£220,000. Soon afterwards the Diplomats played what for them was a pre-season friendly at Highfield Road. The contrast between the English and the American leagues was stark as Coventry trounced the Diplomats 5-1 in front of 2,600 spectators, although the visitors triumphed in an American style 'shoot-out' staged at the end of the match. Five players from each side were given five seconds to score, starting from a distance of 35 yards from goal and the Diplomats won 3-2.

Attendances were down everywhere as an icy football recession gripped the game. The best-supported clubs, Liverpool and Manchester United, saw a 12 per cent slump in crowds and, despite the excitement generated by the League Cup run, City's gates followed suit, falling 2,400 to 16,904. At the club's AGM in December 1980, Hill revealed that the club needed a 28,000 average gate to break even and that the club's books were balanced only by profits in the transfer market, pools and lotteries (that year they generated over £600,000), and the supporters club.

Milne's 'move' upstairs pacified many of the club's critics but Jimmy Hill's decision to convert Highfield Road into England's first all-seater stadium caused uproar. Not only did it take a knife to the whole concept of standing on terraces, upon which generations of football-goers had been reared, and from where most Coventry fans chose to watch their team, but it also reduced the ground's capacity to just 20,500. That figure, although greater than the club's average attendance, was 15,000 below the gate for City's home semi-final with West Ham a few months earlier, and for that reason did not appear to make economic sense. Even more distressing to supporters was the way the decision was reached, without warning or consultation. City had toyed with the idea of a fan registration system in an effort to beat hooliganism, but in March 1981 the all-seater plan was unveiled.

Phase one, planned for that summer, would involve – at a cost of £375,000 – the removal of fences and the installation of seats in the west end, the Sky Blue terracing, and twelve rows of seats at the front of the Spion Kop terracing. The remainder of the Kop would be boarded off ready for development in Phase two, when it was planned to completely seat that end, and roof it, increasing the capacity to 26,000.

The *Coventry Evening Telegraph* printed pages of protest letters for weeks, but Hill and his directors were in no mood to listen. They knew best. The fans were undoubtedly frustrated by the team's slump in form, but many were at a loss to comprehend the direction the club was taking. This encouraged a sense of alienation on their part, as did the farcical attempt to change the club's name, the unveiling of a garish strip incorporating the Talbot logo, not to mention the all-seater stadium – tickets for which were more expensive. Unless purchased prior to Fridays, they would cost a crippling £5 (and £6 for the 'big' games). The new ticketing policy had the effect of raising the number of season tickets sold to 7,500, the highest number for almost ten years.

The new 'Talbot' kit caused more controversy when the television companies banned City from the screens because of its striking resemblance to the Talbot emblem. The ban was lifted three months into the season when the club introduced a different kit without the blatant Talbot trademark.

For their part, the board insisted they had taken account of the broader economic situation. Declining gates and escalating running costs had driven some clubs to the edge of bankruptcy, and many others were carrying huge overdrafts. The board did not want City to become a victim of soccer's recession, but in their efforts to anticipate the various pitfalls, they were caught in a downward spiral, which became increasingly difficult to reverse.

The club's finances were not helped by the collapse of Washington Diplomats less than six months after the move from Detroit. £500,000 of City's money went down the drain when they folded, although Hill at one stage gave an undertaking to bear half of the loss. It was within these tight financial constraints that Sexton began the task of bringing style and consistency to a talented young team.

The **1981-82** season opened with the perfect test for Sexton's young lions – his old club Manchester United. It was also the perfect curtain-raiser for the club's new all-seater stadium. Another youth product, Steve Whitton, playing only his second full game, scored in a 2-1 win. Neville Foulger, a proponent of the ground developments, effused in the *Coventry Evening Telegraph*: 'They [City] were as impressive and successful as the new Highfield Road all-seater stadium which housed a crowd who never once resorted to obscene chanting or swearing.' Things went smoothly on the big day. There were no arrests inside the ground, but many felt it lacked atmosphere and wondered what it would be like on a cold winter's day with few visiting supporters to liven proceedings. A crowd of 19,329 paid receipts of £60,000, not far short of the figure paid by a 36,000 crowd at the West Ham game the previous season.

Hopes that the new-look stadium would eradicate hooliganism were dashed in the second home game, against Leeds. City ran rampant, and two visiting fans ran onto the unfenced pitch before half-time. When Garry Thompson later made it 4-0, Leeds fans, who had been slinging abuse from their section in the right hand end of the Sky Blue Stand, started ripping out seats and hurling them onto home fans in the lower tier. It was the worst violence seen in the ground for years and seemed to convince many that it was too much trouble to watch their team. There was more trouble for the visit of Villa in October, when large numbers of visiting fans somehow sat amongst City's.

A mid-table course was steered until December, with only Liverpool lowering the flag at home, but just two points from eight away games told an age-old story. Mick Ferguson, who had left that summer for £300,000, returned to Highfield Road in an Everton shirt for a League Cup-tie and promptly scored a late winner. The good home form did not translate into bigger crowds, and for the visits of Stoke and Middlesbrough there were just 10,000 rattling around the all-seater ground. The Boro game saw a boycott by the *Coventry Evening Telegraph*'s photographer after the newspaper was 'requested' to take action shots with a full main stand as the backdrop rather than the thinly populated opposite side. Doctoring photographs was obviously not seen as reprehensible. Two weeks later the photos were back as the club backed down.

From mid-December to mid-March City picked up just three points, all from draws, in twelve games. The gloom was pierced only by advancing to the quarter-finals of the FA Cup, thanks to wins over Sheffield Wednesday, Manchester City and Oxford. The Oxford tie, which saw a return to Coventry of Roy Barry as manager of United, attracted 20,264, the largest crowd so far at the modified ground. But the Wembley train came to a shuddering halt at the Hawthorns, where Cyrille Regis's superb goal deserved to win any match.

The poor run, which included six home defeats in a row, saw crowds dip below 10,000 for the first time since 1962, with the nadir 9,677 for a midweek game against Nottingham Forest. City slipped into the bottom five after a 0-1 defeat to what Neville Foulger described as 'the poorest Forest team since Brian Clough brought them back into Division 1'. Peter Shilton in the Forest goal had just one save to make all night.

The *Match of the Day* cameras returned to Highfield Road for a 'plum' game against leaders Ipswich. The weather had wrecked the League programme and when City's scheduled game at Old Trafford was postponed the club hastily rearranged the home game with Ipswich on their perfect heated pitch. City, in a dark blue fronted shirt, led 2-1 with ten minutes left but then capitulated, losing 2-4. It was the third time they had lost after strenuous efforts to stage a game in Arctic weather.

A woeful 1-5 home defeat by Notts County was for many City fans the last straw. The night game was preceded by Hill's public address statement that the board had rejected Steve Hunt's transfer request. On the pitch there were other players who gave the impression that they hadn't the appetite to play for the club. Notts could have scored eight and the fans chanted 'Hill out' at the end.

Originally scheduled for January, the visit of Notts County had been postponed despite the pitch being in perfect condition. Ironically, the heavy snow had drifted into the stands, blanketing seats, and the streets around the ground were treacherous.

Just as things were at their blackest, City mounted a revival. Former England captain Gerry Francis had arrived for £145,000 from QPR in February, and his experience was a major factor in the club's resurgence. City's first win in more than three months arrived, of all places, at Old Trafford.

That win triggered a sequence of thirteen games with only one defeat. Highlights of those glorious weeks included a never-to-be-forgotten 5-5 draw at the Dell, the ending of the Hawthorns hoodoo, and City's biggest First Division winning margin, 6-1 over Sunderland. Almost three years had elapsed since a Coventry player last claimed a hat-trick; now Mark Hateley and Steve Whitton notched one apiece in the space of four days, both away from Highfield Road.

The season ended with horrendous scenes when Birmingham arrived. There were twelve arrests and a pitch invasion. The Blues needed to win to avoid relegation and when Mick Harford scored their winning goal four minutes from time hundreds of visiting yobs invaded the pitch. But for prompt action by the police, a serious incident could have occurred. Again, Hill's critics pointed out that this wasn't supposed to happen in his all-seater stadium.

The good run-in which lifted City to 14th helped attract a few bigger crowds, but the season's average of 13,100 was 3,800 down, and only Notts County had a lower average in the top division. It was also the lowest home average since 1961-62, Hill's first season as manager. The general feeling was that the all-seater stadium was a white elephant.

In March the ground again hosted a Youth international with England drawing 2-2 with Scotland – going out 2-3 on aggregate – in a European Youth championship qualifier. A crowd of 2,295 saw England lead 2-0 through goals from Sheffield Wednesday's John Pearson and Aston Villa's Mark Walters, but goals from Celtic's Paul McStay and Jim Dobbin settled the outcome. City's Martin Singleton played for England in midfield, alongside Arsenal's Stewart Robson, who would play for City ten years later. Singleton would shortly score City's winner on his debut against Everton – his only ever first-team goal.

Coventry Schools team had their best season in years and reached the final of the English Schools FA Trophy for the first time in its 76-year history. They faced Sheffield in the final and despite only losing 0-1 at Bramall Lane in the first leg failed to take advantage, despite wearing the club's garish Talbot shirts, in front of a 3,685 home crowd and lost 1-4. One of the Coventry schoolboys, Gareth Evans, went on to play for the Sky Blues in Division One. For Sheffield, several players made it in the game, including midfield dynamo John Beresford who had a successful career with Portsmouth and Newcastle.

If the form shown at the end of the 1981-82 season was meant to carry over into **1982-83**, it was a forlorn hope. Sexton was given no funds to enlarge what had become the smallest squad in the First Division. Several squad players, including Jim Blyth, Bodak, Hagan, Kaiser and Gooding, carried on their careers elsewhere for little or no fees. Early in the season, with goals scarce, Sexton was given licence to buy, snapping up Leicester's Scottish striker Jim Melrose, though he had to sacrifice Tom English in exchange. English thereby rejoined his former manager Gordon Milne, who after one season had tired of his position as City's general manager and been lured back into the manager's seat at Filbert Street. Melrose, who scored a hat-trick on his home debut in a 4-2 win over Everton, would not be long at Highfield Road.

1982-83's opening fixture against unglamorous Southampton attracted only 10,000 to Highfield Road, and neither the performance nor the result, a 1-0 win, encouraged stay-away fans to return. With goalkeeper Les Sealey injured, Perry Suckling, aged sixteen years 320 days, became the second youngest debutant in the club's history, and the youngest home debutant. Another new record was set at the second home game, against Sunderland: despite a glorious August evening the crowd of 8,910 was City's lowest ever in the First Division.

Season-ticket sales were down by around 25 per cent to just over 5,000 and this was reflected in match attendances, which by the December game with Brighton had dropped to 8,035, and the entertainment on offer at some games could best be described as pitiful. Following the 2-0 home win over Norwich in October the *Coventry Evening Telegraph* was stung into printing an editorial entitled 'a vision blurred', which described Highfield Road as a 'dreary and depressing place to be, with spiritless players failing to lift the crowd and the crowd finding no encouragement to cheer on the players'. According to the editorial, the policies of the board were a clear demonstration that Hill was 'out of touch with the people who like to watch football'. Hill responded with a new publicity campaign for the all-seater stadium but it made little difference to attendances. He then scrapped the £5 on-the-day admission surcharge to little avail. The fans bombarded the *Coventry Evening Telegraph* with complaining letters blaming the prices, the poor quality of football, and the lack of success.

Matters got worse before they got better. City's latest nadir was a humiliating League Cup exit at home to lowly Second Division Burnley, described as 'pathetic and shameful' by Neville Foulger in the *CET*. But then the stormclouds lifted. Eleven games with only two defeats hoisted the team to a heady 5th. The defence – with Paul Dyson and Gary Gillespie maturing, and Danny Thomas (now a full England squad member) bristling with confidence – was more than solid. Steve Hunt was by now also being touted as an England possible, while up front the goals flowed from Hateley and Melrose, with Whitton ably in support.

The biggest crowd of the season, 18,945, turned out at Christmas to watch City thrash Manchester United 3-0, but in the first week of January high winds caused the collapse of part of the roof of the Sky Blue Stand. West Midlands County Council ordered the club to close the unsafe stand just two days before a third round FA Cup-tie with non-league Worcester City, reducing the capacity to 12,000. The club had to devote all their time to sorting out the resulting ticket chaos and re-allocating seats, but the game went ahead. The first non-league visitors to the ground since the apocalyptic visit of King's Lynn in 1961 gave the Sky Blues a run for their money by taking the lead, and it needed a late goal to kill them off and make it 3-1. A full-house of 11,881 watched.

The roof collapse was caused by metal fatigue in one of the nineteen support beams, so that the west end section fell onto the seats of Block A below. Frank Haywood, a structural engineer, said that the support had 'broken into pieces like a bar of chocolate'. Approximately ten tons of debris crashed onto the grandstand, and the roof which hung precariously was ordered to be brought down. The council insisted on engineers testing the remaining beams for stress, which took weeks to be carried out. In the meantime the club investigated reopening the Spion Kop terracing to accommodate larger crowds.

Three weeks later the stand was declared safe and the unaffected sections reopened. The *Coventry Evening Telegraph* launched a campaign to reopen the back of the Kop terracing – to house ticket holders only – for the following season. They believed it would be an excellent PR exercise to placate disenfranchised fans who had never wanted an all-seater stadium, and had boycotted Highfield Road for two seasons.

Another, altogether larger storm was brewing. Following the FA Cup exit at lowly Norwich, the board agreed to sell Garry Thompson – valued at £1 million two years earlier – to West Brom for £225,000. Sexton did not want to lose him, arguing that the motives were purely financial.

Jimmy Hill replied that Hateley and Thompson were ill-matched and that the club were massively in debt, again. One consequence of Thompson's departure was to leave Sexton with just fourteen senior players. For the fans, and no doubt the players too, the loss of Thompson spoke volumes about the club's lack of ambition. All that mattered, apparently, was balancing the books and staying up.

Another problem was that the contracts of half the squad would expire in the summer. Not surprisingly, in the final gloomy weeks several players made their feelings plain – they had no intention of putting pen to paper. For its part, the club gave the impression of not wanting to even negotiate new deals. The whole sorry situation was one which guaranteed a crisis. From late February team spirit evaporated and the side fell apart. City picked up only three points, scoring five goals, in thirteen games. From being outside bets for Europe, the team were nose-diving towards relegation. During the game with Birmingham in April, one fan dashed across the pitch, tore off his sky blue shirt and hurled it to the ground in front of the directors box. The police apprehended him but, significantly, the crowd loudly applauded his gesture.

One way or another the board got the message, and behind closed doors it was clear that harmony was in short supply. By early May the directors closed ranks and – though the circumstances are unclear – Hill either volunteered, or, more likely, was forced, to resign. Hill's demise was largely unlamented among supporters at large, who felt that the man who had rebuilt the club as a manager was burying it as chairman. He had brought success to the city in the 1960s, but though the club was crying out for more of the same spirit, it appeared to have deserted him. Hill lost a fortune for himself and the club in America. He had invested in the Sky Blue Connexion rather than players. His dream all-seater stadium flopped and a misguided soccer tour to South Africa collapsed. The *CET* described him as a 'Visionary who lost the Midas touch'. No doubt the passage of time will encourage a more generous verdict on Hill's second coming, but it is fair to say that in May 1983 most fans greeted his departure rapturously.

The players, meanwhile, had more pressing concerns. The team put Hill's departure out of their minds and in the penultimate game ended their horrific run with a 3-0 win at Stoke, ensuring their survival.

On the last day, rumours were rife that Sexton was about to be sacked and Bobby Gould – manager of Bristol Rovers – would be his successor. The rumours were true. On the pitch City lost 2-4 to West Ham, which only underlined the importance of that win at Stoke. The Sky Blues would enter their centenary season among the elite. Some of the players knew it was Sexton's swansong and keeper Les Sealey, deeply affected by the sacking, made schoolboy errors which some fans later interpreted to be deliberate.

For the disaffected players, the departure of their mentor and coach proved to be the final straw, and within days a trickle had turned into a flood. Mark Hateley signed for Second Division Portsmouth for a derisory £190,000. Within a year AC Milan would pay £1 million for the young striker. Danny Thomas went on an FA tour of Australia, becoming the first City player to be capped by England since Reg Matthews in 1956. Within days of returning he signed for Tottenham for £300,000. With Sealey joining Luton for £80,000, Dyson moving to Stoke for £150,000, and Melrose transferred to Celtic for £100,000, the club's overdraft was slashed.

The saddest departure was that of Gary Gillespie, who appeared to back Gould's new regime, but when Liverpool came knocking the temptation was irresistible. Arguably City's best defender of the decade was gone for £325,000. Hateley, Sealey and Thomas all made parting sideswipes, accusing the club of parsimony and lack of ambition, and those fans with long memories would never forget their cruel taunts. As the *Evening Telegraph* pointed out: 'The determination of those players to go is emphasised by the status of the clubs some of them have joined. It is arguable whether their careers will blossom as freely.'

The club's malaise also spread to the reserves, who failed to win at home until the last week in April. With the playing staff down to the bare bones, this was hardly surprising, and the reserves were forced to draft in three University of Warwick players at the end of the season. In consequence, the team suffered relegation from the First Division of the Central League.

The new chairman was 54-year-old Iain Jamieson, a former City player who had married Harry Storer's daughter and become a successful businessman with Coventry-based textile company Courtaulds. After his first board meeting as chairman, he vowed to rebuild the bridges between the club and its supporters, offer more value to the fans, and announced that the Spion Kop terrace would be partially reopened the following season. The £5 on-the-day admission charge would be scrapped. Within days the club sold 300 standing season tickets for the Kop.

During the summer of 1983 repairs were carried out on the Sky Blue stand roof. A 100-ton crane guided two five-ton concrete beams into position. It was a delicate operation with the beams needing to be 'precise to two or three millimetres'. With the Sky Blue stand swathed in scaffolding, this was just the first stage. Later, seven steel hawsers were threaded through the beams and rigidly tightened to secure them. Finally the section was re-roofed and some of the 750 seats crushed in the collapse were replaced. The whole operation cost £50,000 and was ready for the 19 August pre-season friendly with Zimbabwe. Despite Gould signing ten new players, only three appeared in the 2-0 win, with goals from newcomer Graham Withey and another from triallist Charlie George, the former Arsenal and England striker.

Bobby Gould had no illusions about the task confronting him. It wasn't just a question of who would be in the team but whether there would be a team at all. The club was in a sorry state, and disaffected fans needed reassuring, and quickly. In Gould's words: 'I have been thrown into the lion's den. At the moment this club is taking one hell of a battering and I've got one of the toughest battles of my life on my hands.'

Gould had two things going for him – an encyclopaedic knowledge of the lower divisions and a passionate commitment to Coventry City, his home-town club. In all, he spent about £750,000 over the summer, buying players both from the top division and others who had impressed him in the lower leagues. In the former category were Ashley Grimes, Dave Bennett and Terry Gibson. Among the latter were Trevor Peake, Michael Gynn, Dave Bamber and Micky Adams. Others to come on board included Sam Allardyce, Raddy Avramovic, Nicky Platnauer and Graham Withey. The final purchase, Stuart Pearce, didn't arrive until November, but would turn out, pound for pound, to be the best of them all. Pearce cost just £25,000 from non-league Wealdstone and within minutes of his debut, a 1-0 home win over QPR, he looked an outstanding player. With this band of footballing gypsies, Gould faced up to the seemingly impossible task of keeping City in Division One. Predictably, bookies and the pundits made them favourites for the drop.

On the eve of the **1983-84** season the club took another financial kick in the teeth when Talbot abruptly terminated their sponsorship. That meant another £100,000 annual income went by the wayside.

In Gould's first game, at runners-up Watford, he restricted himself to just five of his summer purchases, preferring to give a few long-servers a chance to stake their claim. Fears were quickly dispelled as City waltzed to victory, and the first weeks flew by in a blur as supporters got used to the new faces. Gould's influence ensured that any shortage of skill was compensated for by heart and guts.

By December City were fourth, following a nine-game unbeaten run highlighted by the 4-0 drubbing of champions Liverpool – their heaviest defeat for a decade. It was a day when everything went right for City and is rightly considered to be one of the club's finest ever results. From the first minute when Bruce Grobbelaar failed to hold Terry Gibson's shot and Nicky Platnauer sank to his knees to head the ball over the line, it was City's day. The *Match of the Day* cameras witnessed Gibson becoming the first Coventry player ever to score three against Liverpool, and the first player to do so to the Reds for eleven years. Joe Fagan, the Liverpool boss, admitted City had outclassed his team in every department and tipped them as championship contenders.

Despite a Milk Cup exit at Everton, City's away form was exemplary, earning wins at Highbury, St Andrews, Luton and Stoke. By now, the likes of Gibson, Pearce, Bamber and Platnauer were genuine Sky Blue heroes.

Few could have predicted that City's win at home to Sunderland on 2 January would usher in a dreadful run that was halted only after another thirteen winless games. City dropped down the table like a stone. From gazing up at the ceiling they were left staring at the floor. Confidence drained away, especially at home, where six out of seven games were lost and all the doomsday chickens seemed to be coming home to roost.

The crowd to see Watford in January witnessed one of football's rarities, a goal scored by a goalkeeper. Steve Sherwood's clearance was carried by a strong wind and bounced once and over City keeper Raddy Avramovic for a freak goal. Watford went on to win 2-1.

Yugoslav Avramovic was in trouble again a few weeks later when his errors contributed to a 2-3 home defeat to Stoke. He palmed a cross into his own net and after the game an incandescent Gould vowed never to pick him again.

In an effort to stem the tide Gould tried everything. He swapped the players around, played different tactics, fiddled with formations, all to no effect. On transfer deadline day the club had to cash in on its assets. The unsettled Steve Hunt went for a song (£100,000) to West Brom, skipper 'Harry' Roberts moved to Birmingham, and Bamber, who had faded badly after a bright start, signed for Walsall.

Relegation became possible, then probable. Two loan strikers arrived in a last frantic effort to avoid the drop. Ex-Chelsea star Tommy Langley arrived from a sojourn in Greece, and on the evidence of his two games looked among the worst strikers ever to have disgraced a City shirt. For injury-prone Mick Ferguson, however, it was a sentimental return after four years away. His club, fellow strugglers Birmingham, strangely saw no reason not to lend him back to relegation rivals.

Ferguson scored in his first two games, helping to defeat Wolves and Forest. But the upturn proved to be brief and illusory. There followed four nightmarish games – one point gained, nineteen goals conceded, eight of them at Southampton.

The upshot was that Coventry had to win their final game to stay up. Mid-table Norwich were the visitors and scored first, but City quickly equalised and, with twenty minutes remaining, Dave Bennett put them ahead. Chris Woods could only palm in his teasing cross, sparking off a pitch invasion. In the dying minutes, Norwich striker Robert Rosario was presented with what should have been a gift-goal. A deathly hush fell as his header bounced off the inside of a post into the arms of the petrified Perry Suckling in goal. In the last moments of the last match, soccer's unpredictable wheel of fortune had swung City's way.

Twenty miles away at St Andrews, Birmingham were being denied victory over Southampton by the width of the post. And that would send them down. To add to the irony, Coventry's first goal against Norwich was scored by – guess who – Birmingham reject Mick Ferguson. Gould had achieved his target. It was both modest and monumental – to keep City in Division One.

The manager also had a small hand in the reserves' successful campaign in Division Two of the Pontins Central League. Under the stewardship of John Sillett, they bounced back from relegation to win promotion. Gould, a sprightly 37-year-old, played a handful of games for the reserves including the final game, an 8-0 romp over Middlesbrough.

Attendances were up – 12,500 saw the home opener against Everton, and the average was 2,000 better at 12,587. The reopened section of the Kop increased capacity by around 1,500 to 22,000. Liverpool (20,649) and Manchester United (21,533) were both close to capacity, the latter all-ticket game brought the biggest crowd to the ground since 1981. This was the first season under new rules, whereby home clubs retained their gate receipts. For clubs like City, this was another potential financial disaster: big clubs no longer had to share the receipts from a 40,000 crowd, and overall it widened further the gap between the rich and the poor in the League.

The season was marred by numerous crowd disturbances, and following the visit of Birmingham in March the club's newly appointed secretary, Graham Hover, warned that fences might well return to Highfield Road. The Football Association were apparently concerned at the frequency of disturbances and the club was compelled to give assurances that security arrangements would be improved for the next season. At a likely cost of £100,000, this was money the club did not have and Gould's hands would be tied in the transfer market. Later, after the Arsenal home defeat, there was a pitched battle in Thackhall Street.

Having had their nerves shredded in 1983-84, the last thing supporters needed was another relegation battle in **1984-85**. Not only was that what they got, the struggle pitched City even closer to the brink. The circumstances of their eventual escape would cement the club's status as the 'Great Houdinis' of the First Division.

Gould had shuffled the pack vigorously in the summer. Six players came in, Steve Ogrizovic (Shrewsbury), Brian Kilcline (Notts County) and Kirk Stephens (from Luton in exchange for Ashley Grimes). Three other players arrived on frees: Bob Latchford from Dutch club Breda, Martin Jol (West Brom), and Kenny Hibbitt (Wolves). Gould failed, however, to land his top target, Burnley striker Billy Hamilton, a failure later cited by Gould as a major contributory factor in him being sacked.

The boardroom was no more stable than the dressing room, with Jersey-based (but Coventry-born) John Poynton taking over the chairmanship from Ian Jamieson. Poynton had the blessing of majority shareholder Derrick Robins, who gave the new man an option to buy the Robins family shares. The *Coventry Evening Telegraph* paid handsome tribute to the outgoing chairman: 'Most of all, Jamieson's one year reign will be remembered for bringing the club back to the supporters. Gone was the arrogance that distanced it from the people of the city – and in its place all the effort the new management team could muster to seek better relations with the local community. What was missing was the risk capital to invest in new players. By persuading John Poynton to return to his home town with some of the fortune he has made since leaving it, the management now have money to invest.'

A month into the 1984-85 season, with City already languishing near the foot of the table after one win in eight games, Gould appointed the Scot, Don Mackay, as his assistant. By October the benefits of Poynton's involvement began to be felt. Gould swooped for Peter Barnes (£65,000 from Leeds), Cyrille Regis (from West Brom for £300,000), and – a month later – midfielder Dave Bowman from Hearts for £175,000. Regis and Barnes were former internationals, keen to rebuild careers with a club prepared to assist them. To the ultra-critical supporters, such buys showed that City meant business.

On the field, however, things were not going well. Successive home defeats by Manchester United and Arsenal were followed by a humbling 0-3 Milk Cup exit at home to Third Division Walsall. Lack of goals and a worrying inability to hold onto a lead had become major problems: in November alone the defence shipped fourteen goals in four games, and saw heavy defeats at Chelsea (2-6) and West Brom (2-5). Hard-fought wins over Watford and Sheffield Wednesday were mere glimpses of light in an ocean of doom. By and large, City's new players were performing no better than the old.

Spineless Christmas losses at Leicester and Luton sealed Gould's fate. At Filbert Street the irate manager strode onto the pitch during play, risking serious retribution from the FA. The calendar year 1984 had been wretched, nine games won out of 42, and the buck stopped with Gould. The fans were largely sympathetic to the beleaguered manager – who was voted Coventry's sports personality of 1984 – insisting that he deserved credit for keeping City up, and more time in which to impose himself. Chairman Poynton thought otherwise: he was ambitious, impatient, and – after Gould's sacking – unrepentant.

Gould's assistant, Don Mackay, took temporary charge, with Frank Upton as his deputy. Without radically interfering, Mackay initially did the trick. The defence stopped leaking goals and Gibson kept scoring them. Five wins in eight games, including a headline-making victory at Old Trafford, ensured Mackay was confirmed as boss in March, but Easter brought him back to earth. A flu virus swept through the club, causing the postponement of three matches. By the time the players were fit to resume, the team's inactivity had seen them slide into the bottom three.

A home defeat by rivals Sunderland made matters worse. City staggered through a tough closing programme and after a 0-0 draw at Ipswich the magnitude of the task confronting them was clear. Sunderland and Stoke were doomed, leaving one other club to join them. Norwich had finished their programme with 49 points, eight more than City, who still had three games to play. Put simply, Coventry had to win all three of their remaining games. Anything less and, come August, they would be playing in Division Two. Almost everyone was resigned to relegation.

The first game was at moribund Stoke. It should have been easy: it wasn't. City scraped home 1-0, thanks to a Stuart Pearce penalty, and only survived when Ian Painter – later to join the Sky Blues – hit the underside of the bar with a penalty. Then Luton came to Highfield Road and fought as if their lives depended on it. The points were settled by a thunderous volley from Kilcline, which flew into the net with just six minutes remaining. All now rested on the visit of Everton, the newly crowned champions of England.

Their title was mainly down to a twenty-game post-Christmas run of which the Toffees had won seventeen, drawn two, and lost only once – the week before their disappointing FA Cup final defeat by Manchester United. Having been robbed of the double, it was not surprising that Everton were hardly fired up. City's Easter virus meant that they would have to play almost into June to round off their League programme, while jaded Everton would doubtless have preferred to be on the beach. They were already incapacitated by injuries to four regulars – Peter Reid,

Gary Stevens, Derek Mountfield and former Villa striker Andy Gray –
and had nothing to play for but pride.

An all-ticket 21,596 crowd packed Highfield Road for a match that,
because of a Scotland v England international at Hampden Park on the
Saturday, kicked off at 11.30am on a sunny Sunday. For City's long-suffering fans, accustomed over the years to a diet of adrenalin, this would
have been another occasion for watching a game through closed fingers,
but they were rewarded with a goal inside four minutes – a strong Regis
header from a Kilcline flick-on. Regis was a constant thorn in Everton's
side, and contributed to a second goal scored by Micky Adams, who beat
Southall with a lovely ground shot. By half-time, however, the champions
had pulled a goal back and could have had more. Mercifully Regis scored
again 90 seconds after the restart, and with twelve minutes left Gibson
sprinted clear to beat Southall from the edge of the area. It was his nineteenth goal of the season. City might have ended up with six or seven.
Not so pleased were the players of Norwich City, many of whom were
relaxing on a beach when they heard the score. Norwich made obligato-
ry protests about Everton fielding a weakened side, but all to no avail. It
was the first time since December 1982 that City had won three games in
a row.

Neville Foulger, in his match report in the *Coventry Evening Telegraph*
pleaded 'never again' but it is sad to record that twelve months hence, for
the third successive season, City would also have to win their final game
to stay up.

Attendances were slightly up to an average of 12,862, although the
lowest – 8,807 – was 6,000 below the club's break-even figure. One reason given for staying away was hooliganism, which raised its ugly head in
the second home game, against Leicester. Rival fans fought on the pitch
soon after kick-off. The game was suspended for eleven minutes while
police cleared the hooligans off. Referee Tony Ward took the players off,
and Bobby Gould appealed via a microphone for peace. As the players
returned, the tannoy announced that under no circumstances would the
game be abandoned. Any further trouble would lead to the ground being
cleared. It was the worst violence yet seen at the all-seater stadium and
prompted immediate action. Poynton ordered security fences for three
sides of the pitch (all bar the main stand) and a visitors pen at the Kop
end. Manchester United were the next visitors, but that was too soon for
the work to be carried out. A 25 per cent increase in match-day tickets
was imposed to help pay for the work. In the meantime, the FA charged
City with misconduct, fined them £1,000, and made it clear that if fences
had not been put up then the ground would have been closed.

At a cost of £50,000, the new ten-foot high fences were in place for the Walsall Milk Cup-tie, but as a temporary measure the standing room on the Kop was given to away fans until the summer, when a segregated area would be constructed. In addition, a double fence was installed in the Sky Blue stand to divide rival fans. Before the seats were removed from the Kop, Manchester City yobs ripped out 500 and hurled pieces on to the pitch near the end of the FA Cup-tie in January. As a result, City were landed with a £2,000 bill.

In an effort to avoid trouble, the Chelsea home game in February was moved to an 11.30am start and made all-ticket. Over 2,500 Chelsea fans travelled, many without tickets, but on police advice they were all let in to avoid trouble outside. With City charging an exorbitant £6 to the visitors it was a lucrative day for the club.

In early September, Brian 'Harry' Roberts was awarded a testimonial and the current team drew 4-4 with an ex-City players XI captained by Harry. It was not a serious game but the crowd of 2,880 gave Roberts a memorable reception.

In January 1985 the ground hosted one of the strangest matches in its history, a behind closed doors FA Cup-tie between Leicester and Burton Albion. The original third round tie, which had been switched from Burton to the Baseball Ground, saw Gordon Milne's Leicester win 6-1. Trouble between 'neutral' Derby and Leicester fans saw a missile strike Paul Evans, the Burton keeper on the head, temporarily stunning him. An FA enquiry ruled that the game should be replayed behind closed doors. Originally scheduled again for Derby, it was moved to Highfield Road because of pitch conditions and was played on a Wednesday afternoon. Paul Ramsey's winning goal Leicester was greeted by eerie silence from the virtually empty stands and terraces.

Another unique occasion occurred in late May when the club hosted the finals of the European Championships of the Telecommunications and Post Offices. Great Britain, Italy, Holland and Switzerland took part in the four-team tournament of two semi-finals, a final and a third-place match over three days. After its completion the teams were guests at a banquet in the club's Grandstand Restaurant. Sadly there is no record of who won the tournament.

In February icy weather caused City's home game with Everton to be postponed, with the pitch, terraces and stands blanketed by snow. It brought City groundsman Joe Forster into the spotlight. At that time he had been at the club for thirteen years and head groundsman since 1980.

The **1985-86** season began badly and got steadily worse. Survival was again the name of the game, with City's Division One status preserved again only by victory in their final match. It was a season in which the coach was sacked, the manager quit, and three different captains were appointed.

By City's standards, transfer activity in the summer of 1985 was quiet. Stuart Pearce and Ian Butterworth left to join Brian Clough's Nottingham Forest for a combined fee of £450,000. Mackay's replacement full-backs were destined to play a part in the club's FA Cup fantasy the following season. Brian Borrows had been a fine youngster at Everton, but found his opportunities limited by the form of Gary Stevens. Borrows moved to Bolton, took wing, and it wasn't long before City paid £80,000 to bring him back to Division One. As for Greg Downs, he had been a member of the Norwich side relegated by City's momentous run in the previous season. He was too good for Division Two, and a fee of £40,000 secured his transfer.

The captaincy issue blew up even before the season started. Trevor Peake was sent home from the club's pre-season base at Crystal Palace Sports Centre after a confrontation between the skipper and manager Mackay. The incident sparked allegations of a behind-the-scenes revolt, though this was vehemently denied by Mackay and most of the players. But Peake relinquished the captaincy by 'mutual agreement' and midfielder Wayne Turner, signed from Luton over the summer, was eventually handed the job. Injury, however, sidelined Turner for the first five matches. He was on the outside looking in as City picked up just two points from a possible fifteen.

The home defeat by Newcastle on 26 August provided a foretaste of things to come. City led through Terry Gibson, but conceded two goals in the last five minutes. 'A disgrace,' fumed an irate Mackay. 'It was down to a lack of discipline – we just didn't do our job properly.' Sadly, he was to say much the same many times in the coming months, with the Sky Blues proving particularly vulnerable in front of their own fans.

Home results went from bad to worse, the total of ten defeats being the worst at Highfield Road in nineteen seasons of First Division football. At one stage Coventry went four and a half months between one home win and the next – they beat Leicester on 6 October but did not win again until the 3-2 victory over Southampton on 22 February. It was hardly surprising that gates plummeted. Never was the ground full to its 22,500 capacity (the Kop having been completely restored to standing terraces) and the biggest gate – for the visit of Manchester United – failed to top 17,000. Two weeks after Watford knocked City out of the FA Cup, the Hornets returned in the League. This time the gate was a paltry 7,478, which still constitutes City's lowest ever top division crowd and the lowest League crowd since 1962. Even the vital last game attracted only 14,080. Around the country attendances were down almost everywhere, following the Heysel and Bradford disasters, as fans turned away from the nation's national sport.

There were other ramifications of Heysel. The Government imposed an alcohol ban on football clubs and John Poynton estimated that it cost the club £30,000 in unlet executive boxes. The ban on British clubs from European club competitions did not affect the Sky Blues, but two years later would deprive the club and its supporters of exciting trips to the continent.

After their poor start, City stemmed the tide, helped by the return of Lloyd McGrath. A run of one defeat in nine games saw comprehensive home wins over West Brom and Leicester and an amazing Milk Cup-tie with Chester. Having earned a one-goal lead from the first leg, City let rip in the second, winning 7-2, with Cyrille Regis setting a League Cup record of five goals – which equalled his total haul the previous season. It was the first five-goal haul by a City player since the 1930s. Sadly there were only 5,500 to witness the feat. In the main, however, the goals continued to fall to his striking partner, Terry Gibson, with the result that City had to fend off numerous enquires about the tiny striker.

December was a shocker, which saw City slip back to 17th, following a Boxing Day home defeat by struggling Ipswich. Skipper Wayne Turner was substituted, and a few days later he handed the captaincy to Brian Kilcline. Continued bad form into January prompted more changes – on and off the field. Three new directors – Ted Stocker, John Reason and Derrick Richardson, all Poynton men – joined the board, which almost in the same breath accepted Manchester United's £650,000 bid for Gibson. Scottish international striker Alan Brazil arrived as part of the deal, and some of the balance was used to buy Nick Pickering from Sunderland and Jim McInally, a full-back cum midfielder, from Forest.

The club had revealed £800,000 debts in December and when a half-baked attempt by Poynton to raise £400,000 by way of a rights issue was scuppered by Derrick Robins, the sale of the prize asset Gibson had become inevitable.

The comings and goings freshened up the side for a while. Excellent wins at Oxford and Tottenham, plus a 4-4 draw with Birmingham, and the long-awaited first home victory for nineteen weeks – 3-2 over Southampton after being two down – hinted at better times. It was not to be. After squandering a lead to lose at Leicester, City sank back into the red zone. Someone had to take the rap, and coach Upton was sacked the week after Easter.

Mackay stayed on – but not for long. Eight games without a win, cul-minating in an abject surrender at Anfield, saw him dramatically leave with just three matches to go, at which point City lay nineteenth. Perhaps Mackay jumped; more likely he was pushed.

Executive Director George Curtis and youth-team coach John Sillett took temporary charge, and a side unrecognisable from the previous game beat Luton 1-0 to ease the pressure. But for the third season in a row City's bid for safety went to the wire. City entered their final game at home to QPR as one of four teams hoping to avoid joining Birmingham and West Brom in Division Two. If they failed, three Midlands clubs would drop together. City had a point more than Leicester and Oxford, who had a game in hand, but one point less than Ipswich.

City were hit by a sucker punch after 28 minutes when QPR's John Byrne scored with a shot that went in off Trevor Peake. City might have crumbled, but Curtis and Sillett were made of stern stuff. Urging on their team from the sidelines, they were rewarded when City won a free-kick on the edge of the box. Up stepped Brian Kilcline to drill home the equaliser. And better was to come. Just before half-time Dave Bennett carved out a shooting chance to fire City ahead.

With Leicester winning, Oxford and Ipswich drawing, it was impera-tive that City held on. The second half saw Rangers at their most men-acing, playing like a side with nothing to lose, while City played in the knowledge that they had everything to lose! Desperate defending kept QPR at bay but in the 77th minute only the crossbar denied an equaliser. After the final whistle blew, all ears turned towards other results. Ipswich had lost and so City were safe.

Once again the fans invaded the pitch for the annual last-match ritu-al. Curtis 'reluctantly' let City players celebrate with the crowd – 'reluc-tantly' because safety was no cause for celebration. The local press spec-ulated about the sort of reaction if City ever won anything. Twelve months later they would find out.

The club had entered a new competition, the Full Members Cup. Thirty-two First and Second Division clubs were initially invited, but when the competition started in mid-September there were only 21 tak-ing part, and only five from the top flight. Despite the lure of a Wembley final, many clubs did not want another domestic cup and the attendances confirmed that the fans did not want one either. City were put in a group with Stoke and Millwall, the teams playing each other once and the group winners progressing to a knock-out stage. City lost 0-3 at Stoke, and when Millwall and Stoke drew it rendered the final game – City v Millwall – meaningless from City's point of view if not Millwall's. In consequence, only 1,111 turned up – the lowest ever for a competitive game, if it could be described thus. Only the main stand was open, plus the Spion Kop. The hardy few saw Terry Gibson score in his seventh successive game – a new post-war club record – in the meaningless 1-1 draw. The competition did not impress anyone, that is until the final at Wembley, when 67,000 watched Chelsea beat Manchester City 5-4.

For the first time in five years the club had a strong youth team. Ably coached by John Sillett, the youngsters – who included sixteen-year-olds Tony Dobson and Steve Livingstone – put together a good FA Youth Cup run. A 7-1 victory over Wolves was followed by wins at Newcastle (4-1) and Tottenham (2-1) to send the kids through to a semi-final. In the home first leg 3,434 watched them lose 0-2 to Manchester United. A 1-1 draw at Old Trafford saw United through to the final. The reserves, too, had a successful season, winning promotion back to Division One of the Central League.

City's previously superb pitch deteriorated through the side-effects of the under-soil heating. Apparently the soil around the pipes had become rock hard, making drainage almost non-existent. Surface water could not escape quickly enough and made for a heavy pitch. Groundsman Joe Forster's remedy was to put tons of sand onto the pitch, to break up the compaction, and also lay additional drainage pipes. The pitch was then re-seeded and the improvements created better root growth. Disaster, however, struck in January 1987 when a faulty boiler burst pipes. The whole system was put out of action for the season.

Coventry fans were fed up with the slogan 'never again', trotted out three seasons running after nail-biting relegation escapes. The appointment of former captain George Curtis as manager and managing director, backed up by John Sillett as first-team coach, was seen by most supporters as unadventurous and unambitious. Terry Yorath had been the name on many lips, but the board veered away from the people's choice and plumped for the option that they believed offered stability.

Nor were supporters reassured by the club's summer transfers. Alan Brazil was jettisoned after only fifteen games, joining QPR for £200,000, at a net loss to City of £100,000. Suspicions that Brazil was unfit were confirmed soon afterwards, when he was forced to retire with back problems. Scots Jim McInally and Dave Bowman, bought by previous managers, were sold to Dundee United for a combined £130,000. This also constituted a loss, particularly as both gave fine service to the Tannadice club and won Scottish caps. Wayne Turner joined Brentford for £35,000.

The net proceeds went towards the purchase of Scunthorpe striker Keith Houchen (£60,000), Manchester City's Welsh midfielder David

Phillips (£50,000, plus Perry Suckling) and Stoke's Under-21 international Ian Painter (£80,000). Phillips and Houchen debuted in an opening-day defeat at West Ham. Painter was forced out of the game through injury the following summer.

The major difference between **1986-87** and the previous season was tactical. McGrath was the lynchpin in midfield, supported by Phillips and Pickering. Up front, Regis started alongside Houchen, but Dave Bennett soon established himself as Cyrille's preferred partner and dazzled in his new role. Sillett appears to have been the first City boss to consult Regis about his preferred style of play, learning that the big man wanted the ball to his feet rather than in the air. High balls into the box would from now on be strictly rationed.

That loss at Upton Park was followed by an eight-game unbeaten run, the highlight of which was the 3-0 defeat of Newcastle in which Regis shone. After so many false dawns, the fans were unlikely to get carried away, and were certainly not returning in droves, as the 11,000 gate testified. The squad was so small that supporters dreaded the inevitable injury crisis that would scythe down the team.

The good run was ended, predictably, by Aston Villa, who could still win at Highfield Road despite having their worst season for years. But the snap purchase of Rotherham's midfield dynamo Dean Emerson – following his eye-catching display against City in the League Cup – was the catalyst for another string of good results, the best being the scalp of leaders Nottingham Forest. A League Cup replay exit at Anfield, and a first round exit at Norwich in the daft Full Members Cup, did little to dampen City's League form. The Liverpool home tie, 0-0, was watched by 26,440, generating club record receipts in excess of £100,000. The Spion Kop terraces were packed like the good old days.

By Christmas, not only had the Sky Blues rarely been out of the top eight, but they also boasted one of the best defensive records in the division. The Christmas win over Tottenham finally won over the doubting Thomas's. Described by some as the game of the decade, City twice came from behind, before Regis clinched a 4-3 win in injury-time. Gynn and Houchen were back in the side, by this time, and Emerson's impact was immense.

The FA Cup run started inauspiciously at home to Phil Neal's Bolton, who were sent packing 3-0 on an icy pitch. Next up were Manchester United, still finding their feet under new manager Alex Ferguson. Keith Houchen, the man destined to be dubbed 'Roy of the Rovers', snatched a goal, City soaked up the pressure and the first signs of Cup fever hung in the air.

The Victoria Ground was the next stop and Michael Gynn scored the winner in front of 8,000 travelling fans. The Sky Blues were now through to only their fifth quarter-final in 104 years. The win over Stoke was the second in a run of six victories which established a post-war club record. Sheffield Wednesday were City's victims in the last eight, in what became known as 'Houchen's match'. Sillett had had to shuffle the side following Emerson's knee injury the previous week, and Bennett took his place to set up all three City goals. Over 14,000 City fans travelled to Hillsborough and a 48,000 crowd meant the club had already netted £150,000 from their Cup exploits.

The semi-final was against Second Division Leeds United. City returned to neutral Hillsborough just four weeks after their quarter-final win, and this time 27,000 supporters made the trek for the Sunday lunchtime confrontation. ITV screened the game in its entirety, but with an hour's time lapse. City needed extra-time to dispose of Billy Bremner's stubborn side, and the tie was rated by David Miller in *The Times* as one of the best the competition had seen in the last twenty years.

David Rennie, later to become a Sky Blue player, headed Leeds ahead and the score remained 1-0 until the 68th minute, when Gynn levelled from Bennett's cross. Houchen then gathered a ricochet off Ormsby, side-stepped Mervyn Day in the Leeds goal, to make it 2-1. When Ritchie crossed and Edwards converted it was back to 2-2 and extra-time. Leeds – with Micky Adams at left-back – looked to have the wind in their sails, but it was City who scored. Bennett was fouled, Gynn floated across the free-kick, Regis headed back at the far post, Houchen shot against Day, Bennett pounced, 3-2. When Ogrizovic then blocked from Edwards, Wembley beckoned.

The League run in to Wembley was largely carefree. City were for once safe from relegation and ended the season unbeaten in seven games. Along the way, Liverpool's title hopes were buried, 1-0, before a gate of 26,657 – City's biggest League crowd for six years. Home gates, averaging a break-even 12,000 in February, rocketed in the last weeks when attendance was necessary to stand any hope of obtaining a Wembley ticket. The team finished 10th, their best for nine years, winning fourteen home games – a club record in the top flight.

Brian Borrows injured a knee in the last home game, Southampton, denying him a place in the greatest day in City's history. Also missing was Dean Emerson, who had suffered a chipped bone in his knee in an earlier League clash with Sheffield Wednesday.

Throughout the Southampton game the fans performed the Mexican Wave – introduced during the Mexico World Cup a year earlier – and everyone seemed to have a flag or banner. In the carnival-like atmosphere there was little interest on the result, and a tame 1-1 draw ensued.

As we all know, the dreams of every Coventry fan came true in a fairy-tale game as City twice came from behind to win the FA Cup in their first final. In a classic contest, City's never-say-die attitude won the day over the superstars from north London.

Perhaps it was clear all along that this would be Coventry's year. John Sillett had been saying since February that City's name was on the Cup and *Old Moore's Almanac* predicted that a team in blue stripes would win it. The bookies favoured logic to astrology, installing Tottenham as firm favourites. After all, Spurs had never lost in seven FA Cup finals.

After just two minutes it looked as though the bookies were right. Clive Allen darted in front of Trevor Peake to net with a near-post head-er. City were soon level: Downs crossed, Houchen flicked on and Bennett was there in a flash, guiding the ball past Spurs' 39-year-old keeper Ray Clemence.

Tottenham restored their advantage five minutes before the break, this time with a messy goal. Hoddle's free-kick caught Ogrizovic in two minds, the ball bounced off Kilcline and ended up in the net. The FA later credited the goal to Gary Mabbutt. It was now that City began to show their mettle. After a quiet first half, Bennett started to impose him-self and it was his cross that eluded Gough for Houchen to equalise with a famous horizontal header. Roy of the Rovers had struck again, with his fifth Cup goal of the season.

It was now anyone's game. Just six minutes into extra-time Rodger – a substitute for the injured Kilcline – sent McGrath clear down the right, and his cross-cum-shot deflected off Mabbutt's knee over the Clemence to put City ahead for the first time.

Doubts about City's ability to hold out and turn the tide of history proved unfounded. It was Spurs who were now on the back foot. Even before the referee blew for time, the Sky Blue Song was echoing around Wembley, and moments later the substituted Kilcline climbed the 39 steps to receive the Cup.

City's fans gave a sporting ovation to Spurs, reserving their taunts for TV pundit Jimmy Greaves, who had predicted Coventry's demise at every hurdle. The media concurred that this had been one of the best FA Cup finals since the war and that the underdogs had merited their win.

The club had been allocated 25,000 tickets, and their sale degenerated into an administrative nightmare. Secretary Graham Hover prophetically described it as 'an impossible task', and so it proved. Season ticket hold-ers, executive club members and shareholders were allocated one ticket each. The club, keen to sign up more season ticket holders, sold tickets to over 2,000 fans who signed up for the following campaign's season ticket. The rest went on general sale to those able to show ticket stubs from five specific recent games.

The general sale was due to start on Tuesday morning. Hundreds were queuing from the Saturday night after the final home game. By Monday morning, with fans packing the VIP car park and spilling into the west end, the club decided, with police advice, to start selling tickets 24 hours early. To compound matters and generate a healthy black market, fans could buy up to ten tickets each. This meant thousands of fans were left without, and whilst it was a practical solution to a potentially serious situation, it was a PR disaster.

Not content with lifting one trophy, the club's youth team, well-marshalled by former player Mick Coop, won the FA Youth Cup for the first time. In a two-legged final against Charlton the Sky Blue babes drew 1-1 at Selhurst Park before winning the second leg 1-0 after extra-time, three days before the seniors did battle at Wembley. Steve Livingstone was the hero, scoring the winner in front of 12,142 fans. Five of the team subsequently appeared for the first team but none, maybe Livingstone apart, made a lasting impression.

Having acquired not just one trophy but two, the club needed somewhere to display them. In August 1987 a 30-foot trophy cabinet was installed in the Vice-Presidents room on the ground floor in the main stand. The impressive cabinet cost several thousand pounds and was paid for by Vice-President Graham Ratcliffe.

Three months after the FA Cup triumph, Coventry fans returned to Wembley for the Charity Shield match against Champions Everton. The size of the City support demonstrated their exaggerated expectations. After the Cup, the League? Europe? Some hopes. Within three months those dreams were shattered. City went through ten games without a win and last season's heroes were this season's villains.

An uncharacteristic Peake error, which led to Wayne Clarke's goal, decided the Charity Shield, which enabled Everton to carve their name on the trophy for a record fourth time. The outing gave City fans a first look at new striker David Speedie, purchased from Chelsea for £780,000. During the summer John Sillett had stepped up from coach to manager, and as he unveiled his prize new signing he uttered the immortal words: 'for too long this club has shopped at Woolworth's, from now on we'll be shopping at Harrods.' The truth was that although the club's Cup run had helped to pay off the overdraft, success would have to come knocking regularly for Sillett to return to the Knightsbridge emporium.

The **1987-88** fixture computer perversely sent Tottenham to Highfield Road on the opening day, and they lost again. Speedie scored after 21 minutes of his League debut. A crowd of 23,947 turned up on a sweltering afternoon to applaud the FA Cup holders and the home crowd took the opportunity to taunt the unfortunate Gary Mabbutt, who had forever endeared himself to City fans for his own-goal at Wembley.

Liverpool, the second visitors to Highfield Road, were made of sterner stuff and outclassed a slapdash and cocky Sky Blues to win 4-1. That result slammed the door on the Cup final party and brought City fans and players alike down to earth with a bump. Any pretensions to a major assault on the title were ruthlessly ended that afternoon.

The real problems, however, started in October, with two bad home defeats in four days. Southampton won at Highfield Road for the first time since 1949, recovering from a two-goal deficit, and Newcastle, with Paul Gascoigne and Mirandinha dazzling, won with something to spare. Luton dashed City's League Cup hopes in a third round tie at Filbert Street (because of Kenilworth Road's ban on away fans), and the large City support was reduced to chanting 'What a load of rubbish'. It already seemed light years from Wembley. As Christmas approached, the side drew five games in a row, three of them without a goal, and doubts about pairing Regis with Speedie in attack intensified.

It was at home that City really suffered. The team went from early October until mid-February without a home League win. Fortunately away results went some way to redress the balance and kept Sky Blue heads above the relegation waters. City began their defence of the FA Cup at home but made heavy weather of disposing of Torquay. Three weeks later lowly Watford ended a feeble defence of the trophy, with the poor Highfield Road pitch shouldering much of the blame.

It had been Coventry's misfortune to win the FA Cup during the five-year penance English clubs served following the deaths at Heysel. Denied a place in the Cup-Winners' Cup, they sought consolation in the Simod Cup, a joke Mickey Mouse competition introduced by the English football authorities to compensate clubs for the lost revenues of competing in Europe. The two teams reaching the final would be granted a Wembley showcase. City defeated Ipswich and Wimbledon in front of small crowds to set up a semi-final at Second Division Reading. The thought of a third visit to the Twin Towers in a matter of months – no matter the reduced circumstances – was enough to entice thousands to queue in the rain for hours to buy tickets. Defeat in a penalty shoot-out, which was not concluded until 10.45pm, denied them their cherished visit to the national stadium, which would otherwise have become a home from home.

Paradoxically, Watford's FA Cup ambush lifted a weight from the City players' minds. Their form picked up, and a sixteen-game League run saw only two defeats, both at home. Injuries and vagaries of form meant that by curtain fall Sillett's line-up contained only five of his Wembley heroes. Dave Bennett and Lloyd McGrath had suffered broken legs, Phillips, Gynn and Downs had lost their cutting edge, while Houchen was picked only intermittently all season. Borrows, when fit again, had regained his full-back place, and Dean Emerson and Steve Sedgley policed midfield. Gary Bannister had returned to the club for £300,000 from QPR, and young David Smith, on the verge of being freed the previous summer, had forced his way into the side in February and made a major impact on the left flank. Regis recovered from a poor autumn, ironically after he had been recalled to the England squad after a six-year break. But as ever, Cyrille Regis seldom threatened to score, preferring to win the plaudits for leading the line with verve and leave the scoring to others. One such 'other' should have been David Speedie, but despite playing in almost every game, he netted only six goals. The club already had one classy striker who did not score his quota, and could not afford two.

City finished 10th, which would have been creditable enough in an earlier era, but not now that Sillett had promised the moon. In fact, City had finished 10th the previous season, too, which meant no improvement at all. The supporters, appetites whetted, looked upon the mid-table not as a glass half-full but as half-empty, which confirmed the extent to which raised aspirations can distort perceptions. Supporters no longer just hoped, they expected, and the attendances reflected the mood. Home gates were the best for seven years, the average of 17,530 being up 10 per cent on the year, boosted by a three-fold increase in season tickets, which at 8,700 was the highest since 1970.

The pitch caused numerous problems. In October the Southampton game was called off two and a half hours before kick-off after the referee Mike Peck decided the surface was unplayable. Sky Blues secretary Graham Hover was stunned: 'As far as we are concerned, our drainage system worked and, in our opinion, the pitch was playable.' By the time of the scheduled kick-off time there was no surface water on the pitch and the game could easily have gone ahead. Peck's decision was hasty, to say the least, and it left the club with a £5,000 bill for catering and police.

On 2 January the situation was repeated after a downpour that morning – at Bablake School 1½ inches of rain was recorded in an hour . The Norwich home game was called off in mid-morning.

Substantial work had been carried out on the pitch over the previous summer, including a new under-soil heating system and new drainage, but the reseeded pitch had not bedded itself properly and was showing signs of serious wear by November. Sillett blamed it for the poor home form and believed the Cup defeat by Watford was down to the beach-like surface caused by pumping 100 tons of sand. Lloyd McGrath has unhappy memories of the pitch: 'John Sillett pulled us to one side before a game and told us we weren't going to like the pitch but that we just had to get on with it. Unfortunately I broke my leg playing on it in a Simod Cup match against Ipswich and was out for nine months.' The Watford game apart, City's home form improved after the sanding, but at the end of March chairman John Poynton declared the pitch would be 'dug up' and relaid at the end of the season. He appointed John Booth, assistant groundsman at Sheffield Wednesday, as ground manager.

Leicester-based consultants WE Hewitt & Son were given the task of restoring the pitch. They had been involved in the sand exercise and, despite much criticism, their director John Hewitt said that without the sand it would have been impossible for the club to complete its home fixtures. Hewitt blamed the problems on a number of causes. These included 'the main stand cutting out sunlight over much of the ground, a peculiar closely locked soil texture and the under-soil heating affecting aeration. His solution, at a cost of £15,000, was to dig a series of 165 ten-inch deep, three-inch wide trenches. These were filled with pea gravel and a special sand, which would aid drainage. The under-soil heating was ripped out and not replaced.

Live TV football came to Highfield Road for the first time on Sunday, 13 December 1987, when the Arsenal game was shown on BBC's *Match of the Day*. The BBC had won a two-year contract in 1986 to show live League games on a Sunday afternoon. In its first season City had featured just once, in a 0-0 draw at Highbury. That score was repeated at Highfield Road in a tepid game.

Ten days later came another Highfield Road first as the Sky Blues met Scottish Cup-holders St Mirren in the first leg of the Anglo-Scottish Cup-Winners' Cup. Owing to the ban on English teams in Europe, the clubs had to get special permission from the Football Association and the Football League to stage the game. City hoped to attract sponsors for the challenge match but it never materialised and after a 1-1 draw in front of 5,331 at Highfield Road, the second leg – scheduled for March 1988 – never even happened.

City were not the only Coventry team successful in 1987. Coventry Bees speedway team won the British League that year, and also lifted the League Cup. At the Chelsea game in March, their captain Tommy Knudsen led their riders on a lap of honour around Highfield Road.

Looking back today, season **1988-89** was not so wretched as it seemed at the time. Back then, the defeat at Sutton blackened everything, hanging like a pall over the club, and it is arguable in retrospect to claim that the club's barren early 1990s was sparked that awful day at Gander Green Lane. The other disappointment at the time was City's failure to clinch their first ever top-four place, though by February that had been within their gasp. Looking on the bright side, 7th place was a considerable achievement, City's highest for eleven years. The club was never out of the top eight. A key factor in the team's form was the conversion of David Speedie from striker to midfield, behind Regis and Bannister, and the little Scot's form was rewarded with a recall to the international scene after a two-year break. Three defenders – Ogrizovic, Borrows and Peake – were also tipped for international honours, but whilst all three were at the height of their powers, the England call never came.

The season had its share of gripping matches – for example, defeating champions Arsenal and finally ending the Villa bogey after 51 years. City also did the double over title-chasing Norwich and Manchester United. On the other hand, City frustrated their fans by losing at home to two relegated teams – Newcastle and Middlesbrough, the latter in a seven-goal thriller – and succumbed early in both cups. To sum up 1988-89 in one word – Sutton – is therefore to oversimplify.

There had been only two significant transfers in the summer. Nick Pickering, unhappy at playing out of position at left-back, moved to Derby for £300,000, and Celtic's reserve winger, Dougie McGuire, signed for £40,000. McGuire soon contracted glandular fever and could not force his way into the first team all season.

City's start was delayed by the postponement of the opening game at Tottenham, when their new east stand failed to receive a safety certificate. Spurs were subsequently docked two points by the FA, later overturned on appeal. A week later, Everton won 1-0 at Highfield Road, courtesy of their new £2 million striker Tony Cottee. He had been a persistent thorn in City's side for West Ham and the goal was his twelfth against the Sky Blues, a record.

By mid-October, however, a good run pushed City up to the heady heights of 3rd. Only Norwich and newly promoted Millwall were above them, and it looked the most open championship races for years.

It was the 1987 hero Keith Houchen who scored the second goal to end the Villa jinx, confirming a first home win over the local rivals in 27 attempts – since Jackie Brown scored the winner in February 1937.

On the Saturday before Christmas, City's home game with Derby was almost abandoned when the floodlights failed during a 0-2 defeat. Just 26

minutes had been played when all four lights went out. There was sufficient light to get to half-time on the shortest Saturday daylight of the season. Behind the scenes, frantic efforts were made to trace the source of
the problems. Just before half-time one of the west end pylons flickered
into life, and afterwards normal service was resumed.

There were further problems at the next game, Sheffield Wednesday,
when the lights only worked to a third of capacity. Graham Hover confirmed that the cause was nothing to do with the new scoreboard but
stemmed from a sub-station in Swan Lane, which the Electricity Board
were rectifying. He also confirmed that the club had an emergency power
supply that could be activated in emergencies, but the halogen floodlights
took 30 minutes to cool down and spark up again.

There was no premonition of the Sutton debacle. The previous week
Speedie had scored a spectacular headed hat-trick – his second headed
threesome of the season – in a 5-0 home romp over Sheffield Wednesday.
The trip to Surrey looked a formality. On the day, City undoubtedly
under-estimated their Conference opponents, and by the time they
realised they were in serious trouble it was too late. It was only the fourth
time since the war that a top division side had gone out of the FA Cup
to non-league opposition.

The one positive outcome of the Sutton disaster was to inspire City
to vent their frustrations on their League opponents. City harvested a
good crop of points over the following weeks. They came from behind
to snatch a win at Norwich, and followed that by beating Wimbledon at
home. In both games Speedie left the fans dazzled with chipped winners.
The most eye-catching result, though, was at home to leaders Arsenal,
destined to win the title in extraordinary circumstances at Anfield in May.
City's hero in this particular match was Brian Kilcline, who recovered
from missing an early penalty to step forward eight minutes from time to
convert a second to earn a 1-0 win. Kilcline had a mixed season with his
penalties – he scored three but squandered four, all at Highfield Road –
and it amazed the fans why Sillett allowed him to keep the job.

The Arsenal win left the Sky Blues dark horses for the championship:
they lay 3rd, eleven points off the top. Four days later Millwall punctured
their hopes and a run of five winless games let the bookies breathe more
easily.

On the transfer front, Sillett was already thinking long-term. Cup final
scorers Houchen and Bennett both left in March. Houchen had been out
of sorts for a while and almost joined QPR, until a red card in a reserve
game resulted in a suspension and the deal collapsing. Hibernian eventually paid £300,000 for him, with Bennett signing for Ron Atkinson's

Sheffield Wednesday in a £250,000 deal that came out of the blue. As for first-team regular Steve Sedgley, he looked set to move on in the summer, but ill-advisedly allowed his agent to pepper the press with a list of grievances, which got everyone's backs up, whereupon Sedgley slapped in a transfer request.

The 1988-89 season – shorter on account of cutting the First Division from 22 clubs to 21, and then twenty – petered out after Liverpool had dished out a lesson in football's finer points, winning 3-1 at Highfield Road in a canter. Although City lost only two of their last nine games, too many were drawn to improve on 7th place. On 15 April, while City played out a 2-2 draw at Luton, 96 Liverpool fans died at Hillsborough. The following Saturday, City and their supporters paid their respects with a minute's silence before the kick-off against QPR. The start was delayed until 3.06pm, the precise time that the Liverpool v Nottingham Forest Cup semi-final had been halted a week earlier.

International soccer returned to Coventry in October with England's Under-21 international against Sweden. Two City players, David Smith and Steve Sedgley, played for England in the 1-1 draw. England's star was goalkeeper Nigel Martyn, then of Bristol Rovers, who foiled a strong Swedish team which included future stars Stefan Scwarz, Martin Dahlin and Tommy Brolin. A wet night kept the crowd down to 4,141. None of the England team became regulars for the England full team.

On a Thursday afternoon in February the club staged a private friendly against Second Division Ipswich. It was organised at short notice to give the team practice with a free Saturday looming. Soviet Union international Sergei Baltacha, the first Russian to grace the Football League, headed an own-goal and Houchen scored City's other in a 2-2 draw.

A new ticket office was opened in Thackhall Street under the Sky Blue stand. The old office had been beneath the main stand since 1936 and moving it made it more accessible. On match-days the old office was opened up for anyone buying tickets for the main stand. Early in the season a new electronic scoreboard, the third at the ground, was erected on the Spion Kop and chairman John Poynton displayed his entrepreneurial streak by getting it 'for free'. The suppliers took advertising revenue from the new board until the costs was recovered, after which the revenue would be shared.

Attendances slipped – hardly a surprise, bearing in mind the several thousand 1987 carpetbaggers who had not renewed the season tickets they had bought in order to watch the 1987 Cup final. The final average, 16,040, was down around 1,500, with the biggest crowd being 23,880 for the visit of Liverpool.

The major problem in **1989-90** was the paucity of goals. In 38 League games City only scored 39, the lowest since 1970-71 when they reached 37. Despite having Cyrille Regis and David Speedie, and the record purchases of Kevin Drinkell and Kevin Gallacher, no City player achieved double figures, the first time this had occurred in fifteen years. Speedie ended the season as top scorer with eight League goals, despite missing eight games through his appalling disciplinary record.

The defence, too, had an off season, conceding 59. If mitigating circumstances are sought, 38 of that total were squeezed into ten games. Liverpool hit City for six, and the Sky Blues were on the wrong end of a 1-4 scoreline on no fewer than five occasions. Yet they still managed to keep thirteen clean sheets.

There was a considerable turnover of players in the summer of 1989. Peter Billing, a young centre-half from Crewe, joined for £120,000, and Kevin MacDonald arrived on a free from Liverpool. David Phillips' contract had expired and he had joined Norwich for a tribunal-set fee of £550,000. Steve Sedgley's transfer request had been granted and he had gone to Spurs – whom he had supported as a boy – for a fee of £750,000. Centre-back Graham Rodger had departed for Luton for £150,000. Transfer fees were escalating, illustrated by Spurs' Chris Waddle signing for Marseille for £4.5 million. Sillett, with a net income of almost £1.3 million, thought the market was overheated and preferred to sit and wait for quality players at affordable prices. When chairman Poynton declared a profit of £770,000 – excluding the summer income – fans questioned the wisdom of waiting.

The season had started brightly, and City's third win in four – over Manchester City with a last-minute goal – lifted them to the top of the table. With a free weekend in the fixture list on account of international duties, City's first occupation of pole position lasted ten days. In their first game as leaders they sank 1-4 at Millwall, who took over the top spot themselves. That game saw Oggy injured, ending his run of 241 uninterrupted appearances, which surpassed Alf Wood's 40-year-old record. Oggy's deputy Keith Waugh made his debut against Luton.

Despite the promising start, Sillett signed Kevin Drinkell, surplus to requirements at Glasgow Rangers, for £800,000. He scored for City after 23 minutes of his debut, a League Cup-tie with his old club Grimsby. His goal sparked a comeback after a 1-3 first-leg defeat had rendered City vulnerable to another early cup exit. Grimsby, with Tony Rees sent off early, collapsed in the face of a five-man forward line, and City won 3-0.

Away wins at QPR and Manchester City saw City through to the last eight of the League Cup where a kind draw sent them to Second Division

Sunderland. A sniff of Wembley was in the air again, but before the tie City suffered more FA Cup embarrassment, this time at Third Division Northampton. The Cobblers made light of a glue-pot pitch and their solitary goal was enough against a sad City who barely created a chance. The supporters vented their anger: nothing seemed to have been learned in the twelve months since Sutton. It was time for action, and but for City being in the quarter-finals of the other cup, that action would surely have been forthcoming. Sillett, off the hook, did nothing other than appoint a new coach, Dixie McNeil. Many fans thought the side sterile and boring, the antithesis of Sillett's principles, and that the man who masterminded the heroics of 1987 had stayed loyal for too long to the under-achievers in his team.

The heated reaction to the Northampton defeat stirred up the players sufficiently to despatch Sunderland, after a replay, in the best home result of the season. Young centre-forward Steve Livingstone – yet to score in the League – scored four of City's five goals. It had been clear from the outset that there were scores to settle after the first game at Roker, where Speedie and Sunderland's Gary Bennett were dismissed, and Speedie was singled out for harsh treatment. This saw two Sunderland players booked and Gary Owers sent off just before half-time for elbowing. Sunderland were already trailing by two goals, so that was that.

City's reward was a potentially mouth-watering two-leg semi-final with Brian Clough's Nottingham Forest. Forest won the first leg 2-1, and then at Highfield Road in front of the television cameras battened down the hatches, securing the goalless draw they sought, *en route* to a successful Wembley final against Oldham. An all-ticket crowd of 25,500, just 300 short of the ground capacity, watched the second leg and paid record receipts of £177,000. Six thousand Forest fans chanted 'You'll never beat Des Walker', as the outstanding English defender of his generation marshalled Clough's miserly troops. The perimeter fences at the west end and in front of the Sky Blue stand were removed for the game, after six years in place, and the response from the fans was exemplary, with no one encroaching on the pitch.

It was typical of Coventry that a cup defeat should spark a winning League run. This time they were boosted by another new record signing, winger Kevin Gallacher, a £900,00 buy from Dundee United. An epic Sunday win over high-flying Aston Villa, with Drinkell coming off the bench to score, was trumped by an improbable 4-2 win at Forest, which saw City climb to 4th with nine games remaining. The Villa game, played on a Sunday, was shown live on ITV's *The Match* and earned the club £150,000, to add to the £200,000 banked from the live transmission of the semi-final ties. The good form had shallow foundations, however, and one win out of the final nine games saw City slip into the bottom half. Home defeats by Charlton and Sheffield Wednesday, both doomed, was an insult to City's pride.

In December, Arsenal's Paul Merson scored one of the finest goals seen at the stadium in years. The Sky Blues were on course for a draw against the champions until Merson's stunningly executed chip from out on the right flank went in off the post.

The Full Members Cup – renamed the Zenith Data Systems Cup after two seasons as the Simod Cup – saw City lose at home to Bobby Gould's hard-nosed Wimbledon, 1-3 after extra-time in front of a pitiful 3,781. It would be City's last home game in the competition, which was wound up the following season with few tears for its demise.

Almost a year after the Hillsborough disaster, the Taylor Report recommended that all First and Second Division grounds become all-seater from 1994. The League estimated that it would cost £130 million to comply with these recommendations but clubs were given a boost when Chancellor of the Exchequer John Major announced a reduction in pools tax from 42.5 to 40 per cent in his Budget. This unexpected move would raise around £100 million for the clubs – money to be spent on the necessary ground improvements.

City set up a three-man board sub-committee and commissioned Coopers & Lybrand Deloitte to carry out a £25,000 feasibility study to consider the club's strategy. Amongst several ideas on their agenda was a roof on the Spion Kop – an idea shelved in the early 1970s – and a ten-year redevelopment plan which would see much of the surrounding property purchased. Preliminary talks with Coventry Council had ascertained, however, that the club would not receive any financial assistance from that source. Another possibility was a suggestion from Bryant Homes that the club re-locate and the stadium be turned into a housing estate.

Overall attendances were down again, by 1,700 a game to an average of 14,312. For the first time in four years some gates were below 10,000, with only 8,294 present to see Wimbledon on the last Saturday before Christmas. Other factors were higher prices, embarrassing Cup exits and a lack of goals. The biggest League crowd, 23,204, was reserved for the finale against Liverpool. The new champions made City suffer for having the temerity to win at Anfield (for the first time ever) earlier in the season, by hammering them 6-1, the Sky Blues' worst home defeat in 71 seasons of League football. Sillett did not help his cause afterwards by running to the Spion Kop to applaud the Merseyside fans, while appearing to ignore City's own supporters. Young City player David Titterton came on as a substitute for a memorable debut, only to receive a yellow card for a foul before he had even touched the ball.

The announcement that ticket prices would rise the following season (the Spion Kop would cost £6 and the cheapest seats £7) did not endear the board to the fans, and three years after the Cup win, despite four seasons without relegation fears, there was a feeling of under-achievement.

1997 artist's impression of the first Arena,
incorporating sliding roof and retractable pitch

April 1936. Photos of the famous Luton game from the *Midland Daily Telegraph.*
Over 42,000 packed into the ground to see a 0-0 draw

An aerial view of Hillfields in the late 1930s.
The Rex cinema is prominently advertised on the roof of the Covered End

August 1919. An advertisement for the first ever Football League game
at Highfield Road, against Tottenham Hotspur

COVENTRY CITY FOOTBALL CLUB, Ltd.

To-morrow (Saturday),

KICK-OFF 3.30.

THE FOOTBALL LEAGUE—2nd DIVISION.

Tottenham Hotspur.

PRICES—3s., 2s., 1s. 6d., 1s.

THE SILVER BAND WILL PLAY BEFORE
THE KICK-OFF.

NEXT MATCH, SATURDAY, SEPT. 6th—

WORCESTER CITY.

1970. An artist's impression of the super stand with clubrooms and other facilities.
It was Derrick Robins' dream, but the Kop stayed undeveloped until 1993

February 1963. Despite the big freeze, City play their first game for two months, against
Barnsley, winning 2-0. Jimmy Whitehouse and Terry Bly put the visitors under pressure

May 1987. City's last home game before Wembley and the players applaud the fans

Coventry City's board of directors and management in the mid-1970s. From left: Jimmy Hill (managing director), Iain Jamieson, Tom Sargeant, Peter Robins, Jack Scamp (chairman), Eddie Plumley (secretary), Phil Mead, Joe Mercer, Gordon Milne (team manager)

November 1919. Despite a woeful start to the season, an almost record crowd of
19,000 watch City hold Blackpool to a 0-0 draw

February 1968. The Sky Blues line-up with an all Scottish forward line. From left: Ernie
Hannigan, Ian Gibson, Neil Martin, Gerry Baker, Willie Carr. Baker, despite his Scottish
brogue, was born in New York, so is not strictly Scottish. City beat Chelsea 2-1

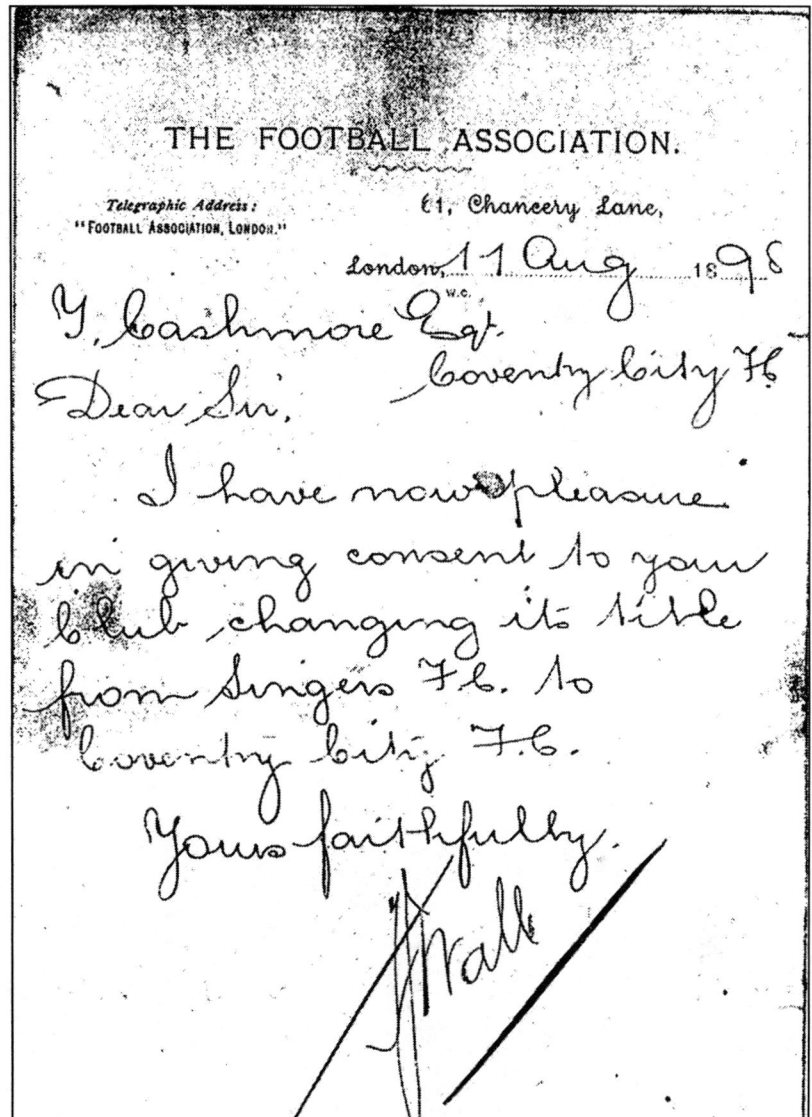

THE FOOTBALL ASSOCIATION.

Telegraphic Address:
"FOOTBALL ASSOCIATION, LONDON."

61, Chancery Lane,

London, 11 Aug 1898
w.c.

Y, Cashmore Esq.
Coventry City FC

Dear Sir,

I have now pleasure in giving consent to your club changing its title from Singers FC. to Coventry City F.C.

Yours faithfully,

Wall

In August 1898 Frederick Wall, Secretary of the FA wrote to City secretary Tom Cashmore, consenting to the club's name change from Singers FC to Coventry City FC

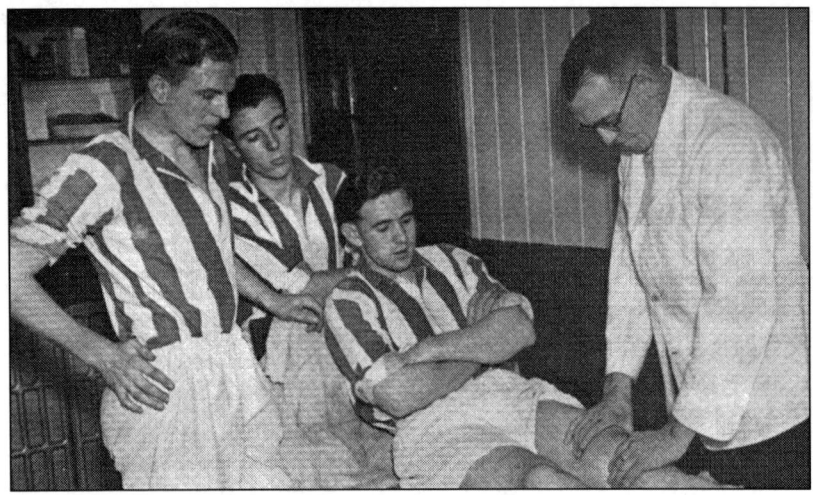

Dick Hill was the first-team trainer at Highfield Road from 1935-50.
He was still helping out in the dressing rooms at Highfield Road in 1967, aged 74.
Here he treats youngsters in the late 1940s

August 1961. Billy Frith's last team picture before his sacking in November 1961.
The players sport their attractive all-white kit

Early 2006. The West Stand, built in 1967, awaits demolition. More memories are erased

Another view of an early refreshment bar at the ground, taken around 1906.
It was operated by local landlords Messrs Tipping and Warden

Summer 1994. The new East Stand is almost complete. It looks good from the outside

April 1936. A view of the Kop before the Southern Section Cup final against Swindon Town. Note the rudimentary terraces, crush barriers and retaining fence

January 2000. A wintry sun on the Premiership game with Wimbledon. The Main Stand is almost full. To the right is the temporary stand from Silverstone, which stood for ten years

August 1981. The ground has been converted to an all-seater and the Kop has been closed, apart from 12 rows of seats

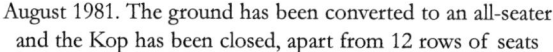

Early 2006. Demolition of the ground is well under way.
The club crest has gone and the Main Stand awaits its fate

August 1975. The team parade their new Admiral 'egg-timer' kit for the first time

April 1983. Hill's reign as chairman is coming to an end. A banner urging him to go is displayed just yards behind the directors' box

November 1974. New England manager Don Revie (left) is the guest at Coventry's Annual Soccer Ball. He chats with City chairman Peter Robins and director Joe Mercer, who had been a successful caretaker manager of England prior to Revie's appointment

April 1964. A 1-0 win over Colchester has clinched the Third Division Championship and the players celebrate. From left: Mick Kearns, goalscorer George Hudson, George Curtis, Dietmar Bruck, John Smith, Alan Dicks (assistant manager), Ron Farmer

May 1917. Highfield Road hosts boxing. Top-billing is the fight between Tango Debney from West Bromwich and Jean Barr, a Belgian residing in Coventry, here facing each other. Debney won on points. The ring was erected in front of the Atkinson's Stand

March 1983. The last team picture of Dave Sexton's fine young team (the youngest in City's history). Three months later seven players were out of contract and left the club

July 1936. Five weeks before the start of the season the steel-work is still being erected for the new 'Promotion' Stand

December 1983. Terry Gibson scores the first of his hat-trick
in the 4-0 victory over Liverpool

January 1913. Jack Cribdon, well-known local boxer and City supporter, as he appeared
when riding around the pitch at the FA Cup-tie with Manchester United. The donkey
was draped in the Bantams colours and Cribdon carried the blue and white umbrella.
The bantam that was perched in the Main Stand sits on the donkey's back

April 1964. City attack the Colchester goal. The old stand will be demolished after the game to make way for the new Sky Blue Stand. Note the invalid cars on the running track. These were a feature at the ground throughout the 1960s and 1970s

February 1912. On a snow-covered pitch, Southern League City are knocked out of the FA Cup by First Division Manchester United

A general view of last February's cup-tie. The figures of Barnacle, Chaplin, Meredith Turnbull, Thomson, and Wall will be easily recognised.

February 1968. Gerry Baker's diving header helps City gain a vital 2-1 win over Chelsea

Summer 1993. A large crane is brought in to put a new roof on the Sky Blue Stand

The old turnstiles at the back of the Spion Kop, shown before their demolition in 1993

July 1979 manager Gordon Milne and his assistant Ron Wylie sport smart yellow away shirts, flanked by their support team of George Dalton, John Sillett and Colin Dobson

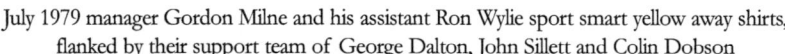

October 1917. The Coventry Ordnance Main Shop Ladies Team pose on the Highfield Road pitch. They reached the semi-final of the Female Munitions Workers Tournament

June 1963. The pitch is levelled during the close season

April 1936. The *Midland Daily Telegraph* makes light of the crowd issues
at the stadium for the Luton game

CHAPTER TEN

The 1990s

The **1990-91** season started with John Sillett talking of championships – and ended with him out of a job, and City finishing in the bottom half. This was an eventful season of sackings, controversial transfers, rows, injuries, highs and lows, and another end-of-season thrashing.

Transfer activity in the summer was thin. Sillett ignored demands for a midfield general and bought central defender Andy Pearce from non-league Halesowen for £15,000. Long-serving defender Greg Downs moved on a free to Birmingham. Sillett was confident his existing squad could arrest the slump they had suffered in the last two months of the previous season and push for a top-six finish.

That notion was exposed in the opening weeks with feeble perform-ances at Old Trafford and Villa Park. The Forest home game was unique for the four penalties awarded – three of them to City. Kilcline scored one and missed one before Brian Borrows took responsibility for the third and pulled the scores level at 2-2.

Controversy raised its head after the Rumbelows Cup-tie with Bolton at Highfield Road in September. David Speedie, who after a poor start to the season had been axed, clashed with a club vice-president after the game – the result of an apparently long-running dispute – and was fined two weeks' wages. The story hit the front pages of *The Sun* but Speedie kept quiet as speculation over his future mounted.

Sillett had enough problems as it was, and pressures on him increased with a home defeat by Southampton. Speedie's return could do nothing to stop City slumping to 16th. On the 50th anniversary of the blitz Sillett was out of work. The club denied he was sacked, but when he said he would quit in the summer unless he could agree new terms, the board didn't give him the chance and he was out. Behind the scenes, Poynton had been negotiating with the big-name manager he coveted, Rangers and England centre-half Terry Butcher. The inexperienced Butcher came as a player-manager and therefore, in addition to the hefty package, Rangers had to be paid £400,000. It was to be an expensive mistake for Poynton and the club.

Butcher did not enjoy a dream start, a home defeat by Liverpool, but he lent a steadying influence to the defence while Kilcline was missing with a hamstring injury. Eleven days later the result of the season arrived, a 5-4 victory over Forest in the League Cup. In terms of 'shock factor', this result ranks alongside the 4-0 victory over Liverpool in 1983. Forest hadn't lost a League Cup-tie for three years, hadn't conceded five goals for two and a half years, and had knocked City out of the League Cup in the previous two seasons. Hero of the hour was Kevin Gallacher, who scored his first hat-trick in English football, as the Sky Blues took a 4-0 lead inside 35 minutes and the travelling Forest fans poured to the exits. Not even Gallacher, however, could match Nigel Clough's eight-minute hat-trick as Forest levelled the scores early in the second half. The winner came from Steve Livingstone, but City were left hanging on.

It would be another month before Butcher registered his first League win as a manager, a Boxing Day victory over Tottenham, but by now relegation clouds were hovering. The New Year was not a happy one. Wigan forced a replay in the FA Cup third round, and another shock looked on the cards until a fighting performance saw City through.

A black week saw Ron Atkinson's Division Two Sheffield Wednesday end the League Cup run and with eight players on the injury list City's FA Cup campaign was brought to a shuddering halt at the Dell. Pitch problems resurfaced prior to the Owls match, when heavy frost caused a postponement at short notice. Irate fans demanded to know why the undersoil heating had failed, until a sheepish Graham Hover revealed that the club no longer had a heated pitch – they had ripped it up three years previously after the earlier pitch problems.

Speedie's season had staggered from bad to worse – he was sent off at Crystal Palace in November – and it was no secret that Butcher and he did not see eye to eye. Speedie looked set to join Aston Villa, which galled many City fans, until Kenny Dalglish came in at the last minute and whisked him to Liverpool for £675,000. Chairman Poynton later revealed that Speedie had repeatedly asked for a move and the club did not want to keep a player whose heart was elsewhere.

By February, with relegation on the cards, Butcher rang the changes. His former England teammate, Kenny Sansom, arrived from Newcastle for £100,000 and midfielder Stewart Robson on loan from West Ham. The team put together a run of ten games with only two defeats to haul themselves up to 9th before sliding back to 16th. They lost two out of their last three games and were sacrificial lambs at champions Arsenal, again losing the final game of the season 1-6.

City had stayed unbeaten at home in fourteen games since Butcher's debut, a creditable achievement. But the away form was dismal. Only one win was recorded, and that was before Butcher took over.

Kevin Gallacher adjusted well from winger to central striker and scored sixteen League and cup goals, the best haul since Terry Gibson in

1984-85, and he deserved his recall to the Scotland squad. Michael Gynn also chipped in with eleven goals and played some of the best football of his career. Cyrille Regis was superb again and many fans were upset when Butcher announced he would be releasing Regis at the end of the season. Robert Rosario arrived from Norwich in the closing weeks for £650,000, with the aim of replacing Regis, but he faced a tall order. Butcher himself had been beset by injuries and had started only seven games. Fans wondered whether he would be seen in a City shirt again.

Gates were marginally down, by 400 a game, to an average of 13,887, with the Christmas visit of Tottenham attracting the biggest crowd – 22,549. One of the Spurs' attractions was the newly elected BBC Sports Personality of the Year, Paul Gascoigne. 'Gazza's' antics at the 1990 World Cup finals, culminating in his tears in the semi-final denouement against West Germany, had won the hearts of the nation. Coventry's fans were not impressed: despite the absence of Lloyd McGrath, who normally policed the Geordie star, Gazza failed to make an impact and the Sky Blues won 2-0.

John Poynton made it clear that he wanted the club to be the first to comply with the Taylor Report, and have an all-seater stadium. He even announced that the Spion Kop would be closed at the end of the season and remain shut while a new stand was built. It would cost £6 million, seat 6,000 and include shops and offices. A £2 million grant from the Football Trust was sought and won, but by the end of the season there was no further news.

In March 1991 the club appointed its first safety officer, bowing to the recommendations of the Taylor Report. Tom Meffen, former Assistant Chief Constable of the West Midlands, was put in charge of 'every aspect of safety at the ground, from fencing to training stewards, and looking at creating an all-seater stadium'. One of his first tasks was to recruit and train twenty stewards, to reduce the policing costs.

The club staged pre-season friendlies against Czech side Banik Ostrava and non-league Halesowen, pulling in 2,752 for the first and 740 for the second, which was part of the deal for signing Andy Pearce from the Black Country side.

Even by Coventry's chaotic standards, the **1991-92** season goes down as one of the most turbulent in the club's history. Most of the action took place off the field in a twelve-month period that saw two chairman, two managers and three assistant managers. Yet despite, or maybe because of, all the changes, the team continued to struggle and City fans were put through the sort of nail-biting final day that they thought they had left behind in the mid-1980s.

Terry Butcher, at 32 the youngest manager in the First Division, started the season with just four additions to his squad. Stewart Robson made
his move from West Ham permanent on a free transfer. Striker Paul
Furlong was signed from Enfield for £100,000. Exciting Zimbabwean,
Peter Ndlovu – spotted by John Sillett in 1990 – signed from Bulawayo
Highlanders for £10,000. Ndlovu quickly showed that he was one of the
most skilful players the club had ever had but Butcher, like his successors,
never quite got the best out of him. Butcher jettisoned 1987 Cup final
heroes Cyrille Regis and Brian Kilcline. To the outrage of many supporters Regis went on a free transfer to join his old mentor Ron Atkinson at
Villa Park. Newly promoted Oldham paid a generous £400,000 for
Kilcline.

There were problems in the camp even before the season started. A
three-match tour of Scotland was overshadowed by the sending home of
Kenny Sansom, Trevor Peake and Lloyd McGrath, who had been out
drinking in Troon less than 48 hours before a tournament in Kilmarnock.
All were heavily fined and transfer listed as Butcher sought to make
examples of them. Peake was quickly on his way to Luton, for £100,000,
a deal that paved the way for the signing of young Wigan defender Peter
Atherton for £300,000.

After nine games City lay 4th, a position distorted by having played six
home games and only three away. Their form was iffy – Manchester City
and Wimbledon had lowered their colours at home, but a shock win at
Arsenal, inspired by Ndlovu's first goal, showed what they were capable
of. The Manchester City loss was the first time City had lost at home on
the opening day since 1953.

A 1-0 home win over Villa, courtesy of a Ndlovu special, and victory
at West Ham left City 5th, but it was the calm before the storm. Despite
Ndlovu's dazzling if inconsistent displays, City embarked on five League
defeats in a row. On 9 November, amid rumours of financial problems
and the possible sale of Gallacher, chairman Poynton resigned. The new
man at the helm was Peter Robins, son of 1960's benefactor Derrick and
his father's successor as chairman in the mid-1970s. Robins, it later transpired, was little more than a front man for the ambitious London-based
former Warwickshire cricketer Bryan Richardson.

Within days Robins made his first pronouncements. These included
the usual platitudes about 'giving the club back to the supporters' and listening. He announced that the £5.5 million plans for the Spion Kop
stand would be reviewed and that merchant bankers Henry Ansbacher
would be examining the club's finances. His most vociferous comments
were reserved for his manager: 'Terry is doing a first class job.'

Within days Butcher was instructed to sack his assistant Mick Mills and reserve team coach Brian Eastick. They were replaced by the vastly experienced Don Howe. Home victories over Arsenal (League Cup) and Southampton were the only respite for the under-pressure Butcher, who announced his retirement as a player in November after a rusty performance in a 0-2 home defeat to Villa in the Zenith Data Systems Cup. He ended that match prematurely with a red card.

At the club's AGM, Robins – who had not exactly set the club alight during his previous chairmanship in the mid-1970s – accused his predecessor Poynton, in terms reminiscent of a Soviet Union whitewash, of letting the club fall into disrepair with a lack of leadership and commitment. Poynton responded by accusing the new regime of lies and exaggeration. The truth remained buried under rhetoric and hubris.

December was grim. Spurs grabbed a late victory to knock City out of the League Cup, and bad defeats at Old Trafford and Luton saw City slide nearer the trap door. On New Year's day, for the visit of Spurs, the club celebrated the new regime with parachutists, chocolate and clowns for kids. However, a 1-2 defeat and a home FA Cup draw with Cambridge forced Robins' hand and Butcher was shown the door.

Robins alluded to Butcher's contractual terms, indicating that he had sought to renegotiate his manager's contract to reflect his retirement as a player, an issue that would provoke a court case. Despite Robins' supportive word two months earlier, the Premier League and all its perceived crocks of gold loomed over the forthcoming season, and the board felt it necessary to make changes sooner rather than later. Assistant Don Howe was asked to take over as caretaker manager, on the understanding that he had no money to buy.

Howe couldn't prevent an FA Cup loss at Cambridge – courtesy of a goal from Dion Dublin – but tightened the defence at the expense of the attack. Drab, dour football was the outcome, and although only one game in nine was lost, there were four goalless draws and just four goals scored. The fans voted with their feet, and for the 0-0 with Norwich the crowd was down to 8,454. The team looked quite comfortable until mid-March, when they were overtaken by surges from Sheffield United, Southampton and Tottenham. Successive defeats against Tottenham and Arsenal meant that City would once again have to fight to the death.

Most worrying was Luton, who were stringing together a fine run to close the gap. They beat Villa in their penultimate game, while City's win over West Ham was their first at home since 10 November. It set up a tense final day at Villa Park. Notts County and West Ham were already down. Luton, two points behind City, were at Notts County. With the Sky

Blues having a superior goal-difference, all they needed was a draw to ensure safety.

Within 21 seconds City's hopes of even a point looked thin, as their former hero Cyrille Regis put Villa ahead. News that Luton were leading at Meadow Lane and a second Villa goal from Dwight Yorke, left City in the bottom three for the first time and the fans seemed resigned. With time running out, Loughborough University student Rob Matthews scored two goals for Notts, sending Luton down and securing City's place in the new Premier League. As Roger Draper put it in the *CET*: 'Another wake but still no corpse.'

Survival was a huge relief, but there seemed no end to the instability at the club. A champagne-swilling Robins vowed that the club would not struggle again, and pledged £2/3 million to ensure it. Where did we hear that before?

The plans for the Spion Kop end were reviewed. The same design – complete with 5,000 seats, executive boxes, restaurants, shops and a health club would cost 'approximately half the £5.5 million' previously quoted, but work would not commence until the close season of 1993. Few fans liked the notion of an all-seater stadium, and at the Manchester United game around 10,000 held up red cards in protest. The Football Supporters Association, which organised the action, said the protest had gone well. In the meantime the club unveiled plans to spend £70,000 refurbishing the west stand, converting it to a family stand with a crèche, various eating places, video games and a souvenir shop. Additionally an exclusive Premier Club was launched – aimed at local businesses – featuring a luxurious lounge in the club's trophy room.

Another initiative launched the club's first Ladies Day, against Oldham in March. Around 3,000 'ladies', boosting the crowd to 13,000, were lured to Highfield Road by the attraction of a free ticket. Following a drab 1-1 draw it was doubtful that many subsequently returned.

Goalkeeper Steve Ogrizovic went from strength to strength. He had missed only two League games in seven seasons, but in March 1992 suffered a rare injury in training and was forced to miss four games. With his deputy, Clive Baker, sidelined with appendicitis, the club were forced to take two goalkeepers on loan. Paul Heald came from Leyton Orient, then Les Sealey – Villa's reserve keeper – played two games. Fans had long memories of Sealey's disparaging remarks about the club when he left in 1983 and gave him a muted reception, despite Howe's appeal to support the Londoner.

John Sillett's compensation package when he left in November 1990 included a testimonial, and it took place on the Sunday following the Villa game. Ten of City's 1987 FA Cup winners (Houchen was delayed by traffic and joined the action midway through the first half) kicked off against a Spurs Select XI, featuring three of their 87 team and supplemented by Tony Dobson, Steve Sedgley, Dean Emerson, Kevin Gallacher and David Speedie. City won 7-5 in front of 4,600 in a fun-filled game.

After the tribulations of the previous campaign, the inaugural Premier League season, **1992-93**, had to be judged a success, even though some of the football was not pretty to watch. With Bobby Gould back in charge, the Sky Blues started with a bang and were the first leaders of the new League. Then came a lull before Mick Quinn arrived and sparked a revival with the best goalscoring sequence in 25 years in the top flight. Although the season petered out, it wasn't until 17 April that City drifted out of the top half.

Bobby Gould had been sacked by West Brom and within days was ensconced at Highfield Road alongside new joint-manager Don Howe. The idea was that Howe, whose record and style had not endeared him to many City fans, would retain the coaching and tactical role. Howe soon decided that the daily round trip from his Hertfordshire home was too much, so Gould recruited axed Bolton boss Phil Neal as his assistant.

Gould's knowledge of the lower divisions again came in handy. Swansea's flying winger John Williams arrived for £250,000, and defender Phil Babb from Bradford City for £500,000. Gould's son Jonathan also signed for a small fee from West Brom. Heading out were Paul Furlong, sold for £250,000 to Watford, Kevin Drinkell and Dean Emerson, both on free transfers.

The start to City's Premier League career was extraordinary. After a tentative home win over Middlesbrough, two away victories in four days produced a maximum nine-point start. Two more successes, at Sheffield Wednesday and Oldham, set a new club record of four successive away wins. A crowd of 12,345 welcomed Middlesbrough, and John Williams' ninth-minute goal was the second fastest in the new League, four minutes behind Brian Deane's penalty for Sheffield United.

Williams, Gallacher and home-grown Lee Hurst all impressed, but the star was the inimitable Ndlovu, who ran defences ragged with his speed and skill. Media interest in the Zimbabwean escalated when he scored a superb individual goal against leaders Norwich on *Match of the Day*. By the end of September City lay 3rd, with Gould picking up the Manager of the Month award and Phil Neal invited to become Graham Taylor's part-time assistant manager.

An early visitor to Highfield Road was Britain's most expensive player, £3.4 million Alan Shearer, signed by newly promoted and Jack Walker-bankrolled Blackburn. Shearer was well marshalled by Lloyd McGrath for almost 70 minutes before City's specialist marker tripped him. Shearer scored from the spot to help Rovers to a 2-0 win.

In September, Sky Television – who had paid a colossal £304 million for the live rights to 60 live Premier League games – sent their cameras to Highfield Road for the first time. Pre-match entertainment included fireworks, Red Devil parachutists in Sky Blue kit, and 100 US-style dancing girls. At half-time Sonia, Britain's choice for the next Eurovision Song Contest, 'entertained' the 15,000 crowd. Sky's anchor-man Richard Keys, a long-time City fan, was ecstatic after a 1-0 victory lifted City to second place in the table.

The familiar cup banana skin was lurking round the corner, and a routine trip to Scarborough in the League Cup – buttressed by a two-goal lead from the first leg – ended in a nightmare 0-3 defeat. Soon after, with League results slipping and Gallacher injured, Gould introduced well-travelled striker Mick Quinn on loan from Newcastle. Quinn's impact was staggering: ten goals in six games kick-started City's season. Christmas wins at home to Liverpool (5-1) and Villa (3-0) were largely indebted to the stocky striker and his rejuvenated partner, Robert Rosario. City's financial situation was so serious – they announced debts of £3 million – that Quinn's eventual fee of £250,000 was rumoured to have been paid by a wealthy supporter.

Before Christmas, at the AGM, chairman Robins boasted of turning the ailing club around, a point not accepted by John Poynton, and not borne out by the dreadful financial results. Nevertheless there were some positives, including the successful refurbishment of the west stand ('the only carpeted stand in the country') now renamed the Cooperative Bank Family Stand, upgraded 'loos' all round the ground, and various initiatives to bring the club closer to the fans and the community.

Robins described a number of ground improvements planned for the summer of 1993. At a cost of £500,000 – largely from the Football Trust and other grants – the Sky Blue stand would have a new roof extending down to the pitch, and have its 30-year-old wooden seats replaced with modern seats. The big news was that planning permission had been granted for the new east stand, to replace the Spion Kop. It would have 5,200 seats and cost £2.3 million, of which – after grants – £1 million would have to be funded by the club. City were unclear how this funding gap would be bridged, so decisions about the project's go-ahead were postponed until nearer the end of the season.

Before the Liverpool game, City fans looked for good omens. After all, Gould had been in charge when City crushed the Reds 4-0 during his first stint, but none expected a repeat. By half-time, Liverpool had large-ly dominated but were a goal down. Amazingly it ended 5-1 to City, who were once again the talk of football as they sent the Reds crashing to their worst defeat in sixteen years.

A week later, on Boxing Day, the team trounced Villa 3-0 in front of the biggest home League crowd for five years – 24,135 paying record receipts of £198,787. Villa, managed by Ron Atkinson, were serious title contenders, so the result – with Quinn netting twice more – severely dented their chances.

After Christmas, City were rarely out of the top six. More away wins, at Blackburn and Middlesbrough, even had fans talking about Europe. Financial considerations, however, took a decisive turn. Rosario was sold over Gould's head to Forest for £500,000, and Gallacher finally left to the fans' chagrin in a part-exchange deal with Blackburn for £1 million, plus £500,000-rated Roy Wegerle.

On Easter Monday the Villa gate was topped as Manchester United came to town. United were set to win the first Premier League title and their first championship since 1967. A goal from Denis Irwin gave then the points in front of 24,410. Mick Quinn was shown 'red' for allegedly striking goalkeeper Peter Schmeichel. TV replays later exonerated Quinn.

One win from the last eleven games was a poor finish. Even on the last day, a 3-1 lead over Leeds was squandered in the last minute, costing the club £250,000 in prize money as they slipped three places in the final table. Gould later blamed the slump on the board for forcing the sale of Rosario.

The final average attendance was 14,950, an increase of 1,100, largely due to the team's good form up until March. The Sky cameras had been at the ground on three occasions – Tottenham; a Saturday tea-time kick-off against Oldham (won 3-0); and a Sunday afternoon defeat by Everton (0-1). With the final away game, at Old Trafford, also televised, City's four Sky appearances were worth £78,000 each. With their merit awards and the £750,000 equal share from the Premier League pool, the first season in the new League earned the club £1.3 million. That was substantially less than the £2.4 million that champions Manchester United pocketed, but still a welcome addition to the coffers.

Quinn could not sustain his scoring rate but he still finished with sev-enteen League goals, the best individual haul since Terry Gibson almost ten years previously. Robins was unable to realise his hopes of releasing large sums of money, although progress was made on the stadium. The Leeds game was the last in front of the Kop: the following Monday a massive summer ground project commenced. It would be the biggest face-lift for the ground in its 94-year history. The Kop would come down over the summer of 1993 and eventually be replaced by the new east stand, built by Alfred McAlpine Construction – who had successfully built new stands at Molineux and Anfield. It would be ready for the opening game of the 1994-95 campaign. The final cost of the whole project was £4.3 million, of which £1.9 million came from a Football Trust and £1.3 million from Midland brewing giants Mitchell & Butlers, in return for a ten-year sponsorship of the Sky Blue stand.

The roof of the Sky Blue stand – renamed the Mitchell & Butlers Stand – would be replaced over the summer. There would also be new floodlights, a scoreboard at the junction of west and Sky Blue stands, TV gantry and public address system. When complete, the ground would again be all-seating and would comply with the Taylor recommendations.

In order to level the site for the new stand, 250,000 cubic metres of soil were removed. The work had started before the Leeds game, with some seats in the Sky Blue stand being removed and four new bases inserted for the new roof, before being concreted over and the seats being temporarily replaced. On the Monday various local clubs – including Coventry Rugby Club, Telford United and Nuneaton Borough – arrived to scavenge any wooden seats they wanted, and by the Wednesday most had gone, saving City a considerable sum in transportation costs. The police control building, which had stood since the mid-1950s, was demolished and the police relocated.

It was rumoured that excavation of the Kop had to be halted for four days because of an unexploded wartime bomb. The 'bomb' turned out to be an old tea-urn buried from the Kop's earliest days.

The project was overseen by stadium manager Derek Chattington, who also had to oversee all the internal changes taking place. For instance all the club's telephone lines and alarms were attached to the electricity sub-station which was linked to the redundant floodlights. These lines had to be rerouted. The old floodlights were demolished and for the first time in almost 40 years it was impossible to spot Highfield Road on the horizon. Witherford Electrical were responsible for removing the floodlights. The steel went for scrap and 106 lights were bought by Hamilton Academical in Scotland.

The club's offices were moved temporarily to King Richard Street. The new roof over the Sky Blue stand was supported by just three vertical supports to the rear of the front seats. A wide lateral gangway was installed, replacing the narrow, barrier-lined passage, which had a tendency to become uncomfortably overcrowded in the past. The whole feel of the stand was an improvement.

In the main stand, a new Public Address room was installed where the dugouts used to be. New PVC dugouts were erected, closer to the pitch. The ground capacity for the new 1993-94 season was reduced to 17,000, but when the new stand fully reopened it would rise to a shade over 23,000.

Highfield Road was a hub of activity that summer, but not everything went to plan. During the removal of the Sky Blue stand's old roof, the crane driver faced a problem with one of the new beams installed in 1983 following the collapse due to high winds. The crane driver discovered it to be two thirds heavier than the rest. It was so heavy it started to bend the jib and he had to release it, causing damage to the invalid enclosure and to the concrete terracing.

The summer also saw boardroom battles. Peter Robins stood down as chairman and local businessman John Clarke, backed by Derrick Robins – who still owned a substantial shareholding – looked set to take over until his bid failed at the eleventh hour. Following a boardroom power struggle, Bryan Richardson took the chair and Clarke resigned. Later in the season, Peter Robins – who had become chief executive – quit the board and sold his shares to Richardson, against the wishes of his father. Consequently, Richardson became the majority shareholder.

When the **1993-94** season opened in August, the Swan Lane end was obscured by a ten-foot fence advertising Carling, the Premiership's new sponsors. As the season progressed the new stand slowly emerged from behind the fence.

Phil Babb, City's latest international, summed up the season perfectly: 'We did well at the start of the season and well at the end of the season – it's just the 25 games in between we struggled with.' It was a fair review of a season that once again saw the Sky Blues propelled on to the back pages of the national papers as the club was rocked by another internal squabble.

Bobby Gould's walkout, characteristically dramatic and unexpected, shook the club to its core and could well have sent it tumbling out of the Premiership. Perhaps the seeds of Gould's departure had been sown during the close season when Peter Robins, his friend and confidante, moved from chairman to chief executive. Gould was now answerable instead to Bryan Richardson, who insisted his relationship with Gould was cordial, although behind the scenes everything was falling apart.

The season started with a glut of injuries. Gould's pre-season trip to an army camp backfired when Lee Hurst injured knee ligaments on an assault course so badly he would never play first-team football again. Ten minutes into the opening game, at Highbury, Stewart Robson collapsed with a knee injury, and the heart of City's midfield had been ripped out. Robson, like Hurst, would never appear for City again. At the time, Robson's injury couldn't mar the celebrations for a 3-0 win, with Quinn netting a hat-trick.

Four days later 15,763 packed the temporarily three-sided Highfield Road to welcome Kevin Keegan's promoted Newcastle. New signing Mick Harford came off the bench to score City's winner. A back injury meant Harford never played for City again. Earlier, Mick Quinn, facing his former club, blasted a penalty over the fence into the building site.

In what was the best start since 1937, City were unbeaten in their first eight League games, even accounting for Liverpool and drawing at Villa, but all was not as good as it looked. In the Coca-Cola Cup, the Football League newboys Wycombe destroyed City at Adams Park, recovering from a three-goal first-leg deficit to lead 4-3 on aggregate. Two late goals saved City's blushes, but the fans were not impressed.

In October, Gould was forced to play himself in the reserves because of injuries. The 47-year-old stunned the Bolton defence by notching the first goal in a 2-1 win – his first goal at the ground since he left to join Arsenal in 1968.

The club had never witnessed a day like 23 October 1993. A 1-5 dousing at QPR was bad enough, but Gould stunned the post-match press conference by announcing his resignation. The reasons were hard to fathom. Gould accused Richardson of forcing him to sell Peter Ndlovu, but the player wasn't sold. Richardson apologised to Gould after claiming his resignation was stress related. A week of claim and counter claim ended with Gould returning as a Sky TV commentator for the home match with Sheffield United on the Sunday. His arrival did nothing to help the team as the game was reduced almost a side-show. Amid angry scenes, protesters scrambled across executive box rooves to confront the directors. The net result was that City got the wrong kind of headlines and lost a hometown manager who cared passionately for the club. The definitive story may never be known, but one school of thought claims Richardson made no effort to dissuade Gould once he had resigned. If true, it perhaps demonstrates that the chairman wanted his own man all along.

His own man, for the time being, was Gould's assistant Phil Neal who, far from being forced to sell players, was encouraged to spend. Lower division players Julian Darby (£150,000 from Neal's old club Bolton) and Ally Pickering (£85,000 from Rotherham) were signed, with Huddersfield midfielder Chris Marsden arriving on loan. Marsden looked the part from the outset; a ball-playing midfielder with a sweet left foot, and with him in the side over Christmas, City looked the genuine article. Roy Wegerle was playing his best football since arriving at the club and Marsden was linking superbly with him and Ndlovu.

City, however, hesitated when Marsden's loan expired, and he slipped away to join Wolves. Instead, City signed Sandy Robertson, another midfielder from Glasgow Rangers (£250,000) who, it was obvious from the start, was totally unsuitable for the Premiership.

If the Gould fracas was not enough for the City board, they then had a court case with Terry Butcher, who was claiming unfair dismissal. The case was settled out of court for a sum believed to be in the region of £240,000.

Mick Quinn's lack of goals, caused in no small part by lack of service, sparked a mid-season dip. From early January to late March City lost their way, winning just two matches and sinking perilously close to the relegation zone. Neal reacted by axing Quinn and John Williams, and playing Peter Ndlovu and Sean Flynn as dual strikers. Ndlovu's brilliance, hidden for most of the season, suddenly exploded and he ended the campaign in devastating form. His goal in the 1-2 home defeat by Wimbledon was judged one of the ground's finest. The Zimbabwean sped away from three Dons defenders before unleashing a left-foot thunderbolt past Hans Segers.

Ndlovu's five goals in the final eight games sparked a late resurgence, climaxing when City out-fought and out-played title-chasing Blackburn. The 2-1 home win, with Phil Neal's signing Julian Darby scoring twice, ensured that Manchester United would pip Rovers' millionaires for the Premiership trophy. United had pulled in the largest crowd in November at the three-sided stadium, a capacity 17,009. The final average of 13,352 was 1,500 down, but in the context of the ground development it was a reasonable figure.

Neal and his new assistant, Mick Brown, had the team playing bright, positive football. In Ndlovu – who equalled the club's record as the most capped international player – and Babb, City possessed two of the brightest stars of the Premiership. Babb made his debut for the Republic of Ireland in the spring and was touted as a candidate for the World Cup squad for the USA. City had already rejected a £1.8 million bid for him from Newcastle.

Chairman Bryan Richardson faced the classic dilemma. If he sold, he could wipe out the club's debts at a stroke – but that would dash the hopes of sceptical supporters used to seeing the best players leave.

Lloyd McGrath was rewarded for ten years' service in November with a testimonial against Birmingham. Only 2,301 turned up to recognise the efforts of one of the club's most hard-working players. Lloyd, who was on a week-to-week contract after rejecting City's terms in the summer, scored the first goal in a 2-1 win. Two weeks later he was stretchered off at Hillsborough and his Sky Blue career was as good as over.

A bigger crowd, 6,363, attended on a Friday night in February to see England Schoolboys beat Wales 2-0, a game covered by Sky cameras.

That same month saw the return to Highfield Road – after an absence of 28 years – of close-circuit television, when City's rearranged League game at Newcastle was beamed back to Highfield Road. Newcastle, undergoing a massive ground redevelopment, had banned away fans from St James' Park. Many City fans had tickets from the original game postponed in November, and were livid when told they could not attend the rescheduled game. Two large screens were erected on a snow-covered pitch in front of the main stand and 1,542 hardy souls braved bitter weather to see their team go down 0-4.

The new stand inched upwards. By late October most of the steel-work was in place and by January the roof was on. In early March, for the Aston Villa game, around 1,300 seats were made available for visiting fans but a poor Villa following made them unnecessary. The Sunday after-noon game, which City lost 0-1, was shown live on Sky and was the only defeat they suffered in four televised home games.

The final stages of the east stand involved fitting out the inside. A huge mall was created and Strategic Leisure were employed to plan the facilities. Government Minister Peter Brooke attended the home game with Sheffield Wednesday, to hand over the cheque for £1.9 million from the Football Trust.

City had a new board member in February, Mike McGinnity, head of PEL, one of Britain's leading seat companies. PEL had supplied all the new seats in the stadium and been paid £400,000 for the east stand fit-out. Now McGinnity was deputy chairman.

In May, the club turned the reserve game with Manchester United into a fun night. A crowd of 7,025 turned up and although disappointed that United did not field any stars, unknown kids David Beckham, Paul Scholes and Gary Neville were on show in the 1-1 draw. The main entice-ment was an autograph-signing by the first team – it took them three hours to satisfy every young fan. When the club shortly opened the new stand for viewing, over 5,000 fans turned up, many queuing for hours in the rain to get a look. The queue for new season tickets was 'between 100 and 200 yards long'. The new stand season tickets were, at £150, the 'cheapest in the Premiership'.

For the **1994-95** season away supporters were penned in the western end of the Sky Blue stand, which meant many disgruntled season ticket holders had to move. The change made sense from a segregation point of view, but a few disaffected home supporters vowed not to renew their season tickets.

From the start of 1994-95 there was a fresh look about the stadium. Every seat in the ground had been replaced, a no-doubt lucrative contract for McGinnity's PEL. The initials 'CCFC' were spelled out in dark blue in three stands, with 'Sky Blues' in the M & B stand. The new east stand mall was truly impressive. Heated, air-conditioned, with polished floors, fast-food outlets, video games, a Ladbrokes betting concession, TVs and bars, it was so enticing that some fans paid for admission just to watch large chunks of the game on the monitors inside. Takings shot up in the new facility, with average spending going up from 26p per head to £1.30. Healthy figures for Richardson and his board, who had to massage a multi-million pound debt.

On the next level up (level three) there was a restaurant for Ladbrokes Club members, two bars and television screens. Membership of the club was £600 for two for the season, and entitled you to specially padded seats in a central dedicated area of the new stand. A similar arrangement could be had for the Premier Club on level four, whose members had access to the carvery restaurant and a panoramic viewing theatre.

Nevertheless, the stand had its critics. Because of the site's irregular shape and the proximity of Swan Lane, a cantilevered roof was ruled out and a 'goalpost' roof would have cost an extra £500,000. The solution was a roof supported by five columns, which inevitably restricted the view of some – it was the only new stand in the Premiership built this way. Stadium expert Simon Inglis described the stand as 'one of the most idiosyncratic designs of the post-Taylor period'. In *The Football Grounds of Britain* he wrote: 'Thus what the fans have won on the swings, they have lost on the roundabout; slick facilities behind the scenes, but a restricted view out front. A shopping mall within, a warehouse without.' Inglis however was complimentary about the predominance of sky blue around the modernised ground: 'the Sky Blue message is now cooler, sharper, more business-like than ever before. No more middle ground, but a stadium in the making.'

The 1994-95 season started optimistically but by Christmas had been replaced by mediocrity. But rarely can a season of struggle have ended on such a high note. The reason? Ron Atkinson!

The arrival of the much-travelled managerial legend revived the season that looked as though it might prove one season too far, with the Endsleigh League beckoning. Phil Neal had done a solid job under Gould and 1993-94's strong finish had raised expectations. But as the injuries mounted and the critics became increasingly agitated, drastic action was needed. Big Ron arrived in a blaze of glory, bought some players, added 5,000 to the first home attendance, and intriguingly acquired Gordon Strachan as his number two.

Before the season kicked off, however, Highfield Road hosted a testimonial for Steve Ogrizovic, almost ten years to the day since he had joined from Shrewsbury. 7,538 fans paid to see City play Aston Villa, preceded by a kickabout between an old Coventry City XI and Jess Conrad's Showbiz XI. Villa won the main game 2-1, but the occasion was somewhat overshadowed by rumours of massive bids being made for City's captain Phil Babb.

Babb went to the 1994 World Cup with only five Republic of Ireland caps and returned having been one of the stars of the tournament. It was no surprise when the transfer stories surfaced, and when he finally waved farewell after the second home game, bound for Liverpool, City had earned more than double what Newcastle offered six months earlier. The fee, £3.75 million, was a British record for a defender and Neal was entrusted with a large slice of it to spend. Striker Dion Dublin arrived for a club record £2 million from Manchester United and promising young central defender Steven Pressley from Glasgow Rangers for £630,000. Dublin was a revelation, scoring sixteen goals in 38 games. Pressley, on the other hand, collected seven bookings and a sending off in his first eleven games. Enough said.

The new stand had duly opened on the first day, against Wimbledon. It was a poor 1-1 draw, but virtually every seat was taken (2,500 of them season ticket holders) even though the overall gate was a disappointing 11,005. Not everyone was happy with the new stand. Dave Long, writing the Terrace Verdict for the *CET* spoke for many: 'the East Stand drummer please note that his task is to get the crowd going and then leave them to get on with it … hammering away like Keith Moon on a particularly bad acid trip for the entire 90 minutes will not endear him to those he is both surrounded and vastly outnumbered by.' The drummer, longtime fan Phil Woods, soon beat a hasty retreat to the west end.

The arrival of Dublin and US international Cobi Jones kick-started the season. In their home debut, against Leeds, Dublin scored one and Jones earned the winning penalty to register the Sky Blues' first win of the season. Trouble erupted when away fans surged to the toilets at half-time. Amid ugly scenes, many suffered crush injuries in a Hillsborough-type incident which prompted many fans to ring David Mellor's 606 programme on BBC Radio. Before the next home game, the wrought iron fence separating the Sky Blue stand from the lower terrace seating was demolished to avoid any recurrence, and away followings were restricted to a maximum 2,000.

In November the club were at the centre of a betting scandal when it was alleged that Southampton goalkeeper Bruce Grobbelaar stood to collect from a betting syndicate if the Saints had lost 0-1 at Highfield Road two months previously. The game ended 3-1 in Southampton's favour and Grobbelaar vehemently denied the allegations. *The Sun* newspaper claimed that it had a taped recording of Bruce admitting to have 'pushed in' City's early goal and how he had collected cash for other 'thrown' games from the syndicate. In 1997, after two trials he was cleared and successfully sued *The Sun* and awarded £85,000 damages. Later on appeal to the House of Lords, the award was reduced to £1 with the judge perhaps implying dishonesty on Grobbelaar's part. A fine career tarnished.

With Dublin netting ten goals in his first thirteen games City lay 10th at the end of November. Injuries to Dublin and David Busst then illustrated how thin City's resources were. Dublin missed six games – none of which were won, and only one outfield goal scored. The results were worst over Christmas, when City were thrashed 1-5 at Hillsborough and then 0-4 at home to Tottenham.

Dublin returned in early January but the first six weeks of the New Year offered only an FA Cup replay win at West Brom to keeps City's fans sane. Richardson asked them to lay off Neal, and the fourth-round tie with Norwich assumed massive proportions. A 0-0 home draw was followed by an extra-time defeat at Carrow Road. With time running out for Neal, Jones and Dublin appeared to have given their manager a lifeline when they earned City's first League win in twelve at Crystal Palace. But ominously it came on the day Ron Atkinson settled his contractual negotiations with Aston Villa following his autumn sacking.

On the Tuesday Neal was dismissed and immediately took a swipe at the local media and some of the fans. Injuries and bad luck had conspired to dethrone an honest man who, in retrospect, was probably a good assistant but not quite up to being a Premiership manager. Twenty-four hours later Atkinson was confirmed City's the new boss and wasted no time in bringing in new players. Kevin Richardson, his former general at Villa Park, arrived for £300,000, and two weeks later Everton full-back David Burrows for a cool £1 million. Gordon Strachan, who arrived as Ron's number two, cost nothing, but the Scot wasn't interested in playing and said that he would only play in an emergency.

Big Ron's impact was instant. Five thousand extra fans watched his first match, a 2-0 win over West Ham, and when he walked out onto the pitch he received a huge ovation. After six games his side were unbeaten and demolished Liverpool at Anfield, thanks to a Peter Ndlovu hat-trick, the first at Anfield by a visiting player since 1962. Perched in 9th position, City looked safe from a relegation battle and on the financial side Big Ron's arrival had attracted three crowds of 17,000-plus.

Then the goals dried up and the Sky Blues lost five out of the next six and slumped to 18th. The biggest crowd ever at the time, and the largest all-seated crowd ever at the stadium, 21,858, saw City lose 2-3 to title-chasing Manchester United. In front of the Sky cameras, the Sky Blues twice came from behind, only to lose to a late Andy Cole effort. Five days later, a 0-2 defeat at bottom club Ipswich was City's worst performance in ages. With four teams going down this season, to reduce the Premier League to twenty, the pressure was on. A superb 3-1 win in the penultimate game at Spurs, inspired by immense performances by Ndlovu and Strachan – who Atkinson had begged to play – ensured safety.

The second highest crowd of the season, 21,787, turned up for the meaningless finale against Everton and Big Ron was feted like a messiah. The final position was 16th, five points clear. City's average crowd was up by 2,000 to 15,980. The smallest was 9,509 for the Ipswich game shown by Sky on a Monday night in October.

In April, for the visit of QPR, the club experimented with a police-free environment, using their own stewards instead of expensive policing. There was a hiccup, however, when a home fan side-stepped the stewards to remonstrate with City players after Ian Holloway scored the only goal. The club hoped to repeat the exercise the following season at low-risk games, subject to approval from Coventry's Chief Superintendent.

The final stage of the ground transformation saw the main stand get a make-over in the summer of 1995. The propped and vaulted roof was replaced by a 'goal-post' supported roof offering an uninterrupted view. The main beam of the new edifice was 129 metres long in a single structure and had to be lifted into place by one of the largest cranes in Europe. The new roof was joined to that of the east stand, which in turn was connected to the roof of the M & B stand. The original executive boxes in the main stand, now an eyesore, were removed and an extra 1,800 seats installed. This extended the seating down to the running track and marginally increased the capacity. The corner between the main and west stands was filled by a 3x3 block of demountable executive boxes on stilts. Formerly sited at Silverstone (but similar to one at Twickenham), they were intended as a temporary feature but would remain in place until the ground closed. In addition, the old wall at the perimeter was removed. This allowed the advertising at pitch level to be uniform and tidier. Every area of the ground not previously reseated would have new seats. The total cost of £1.4 million was helped by a further grant from the Football Trust, £750,000, with the balance funded by the club. Since 1990 an estimated £7 million had now been spent on Highfield Road but few fans complained because the Taylor Report was binding.

Bryan Richardson outlined more plans for the next summer which never materialised. These included moving the dressing rooms and treatment rooms to the area between the main and west stands. The same corner was to have a fixed TV studio, press facilities and players' lounge. Richardson boasted that before the Manchester United game they had served around 1,000 meals, and the catering facilities had taken around £35,000 on the night.

The **1995-96** season, which started with so much expectation, delivered mostly disappointment and ended with City having to get a result on the final day for the ninth time in 29 seasons. It was not exactly a season to savour but certainly one to remember.

In August everything seemed right with the world. City had a manager more accustomed to success than struggle, assisted by one of Britain's finest players, and the two were given serious money by one of the most popular chairmen in the club's history. What could go wrong?

The answer? Just about everything. The bullish talk seemed different somehow. Before the season started Atkinson had splashed the cash to make what, at the time, seemed promising purchases. City rejected offers totalling £10 million for Dublin and Ndlovu, confirming to the fans that they did not intend to be a selling club any more. Ron bought six players: midfielder Paul Telfer, winger John Salako, Paul D Williams, Ghanaian prodigy Nii Lamptey, and – in a close season that saw foreign stars like Bergkamp, Ginola and Gullit flood the Premiership – Brazilian midfielder Isaias and Portuguese youngster Carlita. Of these, Telfer, Salako and Williams were all £1 million players. Out went Sean Flynn, John Williams, Mike Marsh, Paul R Williams, Steven Pressley and Sandy Robertson. Ron's most audacious move, for Wolves striker Steve Bull, didn't come off. Despite the two clubs agreeing a transfer fee, Bull decided to stay at Molineux.

The fans got an early chance to see some of the new faces at Brian Borrows' pre-season testimonial against Birmingham. The season started well: a first-day defeat at Newcastle was quickly forgotten as Manchester City were sent packing, with flowing soccer inspired by Isaias. Creditable draws against Arsenal, Chelsea and Forest seemed to indicate that relegation was not on the agenda this season. However, in a depressing autumn, City's fourteen League-game winless run was a club record in the top flight. The only cheer was a 3-2 home League Cup win over Spurs, pulling back a two-goal half-time deficit. An 18,267 crowd paid record receipts of £272,000.

Two weeks later Manchester United came and handed out a footballing lesson, 4-0, to send City to the foot of the table. The only consolation was the 23,344 attendance, a virtual capacity. Meanwhile, the team was acquiring an appalling disciplinary record with five players sent off in nine games, including Oggy in a miserable League Cup defeat at Wolves, and two players in one game at Highfield Road – for the first time ever – during the 3-3 draw with Wimbledon. Against the Dons, City somehow retrieved a point after being 1-3 down.

The chequebook came out again and Richard Shaw was signed for £1 million to bolster the suspect defence. He was quickly followed by Leeds starlet Noel Whelan, who cost a club record £2 million, and Whelan made an instant impact with three goals in his first four games. The awful run ended on a snowbound pitch with a 5-0 thumping of champions Blackburn and a good Christmas saw City creep off the foot of the table. Whelan became an instant hit, with an impudent winning goal on his home debut in the 2-1 win over Everton. The Christmas chants of 'Noel, Noel' had not been heard around Highfield Road since the days of Noel Cantwell.

The impetus generated by Whelan's signing lasted well into the New Year. Relegation fears seemed to be fading until successive home draws were followed by a ghastly home defeat by fellow strugglers Bolton. By this time Big Ron had taken his spending in twelve months to £13 million, with the addition of two more £1 million signings, midfielder Eoin Jess and Liam Daish, yet another central defender to shore up the persistently porous defence.

The week before Easter it looked all up for the Sky Blues, who had a testing run-in. They were 19th with only one win in twelve, and confidence was at its lowest ebb. They were on the brink.

Incredibly, title-chasing Liverpool were beaten by another Whelan goal. Two days later, however, City could not stop the eventual champions, Manchester United, winning a game marred by David Busst's tragic broken leg. A home win over rival strugglers QPR and a draw at Forest eased the pressure slightly, and roared on by 7,000 City fans Wimbledon were defeated on their own ground, helped by an inspired performance from Peter Ndlovu.

A goalless draw against Leeds was enough for Coventry to survive on goal-difference on a nerve-racking final day. Manchester City recovered from two goals down at home to Liverpool to get to 2-2. Some of their players thought the draw would keep them up at the expense of Coventry or Southampton. At the final whistle at Highfield Road, Atkinson and his men did not know their fate and huddled into the manager's office under the main stand waiting for Teletext to flash up the red FT (full-time) by the scores from Maine Road and the Dell. Draws for all three threatened teams meant they all finished level on points, condemning Manchester City to relegation.

That final game was marred by mindless hooligans posing as Leeds fans, who initiated violent pitch battles at the end and caused the City players' lap of honour to be cancelled. The club, the media and the police were in agreement about the cause: the 4pm kick-off – an innovation for the final day courtesy of Sky TV – encouraged fans to drink to excess. There were fears that the trouble could result in a points deduction which would incur relegation. Instead, the club escaped with a final warning about pitch invasions.

It would have been grimly ironic had the club gone down. Despite the growing debts, around £9 million, under the enthusiastic chairmanship of Bryan Richardson the club exhibited more ambition than for many years. The vast sums put at the disposal of the manager to buy players – funded in part by the novel 'buy a player' scheme, involving among others Coventry North West MP Geoffrey Robinson (who allegedly put up £5 million) – together with investments in ground improvements, had begun to convince the Coventry public that their club meant business. Both Robinson and merchant banker Derek Higgs joined the board during the season. Gates, which averaged 18,505, were up almost 40 per cent in two years and, whilst competition in the Premier League was hotter than ever, the club's ambition deserved some reward.

More planned ground upgrades were unveiled in March 1996, with proposals to provide a community and sports and leisure centre on the site of the Mercers Arms public house in Thackhall Street, purchased by the club in 1994. It would be open to the public seven days a week and become home to the club's centre of excellence, where youngsters would be developed. To help fund the project, Richardson had lined up 'a major retailer' to lease the site's retail centre.

A bad winter, weather-wise, caused more problems for the pitch. For the visit of Southampton a hot-air balloon was used to protect it from snow and frost and although the game went ahead, with the added help of 100 or so volunteers who cleared the pitch, the playing surface deteriorated quickly. Some blamed the easily cut up pitch for poor home performances, but that was a smoke-screen for deeper failings.

In October Willie Boland achieved a novel feat when he scored a hattrick of penalties in the reserve team's 7-3 win over Mansfield Town.

Then in March the ground hosted top Swedish club IFK Gothenburg, in England for their pre-season training, in a 'private' friendly.

After the latest close shave, the Sky Blues management were adamant that there would be no repeat in **1996-97**. During the summer they pulled off the biggest signing in the club's history, not only for the size of the fee, £3 million, but for the profile of the man. Gary McAllister, captain of Leeds and Scotland, would not have joined Coventry but for the persuasive skills of Atkinson and Strachan. Here, most thought, was the sort of playmaker City fans had yearned for during their barren years. Sadly he did not live up to expectations.

Two other signings, Belgian international full-back Regis Genaux and Northern Ireland international winger Michael O'Neill barely appeared for the first team, so another £1.5 million went down the drain.

The signs were ominous in a pre-season friendly when Benfica, inspired by Portugal's Euro 96 star Joao Pinto, won 7-2 in front of almost 11,000. It was a savage beating and might have done greater damage than was realised at the time. A week later Forest won 3-0 with a hat-trick from Kevin Campbell, a rare victory in a miserable season for Frank Clark's team. Atkinson's days as manager were numbered. The side recorded only one home win before, in November, he was replaced by Strachan. As Ron's contract ran until the following June, Richardson gave him a new role as director of football, a non-job which meant he was virtually paid to stay at home and not interfere with Strachan.

Richardson himself was not everyone's cup of tea. First he alienated the supporters club, substantial benefactors in bygone years: 'they do not in any way, shape or form support Coventry City.' He announced the club was setting up its own in-house supporters club, an initiative which sank without trace. Then he made an audacious takeover bid for Coventry Rugby Club, which would have involved the oval-ball men moving to a new stadium at the Butts, yet play high-profile games at Highfield Road. After a war of words the bid was rejected by the rugby club.

In October 1996 the Sky Blues used three substitutes for the first time for the visit of Southampton. Atkinson brought on Paul Williams, Peter Ndlovu and Dion Dublin (dropped after failing to score in the first eight games) and Dublin snatched an equalising goal in the last minute. The rules allowing three subs had been introduced the previous season but Ron had never deemed it necessary to use them all.

Strachan opened his reign with a Coca-Cola Cup home replay against Gillingham, at the end of which City had been dumped by a Neil Smith goal. Strachan's response was typically forthright: 'if players listen and play to the standards I require then they should be all right. If not there will have to be changes. It's up to the players'. Rumours of sloppy training sessions and general indiscipline under Atkinson were rife, but somehow one could not imagine that continuing under the fiery Scot.

After five winless games under Strachan he appointed fellow Scot Alex Miller, Scotland manager Craig Brown's number two, as his assistant. Darren Huckerby had arrived from St James' Park by this time, for £1 million, and the occasion was tailor-made for the tricky striker. City kicked-off bottom, but Huckerby netted after six minutes to lead City to their second win. Richardson looked good in the anchor role, and with Dublin at centre-half City won their next three games to earn Strachan the manager of the month award for December. In the 3-0 victory over Middlesbrough, Oggy overtook George Curtis's club appearance record by playing his 544th first-team game.

Despite missing Dublin for seven games, suspended for two red cards in successive outings, City did well enough in the FA Cup. They reached the fifth round before surrendering a 2-0 lead to lose at Derby.

Once again City endured a dreadful February and March. Eight games without a win left the team with a mountain to climb. When rivals West Ham grabbed the points in the six-pointer at Highfield Road, City faced a Sunday trip to a Liverpool side set to go top of the table.

Strachan, in desperation, called for Big Ron, a man with a good record at Anfield, to motivate his team. The contest was painfully one-sided – City took a thrashing but managed to win, with McAllister's dead-ball delivery allowing Whelan to score, and then, in injury-time, Dublin did the same.

Strachan donned his boots for the third season running and helped City to a 3-1 victory over Ruud Gullit's FA Cup semi-finalists Chelsea. The kick-off was delayed fifteen minutes for 'technical reasons' which became evident as soon as the players appeared. Chelsea were wearing their traditional blue shorts but in order to avoid a colour clash they had not foreseen, they now sported City's red and blue chequered away shirts. Chelsea had not brought their change kit and City had to send someone to the Ryton training ground to fetch their own. When they arrived, Chelsea insisted that City change shirts. Strachan refused to budge. At the final whistle a frustrated Frank Leboeuf threw his Coventry away shirt to the ground to the disgust of Coventry fans who booed him off.

That victory, plus draws against Southampton and Arsenal, lifted City to 15th. One more good display in the final home game against Derby would secure safety. They blew it with a shocking defensive display. With all their relegation rivals winning, it left City not only needing to win at Tottenham, but hoping that Middlesbrough and Sunderland tripped up.

City were closer to the brink than they had ever been. The bookies made them '9 to 1 on' to go down, and all but the hopelessly optimistic had written off City's chances.

In circumstances reminiscent of 1977, kick-off was delayed for fifteen minutes until 4.15 – ostensibly because of traffic on the M1 – thereby wrecking the Leagues rule that the final games must kick-off together. Goals from Dublin and Paul Williams, both from McAllister set-pieces, gave City the advantage before McVeigh pulled a goal back just before half-time.

With tension mounting, City battled out the second half to a backdrop of incessant noise from the 4,500 travelling army. Every other person in the away section seemed to have a radio glued to his ear. With fifteen minutes remaining the image began to clear – Middlesbrough had drawn 1-1 at Leeds and were going down. Then an interminable wait (in reality about three minutes) before learning that Sunderland had lost 0-1 at Wimbledon. The bedlam left City's players in no doubt of the situation. All they had to do was hold out for fifteen minutes. Neale Fenn thought he had scored, but Ogrizovic pulled off a terrific save. Was there ever a longer fifteen minutes? At the end there were tears amidst the roars, but City had done it again and pulled off their most improbable escape.

In light of Highfield Road's ongoing pitch problem, City had decided to play their reserve games at Nuneaton Borough's Manor Park. After just one game, against Sheffield United, which attracted 623 fans – considerably more than attended games at Highfield Road – Strachan requested they revert to Highfield Road. His reasoning was that the reserves would benefit from gaining experience on the ground.

A new under-soil heating system was announced in December, while snow lay on the pitch. Costing £300,000, Richardson explained that although City had sacrificed only one home game to the weather in two years, technology had improved since the disasters of the previous system five years previously. Three days later City and Sunderland played out a 2-2 draw on an ice-bound surface which made the result a lottery and made a mockery of referee Graham Poll's decision to play. On the following Saturday, with the weather no better, the FA Cup third round tie with Woking was postponed. It went ahead on the date of the fourth round, after a second postponement. Referee Gerald Ashby was again criticised for calling off a game an hour before kick-off, with 900 fans already in the ground. All other parties were satisfied with the surface. When the game finally went ahead City were stunned by a late Woking equaliser, and had to travel to leafy Surrey to finish the job 2-1.

Another item on Richardson's agenda was a new stadium – he was reported as saying the club needed to move to a bigger home within five years to maximise its potential in the Premiership – and with England bidding for the 2006 World Cup, the timing was opportune. The derelict 57-acre Foleshill gasworks site close to the M6 was identified by the city council as appropriate for leisure and commercial redevelopment, and preliminary discussions with the football club were reported.

Despite only four home wins all season – the lowest in the club's 77-year League history – crowds increased by 1,100 per game, giving a final average of 19,625, the highest since 1978-79. The largest League gate, 23,080 for the visit of Manchester United in January, was topped however on Friday, 16 May when United returned to play in David Busst's testimonial. An all-ticket 23,326 watched a 2-2 draw and earned Busst a £250,000 pay-day. City fielded a few guest players: Paul Gascoigne was trying to get fit before England's summer games and Les Ferdinand played most of the game. David Speedie came on as a late sub, as did Gordon Strachan – in his final playing appearance at the stadium – and Steve Ogrizovic, who played the last eight minutes as an outfield player. Gascoigne put City ahead before Eric Cantona scored twice, one a penalty, for United, for whom David Beckham and the Neville brothers appeared. With two minutes remaining and the atmosphere becoming more surreal by the moment, City won a silly penalty and on to the field came Busst. His left-foot kick bobbled into the United net to level the scores. The blond centre-half got a wonderful reception as he jogged a lap of honour to cap a memorable night. The following day Cantona announced his retirement from football and his shirt was later auctioned on radio with a further £15,350 raised for Busst's fund.

In April 1997 the club joined the technological age when it launched its first website. Comprising just six pages, it displayed ticket information and availability, a Sky Blue Leisure page, a fans' forum and match reports and statistics.

It is not often that Coventry City fans can have ended a season feeling warm and satisfied, but that was the case a year later in **1997-98**. To finish 11th in the Premiership – one year after the club had pulled back from the brink – and reach the FA Cup quarter-finals was more than most fans dared hope for.

City's relative success was a fitting tribute to the managerial and coaching skills of Gordon Strachan, in his first full season of football management. With a little luck City might have sneaked into Europe, and Wembley was tantalisingly within reach at 9.45pm on 17 March at Bramall Lane.

This season, moreover, Strachan was on his own. Atkinson's contract had expired in June and he slipped quietly away, appearing regularly as a TV match summariser, before being recruited in November to manage Sheffield Wednesday.

Strachan's summer transfer targets included a batch of Scandinavians: Norwegian midfielder Trond-Egil Soltvedt, Swedish goalkeeper Magnus Hedman from AIK Stockholm and Dane Martin Johansen. City's buy of the season however was Swedish international right-back Roland Nilsson, a snip at £200,000, who looked the part from day one, lending composure and style to the defence.

A promising 2-1 pre-season victory over Feyenoord saw goals from Soltvedt and Salako take the Sky Blues home in front of 5,700. A young Ghanaian-born full-back George Boateng replied. A week later in the first home game Dion Dublin's hat-trick, the first by a City player at home for seven years, sank FA Cup-holders Chelsea 3-2 after City had twice fallen behind. A virtual full-house of 22,691 watched on a scorching August day.

But – a 1-0 home win over Southampton apart – that was City's only League win until early November, by which time all the old ghosts were returning. What was different this time was that City were playing conspicuously better than of old. Of seven draws (five at home) in the first twelve matches, City had chances to win them all, and had acquired a self-destructive habit of letting opponents off the hook.

The 2-2 draw against Newcastle in November witnessed one of the strangest goals ever seen at the ground. After a City attack had broken down Dion Dublin reappeared from behind the goal-line, to the shock of goalkeeper Shay Given, who had grounded the ball ready to clear. Dublin darted in to prod it into the unguarded net and referee Paul Durkin allowed the goal to stand.

Following the departure of assistant manager Alex Miller, who took charge at Aberdeen, City lost three successive Midlands derbies – and slid down to 16th. But several factors combined to suddenly turn the season into one of relative success. December alone witnessed five key changes. First, Gary McAllister suffered a bad injury in the Leicester home defeat which he exacerbated against Tottenham. Second, City's £250,000 signing from Feyenoord, George Boateng, provided welcome bite to the midfield. Third, Romanian striker Viorel Moldovan arrived from Zurich Grasshoppers for a record £3.25 million, and many fans felt that his coming lit the fuse under the other strikers. Fourth, a couple of below-par performances from Ogrizovic opened the door for Hedman in goal. Finally, Whelan returned after serious injury.

It is difficult to know which was the most significant and which was the least, but the outcome was that Manchester United got stung in a classic over Christmas. Trailing the champions 1-2 with five minutes left, Darren Huckerby earned a place in club legend, first by winning a penalty – slotted home by Dublin – then, two minutes later, scoring a wonder goal at the end of a mazy 40-yard slalom.

Three weeks later, before another full-house, Arsenal almost got the same treatment, escaping with a 2-2 draw, in a match marred by red cards to Patrick Vieira and Paul Williams, the latter following a blatant dive by Dennis Bergkamp.

That sparked a welcome unbeaten run which – other than a blip at Chelsea – extended all the way to Easter. City set a club record of seven straight wins in League and cup, part of a longer run of fourteen games without defeat.

The threat posed by Dublin and Huckerby sent shivers through opposing defences. Huckerby had won BBC's *Match of the Day* 'goal of the month' in December for his sublime winner against Manchester United. As for Dublin, his six January goals made him Carling's player of the month. He was called up by England, having never previously been in the frame for international honours, and his cap against Chile made him only the fourth City player ever to be capped by England.

February was even better than January. City won five matches on the trot, including the momentous 1-0 victory at Villa Park in the FA Cup – their first in 26 visits to the ground over 62 years. The club sold their full allocation of tickets and a further 2,000 fans crammed into the east stand mall at Highfield Road to watch televised transmission.

Cup fever gripped Coventry, with fans clamouring for tickets for the quarter-final home tie with Division One Sheffield United. It was the first time City had reached the last eight since winning it. Fans camped outside the ground to ensure they got a ticket but some were unhappy at paying an extra £2 for a programme voucher. The rudderless Yorkshire side had lost their manager, Nigel Spackman, days before the tie, but inspired by goalkeeper Alan Kelly held out for a 1-1 draw – thereby bringing to an unwelcome end City's seven-match winning run, an all-time club record. A sell-out crowd of 23,084 paid club record receipts of £375,510, of which City banked 45 per cent.

In the replay the Sky Blues were still overwhelming favourites to meet Newcastle in the semi-final, the more so when Paul Telfer gave them an early lead. City spurned chances to add a second goal, and were made to pay through Holdsworth's late equaliser. The team staggered through extra-time, only to lose a nerve-racking penalty shoot-out that swung first one way then the other. Even the reliable Dublin – with five penalty goals since Christmas – lost his nerve.

That was the worst moment of City's otherwise laudable season. They kept their good League run going, and only Villa lowered their colours in the remaining nine games, but the slim hopes of Europe were stymied by returning to an epidemic of draws – no fewer than six in those nine games. One of them saw the first appearance at the ground of Michael Owen. The eighteen-year-old prodigy had made a big impression in his first season for Liverpool (and scored the only goal of the League game against the Sky Blues at Anfield in December) and scored a stunning goal out of nothing. Dublin's scoring feats continued and won him a share of the Premiership's Golden Boot, along with Owen and Chris Sutton. Too bad Dublin was omitted from England's final 22 selected for the World Cup finals in France.

The final home game, against Blackburn, was played in a carnival atmosphere, with City – for the first time in four seasons free from a relegation dog-fight – winning 2-0 to clinch 11th place. Blackburn however were not in party mood and Dion Dublin's controversial penalty sparked unsavoury scenes. First Rovers' substitute keeper Tim Flowers was shown red on the bench for verbally abusing the linesman who had given the penalty. Then Chris Sutton was lucky to avoid a red when a vicious challenge on Noel Whelan sparked a twenty-man brawl. From then on, referee Steve Lodge – infamous in Coventry for dismissing Paul Williams and Patrick Vieira in the Arsenal game – was abused from all sides.

The club's average attendance continued its upward trend, up by 93 to 19,718 with eight home games attracting over 22,000.

New stadium plans progressed and in November 1997 City unveiled plans for the Foleshill site. A £60 million development would include a revolutionary sliding pitch and retractable roof, making it an all-year venue for football, other sports, concerts and exhibitions. Planning permission was expected before Christmas and the first game was pencilled in for August 2001. Scale models were displayed to shareholders but details of the financing were sketchy, to say the least.

In January a star-studded Bayern Munich team arrived for a friendly. City fans had the opportunity to see some of the Bundesliga's top players including German internationals Kahn, Matthaus and Janker, plus French full-back Lizarazu, who would help his country lift the World Cup that summer. Bayern wanted a warm-up at the end of their winter break and put on an entertaining display for the 8,409 crowd, winning 4-2.

An already sizable City squad was enhanced by four summer signings. They included French centre-half Jean-Guy Wallemme and Belgium's

'Player of World Cup 98', Philippe Clement, a strong tackling midfielder. Wallemme made only six starts before, in December, his son's schooling sent him back to France to sign for Sochaux. Clement's injury problems restricted him to eight starts and he left for FC Bruges in the summer of 1999.

The only significant 1998 summer departure was Viorel Moldovan, whose stock had soared after scoring for Romania against England in the World Cup. He joined Fenerbahce of Turkey for £4 million, netting City a £750,000 profit in five months.

The most bizarre close-season event was the Robert Jarni saga, which saw the wing-back sign for £2.6 million. Within days Real Madrid, desperate to sign one of Croatia's World Cup stars, paid City £3.35 million for a player who never played in a City shirt.

Once again the club laid on a pre-season friendly with foreign opposition, with Spanish club Espanyol providing an entertaining warm up to the season in a 1-1 draw.

The **1998-99** season started with another thrilling win over Chelsea. The Londoners paraded a team of overseas all-stars with just two English players and the eyes of the world were on French defenders Desailly and Leboeuf, who had just helped their nation to success in the World Cup. Gianluca Vialli's side also included three Italians, a Dutchman, a Spaniard and a Uruguayan. Along with Arsene Wenger's Arsenal, they were leading the way with the importation of foreign players. A panoply of international stars played at Highfield Road during the season – Jaap Staam, Peter Schmeichel, David Ginola, Paulo Wanchope, Jimmy Floyd Hassalbaink, Benito Carbone and two other World Cup winners, Petit and Vieira. The Premiership had become truly cosmopolitan.

Huckerby and Dublin brought Desailly and Leboeuf down to earth when inflicting a fourth successive home defeat on Chelsea. However, four defeats in the next five games dumped them into the relegation zone. The rest of the season was spent trying to keep heads above water and after the comparative success of the previous season, 1998-99 was a major let-down. Cup expectations were high, but woeful displays at Luton and Everton dashed them. In all, 31 players were called upon by Gordon Strachan. The transfer merry-go-round saw City continually linked with new players and many arrivals got little chance to show their worth.

The fans, meanwhile, were captivated by Dion Dublin's 'would he stay or would he go' contract talks. With only a year left on his contract and City fearing a walkout on a Bosman, they had agreed a £20,000 per week deal in the summer. But in October Dublin began attracting interest from struggling Blackburn. His advisers had inserted a clause that allowed him to talk to any club who offered a fee of £5 million.

With Dublin's form patchy, City accepted Blackburn's bid of £6.75 million, seen by many to be excessive for a 30-year-old striker. But, once the clause became public, other clubs joined the hunt. Dublin snubbed Blackburn and after a week of impasse, legal threats and the striker's refusal to play for City in a League Cup tie at Luton, he was given permission to talk to Aston Villa, who paid £5.75 million to get their man. The scars inflicted by the episode soured relations between the two clubs for years and many City fans vented their feelings on the man they nick-named 'Judas' at every opportunity.

October's visit by Arsenal was marred by a distressing incident. Ron Reeves, the club's security guard, was hit by the Arsenal team coach as it backed into the gates at the players entrance to the main stand. Ron died at the scene. The accident affected both teams and reminded fans that there are more important things in life than football.

Steve Froggatt, a new arrival from Wolves for £1.9 million, quickly showed his pedigree by scoring a stunning goal in the 3-0 home win over Everton, faithfully recorded by the Sky cameras, but the team earned just three points from the next seven games and did not win again until a new striker, John Aloisi got his chance at Christmas.

Strachan, the subject of autumn speculation linking him with the vacant Leeds and Blackburn manager's jobs, steadied the ship a little after Christmas. Aloisi's arrival, often from the bench, spurred the whole team into action. It was the Moldovan effect all over again. In a turnaround not dissimilar to the previous campaign, following the Romanian's arrival, the side simply clicked. McAllister and Boateng, previously unimpressive in midfield, looked world-beaters. McAllister had been the target of City's boo-boys at West Ham at Christmas, but he responded with a superb spell where he was at the heart of all City's moves. Seven goals were fired past Macclesfield to equal the club's record FA Cup win, and seven days later City put four more past a woeful Nottingham Forest, under the care-taker management of former City man Micky Adams. Huckerby was in devastating form and hit successive hat-tricks, including another dazzling solo goal which revived memories of the Manchester United goal a year earlier.

Cup hopes were high again after a 3-0 win at Leicester, and 8,000 City fans travelled to Goodison Park for the FA Cup fifth-round tie. Whatever happened before kick-off is subject to rumour, but on the pitch the defence played like strangers. A feeble Everton side went through at City's expense.

Six games with only one defeat effectively banished relegation fears. The run included the club's first ever League win at Aston Villa, a thumping 4-1 victory that gave City and their fans even more pleasure in the light of the Dublin transfer wranglings. Villa were one club to buck the trend by not buying lots of foreigners – their side that day contained eleven Englishmen, the last time that happened in the Premiership. City's crucial result, however, came the following week, at home to struggling Charlton. With City a goal and a man down, after Aloisi had been sent off, Strachan brought on substitute Soltvedt, who hit the winner with five minutes remaining.

Strachan set a points target at 40 to avoid the drop, but the team dragged out the agony. With six games left they only needed three points to reach that target, but proceeded to lose three games in a row, one of them bizarrely to Middlesbrough, who took advantage of an injured Hedman to score twice from 25 yards. The Swede appeared to want to come off before half-time but Strachan later insisted that the keeper had asked to stay on.

A home win over Wimbledon, which saw Huckerby score his first goal in fourteen games, earned the 40th point, although in the event the final margin of safety was six points. An emotional final game saw visitors Leeds play their part in a four-goal thriller. Roland Nilsson, who had fractured two ribs and suffered a punctured lung at Arsenal in March, returned for his final game before retiring from English football, and earned a tumultuous ovation from the fans.

The season ended with speculation that linked Huckerby, Whelan and Breen to possible moves. Boateng, whose form had been inconsistent all season, had allegedly been the subject of an illegal approach from Aston Villa. Bad blood had existed between the two Midlands rivals since the Dublin transfer, and the fans were resigned to losing the midfielder.

On a brighter note, plans for the new 40,000-seater stadium and retail complex at Foleshill were given approval by all parties, including the Government, and was expected to be ready for August 2001 at a cost of £135 million. The stadium, dubbed Arena 2000, was also placed on a sixteen-ground provisional list for England's bid for the 2006 World Cup. There was an estimated £20 million to be spent on cleaning up the contaminated land and Richardson remained vague on the funding for the whole project.

Despite no increase in the ground's capacity, gates increased again, with the average up by just over 1,000 to 20,773.

After several years without any major success at Youth level, the club had produced a fine team that, under coach Richard Money, reached the

FA Youth Cup final for the first time since 1987. Bright prospects such as goalkeeper Chris Kirkland, sixteen-year old Gary McSheffrey, who had recently become the club's youngest ever player, and Calum Davenport pulled off excellent victories to reach a two-legged final against West Ham. In the home first leg West Ham won 3-0 in front of 11,118, and the Hammers, boosted by the return of boy prodigy Joe Cole, were in merciless mood at Upton Park, thumping City's babes 6-0.

In **1999-2000,** the team's home form would earn them the tag as the Premiership's 'entertainers'. Twelve wins and 38 goals made it the best home season since the late 1970s. But the downside was an even worse away record, City failing to win for the first time in their history. The cups saw a thrashing at Tranmere and a two-goal home lead squandered against Charlton in the FA Cup.

The summer transfer saga brought in midfielder Youssef Chippo from Porto for £1 million, Moustapha Hadji, a star of the 1998 World Cup from Deportivo La Coruna for a club record £4 million, and a young Norwegian winger, Runnar Normann for £1 million. Following another media war of words, City and Aston Villa finally agreed a fee of £4.5 million for George Boateng.

Lack of goals was still perceived to be the problem. After a one-goal reverse on the opening day to Southampton, Darren Huckerby was sold to Leeds for £5.5 million and Trond Soltvedt offloaded to Southampton for £300,000. This helped raise £6 million for Wolves' Irish international Robbie Keane. It was a major gamble. Other clubs had looked hard at the nineteen-year-old and decided not to take the risk, but on his debut against Derby the most expensive teenager in British football history scored two trademark poacher's goals to clinch City's first win. Another goal at Sunderland meant Keane was the new Coventry hero.

To replace Boateng, Carlton Palmer arrived from Nottingham Forest on loan, but signed for £500,000 after City went unbeaten for his first eight games. Home wins over West Ham, Newcastle, Watford and Aston Villa – the latter two live on Sky – saw the team climb to 11th. Keane and Hadji were on song, but when injuries forced Strachan to seek a loan striker, Euro-scout Ray Clarke found 21-year-old Belgian Cedric Roussel. Roussel shredded the Watford defence on his first start, and in his second he scored a good goal against Villa. His partnership with Keane was a major factor in City's dominant home form, with his aerial prowess providing chances for the nippy young Irishman. In January Roussel rejected other Premiership clubs to sign permanently, the fee £1.2 million.

Apart from a blip against Leicester, the impressive home form continued into 2000, bringing wins over Arsenal and Wimbledon and an exciting draw with Chelsea. The 3-2 win over Arsenal was hailed as one of the finest wins for many years – covered again by Sky. Keane scored City's third, cheekily striking the ball with the outside of his boot from an acute angle.

The new millennium was welcomed with a visit on 4 January from Chelsea, who played their part in a thrilling 2-2 draw. The line-ups showed how foreign players had come to dominate the Premiership. No fewer than fourteen nationalities were represented on the pitch that night. City started the game with only three Englishmen, Williams, Froggatt and Palmer, whilst Dennis Wise was Chelsea's sole Anglo.

January saw the two Moroccans on international duty at the African Nations Cup for the best part of the month, and they were missed. After two good FA Cup wins, First Division Charlton should have been put to the sword at home in round five, especially as City led 2-0 after 21 minutes. Charlton roared back to win 3-2 in a result that might have been avoided had the Moroccans been available. A full house of 22,842 paid record receipts of £405,000 but the result was a watershed and the terrible away form dashed hopes of European qualification. The last nine away games were all lost. They included a 0-5 drubbing at West Ham and a last-day defeat at relegated Watford. Only three goals were scored in this run, two of them by Roussel at Old Trafford. Fans became fed up with Strachan's weekly chiding of players in Monday's press.

Home performances kept most fans happy though, and the first 45 minutes against Sunderland was special. That game, however, also witnessed a dreadful challenge on Froggatt by Nicky Summerbee that inflicted serious ankle damage. Froggatt's season had been patchy, but his form had picked up after November following a surprise England call-up by Kevin Keegan. Froggatt was on the bench for England's European Championship play-off with Scotland and looked set to win a cap in the near future. He took the field several times after the Summerbee incident but by the end of the season he was in pain and forced to rest. A year later he was forced to retire.

In March, Hedman was injured on international duty, so up stepped 42-year-old Steve Ogrizovic for his swansong. He played two blinders and could not be faulted for the defeats. He announced his retirement but returned for the final home game against Sheffield Wednesday to a huge ovation and bowed out with a club record 601 appearances.

Speculation surrounded the future of 35-year-old McAllister. After three questionable seasons he had an outstanding one, being the fulcrum of all of the team's moves, and even outscoring Robbie Keane. Rumours were rife of a move to Liverpool, and Coventry offered him substantial sums to re-sign. In the end it was his desire for medals, not money, that decided his future, and Anfield duly delivered.

For the second season running, City's Under-18s reached the final of the FA Youth Cup, only to lose again. This time a strong Arsenal team were too good. Watched by 10,280 the Gunners won the first leg at Highfield Road 3-1, with Jay Bothroyd setting up two goals, including one for another future Sky Blue, Graham Barrett. Bothroyd scored himself in the 2-0 second-leg victory. City's investment in their academy, however, was beginning to pay off and in the future it was hoped that the vast sums spent in the transfer market would diminish.

There had been no foreign visitors for the traditional home pre-season friendly. Instead the club honoured Cyrille Regis with a testimonial. The former Sky Blue, the joint-caretaker manager with John Gorman of West Brom, did not play and watched as his team were beaten 4-2 by a City side inspired by the first home appearance of the two Moroccans with home fans wearing fezs in their honour.

Attendances at Highfield Road were virtually unchanged in 1999-2000, with an average of 20,785. Unfortunately at Foleshill there was little progress following a grand opening to the project in August 1999. A number of families living in caravans at the gasworks site needed to be relocated and their new site had caused ructions in the local community. As a consequence, work on clearing the site had progressed little through the winter of 2000.

In December 1999 Bryan Richardson struck a deal to sell Highfield Road to McLeans Homes, a subsidiary of Wimpy. McLeans paid around £5.5 million and granted a three-year lease to the club at a cost reported to have been £150,000. The club could not lose either way. Not only did City have an option to stay longer if the new stadium was not ready by 2002, but also had an additional option to allow the club to benefit from any increase in land values.

CHAPTER ELEVEN

The 2000s

By any criteria, Coventry City in **2000-01** were one of the three worst sides in the Premiership: an avalanche of goals against, all too few scored. Result: an appalling goal-difference, only eight wins all season and relegation thoroughly deserved.

It is easy to blame the club's demise on the sales of Robbie Keane and Gary McAllister in the summer of 2000. It wasn't the first time, nor will it be the last, that the club were forced to sell top players. McAllister enjoyed a fine season at Liverpool, but who is to say he would have lasted another of struggle at Highfield Road. Keane and his agent's ambitions were whetted after his superb first season in the Premiership. Amid rumours of the UK transfer system collapsing, City made a sound decision to cash in their chips and sell Keane to Internazionale of Milan for £13 million.

The major factor in sliding from entertainers to relegation fodder was not replacing the two departed stars. McAllister had an eye-catching final season at Highfield Road, but it is easy to forget his undistinguished performances before he was protected by the combative Palmer; and that the team's 1997-98 successes were achieved without Gary. True, McAllister, who was entitled to a free transfer, was virtually impossible to replace. David Thompson was signed from Liverpool for £3 million but he was a wide player, unlike the playmaker McAllister. Keane's replacement was the inexperienced Craig Bellamy, who cost £6 million from Norwich. He was no Keane and his goals were scarce, although the service to him was poor. Add to this the indifferent form of Roussel, Chippo and Hadji – hits the previous term – and you had the recipe for a nightmare.

Hard questions must be directed at the manager. Four years earlier in 1997 Strachan had saved the club from the drop and avoided major relegation worries in the subsequent three seasons. Whilst he had to tolerate the loss of good players, it is debatable whether he got the best out of the rest. His transfer targets also saw many foreign imports fail to make an impact.

Things started badly, only one point earned from the first four home games. On the opening day Middlesbrough ran Colin Hendry ragged and won 3-1. The former Scottish captain was booed off, dropped, and soon offloaded to Bolton. In addition, Thompson became the first Coventry player to be sent off on his debut, for 'over-zealous tackling'.

A 0-3 home defeat to West Ham confirmed the grim task ahead. Fans called for Strachan's head after the game and rumours surfaced that he had offered to resign.

Injuries to key players and suspensions (five players were red carded during the season) did not help, and Palmer left after falling-out with Strachan. Only two home games were won before Christmas – against Spurs and Leicester – but defeats at home to Ipswich and at Bradford City had the fans seething. The team's passing was poor, they surrendered possession too easily, and too many late goals were being conceded. In total, eighteen goals were conceded in the last quarter of an hour – these would prove crucial in the final reckoning and posed questions about the team's fitness.

Christmas was vital, but City missed the chance to put space between themselves and their fellow strugglers by failing to beat Southampton and Manchester City at home. Chances were being created, but none of the multitude of strike partnerships – five different permutations were used in ten games – could capitalise on them. Desperate for a proven goalscorer, the club tried to sign Wimbledon's John Hartson, but the deal snagged. The season's watershed came at home to lowly Everton, who were stricken with injuries and suspensions. City were 0-3 down after 31 minutes and by the end the ground was half empty, with those remaining booing players and management off the pitch.

The Hartson deal was resurrected and the Dons, desperate to reduce their wage bill, accepted a pay-per-play agreement that earned them £15,000 for every match Hartson played, up to a maximum of £5 million. The big Welshman made an immediate impact, helping to draw at West Ham, and scoring on his home debut in a 2-2 draw with Charlton. He demonstrated what had been lacking all season, an ability to hold the ball up – something that Aloisi and Roussel failed to do – and hurt opposing defenders. He also displayed leadership, something lacking on the pitch all season. It was, however, too little too late.

Only two of Hartson's first eight games were lost. He netted six goals (sufficient to finish joint top scorer with Bellamy and Hadji), but home draws with Charlton and Chelsea were not enough; wins were needed. Successive victories over Derby and Leicester gave hope, but defeats at Manchester United and Ipswich, and at home to Liverpool, opened the trap-door wide. The team travelled to Villa Park on 5 May needing not only a win to avoid the drop but others to lose.

In a display which encapsulated the whole sad season, the Sky Blues – who led 2-0 at the break thanks to Hadji's goals (why didn't he score a few more?) – were beaten by two Villa goals in the final minutes. The defending was amateurish and the capitulation embarrassing. Ironically, results elsewhere meant the result was immaterial: if City had won they would have still been relegated. There would be no opportunity to add to their ten last-day escapes. After 34 years in the top flight they were sent down at the one ground the fans would have chosen to avoid.

Attendances averaged 20,535 with thirteen gates over 20,000. The crucial Liverpool home game attracted the largest crowd, 23,063, to see Gary McAllister hammer the nails into City's coffin with a delightful free-kick for the second killer goal.

Pressure to remove Strachan and chairman Bryan Richardson peaked in the following weeks, but the chairman stayed loyal to his manager. He was too busy working on a new budget, one that would compensate for the lost £18 million in Sky television revenue. With City an estimated £30 million in debt, the bankers wanted to know how the club were going to handle relegation.

The **2001-02** season will go down as one of the more tempestuous in Coventry City's chequered history. Two managers, both playing legends in their own countries, were sacked, Richardson was ousted in a boardroom coup after eight years, and the club's first season outside the top flight for 34 years was a roller-coaster that ultimately ended in disappointment.

A number of players were sold over the summer of 2001 to raise funds and reduce a Premiership wage-bill. Mercenaries Bellamy, Hartson, Hadji and Aloisi left, as did Chris Kirkland, who raised £6 million with his move to Liverpool. Some of the proceeds were spent on replacements, who on the whole were disappointing: Julian Joachim started only four games, Lee Hughes, despite scoring fourteen goals was not worth £5 million, and the £1 million Keith O'Neill would earn the tag of the worst City player of all time.

Strachan was axed after just five games when City gathered a measly four points from a possible fifteen. His final game in charge, a dire 0-1 home loss to Grimsby, witnessed massive fan protests against manager and chairman. The following day Richardson, seemingly reluctantly, sacked the man he had appointed. He immediately put Roland Nilsson in charge of team affairs, with academy director Richard Money and chief scout Ray Clarke at his side. Strachan's lieutenants Pendrey and Jim Blyth also departed in a day reminiscent of the day Jimmy Hill joined the club in 1961.

The new threesome produced an immediate turnaround, with City embarking on an eleven-game unbeaten League run which earned the manager of the month award for October and the popular Swede's full-time appointment. The Sky Blues went top of the table for 24 hours after beating Sheffield Wednesday in late October but results took a turn for the worse through November and December.

The experienced Jim Smith was recruited in January to add experience to the backroom and things picked up briefly, but Smith allegedly upset the dressing room and the team's inconsistency cost them dearly. With seven games left the Sky Blues lay 4th, on target for the lucrative play-offs, but only one more point was won and the side finished 11th. During that dreadful run-in West Brom and Birmingham both visited Highfield Road. A tough Albion side, on their way to automatic promotion, showed the Sky Blues what was needed to get out of the division, winning a bruising encounter 1-0. Blues, trailing in City's wake all season, drew, and went up via the play-off final in Cardiff.

A 0-1 defeat in the final home game against Millwall signalled the end of Nilsson's short reign, with Smith also falling victim to new chairman Mike McGinnity's demands for success. Coaches Trevor Peake and Steve Ogrizovic took charge for the final game at Burnley, whereupon Gary McAllister was named as the new player-manager.

Richardson's position as chairman and chief executive had been under pressure all season by the 'Save Our City' campaign. By the autumn of 2001 the media reported that the club was £60 million in debt. In reality, the debt was less than half that, but worsening by the day. A stormy AGM embarrassed more than one board member. In January, Geoffrey Robinson, freed from ministerial duties with the Government, returned ominously to the board. Less than a week later Richardson was 'relieved of his duties'.

Gates had fallen by 21 per cent to an average of 16,137. There were more than 9,000 season ticket holders and 22,406 attended the first home game with Wolves, and the poor winter form saw the crowds slump.

There had been a few memorable, incident-packed home games. In the August 0-0 draw, Nottingham Forest became the first team to have two players sent off at Highfield Road, Stern John and Mathieu Louis-Jean seeing red. Nilsson's first home match in charge against Manchester City witnessed a classic 4-3, with David Thompson scoring the winning goal in the 89th minute. The Portsmouth game saw the worst violence inside the ground for many years. Travelling Pompey fans signalled their intent before the match by causing mayhem in City pubs and had to be bussed to the ground well in advance of the kick-off. Just before half-time the trouble flared in the section of the lower Sky Blue stand next to the west end. Seats were ripped out and missiles thrown at home sup-porters. During the half-time break thugs moved through the disabled area under the scoreboard and into the west end trading punches and causing chaos. Riot police waded in and forced the troublemakers back into their section, but the start of the second half was delayed. In all 28 arrests were made, all males from the Portsmouth area.

February's 4-0 home win over Barnsley saw Youssef Chippo score after just thirteen seconds – that was one second slower than the fastest City goal at the ground, scored by Eddie Brown in 1954.

In the cups, City were unable to benefit from home advantage against Premiership clubs. In the League Cup, Chelsea's 2-0 win was their first win at the ground for nine years. There was a minute's silence for Reg Matthews, who had passed away the previous week. Ironically, Reg had played for both clubs. In the FA Cup, a crowd of 20,633 watched Spurs win by the same score. The 1987 FA Cup-winning team appeared on the pitch beforehand but failed to inspire City.

Progress on the new ground was slow. In December it was announced that the new National stadium would be built on the site of Wembley Stadium – the possibility of it being awarded to Coventry had muddied the waters around the development at Foleshill – but at least brought the project back into focus. Delays caused by design and funding – the club and city council had sunk around £12 million into the project by this time – began to be resolved in March 2002, when the city council stepped in to purchase the land, which the club could no longer afford. The Arena 2001 company appointed football stadium 'expert' Paul Fletcher as chief executive. A fresh stadium design was unveiled, scrapping the sliding roof. It would accommodate 32,000 seats and house an exhibition and conference centre. The target completion date was August 2004.

For the majority of City fans **2002-03** was the worst season in memory. Despite the arrival of Gary McAllister as manager, most were resigned to a tough season because of the financial situation, but few could have anticipated the dreadful post-Christmas results . Following a humiliating FA Cup defeat at Rochdale, the club managed just one win in their last 21 games – and that was against Grimsby, the worst side in the division. The dreadful run saw the team slump from the top six in early January – McAllister won the Manager of the Month for December – to a final position of 20th, one above the relegation places.

McAllister himself could not have realised the extent to which his hands would be tied, but the collapse of ITV Digital and the failed court case against Carlton and Granada left the club around £5 million worse off. The summer had seen a substantial clear-out of players, with the highly paid Magnus Hedman and Gary Breen leaving, followed early in the season by David Thompson and Lee Hughes. The latter two left City nursing substantial losses, but with the bank insisting on a reduced debt the club were over a barrel. Hughes, a major disappointment at Coventry, was sold back to West Brom for around half the £5million he had cost. McAllister and his assistant Eric Black were given none of the proceeds to strengthen the squad.

All told, 44 players were used in all competitions, the highest number in the club's history. Had they managed to get the injury-prone Keith O'Neill off the sick-list they would have equalled the League's all-time record set by Barry Fry's Birmingham in 1997. The Sky Blues' former record had stood for 84 years, in their first ever League campaign in 1919, when the club fielded anyone who could kick a ball! Now, in the two campaigns following relegation from the Premiership, City had fielded a total of 62 players.

Team-changes came thick and fast and the management only named an unchanged starting line-up on seven occasions. With the financial crisis so bad, the loan market was heavily utilised by McAllister. However by February the club had used its full quota of loan signings (the majority failed to impress) and had to start experimenting with home-produced youngsters. Players like Ben Mackey, Mark Noon, Sean Cooney, Andrew Whing, Tom Bates, Isaac Osbourne and Avun Jephcott – all virtually unknown outside Ryton a year previously – were thrown in at the deep end. Only Whing and Osbourne made any lasting impression. At the end of the Stoke game at Easter, City had eight home-grown players on the pitch, the highest figure since Dave Sexton in the early 1980s.

Leamington-born Ben Mackey became the youngest City player of all-time when he came on as a substitute against Ipswich on 12 April. He was sixteen years and 167 days old (31 days younger than Gary McSheffrey back in 1999). Another sixteen-year-old, Isaac Osbourne, debuted two weeks later, becoming only the sixth sixteen-year old to play for the club. At the other end of the scale, two 37-year-olds, Steve Walsh and Vicente Engonga, came briefly on loan.

The team's record at Highfield Road was pitiful, with the eleven home defeats the club's worst ever total. The season ended with failure to win in ten successive home games, equalling the worst run in the club's history set in 1919-20 and 1991-92.

There were a few autumn highlights. The biggest victory was 8-0 over Rushden & Diamonds in the Worthington Cup, a club record Cup victory and the biggest in any competition since 1934. Poor Rushden suffered two red cards, Barry Hunter after 30 minutes for two yellows, then John Dempster 'saw red' for deliberate handball. Many fans wanted Richard Shaw to take the resulting penalty but Robert Betts wouldn't give him the ball, converting himself to make it 7-0.

During the biggest League win, 3-0 home over Derby, a topless female streaker headed for City's new cult hero, Mo Konjic, and planted a kiss on the embarrassed Bosnian.

Gary McSheffrey was in and out of the team all season but overtook Chippo's fast goal the previous season by netting in twelve seconds in the 3-0 home win over Colchester in the Worthington Cup.

The only home win after the New Year was the 3-0 FA Cup replay win over Cardiff. Sky Television sent their cameras along and the club benefited to the tune of around £250,000.

By the season's end chairman McGinnity revealed that the club, like rivals Leicester and Bradford City, could have gone into liquidation at any time during the previous year. What had saved them was that £15 million of the £23 million debt was owed to board members Robinson, Higgs and McGinnity. So whereas Leicester were able, some say unfairly, to leave creditors in the lurch and make a fresh start, the Sky Blues were committed to working their way out of the predicament.

In more cost-cutting actions, fifteen first-team players were either given free transfers or made listed, including popular home-grown stars McSheffrey and Eustace. The club also scrapped the Under-19 team and sacked youth-team coach Trevor Peake and commercial director Ric Allison. Attendances fell by 8 per cent with the average, 14,810, the lowest at home since 1993-94. The biggest crowd was 19,526 for the Boxing Day clash with Reading. It was the first time in ten years that there was no gate above 20,000 at the ground.

In June 2003 after months of rumours it was confirmed that the new stadium would be delayed. The opening, previously planned for August 2004 was now put back to January 2005. The delay was blamed on the original contractors Birse – who were reported to have lost £5.5 million on Leicester's new Walkers Stadium – pulling out. The former gasworks site had been cleaned up, the land would be levelled and prepared for construction work to start in the autumn. Graham Hover obviously had confidence, as he announced that the **2003-04** season would be City's last full season at Highfield Road.

City's third season outside the Premiership was another eventful one, with three managers at the helm and players coming and going through Highfield Road's revolving doors. McAllister cleared the decks for a new batch, and seven players, all either free transfers or small fees, debuted in the opening League game against Walsall. City's typically inconsistent form through the autumn was overshadowed by the activity involving the new stadium. In September it transpired that the Arena company had failed to obtain the £21 million funding required to start the construction and the whole project was at risk. The city council came to the rescue by agreeing to fund the shortfall via a short-term loan, but only after weeks of nail-biting and a seven-hour council meeting on 16 October.

Contracts for the construction to commence were signed, with Laing O'Rourke named as the lead contractor. The delays meant that the opening date was put back again, but the revised date of August 2005 seemed more realistic. The club, meanwhile, had sold their 50 per cent stake in Arena Coventry Limited. This would raise a much-needed £6.5 million, but in the medium term – it later became clear – would deprive them of much income at the new Arena, including catering, alcohol, car parking and ground sponsorship. At Highfield Road, the club exercised the buy-back clause on the old ground, and pocketed a further £2 million from the rising value of the site, which would be used by Wimpy for the building of 175 new homes.

McAllister's new intake rarely gelled and soon the loanees were arriving again. A plum League Cup draw brought Tottenham, and Robbie Keane, back to Highfield Road but the gap in class was embarrassing as 15,474 watched Spurs win 3-0, with Keane earning the respect of City's fans by not celebrating his goal with his trademark somersault.

In early December, following a 1-1 home draw with Sunderland which left the club 17th, McAllister announced he was taking time out from football to be with his sick wife Denise, who was being treated for cancer. His assistant Eric Black took over and a month later was appointed full-time manager after McAllister resigned his post. One can speculate whether McAllister would have lasted until then, but for the board, and the chairman especially, having their minds on the new stadium and the club's financial situation.

Black's appointment had a startling effect on the club's fortunes, apart from the FA Cup defeat at Colchester. They lost only three of thirteen home games and with the previously exiled McSheffrey and Joachim back in favour the goals flowed. At one stage a play-off place, something barely believable in December, became a possibility. The highlight of the winning run was the visit of Preston, when City took a four-goal lead inside half an hour. Although defeats by the top clubs meant a final position of 12th, Black had restored some pride to the club and had the team playing exciting, attacking football.

Then a shock. The day after a 5-2 win at Gillingham in the penultimate game, Black was sacked despite a supposed verbal agreement with the chairman on a new contract. The fans were up in arms and protested at the final home game with Crystal Palace. Many turned up wearing black, signifying a wake and the outgoing manager's name. By this time new manager Peter Reid, who McGinnity believed to be the 'high-profile' figure the club needed, was in place. Reid's reception was muted and despite the team beating Premiership-bound Palace there was an unrest that would prove to be the beginning of the end for McGinnity. Ironically Derrick Robins, the greatest chairman in the club's history, had died just days earlier, and a one-minute silence was preceded by a unique outburst of spontaneous applause.

The full-house of 22,202 for the Palace game, boosted by 4,000 visiting supporters, ensured a final average crowd of 14,632.

In Mike McGinnity's dreams the final season at Highfield Road, **2004-05**, would end with City reclaiming their place in the Premiership alongside the move to the Ricoh Arena. Sadly, his dreams were ill-founded and based more on wishful thinking. The final twelve months would transpire to be McGinnity's *annus horribilis*.

With McGinnity's pledge of promotion ringing in his ears, Reid got down to work. Despite no money to strengthen his squad, he 'freshened' up the playing staff. Moroccan Youssef Safri was in demand and joined Norwich for around £750,000. Big earners Mo Konjic and Joachim moved on, and player of the year Stephen Warnock returned to Liverpool after his loan ended. Two weeks into the season Calum Davenport, a popular home-grown central defender who had always looked destined for bigger things, was sold to Tottenham in a deal worth £1.1 million, rising to potentially £3 million.

Reid's high profile meant City were linked with numerous 'names', including Teddy Sheringham, Dion Dublin and Dwight Yorke. All but Tim Sherwood rejected Reid's overtures, and his arrival on a free transfer with a rumoured hefty signing on fee and two-year contract was to prove disastrous. Although his dodgy ankle somehow escaped the club's medical, he broke down in training and started only ten games. He was also rumoured to be linked with dressing room disruption.

Reid was given £250,000 of the Davenport money for Birmingham's Trinidad striker Stern John, but in the main had to use the risky loan market. The quality of Reid's Premiership loanees was poor, goalkeeper Luke Steele apart. Players like Dean Leacock, Matthew Mills, Rohan Ricketts and Florent Laville did little to improve the team's grim autumn form.

Off the field the antics of Joe Dhinsa shifted the limelight away from the bumbling efforts of Reid. Dhinsa, born and bred in Coventry and supposedly a multi-millionaire, talked of investing £10/12 million in the club and making a takeover bid. He wooed fans with extravagant promises and upset McGinnity and the club's directors with his criticism of their regime. He even talked about installing Gerald Houllier as manager.

When his self-set takeover bid deadline of the end of November came and went, the *CET* did some digging and unearthed the truth that Dhinsa did not have the resources to finance a bid and was nothing more than a self-publicist. He soon disappeared from the scene.

If McGinnity thought his problems had gone away he was mistaken. The club staggered from one crisis to another through the winter. He had accused Dhinsa of disrupting the club, then complained that he was attracting too much flak from supporters, but his credibility plummeted when he threatened the fanzine 'Gary Mabbutt's Knee' with libel after an article questioned his honesty.

Two home defeats over Christmas left City 20th. This was unacceptable to the fans and during the second, the New Year's game with Leeds, with the 'Reid out' chants deafening, the whole ground seemed to be urging him to go. The following day McGinnity, his master plan for instant success in tatters, flew in from his holiday home in Majorca hoping to pour oil on troubled waters. Whatever was said between the two men is not known, but within hours Reid was gone. The club announced that he had resigned but in truth no one had tried to persuade him to soldier on. Reliable sources say that Reid agreed to forego a pay-off to help the financially crippled club, and save himself a torrent of abuse if he had insisted his contract was honoured.

In an unprecedented move, McGinnity – blamed for not consulting supporters over the choice of Reid – asked them to help choose the new manager. The unanimous decision was Micky Adams, who had recently quit from Leicester and had the experience of leading three clubs (Fulham, Brighton and Leicester) to promotion.

Like Reid, Adams had no money to spend and trod the loanee path. Fortunately his choices were a little more astute, and players Richard Duffy, Ian Bennett and Trevor Benjamin helped the club to arrest the slump. On 23 March 2004 City were in the bottom three, with the distinct possibility of the new stadium hosting third-tier football. Two home wins in four days eased the pressure. Fellow strugglers Brighton were beaten 2-1 with a late winner from Steve Staunton, and then City virtually sealed relegation for Nottingham Forest in front of 22,211, the largest crowd of the season to that point. Now, just three points from five games were needed to reach the theoretical 50-point safety mark, but on the morning of the final home game, against Derby, the Sky Blues were still one point short of safety.

In March, City fans suddenly realised that the curtain was slowly coming down on Highfield Road. Gates, struggling around the 13,000 mark, began to rise as non-core fans realised time was running out, and they had to pay their final respects. It had been another miserable home season and not even Adams could regenerate the home form. Just before half-time in the 0-0 draw with Stoke, goalkeeper Ian Bennett was sent off for handling outside the box, the first Coventry goalkeeper sent off at the ground. With no substitute keeper on the bench, Adams put captain Stephen Hughes in goal. For the remaining 50 minutes City's heroic defence, aided by two or three outstanding saves by Hughes, managed to keep the Potters at bay and keep the team's first clean sheet in eleven League games.

The last four home gates at Highfield Road were all over 18,500, producing a final average of 16,131, which was almost 1,500 up on the previous campaign.

On 29 March the last ever reserve game was played at Highfield Road and West Ham won 4-2. The majority of the reserve games had been played at Nuneaton Borough's Manor Park ground.

Three weeks later the ground hosted Michael Gynn's long overdue testimonial. A crowd of 9,435 watched City's 1987 squad draw 7-7 with a Tottenham All Stars XI. Gynn was one of ten of the 1987 starting line-up to play – Keith Houchen had had knee surgery days earlier. One player not of the 1987 vintage, 57-year-old Tommy Hutchison, played for 60 minutes (probably the oldest player to appear in an organised game at the ground) and showed he still had some of his magic. The opposition boasted some famous old names, including Chris Waddle, Steve Bull, Ian Rush and Liam Brady. Gynn's testimonial fund was boosted by £90,000 on that memorable night.

The final day at Highfield Road crept up on many fans, still biting their nails over possible relegation. The club, however, had been preparing for many months and the marketing department had organised a range of 'End of an Era' memorabilia. Programme editor David Antill, in his first season in the post flowing the death of his predecessor David Jones, produced a polished 132-page programme for the final game. It came in two versions: for £6 you could have the basic version, and £10 bought you the deluxe version, one of 2,500 numbered copies personally signed by Mike McGinnity. £19.95 bought you a Highfield Road seat to keep, and for £15.95 you could acquire a square foot of turf.

The final visitors were Derby, virtually assured of a play-off position under the management of George Burley. The game brought Coventry fans' favourite Mo Konjic back to Highfield Road for the first time. He had left for Derby the previous summer and had struggled with injuries all season, but was guaranteed a hero's reception from the fans for whom he was one of the most popular players of the Premiership years. City still needed one point to be mathematically safe and Adams warned the players not to get carried away with the emotion surrounding the final game at the stadium. Police had warned spectators that anyone trying to take souvenirs from the ground could be prosecuted.

The 30th April dawned with glorious sunshine and blue skies. As the 3pm kick-off approached, the streets around Highfield Road buzzed with activity and it was obvious that there was a special atmosphere around the ground. All tickets had been sold weeks before and the club squeezed 22,777 spectators into the ground, the biggest crowd since the club had dropped out of the Premiership. At two o'clock, with the ground already three-quarters full, the entertainment began.

A host of former players had been invited and were introduced on the pitch for the Parade of Legends. Peter Hill, Bill Glazier, Bobby Gould and Dietmar Bruck from the 60s, Carr, Hunt, Hutchison and Cattlin from the 70s, then nine of the 1987 squad, with managers Gordon Milne and John Sillett. Finally the biggest legend of them all, Jimmy Hill, who got a rapturous reception when he skipped towards the other legends waiting in the centre circle. After a quick rendering of the Sky Blue Song the proceedings began.

It was, however, the current crop of players who ensured that the club bowed out after 106 years in style with four goals in 40 scintillating first-half minutes, and two more for good measure after the break. The game had everything the fans could have wished for, from top-class goals to an atmosphere that sizzled, and with scenes of celebration that will hold a special place in supporters' memories for years to come.

McSheffrey, the man of the match, scored the first goal after one of his trademark runs. Six minutes later the impetuous Konjic bundled over Jorgensen in the penalty area and McSheffrey made it 2-0 from the spot. Konjic was exposed again for the third after 36 minutes, Dele Adebola out-muscling him on the by-line before rounding the keeper. A Stern John header from a corner made it 4-0. The home fans had sung their anthem to Konjic before his errors and revelled in the big man's blunders.

The match ended 6-2, and the final twenty minutes were played out in a carnival atmosphere, with Mexican waves and a noisy rendition of the fans' favourite song *Twist and Shout*. For many supporters too young to remember Wembley in 1987, it was the greatest day of their lives, and for many older fans it was up there with the most memorable.

At the final whistle there was a mini pitch invasion which put the players' lap of honour in jeopardy, but the pitch was soon cleared and the victorious players emerged to soak up the history of the occasion. When they disappeared down the tunnel for the last time it was the cue for the fans to pour on to the pitch. A sea of sky blue submerged the green turf as thousands chanted for Jimmy Hill and Micky Adams. Hill emerged in the directors box to conduct the crowd, just as he had done on the day City gained promotion in 1967, in a rendition of the Sky Blue Song. Tears fell, but there was nothing funereal about the day that the fans came to lay Highfield Road to rest.

Steve Evans writing in the *CET* got carried away with his metaphors: 'Saturday was the day of Highfield Road, that grand old lady of grounds, gloriously rose up from her death bed and roared one last memorable time, for all the footballing world to hear.' It could have almost been penned 106 years previously.

The win earned City the performance of the week from the League Managers association and went a long way to clinching the Championship Manager of the Month award for Micky Adams. Remarkably, it was the first time for 23 years that the team had scored six goals in a home League game.

Tommy Hutchison received an award as City's Player of the Century and later was to be seen drinking beer in the garden of Tom Bourke, four doors down from the ground in King Richard Street.

The 5th May saw another 'final' game at the ground, when it hosted the annual Evening Telegraph Challenge Cup final for the last time. Coventry Sphinx, from the Midland Combination, swept Brooklands-Jaguar aside, winning 5-0.

On 7th May came the final, final game, when City's Under-18 side met Newcastle in the play-off semi-final. City's youngsters, coached by former player Brian Borrows, had finished ahead of Premiership sides such as Arsenal, Chelsea and Tottenham to qualify for the play-offs. A noon kick-off with free admission saw City win 1-0. Ulsterman Paul McCrink scored the vital goal to earn a place in the final against Blackburn.

Highfield Road might have staged its final game, but McGinnity's miserable year wasn't finished. He must have been enraged when reading in the local newspaper that Micky Adams' contract was still unsigned. Adams had verbally agreed a two-and-a-half-year deal, but for reasons known only to City's chief executive Graham Hover, the contract remained unsigned and there was a potential risk of Adams being tempted away. McGinnity cut short a holiday in Majorca to take control of a potential timebomb. Within days of the *faux-pas* coming to light, Adams signed the contract and McGinnity was able to relax. Or so he thought.

Within two weeks the news everyone sensed and dreaded was confirmed. The new stadium would not be ready on time. The first game of the 2005-06 season was scheduled for 6 August, but the Arena could not stage a game until 20 August. City's application to the Football League to have their first three games away from home was rejected, and plans to hold a prestigious friendly with Internazionale of Milan in the midweek before the season's start had to be shelved. As City scrabbled around for a contingency plan the options – if the League ruled against the three away games – were to play again at Highfield Road, assuming a safety certificate could be issued, or ask another Midland club to use their facilities. In yet another statement which ruffled City feathers, McGinnity indicated that Villa Park looked a good bet, because the Premiership season did not start until a week later. In a internet web vote, 62 per cent of fans preferred St Andrews, with 21 per cent plumping for Highfield Road, and only 4 per cent backing a game at Villa Park. The issue was resolved when the fixtures were published in late June. Norwich, City's opponents on 6 August, agreed to switch the game to Carrow Road, allowing QPR to be the first visitors at the Arena on 20 August.

The lack of a contingency plan for the failure of the Arena to be open on time, coming on top of the Adams contract debacle, was probably the final nail in the coffin for chief executive Graham Hover. There was no overt criticism of Hover, a loyal servant of the club for 21 years, but just two days after the Arena bombshell the club relieved him of his duties. Perhaps the club's worsening financial crisis, because of the late opening of the Arena, had a bearing on Hover's dismissal. In retrospect, he was an excellent club secretary but perhaps unsuited to the far bigger role as chief executive.

Highfield Road, meanwhile, was still in demand. On 11 June, Elton John played a farewell concert there. A massive temporary stage was erected at the west end of the pitch.

Two weeks later it was the turn of the Jehovah's Witnesses to take over Highfield Road for the last time. The West Midlands branch had held their annual convention there for almost twenty years, and as usual around 8/10,000 flocked to the ground on each of the three days of the event. They, too, erected a stage at the west end, while their members populated the three other stands, and listening to talks and discussing their biblical interpretations for the 21st century. They also were looking forward to the Ricoh Arena and had already booked their 2006 convention at the new stadium.

On 3 July the auctioneers took centre stage at Highfield Road. Over 400 mementoes went under the hammer in a one-off auction on the pitch. Hundreds of fans turned up for the event, conducted by specialist stadium auctioneers SHM Smith Hodgkinson. Amongst the items were turnstiles, programme stands, the dugouts and many signs from around the ground. The larger items went for sale at a public tender in May and included the floodlights, seats (for sale in quantities of 100), the concertina players tunnel, and much of the catering equipment and furniture. In all, around £60,000 was raised from the sales.

In late July a camera crew visited Highfield Road to record an episode of the TV serial *Dalziel & Pascoe*. The storyline centred on a fictional team called Weatherton Wanderers, and was filmed during a City training session.

The demolition of the old ground had started in a small way back in January. The hospitality boxes at the corner of the main and west stands, purchased from Silverstone in 1995, were dismantled and removed to Cheltenham racecourse. It took two days to remove them and they left a bit of a gap at the ground.

The final event took place on Sunday, 21 August. At 2pm the Dean of Coventry Cathedral, the Very Reverend John Irvine, conducted a farewell remembrance service at Highfield Road for around 140 families and friends whose ashes had previously been scattered on the turf. In a largely unpublicised gesture the club had organised for shale from the running track and turf from the goalmouths to be blessed before its removal to a new remembrance garden at the Ricoh Arena.

The Dean spoke for thousands when he said: 'For many Coventry citizens, supporting their football team is about more than enjoying sport. It is a way of showing commitment to the community and finding a sense of belonging. The Highfield Road stadium is the subject of fond memories for lots of local people, and it is fitting for some to make it their last resting place. Everyone is excited about the fantastic new Ricoh Arena and the future, but it is important to take time to acknowledge the past and its people before moving forward.'

The stadium stood empty until January 2006 when the demolition men moved in. In late September it suffered an arson attack on the Thackhall Street offices. Flames soared 20 feet into the air and thick smoke billowed from the blaze. First-floor windows were blown out into the street and it took firefighters two hours to get the blaze – in the social club – under control. A 25-metre stretch of offices were totally gutted. Senior Fire Officers said the fire was started deliberately.

Demolition took just fifteen weeks and by the summer of 2006 the first new Wimpy homes were completed on the old site.

Appendices

Appendix 1: Complete Record 1899-2005: Seasonal Summary

	LEAGUE			HOME					AWAY					TOTAL					
		Div	Pos	P	W	D	L	F	A	W	D	L	F	A	W	D	L	F	A	Pts
1	1899-00	BL	16	30	6	3	6	35	33	0	0	15	12	67	6	3	21	47	100	15
2	1900-01	BL	14	34	9	2	6	42	31	0	4	13	18	70	9	6	19	60	101	24
3	1901-02	BL	16	34	5	4	8	26	32	1	2	14	15	64	6	6	22	41	96	18
4	1902-03	BL	7	34	10	2	5	44	32	5	4	8	31	36	15	6	13	75	68	36
5	1903-04	BL	11	34	5	4	8	20	27	7	3	7	33	33	12	7	15	53	60	31
6	1904-05	BL	17	34	8	2	7	32	28	1	2	14	19	54	9	4	21	51	82	22
7	1905-06	BL	11	34	10	4	3	44	19	3	2	12	20	42	13	6	15	64	61	32
8	1906-07	BL	7	34	11	2	4	51	26	5	2	10	19	34	16	4	14	70	60	36
9	1907-08	BL	4	34	15	1	1	69	17	3	2	12	28	47	18	3	13	97	64	39
10	1908-09	SL	20	40	10	4	6	44	37	5	0	13	20	54	15	4	19	64	91	34
11	1909-10	SL	8	42	11	6	4	50	24	8	2	11	21	36	19	8	15	71	60	46
12	1910-11	SL	11	38	12	4	3	47	21	4	2	13	18	47	16	6	16	65	68	38
13	1911-12	SL	6	38	14	3	2	47	13	3	5	11	19	41	17	8	13	66	54	42
14	1912-13	SL	13	38	9	4	6	42	27	4	4	11	11	32	13	8	17	53	59	34
15	1913-14	SL	20R	38	4	8	7	28	28	2	6	11	15	40	6	14	18	43	68	26
16	1914-15	SL2	5	24	9	1	2	43	10	4	0	8	13	23	13	1	10	56	33	27
17	1919-20	2	20	42	7	7	7	20	26	2	4	15	15	47	9	11	22	35	73	29
18	1920-21	2	21	42	8	6	7	24	25	4	5	12	15	45	12	11	19	39	70	35
19	1921-22	2	20	42	8	5	8	31	21	4	5	12	20	39	12	10	20	51	60	34
20	1922-23	2	18	42	12	2	7	35	21	3	5	13	11	42	15	7	20	46	63	37
21	1923-24	2	19	42	9	6	6	34	23	2	7	12	18	45	11	13	18	52	68	35
22	1924-25	2	22R	42	10	6	5	32	26	1	3	17	13	58	11	9	22	45	84	31
23	1925-26	3N	16	42	13	6	2	47	19	3	0	18	26	63	16	6	20	73	82	38
24	1926-27	3S	15	42	11	4	6	44	33	4	3	14	27	53	15	7	20	71	86	37
25	1927-28	3S	20	42	5	8	8	40	36	6	1	14	27	60	11	9	22	67	96	31
26	1928-29	3S	11	42	9	6	6	35	23	5	8	8	27	34	14	14	14	62	57	42
27	1929-30	3S	6	42	14	3	4	54	25	5	6	10	34	48	19	9	14	88	73	47
28	1930-31	3S	14	42	11	4	6	55	28	5	5	11	20	37	16	9	17	75	65	41
29	1931-32	3S	12	42	17	2	2	74	28	1	6	14	34	69	18	8	16	108	97	44
30	1932-33	3S	6	42	16	1	4	75	24	3	5	13	31	53	19	6	17	106	77	44
31	1933-34	3S	2	42	16	3	2	70	22	5	9	7	30	32	21	12	9	100	54	54
32	1934-35	3S	3	42	14	5	2	56	14	7	4	10	30	36	21	9	12	86	50	51
33	1935-36	3S	1P	42	19	1	1	75	12	5	8	8	27	33	24	9	9	102	45	57
34	1936-37	2	8	42	11	5	5	35	19	6	6	9	31	35	17	11	14	66	54	45
35	1937-38	2	4	42	12	5	4	31	15	8	7	6	35	30	20	12	10	66	45	52
36	1938-39	2	4	42	13	4	4	35	13	8	4	9	27	32	21	8	13	62	45	50
37	1946-47	2	8	42	12	8	1	40	17	4	5	12	26	42	16	13	13	66	59	45
38	1947-48	2	10	42	12	5	4	33	16	4	8	9	26	36	14	13	15	59	52	41
39	1948-49	2	16	42	12	3	6	35	20	3	4	14	20	44	15	7	20	55	64	37
40	1949-50	2	12	42	8	6	7	32	24	5	7	9	23	31	13	13	16	55	55	39
41	1950-51	2	7	42	15	3	3	51	25	4	4	13	24	34	19	7	16	75	59	45
42	1951-52	2	21R	42	9	5	7	36	33	5	1	15	23	49	14	6	22	59	82	34
43	1952-53	3S	6	46	15	5	3	52	22	4	7	12	25	40	19	12	15	77	62	50
44	1953-54	3S	14	46	14	5	4	36	15	4	4	15	25	41	18	9	19	61	56	45
45	1954-55	3S	9	46	15	5	3	50	26	3	6	14	17	33	18	11	17	67	59	47
46	1955-56	3S	8	46	16	4	3	54	20	4	5	14	19	40	20	9	17	73	60	49
47	1956-57	3S	16	46	12	5	6	52	36	4	7	12	22	48	16	12	18	74	84	44
48	1957-58	3S	19	46	10	9	4	41	24	3	4	16	20	57	13	13	20	61	81	39
49	1958-59	4	2P	46	18	4	1	50	11	6	8	9	34	36	24	12	10	84	47	60
50	1959-60	3	5	46	14	6	3	44	22	7	4	12	34	41	21	10	15	78	63	52
51	1960-61	3	15	46	14	6	3	54	25	2	6	15	26	58	16	12	18	80	83	44

	LEAGUE	Div	Pos	P	HOME W	D	L	F	A	AWAY W	D	L	F	A	TOTAL W	D	L	F	A	Pts
52	1961-62	3	14	46	11	6	6	38	26	5	5	13	26	45	16	11	19	64	71	43
53	1962-63	3	4	46	14	6	3	54	28	4	11	8	29	41	18	17	11	83	69	53
54	1963-64	3	1	46	14	7	2	62	32	8	9	6	36	29	22	16	8	98	61	60
55	1964-65	2	10	42	10	5	6	41	29	7	4	10	31	41	17	9	16	72	70	43
56	1965-66	2	3	42	14	5	2	54	31	6	8	7	19	22	20	13	9	73	53	53
57	1966-67	2	1P	42	17	3	1	46	16	6	10	5	28	27	23	13	6	74	43	59
58	1967-68	1	20	42	8	5	8	32	32	1	10	10	19	39	9	15	18	51	71	33
59	1968-69	1	20	42	8	6	7	32	22	2	5	14	14	42	10	11	21	46	64	31
60	1969-70	1	6	42	9	6	6	35	28	10	5	6	23	20	19	11	12	58	48	49
61	1970-71	1	10	42	12	4	5	24	12	4	6	11	13	26	16	10	16	37	38	42
62	1971-72	1	18	42	7	10	4	27	23	2	5	14	17	44	9	15	18	44	67	33
63	1972-73	1	19	42	9	5	7	27	24	4	4	13	13	31	13	9	20	40	55	35
64	1973-74	1	16	42	10	5	6	25	18	4	5	12	18	36	14	10	18	43	54	38
65	1974-75	1	14	42	8	9	4	31	27	4	6	11	20	35	12	15	15	51	62	39
66	1975-76	1	14	42	6	9	6	22	22	7	5	9	25	35	13	14	15	47	57	40
67	1976-77	1	19	42	7	9	5	34	26	3	6	12	14	33	10	15	17	48	59	35
68	1977-78	1	7	42	13	5	3	48	23	5	7	9	27	39	18	12	12	75	62	48
69	1978-79	1	10	42	11	7	3	41	29	3	9	9	17	39	14	16	12	58	68	44
70	1979-80	1	15	42	12	2	7	34	24	4	5	12	22	42	16	7	19	56	66	39
71	1980-81	1	16	42	9	6	6	31	30	4	4	13	17	38	13	10	19	48	68	36
72	1981-82	1	14	42	9	4	8	31	24	4	7	10	25	38	13	11	18	56	62	50
73	1982-83	1	19	42	10	5	6	29	17	3	4	14	19	42	13	9	20	48	59	48
74	1983-84	1	19	42	8	5	8	33	33	5	6	10	24	44	13	11	18	57	77	50
75	1984-85	1	19	42	11	3	7	29	22	4	2	15	18	42	15	5	22	47	64	50
76	1985-86	1	18	42	6	5	10	31	35	5	5	11	17	36	11	10	21	48	71	43
77	1986-87	1	10	42	14	4	3	35	17	3	8	10	15	28	17	12	13	50	45	63
78	1987-88	1	10	40	6	8	6	23	25	7	6	7	23	28	13	14	13	46	53	53
79	1988-89	1	7	38	9	4	6	28	23	5	9	5	19	19	14	13	11	47	42	55
80	1989-90	1	12	38	11	2	6	24	25	3	5	11	15	34	14	7	17	39	59	49
81	1990-91	1	16	38	10	6	3	30	16	1	5	13	12	33	11	11	16	42	49	44
82	1991-92	1	19	42	6	7	8	18	15	5	4	12	17	29	11	11	20	35	44	44
83	1992-93	P	15	42	7	4	10	29	28	6	9	6	23	29	13	13	16	52	57	52
84	1993-94	P	11	42	9	7	5	23	17	5	7	9	20	28	14	14	14	43	45	56
85	1994-95	P	16	42	7	7	7	23	25	5	7	9	21	37	12	14	16	44	62	50
86	1995-96	P	16	38	6	7	6	21	23	2	7	10	21	37	8	14	16	42	60	38
87	1996-97	P	17	38	4	8	7	19	23	5	6	8	19	31	9	14	15	38	54	41
88	1997-98	P	11	38	8	9	2	26	17	4	7	8	20	27	12	16	10	46	44	52
89	1998-99	P	15	38	8	6	5	26	21	3	3	13	13	30	11	9	18	39	51	42
90	1999-00	P	14	38	12	1	6	38	22	0	7	12	9	32	12	8	18	47	54	44
91	2000-01	P	19R	38	4	7	8	14	23	4	3	12	22	40	8	10	20	36	63	34
92	2001-02	1	11	46	12	4	7	33	19	8	2	13	26	34	20	6	20	59	53	66
93	2002-03	1	20	46	6	6	11	23	31	6	8	9	23	31	12	14	20	46	62	50
94	2003-04	1	12	46	9	9	5	34	22	8	5	10	33	32	17	14	15	67	54	65
95	2004-05	C	19	46	8	7	8	32	28	5	6	12	29	45	13	13	20	61	73	52
	TOTAL			3904	986	477	489	3616	2247	403	488	1059	2085	3751	1389	965	1548	5701	5998	4049
	1919-2005			3344	838	423	411	2952	1842	348	448	876	1773	3031	1186	871	1287	4725	4873	3549

DIVISIONAL SUMMARY

		P	HOME W	D	L	F	A	AWAY W	D	L	F	A	TOTAL W	D	L	F	A	Pts
PREMIERSHIP	9	354	65	56	56	219	199	34	56	87	168	291	99	112	143	387	490	409
DIV 1 (NEW)^	4	184	35	26	31	122	100	27	21	44	111	142	62	47	75	233	242	233
DIV 1 (OLD)	26	1036	229	141	148	754	592	102	143	273	463	872	331	284	421	1217	1464	1091
DIV 2 (OLD)	18	756	197	89	92	645	400	82	97	199	405	699	279	186	291	1050	1099	744
DIV 3 (OLD)	5	230	67	31	17	252	133	26	35	54	151	214	93	66	71	403	347	252
DIV 4 (OLD)	1	46	18	4	1	50	11	6	8	9	34	36	24	12	10	84	47	60
DIV 3 (S)	16	696	214	70	64	863	388	68	88	192	415	714	282	158	256	1278	1102	722
DIV 3 (N)	1	42	13	6	2	47	19	3	0	18	26	63	16	6	20	73	82	38
Birmingham League	9	302	79	24	48	363	245	25	21	105	195	447	104	45	153	558	692	253
Southern League	7	258	69	30	30	301	160	30	19	78	117	273	99	49	108	418	433	247
TOTAL	95	3904	986	477	489	3616	2247	403	488	1059	2085	3751	1389	965	1548	5701	5998	4049

^includes Coca-Cola Championship

LEAGUE		HOME					AWAY					TOTAL					
Div Pos	P	W	D	L	F	A	W	D	L	F	A	W	D	L	F	A	Pts

WARTIME SEASONS

	Div Pos	P	W	D	L	F	A	W	D	L	F	A	W	D	L	F	A	Pts
1918-19 War		36	12	0	6	45	33	4	6	8	17	34	16	6	14	62	67	38
1939-40 War		33	11	1	4	56	27	5	2	10	23	35	16	3	14	79	62	35
1940-41 War		10	2	2	1	15	9	3	1	1	13	7	5	3	2	28	16	13
1942-43 War		38	13	3	3	36	13	8	5	6	25	24	21	8	9	61	37	50
1943-44 War		39	11	3	6	53	27	3	7	9	20	33	14	10	15	73	60	38
1944-45 War		38	8	3	8	31	31	4	4	11	28	63	12	7	19	59	94	31
1945-46 War13		42	11	3	7	45	32	4	7	10	25	37	15	10	17	70	69	40
TOTAL wartime		236	68	15	35	281	172	31	32	55	151	233	99	47	90	432	405	245

ALL COMPETITIONS (HOME)

	P	W	D	L	F	A
FA Cup*	109	54	30	25	219	126
League Cup*	71	46	10	15	153	83
Fairs Cup	2	2	0	0	4	1
Div 3s Cup	8	5	2	1	18	10
Texaco Cup	4	1	2	1	7	5
Simod/Zenith Cup	5	2	1	2	6	7
Southern Floodlit Cup	4	3	1	0	9	3
Anglo Scottish	1	0	1	0	1	1
Birmingham League	151	79	24	48	363	245
Southern Lge	129	69	30	30	301	160
Wartime	118	68	15	35	281	172
Football League	1672	838	423	411	2952	1842
Void games+	7	5	2	0	27	8
TOTAL	2281	1172	541	568	4341	2664

Plus 9 games abandoned because of bad weather

APPENDIX 2: LEADING GOALSCORERS

1899-1900	BL	WALKER 12	1900-01	BL	WALKER/CROFT 9
1901-02	BL	WALKER 8	1902-03	BL	PORTER 21
1903-04	BL	CRAYTHORNE 15	1904-05	BL	BANKS 15
1905-06	BL	MCINTYRE 23	1906-07	BL	LEWIS 18
1907-08	BL	SMITH 38	1908-09	SL	BUCKLE 17
1909-10	SL	BUCKLE 19	1910-11	SL	PARKES 12
1911-12	SL	JONES 22	1912-13	SL	PARKES 13
1913-14	SL	DAVISON 19	1914-15	SL2	ALLAN 23
1919-20	2	PARKER 9	1920-21	2	MORGAN 7
1921-22	2	STEVENS 21	1922-23	2	TOMS 19
1923-24	2	HERBERT 12	1924-25	2	PYNEGAR 18
1925-26	3N	PATERSON 25	1926-27	3S	HERBERT 24
1927-28	3S	HEATHCOTE 15	1928-29	3S	TOSELAND 11
1929-30	3S	LOUGHLIN 22	1930-31	3S	LAKE 23
1931-32	3S	BOURTON 49	1932-33	3S	BOURTON 41
1933-34	3S	BOURTON 25	1934-35	3S	JONES 27
1935-36	3S	BOURTON 23	1936-37	2	BROWN 13
1937-38	2	BROWN 13	1938-39	2	CRAWLEY 14
1946-47	2	LOWRIE 26	1947-48	2	LOWRIE 18
1948-49	2	ROBERTS 20	1949-50	2	MURPHY 15
1950-51	2	CHISHOLM 24	1951-52	2	LOCKHART 15
1952-53	3S	BROWN 18	1953-54	3S	BROWN 20
1954-55	3S	CAPEL 18	1955-56	3S	MCPHERSON 14
1956-57	3S	MCPHERSON 21	1957-58	3S	STRAW 14
1958-59	4	STRAW 27	1959-60	3	STRAW 20
1960-61	3	STRAW 18	1961-62	3	DIXON 12
1962-63	3	BLY 25	1963-64	3	HUDSON 24
1964-65	2	HUDSON 19	1965-66	2	HUDSON 13
1966-67	2	GOULD 24	1967-68	1	REES/GOULD/MARTIN 8
1968-69	1	HUNT 11	1969-70	1	MARTIN 14
1970-71	1	HUNT 10	1971-72	1	HUNT 12
1972-73	1	ALDERSON 13	1973-74	1	ALDERSON 9
1974-75	1	CROSS 8	1975-76	1	CROSS 14
1976-77	1	FERGUSON 13	1977-78	1	WALLACE 21
1978-79	1	WALLACE 15	1979-80	1	WALLACE 13
1980-81	1	THOMPSON/DALY 8	1981-82	1	HATELEY 13
1982-83	1	WHITTON 12	1983-84	1	GIBSON 17
1984-85	1	GIBSON 15	1985-86	1	GIBSON 11
1986-87	1	REGIS 12	1987-88	1	REGIS 10
1988-89	1	SPEEDIE 14	1989-90	1	SPEEDIE 8
1990-91	1	GALLACHER 11	1991-92	1	GALLACHER 8
1992-93	P	QUINN 17	1993-94	P	NDLOVU 11
1994-95	P	DUBLIN 13	1995-96	P	DUBLIN 14
1996-97	P	DUBLIN 13	1997-98	P	DUBLIN 18
1998-99	P	WHELAN 10	1999-00	P	KEANE 12
2000-01	P	BELLAMY/HARTSON/HADJI 6	2001-02	1	HUGHES 14
2002-03	1	BOTHROYD 8	2003-04	1	MCSHEFFREY 11
2004-05	C	MCSHEFFREY 12			

WARTIME SEASONS

1918-19	SAMBROOKE 22	1939-40	CRAWLEY 22
1940-41	CRAWLEY/LOWRIE 7	1942-43	LOWRIE 23
1943-44	CRAWLEY 20	1944-45	CRAWLEY 9
1945-46	BARRATT 25		

Divisional Key: P = Premiership; 1 = Division 1; 2 = Division 2; 3 = Division 3; 4 = Division 4; 3S = Division 3 (South); 3N = Division 3 (North); C = Championship; SL = Southern League; BL = Birmingham League;

APPENDIX 3: HIGHEST & LOWEST ATTENDANCES (LEAGUE GAMES ONLY)

		DIV	AVERAGE	HIGHEST	LOWEST
1	1899-1900	BL	N/K	3,000 Shrewsbury	200 Bristol Rovers
2	1900-01	BL	N/K	unknown	unknown
3	1901-02	BL	N/K	unknown	unknown
4	1902-03	BL	N/K	3,840 Ruabon Druids	unknown
5	1903-04	BL	N/K	5,000 West Brom Res	unknown
6	1904-05	BL	N/K	unknown	unknown
7	1905-06	BL	2,200	4,000 Birmingham Res	unknown
8	1906-07	BL	2,700	unknown	unknown
9	1907-08	BL	4,500	5,500 Birmingham Res	unknown
10	1908-09	SL	5,740	7,524 Northampton	2,500 Exeter
11	1909-10	SL	6,300	12,000 QPR	1,500 Portsmouth
12	1910-11	SL	5,900	9,500 Swindon	2,000 Northampton
13	1911-12	SL	6,100	10,000 Northampton	500 Leyton
14	1912-13	SL	6,000	8,500 Portsmouth	3,000 Bristol Rovers
15	1913-14	SL	6,100	8,700 Swindon	2,000 Southend
16	1914-15	SL2	2,700	5,000 Merthyr	1,000 Pontypridd
17	1919-20	2	16,899	23,506 Bury	10,000 Stockport
18	1920-21	2	16,992	22,800 Birmingham	6,000 Wolves
19	1921-22	2	16,679	25,000 Notts County	9,000 Derby
20	1922-23	2	13,491	19,614 Notts County	4,000 Fulham
21	1923-24	2	13,064	20,000 Barnsley	6,000 Leeds
22	1924-25	2	11,896	18,000 Leicester	3,000 Portsmouth
23	1925-26	3N	9,505	15,257 Lincoln	4,744 Hartlepools
24	1926-27	3S	10,274	17,551 Swindon	5,951 Bournemouth
25	1927-28	3S	9,388	15,249 Plymouth	2,059 Crystal Palace
26	1928-29	3S	14,353	21,813 Charlton	11,057 Plymouth
27	1929-30	3S	12,985	26,400 Plymouth	8,755 Gillingham
28	1930-31	3S	10,327	19,569 Northampton	5,329 Brighton
29	1931-32	3S	12,235	23,271 Reading	6,172 Brentford
30	1932-33	3S	12,479	18,909 Brentford	6,016 Norwich
31	1933-34	3S	14,093	27,589 Cardiff	7,036 Bristol Rovers
32	1934-35	3S	15,060	24,226 Gillingham	6,843 Luton
33	1935-36	3S	19,232	42,809 Luton	8,390 Southend
34	1936-37	2	22,744	39,828 Aston Villa	13,061 Plymouth
35	1937-38	2	25,825	44,930 Aston Villa	9,705 Bury
36	1938-39	2	19,506	37,680 WBA	11,869 Tranmere
37	1946-47	2	19,975	29,379 Birmingham	13,047 Luton
38	1947-48	2	22,288	30,558 Birmingham	11,536 Nottm Forest
39	1948-49	2	22,342	39,488 WBA	14,154 Plymouth
40	1949-50	2	22,822	36,981 Leicester	12,611 Bradford PA
41	1950-51	2	26,694	34,918 Blackburn	17,514 Sheffield Utd
42	1951-52	2	22,548	36,337 Sheffield Wed	13,489 Everton
43	1952-53	3S	13,430	19,068 Bristol Rovers	6,869 Norwich
44	1953-54	3S	10,505	16,839 Ipswich	4,785 QPR
45	1954-55	3S	14,202	29,879 Bristol City	3,974 Newport
46	1955-56	3S	17,658	30,020 Millwall	9,037 Torquay
47	1956-57	3S	13,686	20,382 Southend	5,626 Crystal Palace
48	1957-58	3S	11,907	20,375 Northampton	5,846 Aldershot
49	1958-59	4	16,330	28,429 Port Vale	10,059 Oldham
50	1959-60	3	16,348	28,122 Norwich	8,397 Colchester

		DIV	AVE	HIGHEST	LOWEST
51	1960-61	3	11,996	18,213 Bradford City	7,422 Southend
52	1961-62	3	10,256	19,922 Peterborough	5,907 Port Vale
53	1962-63	3	17,098	30,289 Bournemouth	8,876 Carlisle
54	1963-64	3	26,017	36,901 Colchester	19,563 Walsall
55	1964-65	2	26,621	38,278 Derby	18,800 Bury
56	1965-66	2	25,370	36,771 Wolves	19,461 Bolton
57	1966-67	2	28,269	51,452 Wolves	19,682 Cardiff
58	1967-68	1	34,705	47,111 Manchester Utd	28,393 West Ham
59	1968-69	1	33,223	45,402 Manchester Utd	24,126 Southampton
60	1969-70	1	32,043	43,446 Manchester Utd	24,590 Sunderland
61	1970-71	1	26,039	40,022 Leeds	18,377 Burnley
62	1971-72	1	23,724	37,798 Manchester Utd	16,309 Huddersfield
63	1972-73	1	24,623	42,911 Manchester Utd	16,391 Stoke
64	1973-74	1	23,280	35,206 Leeds	16,457 Norwich
65	1974-75	1	19,100	25,460 Leeds	15,217 Everton
66	1975-76	1	19,370	33,922 Manchester Utd	13,777 Sheffield Utd
67	1976-77	1	21,242	38,160 Liverpool	12,893 Middlesbrough
68	1977-78	1	23,353	36,894 Nottm Forest	13,910 Middlesbrough
69	1978-79	1	22,638	28,585 Nottm Forest	15,083 Bolton
70	1979-80	1	19,315	31,644 Liverpool	14,310 Crystal Palace
71	1980-81	1	16,904	27,094 Aston Villa	11,521 Brighton
72	1981-82	1	13,100	19,329 Manchester Utd	9,677 Nottm Forest
73	1982-83	1	10,552	18,945 Manchester Utd	8,035 Brighton
74	1983-84	1	12,572	21,553 Manchester Utd	8,433 Wolves
75	1984-85	1	12,848	21,596 Everton	8,807 Ipswich
76	1985-86	1	11,590	16,898 Manchester Utd	7,478 Watford
77	1986-87	1	16,120	26,657 Liverpool	11,029 Norwich
78	1987-88	1	17,509	27,509 Liverpool	13,711 Luton
79	1988-89	1	16,040	23,880 Liverpool	11,246 QPR
80	1989-90	1	14,312	23,204 Liverpool	8,294 Wimbledon
81	1990-91	1	13,794	22,549 Tottenham	8,875 Wimbledon
82	1991-92	1	13,876	23,962 Manchester Utd	8,454 Norwich
83	1992-93	P	14,950	24,410 Manchester Utd	10,455 Southampton
84	1993-94	P	13,352	17,009 Manchester Utd	9,837 Southampton
85	1994-95	P	15,980	21,858 Manchester Utd	9,509 Ipswich
86	1995-96	P	18,505	23,344 Manchester Utd	12,496 Wimbledon
87	1996-97	P	19,625	23,080 Manchester Utd	15,266 Wimbledon
88	1997-98	P	19,718	23,055 Manchester Utd	15,910 Crystal Palace
89	1998-99	P	20,774	23,091 Tottenham	16,003 Sheffield Wed
90	1999-00	P	20,786	23,084 Liverpool	17,658 Derby
91	2000-01	P	20,535	23,063 Liverpool	17,275 Leicester
92	2001-02	1	16,137	22,406 Wolves	12,441 Stockport
93	2002-03	1	14,810	19,526 Reading	11,796 Wimbledon
94	2003-04	1	14,632	22,202 Crystal Palace	10,850 Wimbledon
95	2004-05	C	16,131	22,777 Derby	11,968 Gillingham

Divisional Key: P = Premiership; 1 = Division 1; 2 = Division 2; 3 = Division 3; 4 = Division 4; 3S = Division 3 (South); 3N = Division 3 (North); C = Championship; SL = Southern League; BL = Birmingham League;

APPENDIX 4: BIGGEST HOME WINS

1919-2005 FOOTBALL LEAGUE ERA

9-0 Bristol City	Division 3 South	28 Apr 1934
8-0 Crystal Palace	Division 3 South	6 Feb 1932
8-0 Rushden & Diamonds	League Cup R2	2 Oct 2002
8-1 Crystal Palace	Division 3 South	9 Nov 1935
8-1 Shrewsbury	Division 3	22 Oct 1963
7-0 Rotherham	Division 3 North	7 Nov 1925
7-0 QPR	Division 3 South	4 Mar 1933
7-0 Scunthorpe United	FA Cup R1	24 Nov 1934
7-0 Macclesfield	FA Cup R3	2 Jan 1999
7-1 Wolves	Division 2	25 Dec 1922
7-1 Bath City	FA Cup R2	14 Dec 1929
7-1 Thames	Division 3 South	13 Sept 1930
7-1 Gillingham	Division 3 South	26 Aug 1933
7-1 Newport	Division 3 South	7 Sept 1935
7-1 Aldershot	Division 4	22 Sept 1958
	(excludes wartime games)	

1899-1919 PRE-LEAGUE ERA

11-2 West Brom Reserves	Birmingham League	29 Apr 1908
10-1 Newport	Southern League Div 2	28 Nov 1914
9-0 Ironbridge	Birmingham League	20 Dec 1902
9-0 Stourbridge	Birmingham League	1 Feb 1908
9-0 Brentford	Southern League	27 Dec 1911
7-1 Darlaston	FA Cup 2QR	5 Oct 1907
7-1 Bishop Auckland	FA Cup 6QR	7 Dec 1907
7-2 Wellington	Birmingham League	7 Mar 1906
7-2 Ton Pentre	Southern League Div 2	13 Feb 1915
6-0 Exeter	Southern League	25 Apr 1910
	(excludes wartime games)	

APPENDIX 5: WORST HOME DEFEATS

1919-2005 FOOTBALL LEAGUE ERA

1-8 Leicester City	League Cup R5	1 Dec 1964
1-6 Liverpool	Division 1	5 May 1990
0-5 Tottenham	Division 2	30 Aug 1919
0-5 Everton	Division 1	27 Sept 1980
1-5 Notts County	Division 1	16 Feb 1982
1-5 Newcastle	Premiership	19 Sept 1998
2-5 Southend	Division 3	13 Mar 1964
0-4 Leeds United	Division 2	4 Feb 1950
0-4 Tottenham	Premiership	31 Dec 1994
0-4 Manchester United	Premiership	22 Nov 1995
0-4 Portsmouth	Division 1	19 Mar 2003

(excludes wartime games)

1899-1919 PRE-LEAGUE ERA

0-8 Wolves Reserves	Birmingham League	15 Dec 1900
2-6 Aston Villa Reserves	Birmingham League	6 Sept 1902
0-5 Aston Villa Reserves	Birmingham League	12 Dec 1903
1-5 Brierley Hill Alliance	Birmingham League	28 Jan 1905
1-5 Manchester United	FA Cup R2	3 Feb 1912
2-5 Dudley	Birmingham League	7 Oct 1899
2-5 Wolves Reserves	Birmingham League	19 Apr 1902
2-5 Southend	Southern League	26 Sept 1908

(excludes wartime games)

APPENDIX 6: PROGRESSIVE RECORD ATTENDANCES

9 September 1899	Shrewsbury Town	Birmingham League	3,000^
10 January 1903	Ruabon Druids	Birmingham League	3,840
31 October 1903	Walsall	FA Cup 1st Qual Rd*	5,000^
7 December 1907	Bishop Auckland	FA Cup 6th Qual Rd*	7,820
11 January 1908	Crystal Palace	FA Cup 1st Round*	9,884
28 December 1909	Queens Park Rangers	Southern League	12,000^
19 February 1910	Nottingham Forest	FA Cup 3rd Round*	12,500
3 March 1910	Everton	FA Cup 4th Round*	19,095
16 January 1913	Manchester United	FA Cup 1st Round replay*	20,042
15 January 1920	Luton Town	FA Cup 1st Round replay*	21,893
1 May 1920	Bury	Division 2	23,506
3 September 1921	Fulham	Division 2	25,000^
24 November 1928	Fulham	FA Cup 1st Round	26,000^
25 December 1929	Plymouth Argyle	Division 3 South	26,400
11 January 1930	Sunderland	FA Cup 3rd Round	31,673
27 April 1936	Luton Town	Division 3 South	42,809
20 February 1937	West Brom	FA Cup 5th Round	44,492
12 March 1938	Aston Villa	Division 2	44,930
29 April 1967	Wolves	Division 2	51,452

^ Attendances are estimates from the *Midland Daily Telegraph*
* Prior to 1925 the FA Cup proper started in January. After 1925 it started in November.
So in 1910 when City reached the 4th Round this was the equivalent of today's 6th Round.

Appendix 7: Progressive Record Receipts

Date	Opponent	Competition	Receipts
7 December 1907	Bishop Auckland	FA Cup 6th Qual.Rd*	£350^
11 January 1908	Crystal Palace	FA Cup 1st Round*	£500^
19 February 1910	Nottingham Forest	FA Cup 3rd Round*	£666
3 March 1910	Everton FA Cup	4th Round*	£1,052
11 January 1930	Sunderland	FA Cup 3rd Round	£1,854
20 February 1937	West Brom	FA Cup 5th Round	£2,798
19 April 1949	West Brom	Division 2	£3,689
27 November 1962	Millwall	FA Cup 2nd Round Replay	£3,816
29 December 1962	Peterborough	Division 3	£3,960
16 March 1963	Portsmouth	FA Cup 4th Round Replay	£4,454
25 March 1963	Sunderland	FA Cup 5th Round	£7,955
30 March 1963	Man United	FA Cup 6th Round	£9,430
29 April 1967	Wolves	Division 2	£10,021
7 January 1970	Liverpool	FA Cup 3rd Round	£14,346
28 October 1972	Birmingham	Division 1	£14,889
27 January 1973	Man United	Division 1	£17,847
27 January 1974	Derby	FA Cup 4th Round	£24,454
24 January 1976	Newcastle	FA Cup 4th Round	£29,672
10 May 1977	Liverpool	Division 1	£31,540
20 December 1977	Liverpool	Lge Cup 4th Round replay	£45,061
9 January 1979	West Brom	FA Cup 3rd Round	£51,568
19 January 1980	Liverpool	Division 1	£52,000
9 December 1980	Watford	Lge Cup 5th Round replay	£58,117
27 January 1981	West Ham	Lge Cup Semi Final 1st leg	£68,029
2 May 1987	Liverpool	Division 1	£101,142
30 January 1988	Watford	FA Cup 4th Round	£101,270
22 March 1989	Liverpool	Division 1	£104,760
24 January 1990	Sunderland	Lge Cup 5th Round replay	£124,840
25 February 1990	Nottm Forest	Lge Cup Semi Final 2nd leg	£177,271
12 April 1993	Man United	Premiership	£179,842
1 May 1995	Man United	Premiership	£216,126
25 October 1995	Tottenham	Lge Cup 3rd Round	£272,134
22 November 1995	Man United	Premiership	£297,000
7 March 1998	Sheffield United	FA Cup 6th Round	£375,510
29 January 2000	Charlton	FA Cup 5th Round	£405,369

In 1980 the Arsenal v Liverpool FA Cup semi-final third replay generated receipts of £115,000.

The receipts are generally those quoted by the *Coventry Evening Telegraph*. They have not been verified in all cases and may not be wholly accurate. Additionally receipts figures from many big games in the pre-war era are unknown. Some marked ^ are contemporary estimates.

APPENDIX 8: ATTENDANCES OVER 40,000

1	51,452	Wolves	Division 2	29-Apr-1967
2	47,111	Manchester Utd	Division 1	16-Mar-1968
3	45,402	Manchester Utd	Division 1	8-Apr-1969
4	44,930	Aston Villa	Division 2	12-Mar-1938
5	44,492	West Brom	FA Cup R5	20-Feb-1937
6	44,000	Manchester Utd	FA Cup R6	30-Mar-1963
7	43,446	Manchester Utd	Division 1	8-Nov-1969
8	42,911	Manchester Utd	Division 1	27-Jan-1973
9	42,809	Luton*	Division 3 South	27-Apr-1936
10	42,207	Liverpool	Division 1	26-Dec-1967
11	41,484	Leicester	Division 1	1-Apr-1969
12	41,281	Derby	FA Cup R4	27-Jan-1974
13	41,212	Nottm Forest	Division 1	29-Aug-1967
14	41,036	Derby	Division 1	16-Aug-1969
15	40,950	Tottenham	Division 1	17-Sep-1968
16	40,746	Sheffield Utd	Division 2	27-Dec-1937
17	40,487	Sunderland*	FA Cup R5	25-Mar-1963
18	40,022	Leeds	Division 1	26-Feb-1971

* In both these games the entrance gates were broken down by spectators and the actual
attendance was probably considerably higher than the official figure

APPENDIX 9: HOME FRIENDLIES

DATE	OPPONENTS	SCORE	ATT	COMMENTS
27-Dec-1899	Gainsborough Trinity	0-5	n/k	
20-Jan-1900	Hinckley Town	2-7	n/k	
17-Apr-1900	Newcastle U	1-5	1,000	
25-Dec-1901	Cov & N Warwicks Lge	3-2	n/k	
28-Feb-1903	Small Heath Reserves	2-0	n/k	
21-Mar-1903	Notts County	0-2	n/k	
14-Apr-1903	Preston	0-1	4,000	
1-Sep-1903	Foleshill Great Heath	8-1	n/k	
6-Apr-1904	Aston Villa Reserves	2-1	n/k	
9-Apr-1904	Pick of Birmingham League	3-1	n/k	
30-Apr-1904	Small Heath	2-1	1,000	
29-Apr-1905	St Michaels	2-3	n/k	
27-Jan-1906	Manchester City	5-2	4,000	
3-Feb-1906	Woolwich Arsenal Reserves	1-2	n/k	
28-Apr-1906	Leicester Fosse	1-3	n/k	
3-Nov-1906	St Helens Town	7-0	n/k	
2-Apr-1907	Burton All Saints	5-0	n/k	Bass Charity Cup semi-final
13-Apr-1907	Midway Albion	6-1	3,624	Bass Charity Cup final
10-Apr-1908	Burton Foresters	7-0	n/k	Bass Charity Cup
27-Apr-1908	Burton United	5-1	1,000	Bass Charity Cup final
30-Apr-1908	Northampton Town	5-0	3,000	
28-Dec-1908	Cov & N Warwicks League	3-2	n/k	
16-Jan-1909	Shrewsbury	6-4	n/k	
26-Apr-1909	Leicester Fosse	0-2	1,500	Bass Charity Cup
5-Jan-1911	Fred Karno's XI	3-2	1,500	Bolton Colliery Disaster
18-Apr-1911	Walsall	3-1	n/k	
25-Oct-1911	Calgary Hillhursts	4-3	n/k	
23-Jan-1915	Munster Fusiliers	8-3	n/k	
11-Mar-1916	Birmingham	1-1	n/k	
24-Mar-1916	Bellis & Morcoms(B'ham)	3-3	n/k	Prisoners of War Fund
16-Feb-1918	Aston Villa	1-1	n/k	
23-Feb-1918	B'ham Works Association	2-3	n/k	
9-Mar-1918	Leicester Fosse	0-2	n/k	
16-Mar-1918	Pennington's XI	2-1	n/k	
2-Apr-1918	Birmingham	3-1	n/k	
18-May-1918	Leicester Fosse	5-0	n/k	
10-May-1919	Birmingham	3-2	6,000	Birmingham C Charity Cup
20-Sep-1920	Birmingham	1-3	n/k	
8-Jan-1921	Port Vale	5-0	7,000	
19-Feb-1921	QPR	1-2	5,000	
7-Jan-1922	Bristol Rovers	6-1	2,000	
1-May-1922	Aston Villa XI	4-0	2,000	
3-Feb-1923	Burnley	2-2	8,000	
12-Jan-1924	Brentford	4-1	2,000	
14-Apr-1924	Birmingham	1-1	4,300	Lord Mayor's Hospital Cup
27-Apr-1925	Northampton Town	2-0	1,570	Coventry Nursing Cup
29-Apr-1925	Birmingham	1-4	2,170	Lord Mayor's Hospital Cup
20-Feb-1926	West Ham	4-3	5,000	
6-Mar-1926	Halifax Town Reserves	0-1	n/k	
26-Apr-1926	Hearts	3-1	3,000	

DATE	OPPONENTS	SCORE	ATT	COMMENTS
31-Dec-1927	Notts County	4-6	1,000	
30-Apr-1928	Birmingham	2-3	2,600	Lord Mayor's Hospital Cup
29-Apr-1929	Birmingham	4-4	3,187	Lord Mayor's Hospital Cup
28-Apr-1930	W BA	1-2	2,650	Lord Mayor's Hospital Cup
21-Apr-1931	Wolves	4-1	500	Lord Mayor's Hospital Cup
27-Apr-1931	Walsall	2-2	1,000	Coventry Nursing Cup
23-Jan-1932	Bradford City	4-0	7,000	
1-May-1933	Notts County	2-0	3,000	Lord Mayor's Hospital Cup
6-May-1935	Leicester C	3-3	3,000	King George V Jubilee
5-Dec-1935	Austria Vienna	4-2	3,000	
14-May-1938	Birmingham	1-1	5,095	Birmingham C Charity Cup
20-Aug-1938	Birmingham	2-0	11,295	Football League Jubilee
21-Jan-1939	Derby Co	2-2	11,381	
19-Aug-1939	Birmingham	3-2	7,979	
30-Sep-1939	Leicester C	3-3	3,236	
7-Oct-1939	Wolves	0-4	6,558	
26-Dec-1939	Notts County	8-2	1,945	
21-Feb-1942	Czech Army XI	4-1	2,500	At Coundon Road
25-May-1942	Birmingham	4-2	5,491	
19-Aug-1944	Tottenham H	3-1	5,147	Red Cross Charity Game
2-Apr-1945	Polish Airforce	2-2	2,892	
17-Nov-1945	Chester	1-5	n/k	
7-Nov-1946	Army XI	3-0	1,623	
29-Jan-1949	Man City	2-1	14,779	
18-Sep-1950	Galatasaray	2-1	9,350	
27-Jan-1951	Portsmouth	2-2	10,897	
21-Oct-1953	Queen of the South	1-1	16,923	Opening Of Floodlights
28-Oct-1953	Wolves	1-0	18,680	
11-Nov-1953	East Fife	2-2	12,644	
6-Jan-1954	Nuneaton B	4-0	4,094	
27-Jan-1954	Hadjuk Split	2-3	4,214	
1-Mar-1954	Leeds United	4-1	5,497	
15-Mar-1954	Hamilton Acad	5-0	4,362	
29-Mar-1954	Portsmouth	5-2	5,250	
23-Mar-1955	Raith Rovers	1-1	6,280	
5-Oct-1955	Birmingham C	2-2	6,823	
10-Oct-1955	Burnley	1-2	11,843	
17-Oct-1955	Sheff United	2-3	6,051	
28-Jan-1956	Preston	1-4	13,731	
30-Jan-1956	San Lorenzo	1-1	17,357	Abandoned 43 minutes
1-Oct-1956	Burnley	1-1	3,222	
15-Oct-1956	Nottm Forest	3-2	10,203	
22-Oct-1956	Huddersfield	3-3	9,688	
29-Oct-1956	Port Vale	0-0	5,678	
6-Nov-1956	Sheff United	0-6	5,728	
6-Mar-1957	A B Copenhagen	1-0	5,572	
25-Mar-1957	All Star Managers XI	1-2	6,036	
28-Oct-1957	Third Lanark	2-2	9,018	Opening of 2nd Floodlights
4-Nov-1957	Partick Thistle	3-2	7,539	
11-Nov-1957	Man City	3-1	8,480	
20-Oct-1958	Luton Town	0-0	6,294	
27-Oct-1958	Sunderland	1-3	4,979	

DATE	OPPONENTS	SCORE	ATT	COMMENTS
24-Sep-1959	Banik Ostrava	2-4	9,657	
29-Jan-1962	Slovan Bratislava	2-1	8,044	
12-Feb-1962	British Army XI	2-1	3,373	
19-Feb-1962	T S V Aachen	5-3	7,100	
10-May-1962	Burnley	2-4	7,416	Cathedral Festival Match
20-Oct-1962	Luton Town	2-1	2,670	
11-Dec-1962	England Youth XI	2-1	3,448	
24-Apr-1963	Aston Villa	2-2	5,500	In aid Coventry Boys club
26-Nov-196	Kaiserslautern	8-0	7,416	
16-Dec-1963	Ferencvaros	3-1	12,163	
24-Jan-1964	Leicester City	0-1	13,560	
2-Mar-1964	British Olympic XI	0-1	4,827	
28-Apr-1964	Tottenham H	5-6	15,638	
30-Apr-1964	America FC (Brazil)	2-5	10,188	
7-Oct-1964	Local Leagues XI	9-0	n/k	
20-Oct-1964	Morton	2-2	17,029	
30-Jan-1965	Fulham	1-2	10,881	Winston Churchill Trophy
29-Apr-1965	Tottenham H	0-3	13,660	
14-Aug-1965	Nottm Forest	4-3	13,493	
1-Oct-1965	Stoke City	5-1	8,180	
18-Oct-1965	Manchester City	4-2	5,757	
23-Nov-1965	Stade Francais	4-1	3,042	
10-Aug-1966	Varna Select XI	1-1	9,739	
4-Oct-1966	Stoke City	2-1	2,248	
29-Nov-1966	Morton	3-2	4,098	
3-Mar-1967	West Ham United	3-3	18,524	Winston Churchill Trophy
2-Aug-1969	Hibernian	1-1	10,853	
30-Mar-1971	Aberdeen	1-0	8,000	
6-Aug-1971	Huddersfield Town	1-2	5,136	
29-Nov-1971	Gornik Zabrze	0-2	6,838	
12-Aug-1975	Coventry Past XI	8-1	3,500	Lord Mayor's Xmas Appeal
17-Aug-1976	Coventry Sporting	8-0	2,000	
14-Aug-1978	Japan	2-0	5,232	
13-Aug-1979	City Past XI	8-2	1,808	In Aid of Sparks Charity
12-Aug-1980	Coventry Suburban League	6-0	391	
24-Mar-1981	Washington Diplomats	5-1	2,626	
19-Aug-1983	Zimbabwe	2-0	1,863	
22-Dec-1987	St Mirren	1-1	5,331	Anglo-Scottish Cup Winners
10-Aug-1990	Banik Ostrava	3-2	2,750	
14-Aug-1990	Halesowen Town	0-1	735	
10-Aug-1996	Benfica	2-7	10,995	
3-Aug-1997	Feyenoord	2-1	5,700	
27-Jan-1998	Bayern Munich	2-4	8,409	
8-Aug-1998	Espanol	1-1	5,436	
12-Aug-2000	Ajax Amsterdam	1-3	11,313	
30-Aug-2000	KRC Genk	1-0	3,406	
25-Mar-2001	Pakistan	2-0	1,871	
4-Aug-2001	KAA Gent	1-0	3,102	
27-Jul-2002	Dundee United	1-1	4,452	
2-Aug-2003	Wolves	2-1	6,822	
31-Jul-2004	Norwich	0-0	5,484	

First Team friendlies only. Note: Attendances in round thousands are estimates)

APPENDIX 10: TESTIMONIAL GAMES

30-Sep-1946	Notts County	4-1	George Taylor	unknown
8-May-1947	Combined Birmingham XI	0-2	Dick Bayliss	8,777
30-Apr-1953	All Star XI	5-8	George Mason	11,143
13-Oct-1958	Derby Co	0-1	Peter Hill	5,748
10-May-1966	Northampton Town	2-2	George Curtis/Mick Kearns	13,576
9-May-1967	Liverpool	2-1	George Curtis/Mick Kearns	25,040
28-Apr-1969	Derby Co	1-1	Brian Hill	10,242
26-Apr-1972	Charlton Athletic	3-4	Dietmar Bruck	5,037
1-May-1973	Aston Villa	1-1	Ernie Machin	4,179
26-Nov-1974	England 1966 XI	6-6	Bill Glazier	15,193
22-Nov-1977	GB XI v Scotland XI	7-5	Mick Coop	7,895
10-Sep-1984	Coventry City Past XI	4-4	Brian Roberts	2,880
12-Aug-1989	WBA	0-1	Jake Findlay	3,596
3-May-1992	1987 team v Spurs 1987	7-5	John Sillett	4,600
15-Nov-1993	Birmingham City	2-1	Lloyd McGrath	2,301
10-Aug-1994	Aston Villa	1-2	Steve Ogrizovic	7,805
5-Aug-1995	Birmingham City	1-1	Brian Borrows	6,036
16-May-1997	Manchester United	2-2	David Busst	23,326
31-Jul-1999	WBA	4-2	Cyrille Regis	5,739
19-Apr-2005	1987 team v Spurs 1987	7-7	Michael Gynn	9,435

APPENDIX 11: MISCELLANEOUS STATS.
SEASONAL RECORDS:LEAGUE 1919-2005

Most Home wins 19 (1935-36)
Fewest Home wins 4 (1996-97, 2000-01)
Consecutive Home wins 11(1952-53)

Most Home Defeats 11 (2002-03)
Fewest Home defeats 1 (1935-36, 1946-47, 1958-59, 1966-67)
Consecutive home defeats 6 (1981-82)

Most home draws 10 (1971-72)
Fewest home draws 1 (1932-33, 1935-36)
Consecutive home draws 5 (1957-58)

Most home goals scored 75 (1932-33, 1935-36)
Fewest home goals scored 14 (2000-01)

Most home goals conceded 36 (1927-28, 1956-57)
Fewest home goals conceded 11 (1958-59)

Longest Unbeaten home run 19 (April 1925- March 1926)
Longest home run without a win 12 (December 2002-August 2003)

Highest average attendances 34,705 (1967-68)
Lowest post war average attendances 10,256 (1961-62)

APPENDIX 12: ABANDONED GAMES AT HIGHFIELD ROAD

DATE	OPPONENTS	COMPETITION	EXPLANATION
28 Nov 1903	Halesowen	B'ham League	Abandoned 82 min 3-1 fog
2 Dec 1905	Stafford Ran	B'ham League	Abandoned 60 min 1-1 heavy rain
4 Dec 1937	Southampton	Div 2	Abandoned 45 min 1-0 snow
19 Nov 1949	Sheffield Wed	Div 2	Abandoned 63 min 1-0 fog
26 Mar 1955	Southend	Div 3 South	Abandoned 68 min 3-1 heavy rain
22 Dec 1956	Crystal Palace	Div 3 South	Abandoned 51 min 0-0 floodlights failed
22 Dec 1962	Colchester	Div 3	Abandoned 45 min 2-0 fog
4 Mar 1972	Sheffield Utd	Div 1	Abandoned 62 min 0-2 heavy rain/snow

APPENDIX 13: OTHER GAMES AT HIGHFIELD ROAD

SEASON	DATE	COMPETITION AND TEAMS	SCORE	ATT
1911-12	23-3-12	RepresentativeBirmingham Jun v Scottish Jun	2-2	1,500
1913-14	4-4-14	RepresentativeBirmingham Jun v Scottish Jun	1-0	1,000
1915-16	5-2-16	Charity gameMidlands v Rest of England	2-4	8,000
1928-29	20-4-29	RepresentativeBirmingham Jun v Scottish Jun	0-1	3,696
1944-45	20-1-45	Charity gameFA XI v RAF	4-6	12,750
1946-47	23-12-46	FA Cup 2R, 2RpNorthampton v Peterborough	8-1	13,150
1947-48	10-4-48	Schoolboy IntEngland v Wales	2-1	25,199
1950-51	3-2-51	Amateur Int England v Eire	6-3	8,067
1956-57	8-11-56	Inter-LeagueDivision 3 (S) v Division 3 (N)	2-1	14,156
1960-61	8-4-61	Schoolboy IntEngland v Eire	8-0	9,108
1962-63	22-11-62	Youth Int England v Switzerland	1-0	*3,200
			*Abandoned after 9 mins, fog	
1964-65	25-11-64	Under-23 IntEngland v Romania	5-0	27,476
1966-67	6-2-67	FA Cup 4R 2RpHull City v Portsmouth	1-3	18,448
1966-67	22-4-67	Schoolboy IntEngland v Wales	3-0	8,465
1968-69	16-4-69	Under-23 IntEngland v Portugal	3-0	13,718
1968-69	5-4-69	Schoolboy IntlEngland v Holland	5-2	6,017
1969-70	17-12-69	FA Cup 2R 3RpBrighton v Walsall	1-2	2,241
1969-70	18-3-70	Inter-LeagueFootball League v Scottish Lge	2-2	26,673
1972-73	28-3-73	World Cup qualNorthern Ireland v Portugal	1-1	11,408
1972-73	10-3-73	FA Amateur SFWalton & Hersham v Highgate	4-0	4,440
1973-74	5-4-74	Amateur Int England v Scotland	1-1	1,211
1975-76	22-11-75	FA Cup 1R Coventry Sporting v Tranmere	2-0	4,642
1975-76	13-12-75	FA Cup 2R Coventry Sporting v Peterboro	0-4	8,777
1975-76	3-3-76	Universities CupAston v Durham	2-0	401
1977-78	29-4-78	Schoolboy IntEngland v Scotland	1-1	4,196
1978-79	6-10-78	Lg Cup 3R 2RpAston Villa v Crystal Palace	3-0	25,502
1979-80	1-5-80	FA Cup SF 3RpArsenal v Liverpool	1-0	35,632
1979-80	12-2-80	Under-21 Int England v Scotland	2-1	15,354
1979-80	26-3-80	Youth Int England v Denmark	4-0	2,464
1981-82	23-3-82	Youth Int England v Scotland	2-2	2,295
1981-82	4-5-82	English Sch F2LCoventry v Sheffield	1-4	3,685
1984-85	16-1-85	FA Cup 3R Burton Albion v Leicester	0-1	BCD
1988-89	18-10-88	Under-21 Int: England v Sweden	1-1	4,141
1993-94	11-2-94	Schoolboy Int: England v Wales	2-0	6,363

SENIOR NON-LEAGUE FINALS

1961-62	Birmingham Snr Cup	Lockheed v Rugby Town	5-1	unknown
1974-75	Birmingham Snr Cup	AP Leamington v Atherstone	0-1	1,844
1977-78	Birmingham Snr Cup	Nuneaton v Redditch	1-1	913
1979-80	Birmingham Snr Cup	Nuneaton v Lye Town	2-0	970

OTHER SPORTS INCLUDE

1916-17	5-5-17	Boxing	Tango Debney v Jean Barr		
			Debney won on points		
1917-18	20-7-18	Baseball	South Canton v Waddington	3-1	4,000
1920-21	26-2-21	Ladies Football	Dick, Kerr's XI v St Helens	8-1	25,000
1924-25	11-12-24	Rugby Union	Warwickshire v New Zealand	3-40	20,000
1925-28		Motor Cycle Football			
			Various games featuring Coventry MCFC		
1944-45	unknown	Baseball	Packington v Stoneleigh		unknown
1947-48	18-5-48	Boxing	Dick Turpin v Bos Murphy	25,000	
			Turpin won KO 1st rd		
1951-52	16-1-52	Rugby Union	Midland Counties v South Africa	8-19	21,326
1957-58	19-2-58	Rugby Union	Midland Counties v Australia	8-3	8,000
1985-86	26-5-86	American Football			
			Chicago Allstars v Leeds Cougars	65-0	1,268

TELEVISED GAMES

1965-66	6-10-65	Live Screening	Cardiff v Coventry	1-2	10,295
1965-66	26-4-66	Live Screening	Charlton Athletic v Coventry	2-0	11,321
1993-94	23-2-94	Live Screening	Newcastle v Coventry	4-0	

APPENDIX 14: HISTORY OF HIGHFIELD ROAD GROUND IMPROVEMENTS

1899   9 September the ground is officially opened for a 1-0 Birmingham and District League win over against Shrewsbury Town. Attendance: 3,000

1905   First refreshments bars opened

1910   Barrel roof stand built on Thackhall Street. Capacity 20,000

1913   Offices moved from Bayley Lane to Highfield Road

1915   Ground closed for duration of war

1919   New entrance built at King Richard Street side of ground, major pitch improvements and new terracing in preparation for League football

1920   Swan Lane end extended creating space for extra 10,000. Capacity 30,000

1922   Waste from Tram tracks building used to build up Spion Kop. Capacity 30,000

1927   Cover bought from Twickenham rugby ground erected at Nicholls Street End

1934   Perimeter wall built at Nicholls Street End

1936   New Main Stand built after promotion to Division Two. Capacity 45,000. Club purchase the freehold from the Mercers Company

1938   Kop improvements include concrete terracing and the erection of the Crows Nest in the north corner

1939   Canopy erected at front of Main Stand

1940   Ground bombed during Blitz & subsequently closed for two years

1953   First floodlights erected on wooden poles

1955   Coventry Evening Telegraph clock erected on the Kop

1956   Corner terracing at Covered end concreted

1957   Second floodlights installed on pylons

1963   Playing surface levelled. Sky Blue wing stands built

1964   Barrel Roof stand demolished & Sky Blue stand completed after promotion to Division Two

1965   Electronic scoreboard erected on the Kop

1967   Covered end demolished and West Stand completed during the close season. Capacity 50,000

1968   Main stand burnt down but new stand erected for the new season

1973   Flat roof replaces original roof on Sky Blue Stand. 12 Executive boxes installed in main Stand

1978   Fences erected around perimeter of pitch after hooliganism

1981   The stadium is made all-seater with the fences removed. Capacity lowered to 21,000

1983   Kop partially reopened for standing spectators

1984   Fences re-built after more hooliganism

1985   Kop totally reopened as a standing area & seats removed

1993   Floodlight pylons removed. Kop demolished. Sky Blue Stand refurbished and new roof

1994   East Stand completed

1995   Major refurbishment of Main Stand. Executive boxes removed and stand extended to pitch. Mini-boxes erected at corner of West End

BIBLIOGRAPHY

Jim Brown: *Coventry City: The Elite Era 1967-2001* (2nd Ed, (Desert Island Books 2001)

Jim Brown: *Coventry City: An Illustrated History* (Desert Island Books 2000)

Derek Henderson: *The Sky Blues: The Story of Coventry City* (Stanley Paul 1968)

David Brassington, Rod Dean & Don Chalk: *Singers to Sky Blues* (Sporting & Leisure Press 1986)

Rod Dean, David Brassington, Don Chalk & Jim Brown: *Coventry City: The Complete Record 1883-1991* (Breedon Books 1991)

Martin & Paul O'Connor: *Coventry City: The Complete Who's Who 1908-1993* (Yore Publications 1993)

Graham Smith & Neville Hadsley: *Sky Blue Heaven Volumes 1 & 2* (Elephant Press 2006)

Jonathan Strange: *Coventry City FC: A History in 50 matches* (Tempus 2004)

Lionel Bird: *History of the Official Coventry City Supporters Club* (2002)

Marshall Stewart: *Miracle in Sky Blue* (Instant Publications 1967)

Jimmy Hill: *Striking for Soccer* (1961)

Jimmy Hill: *The Jimmy Hill Story: My Autobiography* (Hoder & Stoughton 1998)

George Raynor: *Football Ambassador At large* (Stanley Paul 1960)

Simon Inglis: *Football Grounds of Britain* (Collins Willow 1996)

Simon Inglis: *League Football and the men who made it* (Collins Willow 1988)

Simon Inglis: *Engineering Archie: Archibald Leitch: football ground designer* (English Heritage 2005)

John Harding: *For the Good of the Game: the history of the PFA* (Robson Books 1991)

Brian Tabner: *Through The Turnstiles* (Yore Publications 1992)

Arthur Ellis: *The Final Whistle* (Stanley Paul 1962)

Ian St John: *The Saint: My Autobiography* (Hodder & Stoughton 2005)

Gary Imlach: *My Father & Other Working Class Heroes* (Yellow Jersey Press 2005)

Jack Rollin: *Soccer At War 1939:45* (Collins Willow 1985)

Rogan Taylor & Andrew Ward: *Kicking & Screaming: An oral history of Football in England* (Robson Books 1995)

Miscellaneous club history books published by Breedon Books & Yore Publications